SELF-INTEREST

SELF-INTEREST

Edited by

**Ellen Frankel Paul, Fred D. Miller, Jr.,
and Jeffrey Paul**

CAMBRIDGE
UNIVERSITY PRESS

Published by the Press Syndicate of the University of Cambridge
The Pitt Building, Trumpington Street, Cambridge CB2 1RP, England
40 West 20th Street, New York, NY 10011, USA
10 Stamford Road, Oakleigh, Melbourne, Victoria 3166, Australia

First published 1997

Printed in the United States of America

Library of Congress Cataloging-in-Publication Data

Self-Interest / edited by Ellen Frankel Paul,
Fred D. Miller, Jr., and Jeffrey Paul.   p.   cm.
Includes bibliographical references and index.
ISBN 0-521-59892-3
1. Self-interest.   I. Paul, Ellen Frankel.   II. Miller,
Fred Dycus, 1944–   .   III. Paul, Jeffrey.
BJ1474.S39   1997
171'.9–dc21   96-46422
CIP

ISBN 0-521-59892-3 paperback

The essays in this book have also been published,
without introduction and index, in the semiannual journal
Social Philosophy & Policy, Volume 14, Number 1,
which is available by subscription.

CONTENTS

INTRODUCTION

"[T]he good man should be a lover of self," Aristotle wrote, "for he will both himself profit by doing noble acts, and will benefit his fellows. . . ."* Yet in much of contemporary moral philosophy, concern for one's own interests is considered a nonmoral issue, while concern for the interests of others is paradigmatically moral. Indeed, a central issue in ethical theory involves the proper balance to be struck between prudence and morality, between the pursuit of one's own good and the pursuit of the good of others. When deliberating over what action to take, should one weigh one's own interests more heavily than those of others? Or is it possible to accommodate both self-interest and regard for others, to show that we have self-regarding reasons for helping others?

The essays in this volume—written from a range of perspectives—address these questions and examine related issues. Some challenge the assumption that morality is exclusively concerned with the pursuit of the good of others, arguing that self-interest can be a legitimate moral motive. Some ask whether it is possible to resolve the apparent conflict between self-interest and morality by appealing to some third, overarching standard, or by showing that self-regard and regard for others share significant common features or spring from a common source. Other essays seek to determine what values are most likely to contribute to an agent's interest, or what kind of life a self-interested agent should seek to lead. Still others examine the relationship between self-interest and practical reason, or between self-interest and virtue.

In the opening essay, "Beyond Self and Other," Kelly Rogers explores the assumption, held by many contemporary moral philosophers, that an action has no moral worth unless it benefits others, and may not even have worth then, unless it is motivated by altruism rather than selfishness. Self-interested action, on this view, may be rational or prudent, but lacks any genuine moral dimension. Rogers undertakes a comprehensive critique of this "self-other" model of morality, drawing upon Aristotelian and American Pragmatist sources, and offering a number of examples designed to show that self-interested actions can have moral value. A more promising model, she argues, would recognize our need for moral guidance in a wide range of pursuits, not merely in our dealings with others. Morality can assist us in two main ways: it can help us reconcile our passions and our reason in order to pursue the long-range goal of living a good life; and it can help us develop principles for action, so that we can relate new choices and novel situations that we face with those we

---

* Aristotle, *Nicomachean Ethics*, in *A New Aristotle Reader*, ed. J. L. Ackrill (Princeton, NJ: Princeton University Press, 1987), 1169a12–13.

have faced in the past. In the course of the essay, Rogers challenges the view of self-interest as preference-satisfaction; the notion that concern for others is the only proper source of moral motivation; and the idea that regard for others is either necessary or sufficient for morality. While she acknowledges that selfishness is a real moral failing, she characterizes it not as an excessive pursuit of self-interest, but as unreflective pursuit of one's supposed interests, without regard for the wider context in which one acts. The remedy for this failing, she contends, is not to foster an impartial regard for one's own interests and the interests of others, but to recognize that one acts in a world of other people, each pursuing his own ends. By abstracting away from our own concerns, we can gain an appreciation of the situation of others, and can come to see the value of helping them pursue their interests; yet this need not detract from the moral value of pursuing our own interests.

The assumption that morality is primarily other-regarding is also the subject of Jean Hampton's contribution to this volume, "The Wisdom of the Egoist: The Moral and Political Implications of Valuing the Self." Hampton examines theories of self-worth and their impact on how individuals view themselves in society, and she explores the detrimental effects of conceiving morality as a system of impersonal duties owed to others. She begins by distinguishing principle-dependent moral theories from worth-dependent ones: under the former, abstract principles of appropriate treatment are primary, and these principles lead one to the conclusion that all persons have equal worth; under the latter, the notion that people have equal worth is primary, and is used to derive principles of appropriate treatment. Hampton believes that worth-dependent theories offer the more promising approach, since they begin with what she takes to be the proper object of moral concern: the self or the person. The belief in the value of the self is exemplified in the position of the egoist, who places himself at the top of his hierarchy of values. Hampton maintains that the egoist is correct to recognize the self as the bearer of value; his mistake is to value himself exclusively, failing to place any moral weight on the fact that there are other selves, other people in the world. Illustrating her discussion with examples from literature, Hampton argues that the assumptions we make about the source of human value have profound personal and social implications. One's view of one's own worth influences the kinds of interests, talents, and ambitions one develops and the kind of treatment one demands from others; and a society that fails to acknowledge the equal worth of its members will be marked by oppression of those deemed to be of lesser worth. Hampton concludes that by taking self-worth—rather than some impersonal system of duties—as the basis of morality, we can honor both our own value and the value of others.

The assumption challenged by Rogers and Hampton—that morality is primarily or exclusively other-regarding—underlies an ongoing philosophical debate over whether it is always rational to be moral. Thomas E. Hill, Jr. explores the relationship between rationality and morality in "Reasonable Self-Interest," seeking to discover a model of practical reason which accords with widely held common-sense views about moral reasoning. Hill begins by sketching three models of practical reason. On the self-interest model, reason demands that each agent intelligently pursue his own self-interest. On the coherence-and-efficiency model, one is rational if one pursues one's ends, whatever they are, in an informed, coherent, and efficient way. On the consequentialist model, certain ends (such as pleasure, happiness, or friendship) are said to have intrinsic value, and one is rational to the extent that one promotes the greatest possible sum of these values, for oneself and for others. Hill analyzes each of these models, attempting to determine how well each conforms to what he takes to be common-sense views of reason, self-interest, and morality; and he proposes a fourth model, based on the moral philosophy of Immanuel Kant. On this model, one acts rationally if one coherently and efficiently pursues one's ends, subject to certain constraints based on the Kantian idea of treating others as autonomous ends in themselves. The content of these constraints is to be arrived at through "idealized co-legislation," in which conscientious agents deliberate together to arrive at publicly justifiable rules of conduct. This model accords with common sense, Hill argues, in that it recognizes the primary importance of individual moral agents and gives us wide latitude in choosing our ends, while at the same time requiring that we have some regard for others.

While Hill attempts to develop a model of reason which would ameliorate the conflict between self-interest and morality, David Copp takes a different approach to this conflict. In "The Ring of Gyges: Overridingness and the Unity of Reason," Copp assumes that there will be cases in which morality and self-interest conflict, and asks whether, in such cases, the requirements of morality are normatively more important than the requirements of self-interest. A natural way to try to resolve such conflicts would be to appeal to some third standard, such as an Aristotelian standard of personal excellence, which could be drawn on to resolve disputes. Copp argues, however, that the very idea of a standard that would provide a definitive appraisal of the relative normative importance of morality and self-interest is incoherent. Neither morality nor self-interest overrides the other; there simply are judgments and reasons of these two different kinds—there is never an overall judgment as to which action is required *simpliciter* in cases of conflict between these kinds of reasons. In such cases, Copp contends, there is no fact of the matter as to what a person ought *simpliciter* to do. Nevertheless, he maintains that his position does not threaten the significance of morality in guiding our actions: while morality cannot override self-interest, neither can self-interest override morality. Copp concludes with the suggestion that we can minimize the potential for conflict between morality and self-interest, by fostering moral education and social conditions that give people self-interested reasons for acting morally.

The tension between morality and self-interest is also the subject of David Schmidtz's contribution to this volume, "Self-Interest: What's in It for Me?" Schmidtz begins by noting that our faith in the rationality of acting prudently is far stronger than our faith in the rationality of acting morally. "Why should one be moral?" is considered a serious question, which has been the subject of a great deal of philosophical debate; yet the same cannot be said of "Why should one be prudent?" Schmidtz argues, however, that our reasons to be prudent are every bit as contingent as our reasons to be moral: the fact that we have self-interested reasons to perform a certain action in no way guarantees that we will be motivated to do so. The alleged conflict between morality and self-interest is similarly contingent, Schmidtz contends, since the moral perspective does not require that one have a universal regard for the interests of others, and self-interest does not require a wholesale lack of concern for others. Both perspectives make room for a deep, although not universal, regard for others. Indeed, a eudaimonistic view, of the kind Schmidtz defends, suggests that caring for others gives one more to live for, and thus advances one's self-interest. This sort of view, if correct, gives us reasons to reconsider the alleged tension between morality and self-interest, and to reject the common practice of using self-interest as an all-purpose scapegoat for our failures to be moral. Often, Schmidtz suggests, the problem lies elsewhere: weakness of will and social pressure can lead us to act imprudently just as easily as they can lead us to act immorally. Thus, while he agrees that we can be motivated to be moral even when being moral is not in our interest, he also maintains that we can lack motivation to be moral even when morality and self-interest coincide.

The common assumption that self-interest and concern for others are frequently in conflict might seem to indicate that the two sorts of concern are fundamentally different, yet David O. Brink suggests that this need not be the case. In "Self-Love and Altruism," Brink explores what he calls a "metaphysical egoist" attempt to reconcile the demands of self-interest and other-regarding morality. On this view, people's interests are said to be metaphysically interdependent, so that acting on other-regarding moral requirements is a reliable way of promoting one's own interests. The version of metaphysical egoism that Brink develops draws on Platonic and Aristotelian conceptions of love and friendship and on T. H. Green's ethics of self-realization, and it extends the views of these theorists by appealing to plausible claims about persons and their persistence through time. Beginning with a discussion of *intrapersonal* psychological continuity, Brink argues that there is a parallel *interpersonal* form of psychological continuity: a continuity of interdependent beliefs, experiences, desires, and ideals. He suggests that, just as one has a concern for one's own future self, one can and should have a parallel concern for others with whom one shares, or can share, psychological continuity. Thus, Brink's view models interpersonal relations and concern on intrapersonal relations and concern, and thereby extends the boundaries of self-interest so as to include the good of others. Brink concludes his essay by addressing a number of possible objections to his theory, focusing on foundational worries about the value, character, scope, and weight of metaphysical egoist concern for others.

Like Brink, Stephen Darwall attempts to draw out the similarities between self-interest and regard for others, offering an account of self-interest that makes it analogous to a benevolent concern for others. In his essay "Self-Interest and Self-Concern," Darwall begins with a critique of informed-desire accounts of self-interest, in which an agent's self-interest is taken to consist in whatever the agent rationally and informedly takes an interest in. Such theories have a certain appeal as views of what counts as a rational interest, but this appeal does not survive when they are considered as theories of self-interest. Darwall argues that informed-desire accounts include too much within the scope of self-interest, and therefore leave no room for genuine self-sacrifice: anything which an agent informedly judges to be worth some sacrifice is taken to be part of his self-interest, and thus not really a sacrifice at all. Drawing on the work of Henry Sidgwick, Darwall proposes an alternative account of self-interest, which understands a person's interest in terms of what we (or the person himself) would want for him for his own sake. Unlike informed-desire theories, such an account can explain why not everything a person desires is part of his good, since what a person sensibly wants is not necessarily what we (and he) would sensibly want, insofar as we care about him. Darwall concludes with a discussion of the subjective and objective factors that contribute to a good life, arguing that a self-interested agent should desire a life that he can value and derive pleasure from, but one that is also made up of genuinely worthwhile human activities, such as mutual love and creative expression.

The individual's interest in leading a fulfilling life—a subject Darwall touches on—is the focus of the next two essays in this collection. In "Who Is Rational Economic Man?" Jennifer Roback Morse proposes a way of expanding the economist's model of rationally self-interested behavior so that it can give an account of our longings for what she calls the "ultimate goods": truth, beauty, happiness, and love. Morse begins with a discussion of the standard economic definition of rationality, which holds that an agent is rational if he has an internally consistent set of preferences and pursues a given set of ends in a way that minimizes costs. She sets out an alternative model which recognizes that every rational individual plays a dual role: each agent calculates the costs and expected benefits of possible actions, taking his preferences as given; yet, at least on occasion, each agent also takes time to reflect on his values and preferences, and to consider whether he is living the kind of life he wants to live. A person can experience inner conflict, frustration, and disappointment with the course of his life, and these are difficult or impossible to account for on standard economic models. Morse's alternative model attempts to account for these conflicts and disappointments by introducing longings for ultimate goods alongside the appetites (for nourishment, physical comfort, amusements, and so on) that rational agents attempt to satisfy. On Morse's model, the appetites are considered pleasurable in themselves, and are also treated as inputs or contributing factors to the achievement of the longings; but a person can consume too much of the appetites relative to their value in fostering the achievement of the longings. When this occurs, the rational agent must reassess and reorder his preferences if he is committed to achieving the ultimate goods. By conceiving of rationality in this way, Morse argues, we develop an understanding of a number of phenomena that economists cannot currently explain well, including immoderation, self-indulgence, and dissatisfaction with the course of one's life.

The link between self-interest and leading a meaningful life is the subject of Susan Wolf's contribution to this volume, "Happiness and Meaning: Two Aspects of the Good Life." Wolf begins with a discussion of three types of theories of self-interest: hedonistic theories, which identify a person's good with the felt quality of his experiences; preference theories, which emphasize the satisfaction of the agent's desires, whatever they may be; and objective-list theories, which equate a person's good with the achievement of (for example) knowledge, pleasure, friendship, love, and other goods thought to be objectively valuable. The view Wolf offers falls into the third category: she argues that a fully successful life must be a meaningful one, where the concept of meaningfulness has both subjective and objective components, suitably linked. A meaningful life, she says, is a life of active engagement in projects of worth, which might involve such things as moral or intellectual accomplishments, relationships with family and friends, or artistic/creative enterprises. In the course of her essay, Wolf discusses the relationship between meaning and happiness, and between meaning and a subjective sense of fulfillment. She acknowledges that accepting meaningfulness as an important ingredient of a good life makes the identification of what is in one's self-interest less clear and determinate than it might otherwise be: since there is such a wide range of meaningful activities that one might engage in, it will be difficult to make comparative judgments about which are more conducive to one's interests. Wolf concludes by suggesting that, while meaning and self-interest must remain closely linked, the activities that give meaning to one's life will give one reasons for acting that are, to some extent, independent of self-interest—reasons derived from the worth of the activities themselves.

The last three essays in this collection deal in various ways with the relationship between self-interest and virtue. In "Self-Interest and Virtue," Neera K. Badhwar sets out to defend the Aristotelian view that virtue is essential to an individual's happiness or eudaimonia, and thus that virtuous action is in the agent's self-interest. This view has its origin in Aristotle's belief that virtue is necessary for the most effective functioning of our various capacities—cognitive, emotional, social, and physical. Badhwar connects virtue with an agent's self-interest by arguing that virtue is essential to the proper functioning of the agent's capacities, or to what Badhwar calls his "practical efficacy"; this efficacy, in turn, is essential to the agent's happiness. More precisely, she says, virtue is partly constitutive of an agent's happiness, objectively conceived: virtues such as honesty, integrity, justice, generosity, and courage put the agent in touch with various aspects of reality and enhance his relationships with others. Practicing these virtues frees the agent of the control of skewed perceptions and irrational emotions, and thereby enables him to feel at home in the world. Yet if virtue leads to efficacy and happiness, what can we say of tyrants or predators, those who pursue vicious ends? Badhwar argues that such predators cannot achieve the kind of efficacy and self-esteem that are essential for happiness. In choosing to live in parasitic dependence on others, rather than leading productive lives in beneficial cooperation with others, they betray a lack of autonomy and are forced into a pattern of self-deception, rationalization, and evasion that is likely to have devastating psychological consequences. Badhwar concludes that an agent's true interest lies in cultivating a life of virtue and practical efficacy, and that, in the absence of bad fortune, this is the kind of life most likely to lead to happiness.

Michael Slote's essay, "The Virtue in Self-Interest," approaches the relationship between self-interest and virtue from a more abstract, theoretical perspective. An ethical theory, Slote observes, can attempt to understand the relationship between two concepts reductively, by accounting for "higher" concepts in terms of "lower" ones—as utilitarianism accounts for ethical ideals and standards in terms of "mere" well-being or pleasure. Or a theory can take a dualistic approach, analyzing each concept independently. A third method—which Slote calls "elevationism," in contrast with reductionism—understands ethically lower concepts, such as well-being or self-interest, in terms of ethically higher concepts such as virtue. This is the approach taken by some ancient virtue-ethics theorists, including the Stoics, for whom well-being simply *consists* in being virtuous. Slote acknowledges that Stoic elevationism has a number of counterintuitive implications—for example, that appetitive pleasures are not part of human well-being and that pain is not intrinsically contrary to well-being. He suggests a more plausible form of elevationism, influenced by the ethical theories of Plato and Aristotle, which employs weaker assumptions about the connection between well-being and virtue. On this view, every element of human well-being must be tied to or consistent with one or another particular virtue. Although this view does not provide an entirely unified account of an agent's virtue and his well-being or self-interest—since different elements of well-being will be related to different virtues—it nevertheless conforms to some of our strongest intuitions regarding the contribution of at least some forms of pleasure to well-being. Slote argues that this view can also help us explain why some activities that individuals engage in, such as those that waste their talents, or those that involve interactions in which the parties use each other as mere means, do not contribute to the individuals' well-being.

The final essay in this collection, Thomas Hurka's "Self-Interest, Altruism, and Virtue," presents an account of virtue which places self-interest and altruism within a general theory of the intrinsic value of attitudes toward goods and evils. Hurka begins with a welfarist-perfectionist theory of the good, according to which such things as pleasure, knowledge, and achievement are all intrinsically good, that is, good in themselves, apart from their consequences. He defines self-interest as a positive attitude toward one's own good, an attitude consisting of three components: desiring to obtain one's good, actively pursuing it, and taking pleasure in it when it is achieved. Altruism, on this view, consists of a similar attitude toward the good of others. Hurka argues that both self-interested and altruistic attitudes are intrinsically good, since they involve love of some person's good for itself (that is, apart from its consequences). At the same time, he contends, self-interested and altruistic ends can be instrumentally evil if, by being too intense, they prevent a person from dividing his love proportionally between his own and others' good. On this view, excessive self-interest makes for a moral failing of selfishness, excessive altruism for one of self-abnegation. After setting out this theory, Hurka suggests that it should be modified to recognize a subtle asymmetry in the common-sense view of selfishness and self-abnegation, according to which self-abnegation is not always a failing. He also discusses ways in which the theory might be revised to accommodate some other common-sense moral views, such as the belief that parents should care more about the good of their children than they do about the good of strangers.

Reconciling self-interest and regard for others is a central concern of moral theory, one that requires a proper understanding of the nature of self-interest and the relationship between rationality and morality. The twelve essays in this collection offer valuable contributions to ongoing discussions of these issues.

ACKNOWLEDGMENTS

The editors wish to acknowledge several individuals at the Social Philosophy and Policy Center, Bowling Green State University, who provided invaluable assistance in the preparation of this volume. They include Mary Dilsaver, Terrie Weaver, and Pamela Phillips.

The editors would like to extend special thanks to Executive Manager Kory Swanson, for offering invaluable administrative support; to Publication Specialist Tamara Sharp, for attending to innumerable day-to-day details of the book's preparation; and to Managing Editor Harry Dolan, for providing dedicated assistance throughout the editorial and production processes.

CONTRIBUTORS

Kelly Rogers is Assistant Professor of Philosophy at the University of Florida. She has published articles on Aristotle's ethics in *Ancient Philosophy*, *Phronesis*, and the *Southern Journal of Philosophy*, and is the editor of *Self-Interest: Philosophical Perspectives from Antiquity to the Present* (forthcoming from Routledge).

Jean Hampton served as Professor of Philosophy at the University of Arizona. Her books include *Hobbes and the Social Contract Tradition* (Cambridge University Press, 1986) and (with Jeffrie Murphy) *Forgiveness and Mercy* (Cambridge University Press, 1988). She is also the author of numerous essays in moral, political, and legal theory, especially in the areas of contractarian moral theory, history of political theory, retributive justice, and liberalism.

Thomas E. Hill, Jr. is Kenan Professor of Philosophy at the University of North Carolina at Chapel Hill, where he has taught since 1984. He previously taught for sixteen years at the University of California, Los Angeles, and more briefly at Pomona College, at Johns Hopkins University, and (on visiting appointments) at Stanford University and the University of Minnesota. He is the author of *Dignity and Practical Reason in Kant's Moral Theory* (Cornell University Press, 1992), *Autonomy and Self-Respect* (Cambridge University Press, 1991), and a number of recent articles working toward the development of a modified Kantian moral theory.

David Copp is Professor of Philosophy at the University of California, Davis. He taught previously at Simon Fraser University and the University of Illinois at Chicago. He is the author of *Morality, Normativity, and Society* (Oxford University Press, 1995), a book on the foundations of ethics. He has published articles in moral and political philosophy, and coedited *The Idea of Democracy* (Cambridge University Press, 1993), *Morality, Reason, and Truth* (Rowman and Allenheld, 1985), and *Pornography and Censorship* (Prometheus Books, 1983). He is an associate editor of *Ethics* and a former executive editor of the *Canadian Journal of Philosophy*.

David Schmidtz is Associate Professor of Philosophy and (by courtesy) Associate Professor of Economics at the University of Arizona. He is the author of *The Limits of Government: An Essay on the Public Goods Argument* (Westview Press, 1991) and *Rational Choice and Moral Agency* (Princeton University Press, 1995). His articles have appeared in the *Journal of Philosophy* and *Ethics*. He is currently preparing (with Robert Goodin) a book for Cambridge University Press entitled *Individual Responsibility and Social Welfare*.

David O. Brink is Professor of Philosophy at the University of California, San Diego. His research interests are in ethical theory, history of ethics, political philosophy, and constitutional jurisprudence, and his essays have been published in such journals as *Ethics, Philosophical Review, Philosophy and Public Affairs*, and the *Journal of Philosophy*.

Stephen Darwall is Professor of Philosophy at the University of Michigan, where he has taught since 1984. His work has concentrated on contemporary theorizing about the foundations of ethics and practical reason, on the history of fundamental moral philosophy, especially in the seventeenth and eighteenth centuries, and on the connections between these. He is the author of *Impartial Reason* (Cornell University Press, 1983), *The British Moralists and the Internal 'Ought': 1640–1740* (Cambridge University Press, 1995), and numerous articles in moral philosophy, moral psychology, and the history of ethics.

Jennifer Roback Morse is Associate Professor of Economics at George Mason University. She received her Ph.D. in economics from the University of Rochester in 1980 and spent a postdoctoral year at the University of Chicago during 1979–80. She has taught at Yale University, and was John M. Olin Visiting Scholar at the Cornell Law School in the fall of 1993. Her publications have appeared in the *Journal of Political Economy, Economic Inquiry*, the *University of Chicago Law Review*, the *Georgetown Law Journal*, the *Journal of Economic History*, and the *Harvard Journal of Law and Public Policy*. She is currently working on a public choice explanation for the cause of the Civil War, and on models that expand the economists' standard understanding of the person.

Susan Wolf is Professor of Philosophy at the Johns Hopkins University in Baltimore, Maryland. She is the author of *Freedom within Reason* (Oxford University Press, 1990), a book on free will and moral responsibility, and has written numerous articles on ethics and the philosophy of mind for such journals as *Ethics, Mind, Philosophical Topics*, and the *Journal of Philosophy*. Her current research focuses on the relations among happiness, morality, and meaningfulness in life.

Neera K. Badhwar is Associate Professor of Philosophy at the University of Oklahoma. She is spending 1996–97 as a Laurance S. Rockefeller Fellow at the University Center for Human Values at Princeton University, where she will be writing a book on virtue and self-interest. Her articles on friendship, self-interest and altruism, virtue, communitarianism and liberalism, and contemporary moral theory have appeared in *Ethics, Noûs,*

American Philosophical Quarterly, Social Philosophy and Policy, Philosophy and Phenomenological Research, and other journals. Her anthology *Friendship: A Philosophical Reader* was published by Cornell University Press in 1993. She received her Ph.D. from the University of Toronto in 1986, and held a Killam Postdoctoral Fellowship at Dalhousie University in 1986–87.

Michael Slote is Professor of Philosophy and Chair of the Philosophy Department at the University of Maryland, College Park. He has published widely in ethics and moral psychology, and his most recent book is *From Morality to Virtue* (Oxford University Press, 1995). He is currently working on the implications of virtue ethics for political philosophy.

Thomas Hurka is Professor of Philosophy at the University of Calgary. He is the author of *Perfectionism* (Oxford University Press, 1993) and *Principles: Short Essays on Ethics* (Harcourt Brace Canada, 1993). His principal research interest is perfectionist theories of the good and their implications for moral and political philosophy. He is currently working on a book tentatively titled *Virtue and Vice: A Perfectionist Account.*

With deepest sadness, we dedicate this issue to the memory of Jean Hampton, whose untimely passing has left all of her friends greatly diminished. Her piercing intelligence, bemused wit, and unfailing thoughtfulness will be sorely missed.

BEYOND SELF AND OTHER*

By Kelly Rogers

Today there is a tendency to do ethics on the basis of what I should like to call the "self-other model." On this view, an action has no moral worth unless it benefits others—and not even then, unless it is motivated by altruism rather than selfishness. This radical rift between self-interest and virtue traces back at least to Philo of Alexandria (c. 20 B.C.–50 A.D.), according to whom, "lovers of self, when they have stripped and prepared for conflict with those who value virtue, keep up the boxing and wrestling until they have either forced their opponents to give in, or have completely destroyed them."[1] More recently, the distinction between those who value themselves and those who "value virtue" has been drawn sharply by Bernard Williams: "[I]n moral theory . . . it is not the Kantian leap from the particular and the affective to the rational and universal that makes all the difference; it is rather the Humean step—that is to say, the first Humean step—from the self to someone else."[2]

Proof that morality is essentially *about* benefiting others does not usually emerge alongside defense of any particular moral theory. Kantians, for instance, place the categorical imperative at the center of morality— utilitarians, the "greatest happiness" principle—and virtue ethicists, a certain conception of virtuous character. Still, Williams, and most other moral philosophers, conceive of the moral agent as one who has ventured that "first Humean step."[3] The self-other paradigm functions like a back-

* I am grateful to Mark Riebling, R. M. Hare, Frances Rogers, the other contributors to this volume, and its editors for their helpful suggestions in writing and revising this essay.

[1] Philo, *The Worse Attacks the Better*, in *Philo*, vol. 2, trans. F. H. Colson and G. H. Whitaker (Cambridge, MA: Loeb Classical Library, 1929), X.32.

[2] Bernard Williams, "Egoism and Altruism," in Williams, *Problems of the Self* (Cambridge: Cambridge University Press, 1973), p. 265.

[3] For example: Thomas Nagel, a neo-Kantian, asserts: "[M]oral requirements have their source in the claims of other persons" (Nagel, *The View from Nowhere* [Oxford: Oxford University Press, 1986], p. 197); Peter Singer, a utilitarian: "The ethical life is the most fundamental alternative to the conventional pursuit of self-interest" (Singer, *How Are We to Live? Ethics in an Age of Self-Interest* [Buffalo: Prometheus Books, 1995], p. ix); and Lawrence Blum, a virtue ethicist: "Basically, what makes the altruistic emotion morally good is that its object is the weal of another person. Why it is of moral value to have sympathy, compassion, or concern for someone is that one is thereby concerned for the good—the weal and woe—of another person" (Blum, *Friendship, Altruism, and Morality* [Boston: Routledge and Kegan Paul, 1980], p. 163). Classical virtue ethicists, such as Plato and Aristotle, of course, rest ethical theory on the ideal of personal flourishing (*eudaimonia*), but for many modern commentators that is precisely what undermines the Greeks' claim to be doing *moral* theory. Some interpretors have tried to show that certain Greek ethical theories do by and large

ground theory, a riverbed of belief which *constrains what we can count as a moral theory at all*. I take this to be the central reason why egoism is generally considered so unacceptable. It is not so much that egoism is demonstrably false or incoherent—indeed, it is regarded by many as consummately rational—but rather that it contradicts one of our most deeply held dogmas about morality.

Though aspects of the thesis that morality is "other-based" have been questioned by some, in what follows I attempt to develop a thorough-going critique of this idea, and, drawing upon Aristotelian and American Pragmatist sources, to make suggestions toward an alternative model for morality.[4]

I. ROBINSON CRUSOE: BEYOND GOOD AND EVIL?

"For a single man on a desert island, moral reasoning would be un-necessary and pointless, except on the assumption that he is in interaction with persons beyond his island, whether men or gods."[5] So writes Kurt Baier, inviting us to imagine the moral vacuum in which a totally isolated individual would ostensibly exist. A Robinson Crusoe figure, to be sure, would have many prudential concerns: studying his island's flora and fauna, navigating its streams, finding food, building a sturdy shelter; perhaps, after tending to life's necessities, he could develop hobbies and activities, and actually enjoy his new existence. But since nothing Crusoe does affects others, morality on the self-other paradigm is silent concern-ing him. If one accepts this paradigm, it would seem to follow that all Crusoe's activities—at least, until Friday arrives—must be "beyond good and evil."

Can this be right?

Let us imagine that Crusoe, rather than striving to improve his life, sits down in a cave and feels sorry for himself. He gathers berries and plants

---

conform to the self-other paradigm—see, e.g., Terence Irwin, *Aristotle's First Principles* (Ox-ford: Oxford University Press, 1988), esp. sections 208-12—but I have found problems with this idea; see my "Aristotle on Loving Another for His Own Sake," *Phronesis*, vol. 39, no. 3 (1994), pp. 291-302.

[4] An early paper that raises significant criticisms is W. D. Falk's "Morality, Self, and Others," in Hector-Neri Castaneda and George Nakhnikian, eds., *Morality and the Language of Conduct* (Detroit: Wayne State University Press, 1965), pp. 25-67. For more recent discus-sions, see John Cottingham, "The Ethics of Self-Concern," *Ethics*, vol. 101 (July 1991), pp. 798-817; Neera Kapur Badhwar, "Altruism versus Self-Interest: Sometimes a False Di-chotomy," *Social Philosophy and Policy*, vol. 10, no. 1 (Winter 1993), pp. 90-117; and Jean Hampton, "Selflessness and the Loss of Self," *Social Philosophy and Policy*, vol. 10, no. 1 (Winter 1993), pp. 135-65. Cottingham attacks impartialism in ethics; Badhwar challenges the alleged incompatibility of altruistic and self-interested motivation; and Hampton argues that self-sacrifice is not necessarily morally praiseworthy. Michael Slote also raises impor-tant challenges to the self-other approach to morality in his *From Morality to Virtue* (Oxford: Oxford University Press, 1985).

[5] Kurt Baier, *The Moral Point of View*, abridged version (New York: Random House, 1965), pp. 110-11.

when he feels hungry, but beyond that he makes little effort to situate himself, spending his days pining for his old home and deceiving himself about the gravity of his plight. Do we still say there is no moral difference between the two Crusoes?

Perhaps it will be said that even though the former Crusoe exhibits greater virtue—he is more courageous, honest, etc.—his virtue has no specifically *moral* merit, since he exercises it merely in the service of self-interest, which he is already naturally inclined to pursue. Extending his virtue toward Friday, on the other hand, would require special effort. But this objection does not point to a difference between the self and others *qua ends*; it points merely to a motivational difference in pursuing them.

Nor is it obvious that any such motivational gap exists. There are certainly many counterexamples to it, particularly in the very natural affection that parents feel for children, and friends for friends. Does a parent really require "special effort" to concern himself with his child? If anything, parents seem inclined to put their children's good before their own.

In any case, is the pursuit of self-interest really as natural and automatic as is being claimed? The problem of weakness of the will aside, people constantly act in self-destructive ways to gratify their passions, even when they realize this is contrary to their interests. In many cases it would seem that the truly demanding thing to do is to override one's inclinations for the sake of one's best interest. Of course, not everyone succeeds in doing this.[6]

II. THE DARWINIST DOUBLE-STANDARD

In this connection, it is interesting to note the widespread assumption— apparently originated in modern times by Charles Darwin—that if we can only demonstrate the ubiquity of our affection for others and the pervasiveness of altruism in the natural kingdom, we can show that other-concern, and thus morality, is endemic to our nature. In his discussion of the "moral sense" in *The Descent of Man*, Darwin optimistically asserts that inasmuch as we can expect man's "social instincts" to continue developing, "virtue will be triumphant."[7] This idea, however— which is not uncommon among modern philosophers[8]—raises the crucial question: Do our social inclinations provide us with a natural impetus for morality or not? When the inclination is egoistic, the answer seems to be negative; but evidence that we are natural altruists is taken to show our

[6] Cf. David Schmidtz, "Reasons for Altruism," *Social Philosophy and Policy*, vol. 10, no. 1 (Winter 1993), p. 68.

[7] Charles Darwin, *On the Origin of Species by Means of Natural Selection: Or, the Preservation of Favored Races in the Struggle for Life* and *The Descent of Man and Selection in Relation to Sex* (New York: Modern Library, 1948), p. 494.

[8] A recent example appears in Peter Singer, *How Are We to Live? Ethics in an Age of Self-Interest*, ch. 5.

propensity for morality. Proponents of the self-other model thus embrace
the contradictory position that self-interest cannot form a moral end because we are inclined toward it, but that another's interest *can* form a
moral end, because we are inclined toward *it*.

There is a further inconsistency in the denial that a solitary Crusoe can
be moral—namely, that it at once affirms and denies the self's legitimacy
as a moral objective. Consider the following statement of Baier: "Doing
good is doing for another person what, if he were able to follow (self-
interested) reason, he would do for himself."[9] Thus, the agent's self-
interest is a nonmoral end, if he pursues it himself—but also a moral end,
so long as it is pursued by someone else. Against this, I have to agree with
John Dewey when he states: "Consistently you must either say the self is
a nonmoral principle or else that it is a moral principle."[10] If the self is a
nonmoral end, then it is a nonmoral end, "wherever it is found." By the
same token, if it is a moral end, then "the ego and the alter both stand
exactly on the same plane."[11]

Asymmetry between self and other seems to arise on the assumption
that whereas benefiting others is a lofty occupation, to the degree that we
pursue our self-interest, we lead lives that are vicious, materialistic, small-
minded—existing in a condition of "permanent holidaying," as Peter
Singer has put it.[12] But, first, why is *this* sort of life supposed to be to our
advantage? Why is a passion-driven, antisocial life considered *interested*,
instead of just stupid and shallow? Further, why does this assessment of
self-interest not apply to the self-interest of *others*? If this sort of existence
is bad to pursue for ourselves, why is it good to pursue for someone else?
Or, if *their* self-interest is not a "permanent holiday," why must *ours* be?
This is really the gist of Dewey's objection, which seems to leave us with
two options—either (1) to reconceive our own self-interest in a manner
that does not question-beggingly build immoralism right in, or (2) to
banish *all* self-interest from the moral domain, *others' included*.

In any case, it is unclear why certain goods—wealth, bodily pleasure,
etc.—are assumed to be more "of the self" than others. To desire a good
is to have a particular affection for it, and all affections are equally affections of the self.[13] As Henry Sidgwick notes, "all our impulses, high and
low, sensual and moral alike, are so far similarly related to self, that—
except when two or more impulses come into serious conflict—we tend

[9] Baier, *The Moral Point of View*, pp. 107-8.
[10] John Dewey, *Lectures on Psychological and Political Ethics, 1898*, ed. Donald F. Koch (New York: Hafner Press, 1976), p. 210.
[11] *Ibid.*
[12] Peter Singer, *Practical Ethics* (Cambridge: Cambridge University Press, 1979), pp. 218-19.
[13] This observation belongs to Joseph Butler, who deftly observes that "love of our neigh-bor . . . has just the same respect to, is no more distant from, self-love than hatred of our neighbor, or than love or hatred of anything else"; see *Joseph Butler: Five Sermons*, ed. Stephen L. Darwall (Indianapolis: Hackett Publishing Co., 1983), p. 50.

to identify ourselves with each as it arises."[14] There are no grounds for arbitrarily associating self-interest with material as opposed to spiritual goods, or with antisocial as opposed to social affections. Consequently, it begs the question to assume that self-interest is necessarily at odds with morality. And, indeed, as Dewey points out, "unless ideal ends were also rooted in some natural tendencies of the self, they could neither occur to the self nor appeal to the self."[15]

III. A BANKRUPT MODEL: SELF-INTEREST AS "PREFERENCE-SATISFACTION"

Unless we wish to exclude all beneficial activity from the moral arena, clearly we must reconceive the nature of self-interest, questioning the hedonic or "preference" conception that underlies the "permanent holiday" idea. On this conception, a person's interests are determined simply on the basis of his preferences at the time, no matter how absurd or destructive they might be, and a person is "rational" to the extent that he maximizes his preference-satisfaction. Thus, whatever you happen to desire—no matter how harmful it might be to yourself and those around you—*that* is your interest, and since it is "rational" to pursue your interest, it is "rational" to harm yourself and others.

Since it is *not* rational to harm oneself and others simply because one has the whim, however, there is evidently something awry here. Without denying that self-interest does include a subjective dimension, we need to recognize that it contains an equally important objective component, and that when we lose sight of this latter component, we fail to do best by ourselves.[16] Human beings have various needs which must be met in order to flourish, and which their preferences do not necessarily parallel. Thus, for example, whatever he might feel at the time, the heroin addict whose preference it is to shoot himself up with an AIDS-infected needle, is not pursuing his best interest. To claim otherwise is to blur entirely the difference between falsely believing one is doing well and *actually* doing well. Or, if self-interest is to be defined as nothing other than a (potentially delusionary) belief-state about one's condition, then we require an alternative concept to express the idea of *actually* doing well. This concept—be it self-realization, flourishing, or what have you—*may* be inimical to morality, but it cannot be assumed to be so in advance.

---

[14] Henry Sidgwick, *The Methods of Ethics*, 7th ed. (London: Macmillan and Co., 1907), pp. 90–91.

[15] John Dewey and James Tufts, *Ethics* (New York: Henry Holt and Co., 1908), p. 364.

[16] For a fuller discussion of the objective component of self-interest, as well as a detailed consideration of its relation to the agent's subjective state, see James Griffin, *Well-Being: Its Meaning, Measurement, and Moral Importance* (Oxford: Oxford University Press, 1986), esp. part 1.

IV. Moral Courage: The Case of the Disabled Veteran

Consider the case of a certain Vietnam veteran, whose contact with a grenade during the war has left him permanently confined to a wheelchair. Upon returning to the U.S., he decides to enroll in architectural school, to pursue a lifelong ambition. Each school day for four years he wheels himself out to the bus stop at 7 a.m., takes an hour-long bus ride, and then wheels himself, rain or shine, around a large, hilly campus, going from classes to labs to the library. At 7 p.m. he reboards the bus, goes home, fixes himself dinner, studies as long as he can, and goes to sleep. He eventually graduates at the top of his class and becomes a highly successful architect.

This veteran would be widely admired and praised. But why? It is not *despite* the fact that he is pursuing his best interest that we admire his courage, determination, and integrity, but precisely in virtue of the fact. His entire struggle is the product of a decision to make something of himself, instead of letting his life go to waste. Yet on the self-other model, this is precisely why we must deny his actions any moral worth.

But this is absurd. To withhold *moral* commendation on the grounds that it is "his own self" that he aims to improve is to degrade the veteran's achievement.[17] And to assume, in advance, that a person's efforts at self-realization, or flourishing, must be at variance with morality, is manifestly false.

V. Other-Regard: Neither Necessary nor Sufficient for Morality

The desirability of rethinking the relationship of self-interest to morality may be further illustrated by two examples.

(1) A woman's husband has recently gone to jail for armed robbery. She visits him in prison on several occasions, and feeling pity for his unhappiness, agrees to assist him with an escape plot, thereby abetting a criminal and risking her own incarceration. The fact that the wife is "selflessly" pursuing her husband's good imbues her activity with no particular moral value.

(2) A student cheats on a final exam because he has not studied enough during the semester. The exam is not graded on a curve, so he is not causing others' grades to drop; nor is he deceiving his professor, who is "on" to him. But he *is* sabotaging his own education and his future. Now, clearly, there is something morally wrong with this student's behavior that has nothing to do with whether he is concerned with others—indeed, it would be natural to remind him that he is actually harming himself.

We require a broader conception of self-interest and morality than that assumed by the self-other paradigm to handle such cases as these. This

---

[17] See Hampton's "Selflessness and the Loss of Self" for further discussion of this idea.

model arises on the assumption that morality's function is, as one philosopher has put it, to resolve "the problem of ordering our relations with
other people."[18] Since self-interest is the root of the problem—supposedly,
if we were like the self-sacrificing ants or bees, we would all live in
harmony—altruism is thought to be the solution. Morality is consequently seen as an end-specific pursuit—to wit, a pursuit aimed at others'
welfare—that has no application outside society. On this view, morality
has no role to play in cases like that of the veteran, who strives for
personal success. On the other hand, such agents as the wife are at least
in the "moral ballpark," inasmuch as they are trying to further the good
of someone other than themselves.

VI. AN ALTERNATIVE MODEL: THE METAPHYSICS OF VIRTUE

There is an alternative way to conceive of morality, though—viewing it
not as a substantive pursuit itself, but as a structural program for doing
the things one already does, only doing them in a certain *way*. This
approach denies that morality is a specific activity set alongside all the
rest of our activities—artistic, philosophical, scientific, and so forth—and
distinguished by its end; rather, it is a system of principles for guiding
action which is potentially applicable to *anything* we undertake.[19] On this
view, morality's function is not merely to resolve self-other conflict, but to
foster harmonious interaction with our *total* environment. This environment includes a social dimension, but also a great deal more, including
each person's relationship to himself, his work, science, art, and the natural world.

In this wider context, the problem which morality exists to solve stems
from a basic fact about human beings—viz., that we are beings who *think*
conceptually or abstractly, but who must *act* in a world of particulars.
This fact creates a gap between the *director* and the *circumstances* of our
action. Morality assists in bridging this gap, enabling each of us to function as a coherent and integrated unit. It does this in two central ways.
First, it helps synchronize our passions—which are always for particular
things—with our reason—which is capable of forming a long-term or
"enlightened" vision of the good life as a whole. Second, it enables us to
develop principles for action, so that each time we a face a choice similar

[18] Harry Frankfurt, "The Importance of What We Care About," *Synthese*, vol. 53 (1982),
p. 257.
[19] I say "potentially" in order to leave open the question of what pursuits may have moral
import in a given situation; for as the case of the veteran suggests, something as mundane
as getting oneself to school can be morally significant. This approach rejects any intrinsic
moral/nonmoral divide, though it need not make a moral issue out of every step one takes.
Whether a given item or issue will have moral significance will depend in a given circumstance on such things as whether it conflicts with any of one's other values, the sorts of
choices and struggles it involves, its importance to one's well-being and/or that of others,
and so forth. Unfortunately, I can do no more here than allude to these issues, which merit
a separate discussion of their own.

to one we have faced before, it is not like facing a new particular for the first time. On this account, being "moral" is a question not of choosing others over self, but of committing oneself to achieving an integrated personality and a principled way of life.

Seen this way, the moral virtues will be defined in terms of an appropriate relation to the *world*—rather than merely to other people—thus rendering virtue morally significant even for individuals acting in isolation.[20] Consider, for instance, the virtue of honesty. The problem with dishonesty on this view is that of willful misrepresentation of the facts, not that of *who* the facts are misrepresented to. Thus, to return to the case of Crusoe, he is equally dishonest, and morally blameworthy as such, if he lies to himself as if he lies to Friday. Or consider the case of courage: its function is to handle fear, and this is independent of what one's fears are *about*—say, being attacked oneself or being afraid for another's sake. If someone is in control of his fears, he is in control of his fears; their content does not alter that fact. The question of the beneficiary of one's virtue is a separate matter from whether one has and exercises that virtue.[21]

VII. Social Virtues, or Hume's "Egregious Blockhead"

So far we have considered virtues which are essentially personal, but which may be extended toward others as well. But there are certain virtues—e.g., generosity—which involve others' welfare in a far more immediate way, making essential reference to beneficiaries. Are these sorts of virtues best defined on the basis of the self-other model? I would suggest not. To be sure, part of the reason that a generous person benefits others is a concern with their welfare, but there is a good deal more to the virtue than providing benefit. In particular, as Aristotle observes, it involves a certain attitude toward a *third* object, namely, one's wealth.[22] One who cares about others and *wishes* he could give to them, but who compulsively hoards his money, is not generous. Likewise, the person who

[20] This approach is broadly Humean in refusing to recognize any fundamental difference between the personal and social virtues qua virtues, concurring with Hume that "[i]t is probable that the approbation attending the observance of both is of a similar nature and arises from similar principles . . ." (Hume, *An Inquiry Concerning the Principles of Morals*, ed. Charles W. Hendel [New York: Macmillan Publishing Co., 1957], p. 139).

[21] What happens, though, when we turn our attention from the benefits of virtue to the costs of vice? Crusoe may be praised equally for all his displays of honesty, regardless of their beneficiary, but does he not commit a more serious moral offense when he lies to Friday than when he merely deceives himself? (I am grateful to David Schmidtz for raising this objection.) Surely the two cases are not equivalent, but their inequivalence does not, I think, lie in any difference between them qua instances of dishonesty. Rather, forcing another to pay the price of one's own misdeeds involves the additional vice of *negligence* or indifference toward the consequences of one's actions. Negligence may occur in self-confined cases as well—Crusoe may ignore the fact that self-deception tends to result in various psychological maladies—but we tend to think of him as being free to inflict these evils upon himself in ways he is not free to inflict them upon others.

[22] See Aristotle's entire discussion of generosity in the *Nicomachean Ethics*, book IV, ch. 1. Its lack of an other-regarding focus is quite striking, as I discuss in "Aristotle on Beneficence" (unpublished manuscript).

cares nothing for his wealth and indiscriminately gives it all away is not necessarily so either. Generosity is not simply helping others by shuffling one's goods toward them, but knowing how and when to give and how and when *not* to. As Aristotle suggests, the idea is to strike a correct balance in one's giving, and this includes paying attention to how well-off one is leaving oneself. Finally, we do not want to call such agents as the wife who assists with her husband's jailbreak "generous," even though this is an instance of selfless giving to another. The self-other model makes it seem as if the virtue of generosity is essentially about attaining others' good—whereas in fact it seems to be more about the general attitude one takes toward one's possessions vis-à-vis the good of both others *and* oneself, as well the wider environment in which one acts. One who possesses this disposition will most likely do the best job of securing the good for both his fellows and himself, but that is something of a different point.

In general, the approach to morality sketched here differs from the self-other model in that it refuses to allow a narrow conception of social excellence to supplant a general one of *human* excellence. It proposes grounding morality and virtue on what we may call the axiom of *life*, not that of society—recognizing that one could have one's social relationships in order and still have much moral work left to do. Thus, as Hume points out in the *Inquiry Concerning the Principles of Morals*, whereas we certainly heap moral praise upon the possessor of social virtue, "[i]t is at the same time certain that any remarkable defect in courage, temperance, economy, industry, understanding, dignity of mind, would bereave even a very good-natured, honest man of this honorable appellation. Who did ever say, except by way of irony, that such a one was a man of great virtue, but an egregious blockhead?"[23]

VIII. The Myth of "Pure" Motivation

If the self-other paradigm emphasizes the importance of making others' good one's moral *object*, it equally stresses the importance of making their good one's *motive*.[24] What is it to be motivated by others' interests? Typically, altruistic motivation is thought to involve either a particular sort of sentiment—such as sympathy or love[25]—or a certain rational at-

---

[23] Hume, *Inquiry*, p. 130. This passage—which is one of many passages exemplifying Hume's belief that virtue "consists altogether in the possession of mental qualities, *useful* or *agreeable* to the *person himself* or to *others*" (*ibid.*, p. 89; cf. note 20 above)—makes it difficult to see why Williams would regard Hume as a proponent of the self-other model (see the text accompanying note 2 above). Hume places great value on benevolence, but clearly he does not regard morality as exclusively other-regarding.

[24] As Bernard Williams has stated: "[T]he *point* of selecting certain motives for *moral* approbation: we are concerned to have people who have a general tendency to be prepared to put other people's interests before their own" (Williams, *Morality: An Introduction to Ethics* [New York: Harper Torchbooks, 1972], p. 74).

[25] Though sympathy and love doubtless enhance our sensitivity to others' plights, I must concur with Bernard Mandeville when he says of the related sentiment, pity, that, "as it is

titude: a recognition that one's reasons for caring about one's own good give one reasons for caring about others' good, too. It is not my purpose to deny the importance of either of these sorts of motivations in fostering proper other-regard. My question is rather: Why is such motivation alone to be regarded as "moral"?

Clearly it has much to do with the fact that morality's purpose according to the self-other model is the protection and fostering of others' good. Nonetheless, we can benefit ourselves while we benefit others, and, in light of this, the lengths to which philosophers have gone to exclude self-interest from moral motivation seem quite extreme. Francis Hutcheson took the idea so far that he came up with a calculus for subtracting self-interest from one's motivation to determine exactly how moral, i.e., altruistic, it was.[26]

But why is concern with self-interest considered so inimical to moral concern for others? Why the stress on motivational "purity"?

Purity seems required for two reasons. The first is that it is demanded by the "permanent holiday" conception of self-interest. If the pursuit of self-interest breeds an indulgent, materialistic, antisocial lifestyle, there is indeed cause to doubt its compatibility with moral motivation. Yet, as I have suggested, such a conception of self-interest is faulty. There is a second reason for doubting the compatibility of self-interest and morality, however, that would obtain even on a richer conception of self-interest. This is the perception that benefiting others from a motive of self-interest entails valuing them *instrumentally*, as mere fodder for our own pursuits. This is a legitimate concern, but is it a corollary of self-interested motivation?

There are different ways of benefiting others self-interestedly, after all. One can, to be sure, manipulate and defraud another person, making it seem as though one has his best interests at heart, when in fact he is being coldly used for some ulterior purpose of one's own. But one can also benefit another self-interestedly in a way that does not reduce him to a mere tool, but rather respects his purposes and autonomy. Consider, for instance, a small-town grocer who takes great pride in stocking his shelves with fresh, colorful produce, and who regards the upkeep of his shop as his greatest personal interest. He does not run his grocery store in order to further others' good, but he does deal with his customers fairly, honestly, and respectfully. What is the difference between these two cases? Why do we feel contempt for the first agent, but respect for and gratitude toward the latter?

---

an Impulse of Nature, that consults neither the publick Interest nor our own Reason, it may produce Evil as well as Good" (Mandeville, *An Enquiry into the Origin of Moral Virtue*, in *The Fable of the Bees, Or, Private Vices, Publick Benefits*, ed. F. B. Kaye [Indianapolis: Liberty Classics, 1988], p. 56). For a person who cannot properly regulate his passions, it is strictly a matter of chance whether his sympathy and love will lead to virtuous action or the reverse; so-called "altruistic" sentiments are not privileged in this respect.

[26] Francis Hutcheson, *An Inquiry Concerning the Original of Our Ideas of Virtue or Moral Good*, 4th ed. (1738), in *British Moralists 1650–1800*, ed. D. D. Raphael (Indianapolis: Hackett Publishing Co., 1991), p. 273.

Clearly, the difference cannot be traced to self-interested motivation, since this is exhibited by both. The difference lies, rather, in the *way* each views other people in respect of his self-interest. The first agent sees them as nothing more than tools to further his own ends, and has no sense of their autonomy. The grocer, in contrast, respects his customers as ends in themselves. He respects their right to think for themselves and form their own judgments—hence he deals with them honestly. He respects their independent values and purposes—hence he stocks his shelves with a wide variety of items, and responds to special orders. He respects their feelings—hence he deals with them politely and expresses his gratitude for their patronage. The grocer's self-interest is every bit as strong as that of the scoundrel; the difference is that whereas the latter underhandedly uses other people for private ends of which they may not be aware and of which they may disapprove, the former pursues his self-interest regardful of their plans and values.

It may be objected that despite his virtues, the grocer's overall purpose is to make a profit, and hence that he is not really treating his customers as ends in themselves, but as means to this further end. But this objection fails to distinguish between treating other people *as* ends and making them one's *own* end. The fact that the grocer has ends independent of his customers does not entail that he fails to treat them as ends in themselves. This requires only that he respect their independence and commitment to their own, private goals, not that he make their goals his own.

Notice how this objection moves the discussion back to the question of morality's object. The grocer's case reveals that self-interested motivation is compatible with treating others as ends, which I take to be the central moral requirement vis-à-vis them.[27] Even though the customers are being respected as ends, however, the grocer is criticized for not making their good his *object*. The assumption, which I have already criticized at length, is that if his object is merely his own good, there is something morally less worthy about his activity.

It might further be objected that the grocer example shows only that genuine other-regard is *compatible* with self-interest, not that self-interest is *itself* a moral motive. This objection is premised squarely on the self-

---

[27] I thus disagree with Kant, who wrote:

> As regards meritorious duties to others, the natural end which all men seek is their own happiness. Now humanity could no doubt subsist if everybody contributed nothing to the happiness of others but at the same time refrained from deliberately impairing their happiness. This is, however, merely to agree negatively and not positively with *humanity as an end in itself* unless every one endeavors also, so far as in him lies, to further the ends of others. For the ends of a subject who is an end in himself must, if this conception is to have its *full* effect on me, be also, as far as possible, *my* ends. (Immanuel Kant, *Groundwork of the Metaphysics of Morals*, trans. H. J. Paton [New York: Harper Torchbooks, 1964], section 69)

Not only does this involve an untenable self-other asymmetry of the sort identified by Dewey, but, as Sidgwick observes: "It is hard to see why, if man *as a rational being* is an absolute end to other rational beings, they must therefore adopt his subjective aims as determined by his non-rational impulses" (Sidgwick, *Methods of Ethics*, p. 390n.).

other model: it assumes that the grocer's virtue would be self-evident if he were motivated by the good of his patrons, but uncertain if he were motivated by his own good. I have already addressed this issue in connection with the veteran, however, whose case illustrated the absurdity of denying moral worth to a person's motives merely on the grounds that they aim at his own improvement or fulfillment.

Inasmuch as self-interested motivation entails neither instrumentalism nor amorality, the "purity of motive" assumption is misguided. When we deal with others respectfully and forthrightly, we can compatibly pursue our own interests and make it possible for them to pursue theirs, or, when we so choose, pursue their good jointly with our own. (The matter of the extent of our positive obligations toward them is a separate question.) We do not do right by others—or right in general—only when we ignore our self-interest. Indeed, as Bentham observes, if we are concerned with increasing the amount of happiness in the world, the less call for the disregard of self-interest, the better.[28]

IX. Self-Interested Altruism

Philosophers who stress purity of motivation sometimes observe that when we deal justly and benevolently with others, we tend to do best by ourselves. They point out that we will form meaningful relationships with others, be able to trust and be trusted, and so forth. In that sense, they argue, morality (understood in the restricted sense of "other-benefiting activity") is ultimately in a person's self-interest. But there is a catch. One will only reap the self-interested rewards of morality if one does not act morally for self-interest's sake. Thus, self-interest is an acceptable moral object after all, but only if one is not *motivated* by it.

This is a confusing recommendation, to say the least. It tells us that morality will further our interest, but that in order to act for our interest, we cannot act for our interest. Is the agent then supposed to block from his mind any thought of his own interest and enjoyment at the time of action? What if he accidentally "remembers" that he enjoys and values his other-benefiting activity? Should he stamp the memory out of his mind until later? Should he try to make sure this is playing no role in his motivation? Is that even possible?

More importantly, is it desirable? If you were in distress, would you feel slighted if you knew that your benefactor valued your welfare as part of his own and took a personal interest in helping you? Would you object to knowing that his motivation to assist you was "wholehearted," as

---

[28] Jeremy Bentham, *Deontology*, in *Deontology Together with A Table of the Springs of Action and the Article on Utilitarianism*, ed. Amnon Goldworth (Oxford: Clarendon Press, 1983), p. 121f.

Neera Badhwar has nicely put it?[29] I, personally, should prefer such an attitude, far from morally condemning it. Further, I believe that moral philosophers should capitalize on it, recognizing that far from a burden and duty, benefiting others is one of the central pleasures of life. The only argument against encouraging people to benefit others as a way of fostering their own well-being (in addition, of course, to other people's) is the worry that they will start to engage in sham benevolence simply to please themselves. But sham benevolence is not benevolence, nor can it provide the pleasures of benevolence. In this sense, there is truth to the idea of an egoistic paradox: you cannot fail to find gratification in external things and also expect to enjoy them.

On the other hand, it does not follow that full "disengagement" is necessary for attaining one's interest, as Butler suggests.[30] This falsely assumes that the activity and one's interest are two separate items, the former being a means to the latter. For truly kind people, however, benevolence is not a means to their interest; it *is* their interest. Or, as Dewey expresses the distinction, benevolent activity is pursued *as* their interest, not *for* it.[31]

The egoism/altruism distinction generates a false alternative, assuming that our choice is between valuing others instrumentally, on the one hand, or disinterestedly, on the other. Yet, though exhibiting true concern for another surely involves respecting his independence in some sense, the *Oxford English Dictionary* reminds us that to concern oneself with something is precisely "to interest oneself" in it. We have no difficulty grasping this idea when we speak of concern for such things as art or the environment, but for some reason matters are assumed to be different when the object of concern is another person. It is not clear, however, why the basic nature of concern should alter with the *object* of concern. As Butler himself notes, *all* concerns are "equally interested or disinterested, because the objects of them are equally self or somewhat else."[32]

Requiring unself-interested concern for other people borders on the oxymoronic: it tells one to act toward them in a concerned—i.e., interested—way, but not to be motivated by that concern, i.e., interest. The proper alternative to this, however, is not instrumentalism, but rejection of the underlying assumption that benevolence must be monolithically self or other. Seeing it as involving *both* the self *and* others yields a far richer conception of other-concern than is possible when one tries to ignore or block out the connection between benevolence and one's other values and interests. It says to one's beneficiaries: your good is not just something I am obligated to pursue in the ethical abstract, but something that matters to me *personally*.

---

[29] Badhwar, "Altruism versus Self-Interest," p. 115.
[30] Butler, *Five Sermons*, pp. 48–49.
[31] Dewey, *Lectures on Psychological and Political Ethics*, p. 209.
[32] Butler, *Five Sermons*, p. 51.

X. IMPLICATIONS FOR MORAL SKEPTICISM

The self-other paradigm has played a pivotal role in making credible a certain version of moral skepticism. As noted, the paradigm attempts to circumscribe the end of morality to include only the good of others, relegating all other pursuits to the realm of nonmorality. By arbitrarily dividing human ends in this way, however, it deprives us of guidance and principle in pursuing all ends beside others' good, placing these ends under the direction of "prudence"—or, what amounts to the same thing on the modern understanding of prudence, of expedience.[33] How an unprincipled pursuit of ends generally is supposed to be reconciled with a principled pursuit of other-regarding ends, though, is never explained, and indeed, is precisely what enables the skeptic to quip, "Why be moral?" For what this question amounts to is: Why should I add "moral" ends to the set of ends I already have?

Suppose, however, that we refuse thus to categorize actions on the basis of their ends, recognizing, moreover, that, *contra* Hobbesian conventional wisdom, it is both natural and pleasant to seek the good of others as well as of oneself. On this approach, morality is not a question of selecting the first of these ends over the second, but of regulating and balancing our natural desires, including our desires for *both* ends. Others' good does not enter as an alien presence, in need of special integration with "normal" life. There is no need to ask: "Why care about others?"—one already *does*.

This is not to say, of course, that we have innate knowledge of how to develop that care into the correct *treatment* of them. Our natural affection for others is just that—an *affection*—and as such is not a guide to action. Such a guide is provided by virtue, which we need, not in order to transform us from Hobbesian warlords into Christian philanthropists, but to help bring reason and order to what would otherwise be nothing but a jumble of feelings.

Rather than attempt to explain to a sociopath why he should concern himself with his fellows, I think the question ought to be reversed: Why exclude every facet of life except the other-regarding from the domain of the moral? If we refrain from arbitrarily restricting morality in this way, morality justifies itself: one should be moral—i.e., should cultivate an integrated personality and principled way of life—because the opposite of these will sabotage and undermine the successful pursuit of *all* one's goals, be they self- *or* other-regarding (or both). The dishonest, intemperate, miserly coward is no more able to help himself than anyone else. Looked at this way, the burden of proof is switched back to the sociopath. Life can be lived well or poorly; morality makes us live it well; it is up to the sociopath to show us why we should live it poorly instead. The

---

[33] On the radical transformation of prudence since antiquity, see Douglas Den Uyl, *The Virtue of Prudence* (Bern: Peter Lang, 1991).

question to ask is not "Why be moral?" but—as a friend of mine (who never expected to be quoted) once put it—"Why be shitty?"

XI. SELFISHNESS: AN EPISTEMOLOGICAL PROBLEM?

If we cease to identify morality with concern for others and immorality with self-interest, what are we to make of the phenomenon known as selfishness? Surely we do not wish to deny that selfishness exists and is objectionable? The point, however, is not to deny the existence of selfishness but to rethink what such behavior actually consists in. It is not simply the pursuit of self-interest—for we all pursue self-interest, and wisely so. Nor is it simply self-interest "excessively" pursued; that will depend on how one's interests are conceived. Selfishness in the commonly derided sense refers not to the pursuit of our interest as such, but to our *conception* of our interests in relation to the larger context in which we operate. It is fundamentally an *epistemological* problem. Dewey explains:

> It is comparatively rarely that a man says: "I am going to have my own good at all hazards and I do not care how much I sacrifice other people." It comes in a much more subtle way than that. One is engaged in something which has a positive value; it is a good so far as it goes. Then the person becomes so absorbed in that immediate occupation which has defined himself in the past that he is not observant of new stimuli which would compel a broadening of the scope of activity, and which would involve that he subordinate this particular line of interest to something more comprehensive. The judgment that a man is selfish means that he ought to be defining himself on the basis of a wider situation, that he ought to be taking into account factors which as a matter of fact he is neglecting. It means inadequacy almost always.[34]

This is of course not to deny the existence of what we might call "sociopathic selfishness," where a person *is* aware of the harmful effect of his behavior on others and either ignores this fact or positively revels in it. But, first, to injure another is not necessarily to act selfishly; sometimes people harm others out of spite or vengeance, and in doing so pay no attention to the self-harm they are inflicting. Medea, for example, seems to have been driven to murder her children less out of selfishness than out of an all-consuming hatred for her adulterous husband, Jason. One might object that she *was* selfish insofar as she placed her desire for vengeance above the welfare of her children, but this assumes that acting on a hateful emotion is more selfish than acting on a benevolent one, and, as we have seen, this is simply untrue.

[34] Dewey, *Lectures on Psychological and Political Ethics*, p. 213.

Second, those who harm others in pursuit of their own personal advantage tend to depersonalize or vilify their victims, as a way of assuring themselves that they are not really harming anyone after all. Shoplifters, for instance, frequently excuse themselves on the grounds that their "victim" is a large store or corporation that can "painlessly" absorb the loss of a few trinkets. Similarly, rapists and other criminals consistently rely on depersonalization as a way of evading the fact that they are injuring fellow human beings. Alternatively, they tell themselves that their victims "deserve" the treatment they get, and that since their victims are being brought to justice, they should not be thought of as being harmed. This sort of rationalization appears in more mundane contexts as well—for instance, among those who switch higher for lower price-tags on merchandise they wish to purchase, on the grounds that the original price was "unjustly" high. These common rationalizations are a psychological defense that allows wrongdoers to evade the fact of their own immorality. Few people are comfortable acknowledging themselves to be scoundrels, after all, and this discomfort ensures that while the devil-may-care attitude of the sociopath surely exists, it must remain relatively rare.

The problem with the person ordinarily called "selfish," as Dewey suggests, is not that he is pursuing his self-interest in open disregard of the harm he inflicts on others, but that he casts his net too narrowly, failing to appreciate the "comprehensive situation."[35] Selfishness is thus, in most cases, a form of obliviousness. William James—whose discussion of self-love in *The Principles of Psychology* Dewey well describes as "very important"—goes further, suggesting that it involves a measure of obliviousness even toward the *self*. James observes that, "[w]hen I am led by self-love to keep my seat whilst ladies stand, or to grab something first and cut out my neighbor, what I really love is the comfortable seat, is the thing which I grab."[36] Self-love in this sense is nothing more than "a name for certain reflex acts": "something rivets my attention fatally, and fatally provokes the selfish response." Ordinary selfishness is really not focused on the self at all, but on external objects. "[T]he more utterly 'selfish' I am in this primitive way, the more blindly absorbed my thought will be in the objects and impulses of my lusts, and the more devoid of any inward looking glance."[37]

The "pragmatist" analysis of self-love (as we might call it) suggests that the moral problem is not with self-regard, but with *subjectivity*. The selfish person is one who refuses or fails to take into consideration all the facts relevant to assessing how to act. That is, he fails to be objective, in the sense that he rests his choices on an incomplete collection of facts—usually selected on the basis of whether they reinforce his present desires.

---

[35] *Ibid.*, pp. 210–11.
[36] William James, *The Principles of Psychology*, vol. 1 (New York: Henry Holt and Co., 1890), p. 320.
[37] *Ibid.*

The foundation of this view of selfishness is of course Aristotle, who famously distinguishes "bad" self-love from "good" precisely on the grounds that the bad self-lover pursues every whim and fleeting passion as his interest, whereas the good self-lover forms a conception of his interests by rationally evaluating his passions, purposes, and all other facts relevant to his condition—including the fact that he lives in a cooperative society with other independent agents like himself.[38] He may, of course, be mistaken from time to time, but the important thing is that he does not let subjective impulses dominate his life; rather, he employs reason to regulate these and, as best he can, bring them in line with his total context.

XII. THE IMPARTIALISM TRAP

To the extent that we stress the moral importance of an objective viewpoint, it may seem natural to move toward an impartialist position, but I think this move should be resisted. Refusing to conceive of the moral life along self-other lines does not entail that the self's interests be treated with impartial concern. Not only is the psychological possibility of this doubtful, but I do not think it is desirable, for reasons that have been raised in recent years by Bernard Williams, John Cottingham, and others, who stress the sort of alienation this engenders.[39] *Objectivity*, not impartiality, is the appropriate remedy for self-absorption. We should not advise agents to take an impartial attitude toward their own interests, but rather to appreciate the position of their interests in the larger context in which they act. As in the case of the grocer, this calls for a recognition of others as ends-in-themselves, but it does not dictate that one pretend as though oneself and one's values were not particularly special to one.

James outlines the process involved in attaining the objective[40] viewpoint in his *Principles of Psychology*, indicating that it is ultimately a matter of uniting the abstract with the concrete—the very thing I earlier suggested was morality's basic function. In particular, judging one's own case involves moving from the concrete to the abstract, whereas judging another's involves the opposite transition. To elucidate the nature of, and need for, these cognitive passages, James refers us to the work of the now-obscure nineteenth-century German psychologist, Adolf Horwicz, who explains the phenomenon of self-preference in what are essentially epistemological terms. The reason we tend to be biased in favor of "our own," says Horwicz—where by "our own" he means: our own posses-

[38] See Aristotle, *Nicomachean Ethics*, book IX, chs. 4 and 8.

[39] See, e.g., Bernard Williams, "Persons, Character, and Morality," in Williams, *Moral Luck* (Cambridge: Cambridge University Press, 1981); and Cottingham, "The Ethics of Self-Concern" (*supra* note 4).

[40] James refers to it as the "impartial" viewpoint, but the surrounding context indicates that he is referring simply to making an objective judgment about oneself, not viewing oneself with impartial concern.

sions, children, work, and so forth—is *not* that we have impressed the
stamp of our Ego upon these things or that they are *ours*, but that "we
know them better, 'realize' them more intimately, feel them more deeply.
We learn to appreciate what is ours in all its details and shadings, whilst
the goods of others appear to us in coarse outlines and rude averages."[41]
James notes how this epistemological disparity threatens objective self-
judgment as well as our ability to give proper consideration to others'
good, and this is the meaning of his belief that objectivity requires a
uniting of the abstract with the concrete. On the one hand, it requires
"abstraction from the vividness with which . . . things known as intimately as our own possessions and performances appeal to our imagination," while, on the other hand, it demands the vivid representation of
others' affairs, making their good seem more tangible and urgent.[42] On
this account, failure to balance the good of self and others is due not to
partiality as such—though it manifests itself as this—but to what is essentially an epistemological failure to represent things in their proper
perspective.

Of course, it may be that the *reason* we best know "our own" in the first
place is precisely that it is *our own*.[43] True, I know (for example) my own
children better than anybody else's, but *why* do I know them better? Is it
simply that I spend the most time with them, or is it also that they are *my*

---

[41] Adolf Horwicz, *Psychologische Analysen auf Physiologischer Grundlage* (Theil II, IIte Hälfte,
section 11), quoted in James, *Principles of Psychology*, p. 326. It is worth quoting the remainder
of this most interesting passage:

> Here are some examples: A piece of music which one plays one's self is heard and
> understood better than when it is played by another. We get more exactly all the
> details, penetrate more deeply into the musical thought. We may meanwhile perceive
> perfectly well that the other person is the better performer, and yet nevertheless—at
> times—get more enjoyment from our own playing because it brings the melody and
> harmony so much nearer home to us. This case may almost be taken as typical for the
> other cases of self-love. On close examination, we shall almost always find that a great
> part of our feeling about what is ours is due to the fact that we *live closer* to our own
> things, and so feel them more thoroughly and deeply. As a friend of mine was about
> to marry, he often bored me by the repeated and minute way in which he would
> discuss the details of his new household arrangements. I wondered that so intellectual
> a man should be so deeply interested in things of so external a nature. But as I entered,
> a few years later, the same condition myself, these matters acquired for me an entirely
> different interest, and it became my turn to turn them over and talk of them unceas-
> ingly. . . . The reason was simply this, that in the first instance I *understood* nothing of
> these things and their importance for domestic comfort, whilst in the latter case they
> came home to me with irresistible urgency, and vividly took possession of my fancy.
> So it is with many a one who mocks at decorations and titles, until he gains one
> himself. And this is also surely the reason why one's own portrait or reflection in the
> mirror is so peculiarly interesting a thing to contemplate . . . not on account of any
> absolute "*c'est moi*," but just as with the music played by ourselves. What greets our
> eyes is what we know best, most deeply understand; because we ourselves have felt
> it and lived through it. We know what has ploughed these furrows, deepened these
> shadows, blanched this hair; and other faces may be handsomer, but none can speak
> to us or interest us like this. (pp. 326–27; passage translated by James)

[42] James, *Principles of Psychology*, p. 328.
[43] I am grateful to Thomas Hurka for raising this objection.

children, the reflection of *my* image? To extricate ourselves from this chicken-and-egg quandary, it may be useful to distinguish self-love from selfishness. It would seem to be the former—our natural affection for ourselves—that explains the origin of our extensive self-knowledge. Each of us is naturally dear to him- or herself, and, as Aristotle observes, this endearment extends to such things as our children and handiwork inasmuch as they are concrete actualizations of our personal potentials.[44] These endearments, in turn, lead us to spend more time reflecting upon ourselves and our personal concerns, explaining why we know them better.[45] Self-love need not consequently issue in selfishness, but it does create the discrepancy between self-knowledge and knowledge-of-others that *can* issue in selfishness.

XIII. CONCLUSION

If on the conception sketched above morality turns out looking somewhat mundane, that is quite intentional. For the recommendation is precisely that we cease to view it as a pursuit elevated above our other ordinary pursuits and aims; it is a call to *naturalize* morality, viewing it as a structure for guiding the whole of action, not as itself a substantive pursuit—to wit, the pursuit of others' good—set uneasily and insecurely alongside everything else we do. One has a need for guidance by moral principles, and a need to exhibit good character, whether one is choosing a career, writing a paper, or walking down the street. Divorcing morality from these domains serves only to abandon them to rule by a random muddle of desires.

It also serves to marginalize morality, rather than seeing it as our greatest single resource for discovering and living the "good life." On the self-other model, morality is ultimately reduced to a church-on-Sunday routine, an activity that we must find time to squeeze into "real" life. It fosters the kind of scenario wherein a person who acts morally irresponsibly all week can feel good about himself by "selflessly" working at a

[44] Aristotle, *Nicomachean Ethics*, book IX, ch. 7. Interestingly, Aristotle argues that this principle also explains why benefactors love their beneficiaries more than vice versa:

> Each [craftsman] likes his own product more than it would like him if it acquired a soul. Perhaps this is true of poets most of all, since they dearly like their own poems, and are fond of them as though they were their children. This, then, is what the cause of the benefactor resembles; here the beneficiary is his product, and hence he likes him more than the product likes its producer. The cause of this is as follows: (1) Being choiceworthy and lovable for all. (2) We are in so far as we are actualized, since we are in so far as we live and act. (3) The product is, in a way, the producer in his actualization. (4) Hence the producer is fond of the product, because he loves his own being. And this is natural, since what he is potentially is what the product indicates in actualization. (*Nicomachean Ethics*, 1167b34–1168a9, trans. Terence Irwin [Indianapolis: Hackett, 1985])

[45] Survival itself would also seem to demand that we spend the most time trying to understand our own selves and affairs.

soup kitchen on Saturday mornings; this becomes for him a form of penance. Morality for such a person is not part of the fabric of life, but an occasional ornament to it. What he needs to realize is that morality is about *everything* he does, and that his weekend charity work does not override his weeklong behavior, and is arguably not even commendable, unless it proceeds from a character which is good.

Not only does the self-other paradigm marginalize morality, but it erects what is in effect a *moral glass ceiling*. We can peer at the heights of extreme virtue, but are psychologically structured so that we cannot attain them. Even philosophers who wish to "vindicate the autocentric perspective," such as Cottingham, continue to view self-"transcendence" as the essence of "heroic sainthood." Cottingham's only problem is that most of us are incapable of self-overcoming. He is thus not vindicating self-concern at all, so much as identifying it as a necessary compromise—not exactly a cure for the lives of "hypocrisy" and "neurotic self-flagellation" to which he complains anti-self moralities condemn us.[46] Moral excellence, as Aristotle said, should be a "hard target" to hit, but not an *impossible* one.

The "self" is not the basic problem in morality and the "other" is not the solution. The welfare of others is just one of many possible human concerns and pursuits, and as such can be undertaken for better or for worse, consistently with morality or not. Inasmuch as the value it involves— human life—is especially important, helping others can form a particularly excellent activity. But then again, by the same standard, so can helping oneself.

Philosophy, University of Florida

---

[46] Cottingham, "The Ethics of Self-Concern," pp. 815–16.

THE WISDOM OF THE EGOIST:
THE MORAL AND POLITICAL IMPLICATIONS
OF VALUING THE SELF*

By Jean Hampton

I. Introduction

There is a traditional understanding of what morality is, an understanding that most contemporary moral philosophers take for granted.
This understanding is not itself a theory, but rather an account of the
phenomenon of morality, to which these philosophers have thought any
theory of the phenomenon must conform if it is to be considered successful as either an explanation or a justification of our moral life. According
to this account, there are three prominent features that, together, characterize the moral:

First, moral action and moral regard are taken to be other-regarding.
While some philosophers have identified a certain kind of self-respect as
part of morality,[1] in general morality has been thought to involve duties
to others, requiring that they be treated with respect. Self-interest is generally taken to be outside the province of the moral.

Second, morality is supposed to be highly authoritative. In any contest
between reasons derived from morality and other sorts of reasons, particularly demands of self-interest, the moral reasons are thought to be
almost always the rightful winner (albeit often not the de facto winner).
The idea that morality should be accorded such authority has been criticized in recent years by philosophers who accept the idea that morality is
largely other-regarding in nature, and who are concerned that individuals
will be stifled in their self-pursuits by an overdemanding moral sense.[2]

* I am grateful to an audience at Colgate University, where an earlier version of this essay
was presented, for helpful comments and criticisms. For their comments on some of the
essay's themes, I am also grateful to Neera Badhwar, Maudemarie Clark, Stephen Darwall,
Daniel Russell, Don Scherer, David Schmidtz, the other contributors to this volume, and its
editors. Finally, I want to thank the Pew Foundation for their fellowship support of my work
(through their Pew Evangelical Scholar's Program) during much of the time when I was
writing this essay.
  [1] For example, see some of the works of Neera Badhwar, Thomas Hill, Kelly Rogers, and
David Schmidtz, all of whom have essays in this volume. See also Julia Annas's *The Morality
of Happiness* (New York: Oxford University Press, 1993), which explores the way in which an
individual's happiness is associated with morality in the thinking of ancient Greek and
Roman philosophers.
  [2] See, for example, Susan Wolf, "Moral Saints," *Journal of Philosophy*, vol. 79, no. 8 (August
1982), pp. 419–39; reprinted in *The Virtues: Contemporary Essays on Moral Character*, ed. Robert
B. Kruschwitz and Robert C. Roberts (Belmont, CA: Wadsworth, 1987), pp. 137–52.

Note that these attacks on the authority of morality presuppose acceptance of the idea that it is largely or exclusively other-regarding in nature.

Third, morality is supposed to be "impersonal" in two senses. First, its content is supposed to be impersonal: whereas we care for our friends or our family because we love things about them that are personal and distinctive to them, our moral attitudes toward people are supposed to be disengaged from the contingencies of their personalities, and responsive to something about them (e.g., their reason) that is common to all human beings. Second, this responsiveness is supposed to be impersonal in the sense that it is motivated by morality itself: that is, the moral worth of our actions is supposed to arise from the fact that we do them "for the sake of" duty, and not for the sake of some interest or affection we have that just happens to accord with moral demands.

In this essay, I will be attacking the first and third tenets, claiming that morality involves considerable self-interested concern, and is much more particular and personal in both content and motivation than it is standardly thought to be. This means that I will be leaving the second tenet largely intact. However, the import of the second tenet will be substantially different once the subject matter of morality is revised, and the considerable authority of morality will be much less personally threatening when moral concerns extend to the well-being of the self as well as to the well-being of others. In the end, the search for a way to accommodate self-concern within morality enables us to rethink what is at stake when we use the notion of the moral, and what moral theories should ultimately be trying to capture in order to be successful. If I am right, our moral theorizing should be substantially different from what it is now; and while I cannot develop this new kind of moral theory in any full or complete sense in a single essay, I can at least present in a preliminary way the directions this sort of theory would take.

II. The Political Aspects of Our Self-Concern

One way to see how self-concern is part of the realm of the moral is to appreciate the extent to which unjust political structures can affect human beings such that they are disabled from pursuing their self-interest effectively. Consider the following quotation from a novel by Zora Neale Hurston, in which a dying African-American mother speaks to her daughter:

> "Stop cryin', Isie, you can't hear what Ahm sayin', 'member tuh git all de education you kin. Dat's de onliest way you kin keep out from under people's feet. You always strain tuh be de bell cow, never be de tail uh nothin'. Do de best you kin, honey, 'cause neither yo' paw nor dese older chillun is goin' tuh be bothered too much wid you, but you goin' tuh git 'long. Mark mah words, You got de spunk, but mah po' li'l' sandy-haired chile goin' suffer uh lot 'fo' she git tuh de place

she kin 'fend fuh herself. And Isie, honey, stop cryin' and lissen tuh me. Don't you love nobody better'n you do yo'self. Do, you'll be dying befo' yo' time is out. And Isie, uh person kin be killed 'thout being struck uh blow."[3]

This mother appreciates the extent to which her daughter's future ability to fend for herself, pursue her own interests, and have ambitions that she effectively achieves, is directly linked to the extent to which she believes in her own worth—that is, the extent to which she thinks she is someone who matters, whose talents are real, whose interests are important to satisfy, whose ideas and ambitions are something that others should take seriously. This mother knows, however, that once she has died, her daughter's sense of her own worth as a person will be imperiled in the environment in which she is growing up. As the youngest female in a family that doesn't take females to be the equals of males, and as a member of an oppressed group in her society, the child will be sent message after message telling her that she doesn't matter, that her educational and occupational horizons are limited, that her concerns, her views, and her words should not be taken seriously. Hence, the mother tries from her deathbed to bestow upon the child the courage to resist the denigrating messages that she is sure to receive.

The mother's concern is not that such messages might be true, but that her child might (falsely) come to believe them. Hence, she is determined to teach the child that such messages can be fought as long as the child has faith in herself. "Don't you love nobody better'n you do yo'self," she counsels her daughter, whose "spunk" she fears will be sorely tried in the years to come. "Loving" oneself is understood by the mother in a special way here: it refers not to narcissistic adoration but to an attitude of appreciation of oneself and a belief in one's (real) value and importance. Loving oneself in this sense is a way to be the "bell cow" rather than the tail of the herd; and it is a way to steel oneself against the sufferings that can sap one's ability to pursue what one wants and needs. Even more fundamentally, it is a way to ensure that one will not die inside, losing the ability to achieve, to enjoy, perhaps even to survive. The mother knows, however, that this love is something that will, for this child, be hard to sustain in the face of all the failures of love she will experience from others. The child will therefore have to cling to an appreciation of herself; she will have to consistently choose to believe something about herself that other people are going to be telling her isn't true.

Contrast this passage with a discussion by John Stuart Mill in *The Subjection of Women*, describing how certain boys in his society are raised to think about themselves in relation to women:

[3] Zora Neale Hurston, *Jonah's Gourd Vine* (1934; reprint, London: Virago, 1987), pp. 206–7.

[H]ow early the notion of his inherent superiority to a girl arises in his mind; how it grows with his growth and strengthens with his strength; how it is inoculated by one schoolboy upon another; how early the youth thinks himself superior to his mother, owing her perhaps forbearance, but no real respect; and how sublime and sultan-like a sense of superiority he feels, above all, over the woman he honours by admitting her to a partnership of his life.[4]

Particularly insofar as Mill had middle-class and upper-class British men in mind when he wrote this passage, he is portraying the kind of self-conception held by human beings who occupy a high place in the hierarchy of their society. A bit later, Mill refers to these people as enjoying not self-love—which is what Isie's mother wants her to strive for—but rather "self-worship":

It is an exact parallel to the feeling of a hereditary king that he is excellent above others by being born a king, or a noble by being born a noble. . . . The self-worship of the monarch, or of the feudal superior, is matched by the self-worship of the male.[5]

Reared to believe in their own superiority, Mill says, these males receive training in "arrogance and overbearingness."[6]

How remarkably different are the messages about self-worth that Mill's boys and Hurston's Isie hear. To the extent that each kind of child accepts either message, each will differ markedly not only in how each regards himself or herself, but also in how well each of them is able to pursue certain interests. Whereas a kind of death of the self is something that a child in Isie's situation risks, Mill's boys are given the chance to enjoy lordship and aggrandizement (although, in tones reminiscent of Hegel's discussion of the fate of the master in his master/slave dialectic in *The Phenomenology of Spirit*, Mill argues that because this self-worship perverts these boys' relationships with a considerable part of humanity and causes them to have a false sense of their own importance in the world, it is bad for them over the long run).[7] Henceforth I will call the regard that Isie's mother wants her to have "self-honor" and the regard that Mill's boys are taught "self-worship." The term "pride" can refer to either self-honor or self-worship. Criticisms of "pridefulness" commonly found, for example, in Christian religious literature are appropriate, in my view, as criticisms of self-worship, but never of self-honor. As I will explain more fully below, this is, in part, because self-honor is a way to fight against the

---

[4] John Stuart Mill, *The Subjection of Women*, ed. Susan Moller Okin (Indianapolis: Hackett, 1988), p. 87.
[5] *Ibid.*, pp. 87–88.
[6] *Ibid.*, p. 88.
[7] *Ibid.* For the master/slave dialectic, see G. W. F. Hegel, *The Phenomenology of Spirit*, trans. A. V. Miller (Oxford: Clarendon Press, 1977), pp. 111-19.

lack of self-regard which threatens Isie, and which I will henceforth call "self-denigration."

Each of these attitudes reflects the view one takes about one's own value and how that value is related to the value of others. What actions one takes, what aims one develops, what ambitions one believes one is allowed to have, all depend upon the kind of worth one is prepared to accord oneself and others. If Isie thinks she is too unimportant for a certain career, she will not pursue it; if she thinks that her race or gender makes her too "low" or "the wrong sort of person" for certain kinds of interests, she will not develop them. Even if she refuses to believe these messages, the rest of her society may contain enough people who accept them to make it virtually impossible for her to get access to what she needs in order to pursue activities thought inappropriate for "her kind." (For example, in my mother's high school in the 1940s, girls were not allowed to take physics; for much of this century, African Americans were effectively prohibited from pursuing many careers in the United States.) Indeed, merely being poor can be taken as reflective of a person's importance in societies where worth tracks wealth, so that the fact that a person such as Isie comes from the "wrong side of the tracks" (where this fact may be manifested in her accent, her clothes, or her level of education) can be thought, by her or by others in society, to preclude her from pursuing certain kinds of occupations or from getting into certain kinds of colleges. People on the receiving end of messages branding them as "low" in value are in danger of learning to accept being the "tail of the herd."

As these examples show, society can link worth to its members in a variety of ways. If worth is tied to how much money one has, the rich will take themselves to have more worth than the poor. If worth is tied to race, or gender, or religious belief, then one's membership in a racial, gender, or religious group will likely affect one's conclusions about where one fits in one's society's hierarchy of worth. To the extent that there are cross-currents in a society's value hierarchy, this will make the task of ranking harder: for example, if race and gender both matter, it may be hard to determine the relative ranking of two people, one of whom is from the lower-ranked gender but the higher-ranked race and the other of whom is from the higher-ranked gender but the lower-ranked race. Such confusions can cause social struggles, quarrels, restlessness, and rebellion. And if those at the bottom of the heap decide not to acquiesce in their low status, the hierarchy may tumble.

Social and political construction of the value of human beings can also work through the defining of the value of certain *roles*, which people will be steered toward, depending upon how they are categorized (e.g., their gender, their ethnicity, their religion, their caste, their IQ test results). A level of worth will be identified with these roles, which will play a part in defining what kind of interests a person has, and when these interests can be legitimately pursued. Plato's *Republic* defines this process in some detail; types of people are steered toward specific social roles, whose value Plato indicates by using the metaphor of precious metals: rulers are "gold" people, soldiers are "silver" people, and workers and artisans are "iron" people. While contemporary American society is not nearly so explicit in its ranking of people by roles, such ranking still goes on. Certain occupations are commonly taken to be more valuable than others, and those who are fitted for these more valuable jobs enjoy a higher rank than those who are not. This can affect people's self-interest in a variety of ways: consider the extent to which women are commonly steered toward assuming all or most of the parenting responsibilities in a family; and yet such parenting is not regarded as a prestige position in our society, and those who engage in it report having difficulty acknowledging the legitimacy of pursuing their own interests.[8]

To summarize: Social and political forces can indirectly affect what interests we have and our sense of the importance of these interests, by playing a part in constructing our sense of our own worth. This construction can work by relying on certain intrinsic features we have (e.g., our race, our gender), so that we think: because I'm a female, I'm not worth all that much; or because I'm white, I'm very important. Or that construction can work by defining the worth of roles, to which certain kinds of people are steered (e.g., I'm only a mother, and hence I'm not as important as that lawyer over there). The kind of self-worth you believe that you have can affect any or all of the following:

(1) the kind and extent of the talents you believe you have, or are supposed to have;
(2) the kind of interests and desires you have, or believe you are supposed to have, and the extent to which you believe these interests or desires should be taken into account in any practical calculation about how to allocate resources or define policies for a group of which you are a member;
(3) the kind of treatment you believe you can demand from others;
(4) the extent to which you believe your views, ideas, and beliefs count in any theoretical reflection or in any discussion with other people;

---

[8] One advocate of mothers, who recently founded an organization called "Mothers Matter" (a name that nicely indicates the extent to which, in our society, mothers do *not* matter very much), gave an interview in which she lamented the way in which "mother and martyr are treated like the same word," and joked that mothers "feel guilty about running through the park on a spring-like day when there's laundry to be done." (See Donna de las Cruz, "Program Teaches Motherhood as a Profession," *The Davis Enterprise*, July 6, 1995, p. 8; the quote is from Kay Willis, founder of "Mothers Matter.") Her organization strives to enable mothers to give themselves some time off each week to pursue their own interests—a task that she reports is not particularly easy, not merely because many fathers fail to be sympathetic to such requests but also because many mothers persistently feel guilty if they put their own interests before the interests of others in their families.

(5) the kind of ambition(s) you have, and the extent to which you believe you are entitled to have it (that is, believe this ambition is appropriate for one such as you).

However, the construction of your sense of your own worth is not entirely a social and political product—indeed, that is why the mother in Hurston's story is speaking in such an impassioned way to her daughter. Each of us has to choose the kind of worth we wish to accord ourselves, and the kind of worth we are willing to fight to have others accord us. The social and political pressures against the worth we would accord ourselves can be considerable, so that maintaining a belief in that worth can require significant inner strength. That fact does not make the choice impossible, and in my view, does not remove responsibility from those who "give in" and accept a conception of worth that is too low (any more than the social pressure that encourages self-worship in certain classes of men exculpates them from responsibility for the denigrating attitudes they take toward women and the arrogance they assume for themselves). However, I shall leave such issues of responsibility aside for now.

In any case, the implications of one's sense of self-worth are enormous. So what is self-worth? What is the right conception of worth? How should a social and political environment affect children such that they get the right sense of worth? And what does talk of worth have to do with *morality*?

III. Theories of Worth

When I speak of the notion of self-worth, I do not mean the (currently trendy) concept of self-esteem. To the extent that I can figure out what self-esteem is supposed to be, it is either pride in accomplishment, or else some kind of "feel-good-about-myself" sentiment that we are supposed to promote in ourselves and others (especially our children) so that we and they will be happy.

But the notion of self-worth need have nothing to do with personal effort and is not a kind of feeling. It is defined by a theory of human worth, a theory that sets out, among other things, what the criteria of worth are, such that each of us can evaluate our own worth. There are many possible theories of human worth, some of which I will discuss below. But the worth such theories accord each of us is generally understood to be a worth that each of us has, whether we know it or not, and whether others accord it to us or not. Self-worth is, in that sense, "objective," by which I (merely) mean that it is generally not based on how we feel about ourselves. Of course, it is possible for a theory of worth to equate our value with how much we esteem ourselves, in which case the theory would deliberately identify how we feel about ourselves given our accomplishments, with what our worth actually is. In general, however, a theory of human worth will want to separate subjective understandings of value from the value the theory accords a person on the basis of certain criteria, in part so as to provide grounds for criticizing someone whose sense of her own value is incorrect given what the theory identifies as her true value (which may be higher or lower than the person realizes). Advocates of such theories hope we will believe in the value that their theory accords us, but they also insist that this value doesn't disappear if we don't believe in it. Indeed, many theories of worth (e.g., of the sort held by Kant) also insist that this value does not and cannot diminish no matter what we do (so that even a wrongdoer is held to be valuable, and deserving of our respect).

As I have discussed elsewhere,[9] there are many different possible theories of worth, each of which has a number of components.

First, a theory of human worth takes a stand on the *kind* of value each of us has: Are human beings only instrumentally valuable, such that their worth is defined by how well they can be used to accomplish certain desirable goals? Or are we intrinsically valuable, that is, valuable apart from any instrumental uses we have? If the latter, is that intrinsic value something that we project onto one another, so that it is agent-relative in nature, or is it something that is inherent within us? And is it something that is permanent, or can it be degraded or lowered by certain actions (on the part of either the person himself or some external agent)?

Second, the theory takes a stand on whether or not human value is equal. Is one race, or gender, or "kind" of human more valuable than another? Are smart people better than stupid people, virtuous people better than vicious people, rich people better than poor people, able-bodied people better than disabled people, aristocratic people better than commoners? Or is the value of every person (no matter his or her wealth, talents, virtues, physical abilities, or background) the same as that of every other? Clearly, the theory's view of the kind of value each of us has can have implications for how it determines whether the value of all human beings is the same. For example, if each of us is merely instrumentally valuable, our values will differ insofar as our usefulness differs. On the other hand, those who say that our value is noninstrumental may insist that it is also equal, regardless of how useful any of us is.

Third, the theory must take a stand on how human value is aggregated. Can we simply add the values of people together, so that a group of ten people constitutes five times the value of a group of two, or is the value possessed by human beings something that cannot be neatly added together, making the issue of aggregation complicated?

Fourth, a theory of human worth must say why any of us has value. In virtue of what feature are we supposed to have worth? Is it our gender,

---

[9] See Hampton, "The Retributive Idea," in Jeffrie Murphy and Jean Hampton, *Forgiveness and Mercy* (Cambridge: Cambridge University Press, 1988); and Hampton, "Correcting Harms versus Righting Wrongs: The Goal of Retribution," *UCLA Law Review*, vol. 39, no. 6 (1992), pp. 1659–1702.

our race, our talents, the goods we possess? Again, depending upon the kind of value the theory accords us, what properties count as value-giving will differ. An instrumental account of our value will identify properties as value-giving to the extent that they make any of us useful; an intrinsic account of our value will not do so—indeed, such a theory need not identify any property as that in virtue of which we have value, if it regards that value as a kind of primitive property in its own right. The intrinsic value can also be regarded as a property that we project onto our fellow human beings, and there can be various accounts of why and when that projection will occur. In contrast, a Kantian-style theory will regard the value as something we discover in the person, not something we project onto her.

Fifth, the theory must identify the kinds of treatments that are owed to human beings by virtue of their value. If every human being is taken to have equal value, the treatment owed to every human being will be taken to be the same. In contrast, an inegalitarian theory will require different behavior toward people who are valued differently: in the same way that we think a painting by Picasso should be treated with more care and respect than a painting of Elvis on velvet, so too an inegalitarian theory will say that we should treat a more valuable person with more care and respect than a relatively worthless person.

Sixth, the theory can take a metaphysical stand on the source of the value it accords us. For example, it may take our value to be inherent in our natures (like some kind of property). Alternatively, it can represent that value as merely a social invention, albeit a highly important invention with social, political, and personal implications.

In many societies, some kind of egalitarian theory of human worth is standardly advocated (especially in societies influenced by the Judeo-Christian religious tradition, since an egalitarian theory of worth is implicit in prominent strands of that tradition). However, such official endorsement often betrays the reality of a variety of views of worth in those societies that are inegalitarian, and that place people of certain sorts (e.g., those in a certain racial, gender, or ethnic group) higher than people of other sorts (e.g., those belonging to other racial, gender, or ethnic groups). Indeed, an inegalitarian theory that, in my experience, is particularly attractive to some American philosophers is one that links value with moral excellence or virtue, meaning that good people are supposed to be more valuable than bad people. Of course, even egalitarians accept the commonplace idea that our moral evaluations of people will differ, such that some will get better evaluations than others (something that also happens when we evaluate people along other dimensions—e.g., intelligence, athletic skill, artistic talent, and so forth); egalitarians deny, however, that such evaluations have anything to do with our worth as human beings. In contrast, on a moral-inegalitarian view, moral evaluation actually determines where a person falls on the scale of human worth: the higher the moral evaluation, the higher the worth, and vice versa.

All theories of worth, as I noted above, identify what treatments are appropriate for people depending on their worth. For example, an inegalitarian theory that links value to moral worth will insist that good people merit better treatment than bad people, where the latter may be so bad that we are justified in inflicting harm upon them (which is one conception of the way in which punishment can be "deserved"). Such a view is, in my experience, commonly espoused by certain television preachers, who promise viewers that they will get great material rewards from God if they are "good" in the way that God wishes. Other inegalitarian theories develop quite different conceptions of appropriate treatment, depending upon their conceptions of the nature of worth and their criteria for according someone worth: for example, white supremacists will demand that white people be treated (both personally and politically) as superior to nonwhites. Henceforth I will call these "theories of rightful treatment." They are normative theories establishing appropriate behavior toward human beings (and perhaps also other entities) on the basis of a theory of their worth. Thus, for example, a Kantian theory of worth, which regards us all as ends-in-ourselves, regardless of our moral merit, insists that each of us is owed the same kind of respectful treatment as every other person by virtue of the fact that each of us has the same noninstrumental value. Note that such a theory understands punishment not as a treatment deserved by the offender by virtue of his low value, but as a treatment which is responsive to his actions (not his worth) and which must be constructed so that it does not deny his equal worth by being degrading or inhumane.[10]

Different attitudes toward the self are generated by the theory of worth one accepts. Mill's boys, who are reared to self-worship, accept a hierarchical theory of worth that places them at or near the top, and places women well below them. Isie's mother worries that Isie will come to regard herself with self-denigration by accepting her society's view that, because of her race and gender, her value is well below that of others of a different race or gender. Both Mill and Isie's mother are implicitly pushing an egalitarian theory of worth, one that defines the nature of the self-honor which they wish all of us to accord ourselves, and which they believe many in their society are wrong to reject.

It is important to recognize the hold that inegalitarian theories of worth have exercised over people, if we are to understand the history of oppression and injustice. Consider Harper Lee's portrayal of the inegalitarian structure of the American South during the 1930s in her book *To Kill a Mockingbird*. In one passage, twelve-year-old Jem attempts to explain to his eight-year-old sister Scout the facts about value in their society:

---

[10] I develop such a theory in "Correcting Harms versus Righting Wrongs."

> There are four kinds of folks in the world. There's the ordinary kind like us and the neighbors, there's the kind like the Cunninghams out in the woods, the kind like the Ewells down at the dump, and the Negroes.[11]

Scout struggles to figure out where she will fit in this hierarchy given that she will be a woman some day in a town where women are supposed to be "ladies" and are thereby precluded from a variety of jobs and positions. She also knows that Jem's ranking cannot be complete, because it leaves some people out: "What about the Chinese, and the Cajuns down yonder in Baldwin County?" she asks her brother. And in the end, she rejects her brother's assessment of the facts about value, in part because of her acceptance of her father's egalitarian point of view, and in part because of her own experiences. She insists, "Naw, Jem, I think there's just one kind of folks. Folks."[12] The collision between the inegalitarian ranking accepted by most folks in this society and the egalitarian ranking endorsed by Scout and her father (and a few other people in their county) is the central theme of the novel. Harper Lee, who comes down clearly on the side of the truth of the egalitarian theory, is nonetheless concerned to show how the popularity of the false hierarchical theory has profound implications for nearly all the social and political institutions of Maycomb County, including its criminal justice system, its employment practices, its educational system, and its religious life.

An inegalitarian theory of worth can generate behavior that, for those of us committed to an egalitarian theory, is truly ghastly. Consider the following story told by the dancer Bill T. Jones, originally related to him by his mother.[13] In her youth, Jones's mother knew a white farmer who employed a black farmhand and his four sons. When one day the farmhand did something that enraged the farmer, the farmer apprehended him and his four sons, put them in burlap bags, and began burning them. Before he was burned, one of the men asked for a cigar. The farmer answered him by cutting off his penis, and then sticking it in his mouth, saying, "Here, smoke that." The message conveyed by this farmer's behavior is that these men had no value, and thus deserved no respectful treatment. Even mere objects can be taken by us to have worth; this farmer denied that these men had anything that one should respect. By constructing an event that represented the people he killed as degraded and worthless, the farmer demonstrated that, to him, burning them to death seemed no more significant than burning a pile of trash. Note how many details of the entire event accomplish this diminishment: not only

[11] Harper Lee, *To Kill a Mockingbird* (Philadelphia: J. B. Lippincott, 1960), p. 239.
[12] *Ibid.*, p. 240.
[13] I related this story in "Correcting Harms versus Righting Wrongs," p. 1675. The story was told by Jones on *Great Performances—Dance in America: Bill T. Jones/Arnie Zane and Co.* (PBS television broadcast, February 12, 1992).

the killing but also the containment in bags; not only the castration, but also the mocking reference to the penis as a cigar. Those of us who accept an egalitarian point of view will believe that the difference between the value these people actually had, and the (almost nonexistent) value the farmer falsely represented them as having, is what makes his action so horrendous. We will therefore be committed to fighting such inegalitarian views, lest they infect the minds of yet more people, precipitating more ghastly actions by people who take themselves to "matter" far more than those whom they abuse.

As these examples show, one reason it is important to recognize the reality of inegalitarian theories of worth is in order to explain certain aspects of the nature of oppression. When people oppress other people, they generally take their mastery to be *rightful* and legitimate. Hence, they work from a theory of relative value which justifies their advantages and their control over people whom they regard as their inferiors, and which defines the sorts of behavior appropriate to both the oppressors and the oppressed.

There is an interesting passage in *The Subjection of Women* in which Mill implicitly recognizes the reality, in many societies, of oppression-producing inegalitarian theories of rightful treatment that presuppose, and are derived from, theories of human beings' differing value:

> The moral education of mankind has hitherto emanated chiefly from the law of force, and is adapted almost solely to the relations which force creates. In the less advanced states of society, people hardly recognise any relation with their equals. To be an equal is to be an enemy. Society from its highest place to its lowest, is one long chain, or rather ladder, where every individual is either above or below his nearest neighbor, and wherever he does not command he must obey. Existing moralities, accordingly, are mainly fitted to a relation of obedience.[14]

Note Mill's characterization of inegalitarian theories of rightful treatment as "moralities." Mill uses this word because he regards these theories as establishing norms of rightful treatment (for example, norms designating who has the right to command, and who is obliged to obey) that operate so as to define right and wrong behavior in that society. We are used to reserving the term "morality" for a theory of rightful treatment that assumes the equality of all human value, but oppressive regimes will insist on the rightfulness of unequal treatment, as Mill appreciates. Although those of us reared in the culture of contemporary moral philosophy are unused to thinking of any inegalitarian theory of rightful treatment as a "morality," anyone who, like Mill, is reared in a society many of whose members accept such a theory—particularly those who are told they are near or at the bottom—will tell you that such a system encourages people to "see" one another, and to act toward one another, with that value-

---

[14] Mill, *The Subjection of Women*, pp. 45–46.

ranking always in mind, convinced that the normative expectations of the theory appropriately govern people's behavior. One reason Mill wanted to expose the inegalitarian views of his own society was to overthrow them, and to substitute in their place an egalitarian view of human value, which he thought mandated legislation from the principle of utility.

In what follows, I will follow Mill and use the term "morality" to refer to what I have been calling a "theory of rightful treatment," defining it as *a normative theory that establishes the kinds of treatment that people, by virtue of their worth, deserve.* So defined, both inegalitarian and egalitarian theories of rightful treatment qualify as moralities, although these days most moral philosophers will be convinced that only some form of egalitarian theory can be correct.

But how do we know that *any* egalitarian theory is right? From where do theories of worth, and their attendant theories of rightful treatment, come? Are they basic, or are they derived from some more fundamental moral law?

IV. The Primacy of the Idea of Worth

Generations of readers of Kant have puzzled over which of the first two formulations of his Moral Law is the better and more fundamental characterization of the foundations of morality. The first formulation asks us to test our courses of action, implementing them only if we could "will" a world in which everyone pursued that course of action for the purpose for which we want to pursue it. As Kant puts it, this version of the Moral Law says: "Act only on that maxim through which you can at the same time will that it should become a universal law."[15] The second formulation works rather differently. Kant states it as: "Act in such a way that you always treat humanity, whether in your own person or in the person of any other, never simply as a means, but always at the same time as an end."[16] Note that this formulation works by establishing that human beings are "ends" in themselves, and calls upon us to accord them certain treatment by virtue of their standing as "ends."

Whether or not these two formulations generate the same set of permissions and prohibitions, they are nonetheless different by virtue of the way they ground those permissions and prohibitions. The first formulation represents morality as arising from a kind of reasoning procedure, from which it follows that human beings have a certain kind of equal standing. In contrast, the second formulation represents morality as arising from the fact that human beings have a certain kind of equal standing, from which it follows that we must reason a certain way prior to determining how we should act. Thus, both formulations involve a theory of human worth and a theory of rightful treatment, but the first formulation

---

[15] See Immanuel Kant, *Groundwork of the Metaphysics of Morals*, trans. H. J. Paton (Indianapolis: Bobbs-Merrill, 1964), p. 88.
[16] *Ibid.*, p. 96.

derives the first theory (i.e., the theory of human worth) from the second (i.e., the theory of rightful treatment, which, in turn, is itself defined via a reasoning procedure), whereas the second formulation takes the theory of human worth to be more basic, so that specific moral reasoning procedures and policies dictating rightful treatment are derived from it.

It is not only Kant's theory that admits of these two theoretical interpretive alternatives. Mill's remarks above show the extent to which utilitarianism can be understood to be based on a theory of worth, rather than on a principle from which that theory of worth is derived. If it is principle-based, utilitarianism grounds its moral recommendations in the principle of utility, whose recommendations define a theory of moral treatment which we can take to express a certain kind of egalitarian theory of worth. On this interpretation, that theory of worth (as well as the recommendations for treatment) can be considered correct only because the principle of utility is the correct foundation for all action. In contrast, if we take Mill's remarks in *The Subjection of Women* seriously, his principle of utility is not basic but derived, following from the fact of equal human value, so that the principle of utility is conceptually posterior to a certain kind of egalitarian conception of human value. On this view, the principle of utility simply expresses the equality of human value, while taking a certain stand on the way that value can be aggregated.

Which kind of interpretation of these two moral theories is better, the principle-dependent kind, or the worth-dependent kind?

The standard way of interpreting both sorts of theories is principle-dependent. Somehow contemporary moral thinkers have taken it as obvious that moral behavior is commanded fundamentally by some sort of principle or abstract norm. If the principle or norm directs our attention to the consequences of actions, the theory is called consequentialist; if the principle or norm directs our attention to the "rightness" or "wrongness" of the actions themselves, considered apart from their consequences, the theory is called deontological.

Michael Stocker argues,[17] however, that principle-based moral theories portray moral action in a way that is divorced from the nature of the actual moral motives people have, producing a kind of "schizophrenia" with respect to moral reasons and moral motives in those who believe contemporary moral theories. Whether the theory is consequentialist or deontological, what such a theory values, says Stocker, is something abstract and impersonal—e.g., some principle, or moral law, or duty—from which we are supposed to act. Yet he notes that real moral action seems motivated not by austere moral principles but by concern for the person or persons who will be affected by the moral action:

[17] See Michael Stocker, "The Schizophrenia of Modern Moral Theories," in *The Virtues: Contemporary Essays on Moral Character*, ed. Robert B. Kruschwitz and Robert C. Roberts (Belmont, CA: Wadsworth, 1987), pp. 36–45; reprinted from *Journal of Philosophy*, vol. 73 (August 12, 1976), pp. 453–66.

What is lacking in these theories is simply—or not so simply—the person. For, love, friendship, affection, fellow feeling, and community all require that the other person be an essential part of what is valued. The person—not merely the person's general values nor even the person-qua-producer-or-possessor-of-general-values—must be valued. The defect of these theories in regard to love, to take one case, is not that they do not value love (which, often, they do not) but that they do not value the beloved. Indeed, a person who values and aims at love, that is, love-in-general or even love-in-general-exemplified-by-this-person "misses" the intended beloved as surely as does an adherent of the theories I have criticized.[18]

It is as if, says Stocker, such theories are "devoid of all people." In contrast, he notes that an egoistic theory at least recognizes the value and the appeal of *one* person, namely, the self. The egoist welcomes certain actions or events not merely because he takes them to be good, but more fundamentally because he takes them to be good *for him*—the one person he values.

Philosophers have been leery of making moral regard too personal, lest they fail to capture the phenomenon of moral regard: thus, my love for my spouse or my child or my friends, they say, cannot be the same as moral regard because it is too particular, too contingent on features not possessed by everybody, and we believe moral regard is something that we owe all persons, by virtue of the fact that they are human beings. But this interest in universality is really only an interest in preserving the *extent* of moral regard. Might we be able to accommodate the idea that moral treatment is owed to everyone within a theory that nonetheless makes this treatment responsive to something personal? And in particular, might a moral theory founded on a theory of human worth enable us to construct this more personalized account of morality, in a way that will fit our intuitions about what drives us when we act morally?

Suppose we say that moral regard is something that we ought to accord a person not because some moral law or principle requires it, but because something about *this person* requires it: and suppose we describe the nature of that requirement by saying that this person has value. On this view, morality is not required by some set of abstract principles which we honor by giving people certain forms of treatment; instead, moral regard and moral actions are required by virtue of the value possessed by each of us, and any moral principles we recognize merely articulate the requirements this value places upon us.

But such a theory may only be impersonal in a new way. Even if moral behavior is no longer undertaken in honor of some abstract principle, does this theory still represent our moral regard as responsive only to the value-

---

[18] *Ibid.*, p. 40.

within-each-of-us, and not to the particular person? If, for example, the carrier of value is someone's race, or gender, or ethnicity, then it is one of these things that is really valuable. It would seem, then, that rightful treatment on any of these theories is responsive to one of these generic features (e.g., a person's whiteness, or maleness, or ethnic heritage), and not to anything personal with respect to him. Or alternatively, if the carrier of value is the person's rationality, or his capacity to experience a certain kind of pleasure or happiness, then it is that rationality, or that capacity, which we are really honoring when we treat him with respect. In all of these cases, treating him right turns out not to be done because we have regard for *him*, but because we have regard for that within him which is the carrier of value. So can we construct a value-based moral theory so that it is more particularized in content and motive but still universal in scope, impartial in operation, and egalitarian in its assumptions?

Perhaps we can. Consider Stocker's discussion of the egoist, who at least loves one person, unlike contemporary moral theorists, whom Stocker accuses of loving no one. We can think of the egoist as accepting a certain kind of theory of value, one that makes him vastly more valuable than any other human being. But there may be some wisdom in the egoist's point of view after all. If we can figure out exactly how the egoist's perspective avoids impersonality, we may be in a position to figure out how to reconstruct moral theory so that it becomes genuinely person-centered, although in a universal and egalitarian way. In what way, then, and why, does the egoist value himself? Now there's a question rarely asked in moral philosophy these days! It is that question that I shall attempt to answer next.

V. EGOISM

In order to understand what the egoist values with respect to himself, we need some portraits of egoists to work from. There are a number of such portraits in George Eliot's *Middlemarch*,[19] in which egoism, and its attendant evils, is a central theme.

Two of the major characters in the novel are Dorothea and her first husband, Mr. Casaubon. While Dorothea eventually escapes the egoistic point of view, poor Casaubon never does, retreating more and more into a kind of prison of egoistic loneliness as he ages. Happy with his own dreams of his brilliant scholarship, and frightened of the possibility of outsiders who may well have different views of that scholarship, he hides in his study, particularly from Dorothea, his observant new wife, who rather too quickly divines the sterility of his work. Eliot presents us with a sympathetic but unyieldingly critical analysis of his egoism. Lest we judge him too harshly, however, she continually invites us to compare

---

[19] George Eliot, *Middlemarch* (1871), ed. W. J. Harvey (Harmondsworth: Penguin, 1965); all page references to this work will be given parenthetically in the text.

ourselves with him: "Mr Casaubon, too, was the centre of his own world; if he was liable to think that others were providentially made for him . . . this trait is not quite alien to us, and, like the other mendicant hopes of mortals, claims some of our pity" (p. 111). And: "Mr Casaubon had an intense consciousness within him, and was spiritually a-hungered like the rest of us" (p. 312). For this man, who insisted he was not to be disturbed in his library or in his own thoughts, and who could not tolerate criticism or the evaluations of others, being married was a difficult and frightening experience, because it meant that another person, with another point of view unlike—and sometimes opposed to—his own, was continuously foisted upon him.

A different kind of egoist is presented in the person of Rosamond Lydgate, who is even more taken with herself than Casaubon is taken with himself, knowing few of his fears, and displaying even more "hunger" for her own way. In one amusing passage, she displays her remarkable self-centeredness by evaluating everyone *else* she knows as selfish.

> [She complained of the] disagreeable people who only thought of themselves, and did not mind how annoying they were to her. Even her father was unkind, and might have done more for them. In fact there was but one person in Rosamond's world whom she did not regard as blameworthy, and that was the graceful creature with blond plaits and with little hands crossed before her, who had never expressed herself unbecomingly, and had always acted for the best— the best naturally being what she best liked. (p. 716)

Rosamond's self-centered perspective is in many respects matched by that of her husband, Dr. Lydgate, whose other-regarding profession belies a selfish ambitiousness and contempt for women that leads him into a disastrous marriage with Rosamond: "Poor Lydgate! or shall I say, Poor Rosamond! Each lived in a world of which the other knew nothing" (p. 195).

What is it that Casaubon, Rosamond, and Lydgate have in common that makes them egoists? It is not, as in the account of egoism suggested by some philosophers,[20] that they have a solipsistic point of view. Each of them is very much aware that there are other people in the world: for example, Casaubon fears these potentially critical centers of subjectivity, and Rosamond is a very social creature, who needs and thrives on the company of others. However, both perceive other people as "providentially made" for them (and both curse their bad luck if these other people behave in a way that hurts their interests). As Eliot puts it, each of them is at the center of his or her own world, which means that each takes himself or herself to be the only person who matters to any significant

---

[20] For example, Thomas Nagel suggests that egoism is the "analogue of solipsism" in the practical sphere; see Nagel, *The Possibility of Altruism* (Oxford: Clarendon Press, 1970), p. 107.

degree. Hence, each of them views other people as deriving what value they have from the fact that they are useful in some way to the one person—namely, him- or herself—who really matters. Lydgate is valued by Rosamond as a pleasant, handsome companion and source of money and social status; Dorothea is valued by Casaubon only to the extent that she is a pleasing, uncritical, and nonjudgmental helpmate at the margins of his world.

These egoists are not without their virtues. Even horrible Rosamond is impressive in the power of her will. Although Lydgate assumes that, as the man of the family, he will be the master of it, the reality is quite otherwise:

> As to saying he was master, it was not the fact. The very resolution to which he had wrought himself by dint of logic and honourable pride was beginning to relax under her torpedo contact. (p. 711)

By the end of the novel, Lydgate realizes that he has lost the helm to her, and practices medicine as she likes him to do (that is, in a way that brings in good money), rather than in the way that he would have liked (that is, pushing the frontiers of medical research). Thus, he considers himself a failure; yet Rosamond does not countenance any whining from him about it:

> He once called her his basil plant; and when she asked him for an explanation, said that basil was a plant which had flourished wonderfully on a murdered man's brains. Rosamond had a placid but strong answer to such speeches. Why then had he chosen her? (p. 893)

Rosamond's self-assertion is something we are meant to admire; it is something that the main heroine of the book, Dorothea, has to learn.

Dorothea has to learn it because, unlike Rosamond, Dorothea is intent on not being selfish, which she initially thinks means that she must sublimate her will to others. Dorothea learns, however, that selfishness and self-assertion are not the same, and that the latter can be not only admirable but even required in the selfless person. Dorothea's interest in devoting herself to others comes perilously close at various times in the novel to servility and loss of self. Professing "the necessity of some individuals to hold fast to their personal view of the nature of things" (p. 96), she eventually learns to stand up to the bullying commands of Casaubon, finally telling him: "Do you not see now that I could not submit my soul to yours, by working hopelessly at what I have no belief in?" (p. 583). This resolve is something that comes hard for Dorothea, whose fervent belief that she needs to help others—particularly her husband—tends to cripple her ability to stand up for herself. Eliot's message, however, is that the healthy soul is capable of self-assertion—albeit for the right cause. In a letter, Eliot once wrote:

The martyr at the stake seeks its gratification [i.e., the gratification of ego] as much as the court sycophant, the difference lying in the comparative dignity and beauty of the two egos. People absurdly talk of self-denial—why there is none in Virtue to a being of moral excellence—the greatest torture to such a soul would be to run counter to the dictates of conscience. . . .[21]

Thus, Eliot's cure for the egoist is not to give up asserting herself, and not to engage in self-denial. Her cure is to get the egoist to take up a new cause.

But what is the nature of this better cause? The novel suggests that it has to do with letting other people into one's world such that their points of view, their desires, their welfare, their ideas, *matter*. Dorothea's growth toward moral maturity is instructive. At first she is filled with a romantic vision of helping other people, leading her to marry Casaubon, whom she believes is striving for truth and wisdom. What she discovers in her marriage is that helping other people is *hard*, in part because seeing them as they really are, and not as one might wish to see them, is hard. At one point in the novel, full of understandable temper at Casaubon's exasperating behavior, she comes to see him in a new and more sympathetic light, imaginatively producing within herself "a shadowy monitor looking at her anger with sad remonstrance" (p. 464). So she waits for him one evening in the hallway outside her room, where he habitually passes after leaving his library, and her act of friendship toward him is rewarded when he finally emerges. He says to her:

> "Come, my dear, come. You are young, and need not to extend your life by watching."
> When the kind quiet melancholy of that speech fell on Dorothea's ears, she felt something like the thankfulness that might well up in us if we had narrowly escaped hurting a lamed creature. She put her hand into her husband's, and they went along the broad corridor together. (p. 465)

Dorothea learns that helping even one person is a mighty struggle, because it is hard to get the yearnings and feelings and being of even one person into one's sight; and this is because it is hard not to be preoccupied with one's own yearnings and feelings and being, insofar as one's own person seems so much more important than others. *Middlemarch* is, in part, a novel about the struggles of being married, a state in which two people have to learn to admit another's point of view into their lives. Both Rosamond and Casaubon are so absorbed in themselves that they struggle to get any glimmer of the perspectives and interests of their partners

---

[21] George Eliot, letter to Maria Lewis dated February 18, 1842, in *The George Eliot Letters*, ed. Gordon S. Haight (New Haven, CT: Yale University Press, 1954), vol. 1, p. 127.

(although Casaubon's kind words in the passage above, and Rosamond's one act of kindness toward Lydgate late in the novel, suggest that each might not be completely ignorant of his or her spouse's point of view). Dorothea learns more, appreciating that true service to others requires not self-denial but rather what might be called a "roving sympathy" toward others,[22] a sympathy which may not generate agreement or unity or harmony, but which enables one partner to honor and understand the other, and which presupposes, to a considerable extent, one partner's sense of the other as *mattering*.

All of this provides interesting lessons for us moral theorists; for what Dorothea learns is quite unlike the kind of lesson that a contemporary moral philosopher would preach to her.

VI. A Personal Moral Theory

The first lesson Dorothea learns is that moral regard is strikingly *personal* rather than impersonal. There is a marvelous line in which Eliot describes Dorothea's progress in her view of her troubled husband: "[S]he seemed to be looking along the one track where duty becomes tenderness" (p. 400). Dorothea learns to act not from grand principle, but from concern for *him*. She comes to understand his difficulties, his needs, his point of view, so that her behavior comes to reflect not just *her* needs, beliefs, and interests, but also his—although not necessarily in a way that he likes or wants. Learning to admit another—as that person really is—into one's view of the world often does not produce saccharine harmony or untroubled unity, particularly if the other person hungers after something harmful for himself or others. Once Dorothea understands Casaubon, she is empowered to resist his selfish bullying; but she is also empowered to feel compassion toward him, in a way that genuinely does him some good (far more good than her youthful romantic visions could provide him).

The personal nature of Dorothea's moral perspective is one that George Eliot herself may have had trouble embracing. Consider the following story written by a friend of Eliot's, remembering a conversation he had with her toward the end of her life:

> I remember how, at Cambridge, I walked with her once in the Fellows' Garden of Trinity, on an evening of rainy May: and she, stirred somewhat beyond her wont, and taking as her text the three words which have been used so often as the inspiring trumpet-calls of men,— the words *God, Immortality, Duty,*—pronounced with terrible earnestness how inconceivable was the *first*, how unbelievable the *second* and yet how peremptory and absolute the *third*. Never, perhaps, have sterner accents affirmed the sovereignty of the impersonal and un-

[22] The term is that of Karen Chase, *George Eliot: Middlemarch* (Cambridge: Cambridge University Press, 1991), p. 44.

THE WISDOM OF THE EGOIST

recompensing Law. I listened, and night fell; her grave, majestic countenance turned towards me like a sibyl's in the gloom; it was as though
she withdrew from my grasp, one by one, the two scrolls of promise,
and left me with the third scroll only, awful with inevitable fate.[23]

Here is a vision of the impersonal, commanding, authoritative, awful
Moral Law about which we contemporary moral philosophers have theo-
rized. In a way, it is a "scientific" view of morality, in that morality is
presented as directing us—controlling us—via a moral law governing our
will, analogous to the way in which scientific laws direct, control, and
govern matter—with the exception, of course, that we can flout the moral
law but not the laws of nature.

In *Middlemarch*, however, where duty shades into tenderness for the
most successful characters, the lesson is different. Morality certainly calls,
but it has a personal face. It is not duty, but Casaubon himself, to which
Dorothea finally responds. It is not duty, but the viewpoints, aspirations,
and desires of Lydgate, that Rosamond determinedly keeps at bay. Marriage turns out to be a kind of moral test for these characters, in which the
close proximity of another person challenges them to learn either to admit
the other as an equal into their own world, or else to fashion an egoistic
sphere of movement, such that they can still dream their own dreams
about themselves despite living with another.

The novel also expresses a profound appreciation of how hard it is to
admit even *one* person into one's world:

> If we had a keen vision and feeling of all of ordinary human life, it
> would be like hearing the grass grow and the squirrel's heart beat,
> and we should die of that roar which lies on the other side of silence.
> As it is, the quickest of us walk about well wadded with stupidity.
> (p. 226)

Eliot is impressing upon us how much emotional impact is involved in
fathoming, and taking seriously, other people as they are, with their distinctive views and experiences of the world. As the passage suggests,
were we to be perfectly successful in doing all this, we would likely
experience a great deal of pain—probably too much for our own good.
Few of us seem psychologically or emotionally able to put more than a
few people into the center of our worlds alongside ourselves.

The second lesson *Middlemarch* teaches us through its portrait of egoism
is the importance of retaining the self in the moral point of view. Dorothea's story warns us about the danger of too little ego, too little self-

[23] From "A Memory of George Eliot by F. W. H. Myers," quoted by Catherine Neale,
Middlemarch by George Eliot (Harmondsworth: Penguin, 1989), p. 39; Neale drew the quote
from Basil Willey, *Nineteenth Century Studies* (Cambridge: Cambridge University Press, 1977),
p. 204.

assertiveness, and the risks of annihilating oneself if one gives oneself too thoroughly to others. If the center of your world only includes others, then you yourself are lost. Hence, the moral person must retain the self-assertiveness, the self-enjoyment, and the self-definition of the egoist, but expand the "cause" for which she acts to include the interests, needs, and beliefs of others as well as her own. Again, Rosamond teaches us something here. Whereas Dorothea's life is in danger of being joyless and dour, Rosamond has fun. She sings, she rides, she converses with friends while Dorothea frets in monastic dress about how to serve others. Whereas Dorothea decides to give up horseback riding because she concludes it is unfair to have such enjoyment given the plight of the poor in the countryside through which she rides, Rosamond enjoys a good gallop in the country. We are meant, I believe, to judge both of them as making a mistake, albeit in different directions. Rosamond eventually has a miscarriage because she rides while she is pregnant—a telling indication of the extent to which she puts her own desires first. On the other hand, Dorothea's gray life (which reflects, in part, the strictures of a sexist society that gives her very little opportunity to spend it in pursuit of something fine) makes us anxious and exasperated. Were she not so sweet and well-meaning, we would find her tedious.

Thus, the second lesson of the novel (which I suspect George Eliot herself may have had great difficulty learning) is that morality should not be understood as some impersonal law whose "inevitable fate" is destined to kill us off with its relentless other-regarding commands.

In the rest of this essay, I will consider how both of these lessons can be incorporated into a successful theory of our moral life.

VII. ACTING FOR THE SAKE OF THE SELF

What do egoists like Rosamond and Casaubon teach us? They do *not* teach us that we should all like ourselves. This is, in part, because not all egoists do like themselves. Many egoists (like Casaubon) are dissatisfied with who they are, often working relentlessly to remedy what they regard as their deficiencies (think of self-absorbed dieters, or discontented business executives who continually go to self-improvement classes). What marks someone as an egoist, then, is not an attitude of approval or adoration toward herself (an egoist needn't be a narcissist). More importantly, we are sometimes right not to like ourselves, particularly when we have attitudes or character traits basic to our personalities that are morally disreputable, and thus worth condemning. Such dislike can even be valuable, if it instigates a decision to try to change for the better.

Nor do egoists teach us the correct theory of value. Egoism is generated by an extreme form of a hierarchical theory of value: whereas the males in Mill's world accept a hierarchical theory of worth that puts all males (or at least all males of a certain class) at the top of the ladder of value, the egoist puts only himself at the top, regarding other people as (to use

Eliot's phrase regarding Casaubon) "providentially made for him." More-over, as the character of Casaubon illustrates, deep dissatisfaction with some or all of his traits can coexist in the egoist with the view that he matters far more than any other. One might also speculate about the extent to which an egoist's view of his value feeds off a conception of others as mere servants of his interests, such that his sense of his own high worth is dependent on his view of others as radically lower than him. (Compare the way in which, in Hegel's master/slave dialectic, the master derives his higher value from his perception of the slave's vastly lower value.)[24]

Finally, we cannot learn from egoists any sound lessons about what really counts as good for oneself, or what will be truly self-advancing. People such as Rosamond or Casaubon have little idea what the good really is, in part because, like all people who leave out the well-being of others from their view of the world, they are invariably going to miss important components of the good life. (At the end of *Middlemarch* it is striking that the person who achieves the most happiness and personal satisfaction is Dorothea.)

However, we can learn from egoists what I will call the correct "object of concern" of moral behavior. While egoists have the wrong theory of human worth, and hence the wrong understanding of self-worth, they are nonetheless correct in thinking that what it is important to be concerned about is the *self*. Of course, they are concerned with only one self, and it is a self that they may not like, and may wish to improve, upbraid, punish, or even loathe. But what makes them egoists is that they act for the sake of that self, and not for the sake of some abstract principle, rule or object. As I shall now discuss, it is the idea of "acting for the sake of the self," rather than acting for the sake of a principle, that I take to be important for moral theory.

What is a self? (I take the terms "self" and "person" to be synonyms, but in what follows I will generally use the term "self.") As Wittgenstein noted, none of us learns a language by simply following a set of rules, and similarly none of us learns what a self is, or what a particular self is like, by internalizing and then applying certain rigid criteria.[25] Thus, we can-not try to define a self by exhaustively listing a set of traits that are taken to be necessary and sufficient for selfhood. Each of us has learned what a self is by interacting with selves, where these interactions are dynamic, distinctive, and often full of surprises. Such interactions teach us not only to recognize selfhood in others but also to recognize it in ourselves. Even-tually we learn to characterize the self in certain general ways by saying, among other things, that it is both conscious and self-conscious, that it thinks, feels, and chooses—in a distinctive and particular way—and that it has a certain experience with life. But to try to reduce the self to any one

---

[24] See G. W. F. Hegel, *The Phenomenology of Spirit*, trans. A. V. Miller (Oxford: Clarendon Press, 1977). I am indebted to Stephen Darwall for discussions of this point.

[25] I am indebted to Don Scherer for discussions of this point.

of these traits would be like trying to reduce a Mondrian painting to one of its lines, or one of its shapes. It would be to fail to understand the fluid composite shape of personhood.

Why is something such as this valuable? Some might insist that the content of the claim that a self is valuable has to be defined by one or more principles, such as "One ought to respect this entity, e.g., by doing such-and-such a thing." If this is right, moral theory would have to be principle-dependent, because to say that a self is valuable would simply mean accepting certain principles regarding its treatment. Indeed, this is, I take it, how the typical moral objectivist theory works (where it is assumed that these principles have some kind of independent reality). The view I am advocating, however, insists that any substantive principles with regard to the treatment of a self (e.g., "Do not murder it," "Do not steal from it," etc.) are derived from the value of that self. Hence, on this view, to say that the self has value is to say something that cannot be cashed out in terms of some principle of treatment, since all such principles are derived from the fact of that value. What, then, is the substantive content of such a prior attribution of value?

In a preliminary way, we can try to unearth that content by thinking about what we mean when we call some artifact a "treasure." It is *because* we consider something a treasure that we conclude it must be cared for, cherished, preserved. It is perfectly wonderful, we think, *and therefore* we must respect it. Similarly, when we call a painting a work of art, what we mean by that attribution is not simply that we must hang it carefully, keep it from damaging light, and so forth. Instead, it is *because* we take it to be a fine thing that we believe we have a variety of substantive duties with respect to it. To say, therefore, that a self is valuable is to say that it is something like a treasure, a wonderful thing, *and therefore* we have a variety of substantive duties with respect to that self.

I do not know if we can say more about what it is to be a "wonderful thing"; I doubt that such an idea can be analytically dissected. It may be that if something is valuable, it is something that we have to come to see *as* valuable. But we can at least better understand that idea by thinking about how the egoist regards herself as a "wonderful thing." Rosamond's egoism, for example, is not explained by her acceptance of some abstract principle by virtue of which she is supposed to be valuable. Instead, her value is something that, in her view, simply presents itself to her. She is, she thinks, perfectly wonderful, *and therefore* other people are under various obligations to treat her in certain ways. Moreover, it is the fact of her selfhood, rather than the particular content of her thoughts, feelings, or choices (which she may not like), which absorbs an egoist like Rosamond, and which she takes to matter far more than anything else.

Now imagine a moral theory that accepts the egoist's view that the self is what has value, even while insisting that *every* self has value. On such a theory, egoists such as Rosamond are not wrong to value themselves, and are not wrong to think that the source of their value comes from their being selves; they are only wrong to value themselves exclusively. Many different religious and moral traditions recognize some formulation of the Golden Rule: i.e., love others as you love yourself. We can imagine an interpretation of that rule such that it expresses the attitude each of us should take toward others in the face of the reality of our own value. If "love" is defined here as the attitude of recognition of value, then the egoist stops too soon—the value he accords himself points toward the value he should be prepared to accord all other human beings because that which makes appropriate an attribution of value to himself is also what makes appropriate the same attitude toward others—namely, that they too are selves. On this view, then, the egoist's mistake is the hierarchical nature of his value-scheme, which drops others far below himself; but unlike people grandly planning to benefit "humanity" in the abstract, he is at least alive to the value of one human being, namely himself. Were he also alive to the value that all other persons possess, then he would begin to assume the moral point of view.[26]

Recognizing the value of other selves does not necessarily mean liking them. A self that has worth may also be a self that is maddening, irritating, evil, disreputable, ugly, or unfriendly—these characteristics do not detract from the fact that it is still valuable, so that certain kinds of treatments of it are precluded. Or to use Kantian language, the fact that the will of this self may be bad does not lessen the fact that the self is still an "end in itself."

Can we construct an argument that proves the egoist ought to value others besides herself? This holy grail of normative ethics has yet to be achieved. Indeed, anyone who believes that theories of human worth are (merely) social inventions will likely regard such a proof as impossible (but then such theorists will have to explain in what sense racists or sexists who are prepared to radically devalue some human beings are "wrong"). But those inclined to see value as "natural" rather than invented might get some clues about how to construct such a proof by reflecting on how implausible the egoist's theory of human value is. Egoists are not subjectivists about value: if value is in the eye of the beholder, the egoist would have to admit that she is only valuable in her own eyes, even while being relatively worthless in the eyes of others. And that is not her point of view: someone like Rosamond does not take her importance to be something that she only *thinks* she has. Instead, it is something with an independent reality, that everyone is supposed to acknowledge. Why?

Suppose the egoist contends that there is something about herself that means that only she is valuable. This will not work, for two reasons. First, if this distinctive thing is some trait or characteristic, it will likely be found in at least one other person, so that this other will also have value,

---

[26] Again, the point I am making here could be construed as Hegelian; think of the evolution of consciousness in *The Phenomenology of Spirit*. I am indebted to Maudemarie Clark for pointing this out to me.

or perhaps have even more value than she has. Second, on such a view, the egoist would ultimately be valuable only because this trait is valuable, not because there is anything worthwhile about *her*. Suppose, then, that the egoist claims she is valuable by virtue of being the particular self that she is. But then, since everyone else is also a particular self, why wouldn't each other person be just as valuable as she is?

In the end, the egoist is hard-pressed to explain why she is warranted in according herself such overwhelming value. (Although, interestingly, most real egoists do not seem particularly worried about this. Do they take their overwhelming value to be obvious?) It is worth pressing this point: moral theorists have traditionally been challenged to explain why any of us should have regard for others, but what I take to be much harder, indeed impossible, to explain is why an egoist should be justified in according such extreme regard to herself. The absurdity of the egoist's hierarchy of value is at least one consideration relevant to constructing an argument for the plausibility of the moral point of view.

Thus far, I have been concerned to argue that the self is the source of value; but although it certainly lends support to the egalitarian theory of worth, this thesis about the source of our value does not automatically vindicate that theory. For example, one might believe that while, under normal circumstances, all people have equal value, radically evil people such as Hitler or Stalin cannot be as valuable as the rest of us, given what they have done. On this view, extreme evil can actually lower the value of the evildoer by damaging his selfhood, meaning that our value as persons can be crippled (or perhaps even destroyed) by extreme and/or sustained wrongdoing. For the record, I do not think this is right, nor do most of us behave as if we accept it. For example, the anger we feel toward radically evil wrongdoers betrays a belief in their importance as selves. (Why bother being angry at some valueless harmdoer?) When we say "How could you do such a thing?" to a wrongdoer, we are taking him to be important enough to merit our wrath. Moreover, we also show that we value the wrongdoer when we oppose a variety of punishments that are degrading, humiliating, or cruel on the grounds that "one cannot do that sort of thing to a human being." This reaction shows that there is something about the fact that a wrongdoer is still a person that restrains us from cruelty, suggesting that value survives even the most wretched conduct.

In the end, however, I am less concerned with the issue of whether human value survives all wrongdoing than I am with the issue of where the value *is*. I have been arguing that this value is *in the self*, so that, whether this value is permanent or can in some way be lost or damaged, our treatment of another must respect him as valuable in order to be morally sound. And this theoretical point is one that, in my view, accords with the reality of our moral practice. As *Middlemarch* documents, real moral growth is not growth that comes from grasping and acting from principles, but from grasping and acting for the sake of the value of other selves.

Using the egoist's idea that the self is the carrier of value, we can construct an alternative to the impersonal portrayal of Kantian morality suggested in the first formulation of the Moral Law.[27] On a personalized interpretation of the Kantian theory (an interpretation hinted at in the second formulation of the Moral Law, which calls on us to treat human beings as ends in themselves), morality concerns the value of each individual understood as a self (for now, I mean each human individual, but we might extend the realm of the moral to include animals by arguing that a theory of morality also concerns their value, given the nature of their selves—a value that we may not think is the equal of humans, but which is considerable nonetheless). On this view, to speak of a person's value is not to speak of something that is contingent; nor is it to speak of something that is possessed in full by only some. In that sense, value is impersonal. On the other hand, doing something "for morality's sake" on this view comes down to doing it not because one is moved by some abstract moral principle or norm, but because one is moved by the value of *that self*— a value that engages us in a variety of ways, perhaps not only rationally but also emotionally. Thus, even if I dislike a person and eschew friendship with her, a certain sort of treatment of her is still mandated because of something about *her*, not because of some abstract moral principle. Moreover, on such a Kantian theory, this worth is also something which I have myself, and which I must respect in myself just as much as I must respect it in others.

Defenders of Kant's second formulation tend to want to find some trait or characteristic we have, by virtue of which we are valuable—and usually this trait is taken to be our capacity to reason. But this suggests that, in actuality, only *that trait* is valuable, rather than the person who carries it, and even worse, that human value really comes in degrees. For example, if reason is supposed to be what gives us value, it would seem that more-rational people have greater value than less-rational people, which would mean that the theory was actually inegalitarian in nature. But if we say simply that it is our personhood itself which is valuable, and not any particular trait we have, then we avoid such inegalitarian implications, so long as we believe that selfhood does not come in degrees.[28]

This version of Kant's theory is "impersonal" in the sense that it mandates equally respectful treatment for all selves, but it is "personal" in the sense that the mandate is coming from the fact that each is a self, so that it is this personhood or selfhood that is prescriptive with respect to our

---

[27] One can interpret Alan Donagan's work as advocating such a version of Kantian moral theory. See Donagan, *The Theory of Morality* (Chicago: University of Chicago Press, 1977).

[28] Note that if selfhood does come in degrees (e.g., if it makes sense to say that, say, late-term fetuses or young babies are only partial selves), then it would make sense to say that, in this sort of case, value is also partial.

conduct. Or in other words, it is the self which is supposed to move us, and not some abstract principle. Moreover, this theory is consistent with the idea that the more commitments we have to another self (e.g., through marriage or parental bonds), the more responsibility we have in preserving, promoting, or protecting that valuable self. Eliot's *Middlemarch* also suggests that those commitments may play a role in teaching us that other people have value in the first place: because these commitments force us to interact with, learn about, or care for another, they force us to confront the reality of another self (in the way that marriage does for the central characters of the novel), thereby helping us to come to see this other person as mattering.

Not only Kantian theory but also utilitarianism admits of a "personalized" version (which I have suggested may be the version animating Mill's moral theorizing). This version of utilitarianism agrees with the personalized Kantian theory of the equality of human value, but differs on the question of how our values can be aggregated. The fact that aggregation is possible allows us, according to the utilitarian, to calculate the answers to moral questions using the principle of utility, which, on this view, is not foundational but rather derived from a theory of how and why people are valuable. Henceforth, I will call the Kantian and utilitarian value-based theories "personalized" alternatives to the utilitarian and Kantian theories that Stocker criticizes.[29]

VIII. SELF-INTEREST

The egoist teaches us a second lesson: that our own selves are valuable. This lesson has been taken by moral theorists to be blatantly obvious, but it is nonetheless not obvious to many people. Probably because most philosophers have, up until now, been males from relatively privileged social positions—a background that encourages people to think well of themselves—there has been virtually no recognition of how difficult it can be for some people to believe in their own worth. For a person like Isie in Hurston's novel (quoted at the beginning of Section II)—that is, a person who is subjected to social and political forces that attempt to construct her conception of her own worth so as to make her feel lower than others, thereby affecting her ability to accomplish certain tasks, ac-

[29] See Stocker, "The Schizophrenia of Modern Moral Theories." A personalized worth-based moral theory is neither consequentialist nor deontological, although it can generate consequentialist or deontological moral principles, depending upon the kind of "theory of rightful treatment" the theory generates. A utilitarian theory of rightful treatment begins with well-being, because on this view the way to honor the equality of human beings is to work toward maximizing human happiness in a community, where each person's well-being counts in our calculations once, but only once. A Kantian theory defines a theory of rightful treatment that focuses on actions more than on well-being, although that is a bit misleading because treating someone as an end is going to involve concern for his or her welfare as well as concern that he or she not receive certain kinds of treatments deemed "demeaning."

quire certain interests, or develop certain ambitions—maintaining a belief
in one's self-worth can be hard. This shows that the content of a person's
self-interested concerns is not part of the moral in any direct sense. But
the ability of a person to be *appropriately* self-concerned, and to develop
interests and objectives, is a moral matter. Our self-concerns are indirectly
part of the moral to the extent that they reflect our sense of our self-worth,
which *is* a moral matter. It is a moral matter at the personal level, requiring certain kinds of choices from us; but it is also a social and political
matter, insofar as our sense of our self-worth can reflect powerful (and
perhaps virtually inescapable) sociopolitical messages of inferiority or
superiority, or messages about our "place" or proper role, that we may
find it difficult to resist or fight.

Can we accommodate these reflections by saying, in Kantian fashion,
that each of us has duties not only to others but also to the self? Not
completely. We can certainly speak of each of us having a duty to accord
ourselves worth that is the equal of every other person's, entailing a duty
to resist servility and a duty to develop self-respect. But doing things for
oneself, e.g., giving oneself a gift, should not be a "duty," any more than
giving a good friend a gift should be a duty. Kantian ethics has been
criticized because it encourages, at least in certain forms, an impersonal
portrayal of moral action that removes it from the emotional engage-
ments that we want moral persons to have. But one should be able to
enjoy one's gifts both to others and to oneself, whether those gifts be an
extra round of golf, a trip to see a good friend, or a second topping on
one's pizza. And one should not be ashamed to want a good education,
or a good career, or a good time. I would argue, then, that an inability to
feel joy when you give yourself a gift *is* a moral matter, just as an inability
to enjoy gift-giving to others is a moral matter. The joy is a marker for
something: not only does it mark a wholeheartedness in the giving of the
gift, but it is also the emotional sign that you value the recipient of the
gift. You are delighted because you are pleased to do something for *him*
or *her* or *you*—a person whom you believe to be worth the gift. So your
emotion of pleasure is signaling your awareness of the person receiving
the gift as valuable.

These remarks illustrate the larger point that there are moral dimensions to gift-giving whomever the recipient is, and whatever our relationship is to that person. In every friendship, a relationship is constructed in
which each person's value is at stake. The same is true within the family,
or church, or school. Even highly attenuated relationships, e.g., being part
of the same political society, involve each person's value (as the discussion in Section II illustrated). Obsequious or servile gift-giving raises
concerns about how the people involved in the gift-giving think about
their own value, and about how the recipients of the gifts view the value
of those who are giving the gifts to them. We should beware of relationships in which our gifts to others can come to mean that we matter less

than they do. And we should beware of taking an attitude toward ourselves which, by making it difficult to give gifts to ourselves but easy to give gifts to others, betrays our sense of ourselves as mattering less than they do.

If the value of the self and the values possessed by other selves are equal, then how is it that we should work out whose interests matter more when the interests of the self and the interests of others conflict? This is the subject matter of normative ethics: any normative theory needs to provide principles for adjudicating the conflicting interests of different people. It is an issue we face on a daily basis when we are worried only about the conflicting interests of people other than ourselves, for example, when deciding how to resolve the conflicting interests of our children, or our friends, or our employees. We have the same type of problem when we put ourselves into the equation: adjudicating competing interests—including situations when some of these interests are our own—requires a normative moral theory, which expresses a conception of how to weight the interests of equally valuable people.

Note that in the passage quoted at the start of Section II, Zora Neale Hurston presents one principle of such a normative theory: that is, "Never love others more than you love yourself"—which is not to say that you cannot love others as much as you do yourself, but only that you should never love them more. It is a principle that one does not find clearly stated in either the utilitarian or the Kantian tradition, although each can be interpreted so as to be consistent with it. I have argued elsewhere that something like this principle can be thought to animate a contractarian moral theory, and I have commended a certain kind of contractarian reasoning procedure as a way of adjudicating conflicting claims—even (indeed, especially) when some of those claims are your own.[30] In any case, whether or not I am right about the structure that a good normative theory should have, my point here is that it must recognize and accommodate self-worth and the self-interest that worth mandates, lest it fail to acknowledge correctly the value that any acceptable moral theory should accord each of us.

IX. CONCLUSION

In order to investigate the source and nature of any value human beings are thought to have, we need to do meta-ethics. Whether our value is projected or constructed or discovered is not something that I can pursue further here. Certainly some kind of sound meta-ethical theory will be necessary to vindicate the intuition that human value is equal. Exactly *why* racists and sexists and egoists are wrong about who has value

[30] See Hampton, "Feminist Contractarianism," in *A Mind of One's Own*, ed. Louise Anthony and Charlotte Witt (Boulder, CO: Westview Press, 1993), pp. 227–55.

is something any good theory of morality should explain, and I have at least tried to offer some preliminary ruminations on this topic.

What I have been mainly concerned to argue in this essay, however, is that assumptions about human value form the heart of the moralities that actually animate people's views and actions in any society, that they are basic both to other-regard and self-regard, that they are fundamental to people's actual motives to do the right thing, and that a just society accepts a thesis of equal value whereas an unjust society accepts an inegalitarian theory of value that licenses the oppression of those at the bottom. I have also insisted that unless each of us takes responsibility for acknowledging value not only in others but also in ourselves, we will be in danger not only of harming others but also of harming ourselves. Or to use the language of Isie's mother, unless we honor our own worth, the self in each of us will die without being "struck a blow." Indeed, the sort of self-regard that I have called "self-honor" is, as she appreciated, a critical tool in the fight against sociopolitical oppression.

Finally, I have tried to show that an impersonal conception of morality is harmful to the moral cause: to see morality as some kind of unrelenting force of duty, which commands us as surely as the law of gravity, is the worst way we could try to sell the moral life to egoists such as Rosamond or Casaubon, who have a real fear that their selves and their points of view are at risk, and whose egoism may be in part a protection against the kind of loss of self that threatens "selfless" people such as Dorothea. A personalized view of morality protects, above all else, the agent to whom we are commending the moral life; for if that self can be a casualty of "duty," then why should we respect its commands or its authority over us? Why shouldn't it be hated, fought, rebelled against? Whatever morality is, it should not be construed as a force that is out to get us, but rather as a way of regarding human beings, ourselves included, that seeks to generate individual actions and social policies that will bring us a finer and richer world.

Philosophy, University of Arizona

REASONABLE SELF-INTEREST*

By Thomas E. Hill, Jr.

I. Introduction

Philosophers have debated for millennia about whether moral requirements are always rational to follow. The background for these debates is
often what I shall call "the self-interest model." The guiding assumption
here is that the basic demand of reason, to each person, is that one must,
above all, advance one's self-interest. Alternatively, debate may be framed
by a related, but significantly different, assumption: the idea that the basic
rational requirement is to develop and pursue a set of personal ends in an
informed, efficient, and coherent way, whether one's choice of ends is
based on self-interested desires or not. For brevity I refer to this as "the
coherence-and-efficiency model." Advocates of both models tend to think
that, while it is sufficiently clear in principle what the rational thing to do
is, what remains in doubt is whether it is always rational to be moral.
They typically assume that morality is concerned, entirely or primarily,
with our relations to others, especially with obligations that appear to
require some sacrifice or compromise with the pursuit of self-interest. If
there are any self-regarding moral duties, on this view, they must be
derivative from duties to others—they must be understood, for example,
as what we must do to remain fit to fulfill our responsibilities as parents,
friends, citizens, etc.[1] Moral philosophers who share these assumptions
have naturally supposed that their primary task is to answer the question
"Why be moral?" or, in other words, "How can we show that fulfilling
one's moral obligations to others will also satisfy reason's nonmoral demand that one always advance one's self-interest or pursue one's personal ends in an informed, efficient, and coherent manner?" Any attempted
answer, obviously, must appeal to contingent facts, such as the (supposed) inner rewards of virtue and the personal benefits of having a

* I would like to thank David Brink, Stephen Darwall, Chris Morris, Michael Slote, the
other contributors to this volume, and its editors, for their helpful comments on an earlier
draft of this essay.

[1] By "self-interest" I mean to include, roughly, one's welfare, what is good for one, what
is beneficial to one insofar as one is concerned with one's own well-being. "Self-regard" has
broader uses. For example, a self-regarding duty may be simply to treat oneself in a certain
way (e.g., protecting one's health) even if the justification has nothing to do with one's
personal interest in one's own welfare but stems instead, say, from one's promise to a
spouse. To act out of "self-regard," however, seems properly understood as the same as
acting out of self-interest. My understanding here, I hope, simply follows ordinary usage.

secure reputation for honesty and fair dealing.[2] Despite heroic efforts of philosophers to "defend" morality along these lines, there seems to be an emerging consensus that, although such contingent arguments may be adequate to convince most of us under normal conditions, they fail to show that it is *always* rational to be moral.

A radically different picture of the relations between reason, self-interest, and morality draws both (moral) other-regarding requirements and (nonmoral or moral) self-regarding requirements from a common source, our judgments of intrinsic value. According to this picture, which I label "the consequentialist model," we judge many things to be good as means (e.g., money, possessions, reputation, and power), but their value ultimately depends on their usefulness in promoting what we judge to be good as an end and "intrinsically valuable" (e.g., pleasure, happiness, friendship, and/or intellectual activity). Having a good reason to do something, on this model, amounts to being able to promote an intrinsic value (e.g., pleasure) or hinder an intrinsic disvalue (e.g., pain). The most rational thing to do would be whatever, on balance, one has the most good reason to do, that is, whatever contributes most to the greatest possible sum of intrinsic value. From this basic requirement of reason, we can derive both self-regarding and other-regarding requirements. Some hesitate to use the label "moral" for the rational requirement to promote intrinsic values, such as pleasure, *in oneself*, but such self-regarding imperatives have the same *source* as other-regarding imperatives and the same *strictness*, assuming comparability in other respects. To show that it is reasonable to fulfill our other-regarding obligations, on this account, one must use the same method needed to show that limited pursuit of self-interest is reasonable. In both cases, that is, one needs to argue that the conduct in question maximizes (positive) intrinsic value. This general picture underlies utilitarianism of many kinds and, more broadly, most consequentialist theories. Like the first approach, the consequentialist model has a long history but remains open to serious doubts: for example, doubts about whether *objective* intrinsic value judgments are possible, about whether (even if so) rationality requires each person to maximize such "agent-neutral" goods, and about whether the prescriptions justified by such a method would closely resemble what we recognize as "morality."

Regarding the relations among reason, self-interest, and morality, various forms of the self-interest model, the coherence-and-efficiency model, and the consequentialist model have largely dominated contemporary discussions; but there is an alternative worth considering. I label this alternative "the Kantian model" because its main elements are drawn from Kant's work, but I do not to intend to explicate, or even to endorse,

---

[2] According to the coherence-and-efficiency model, one can also appeal to empirical facts about our other-regarding desires, because this model does not assume that the ends one wants to fulfill are all benefits for oneself.

all aspects of Kant's views about practical reason. My aim, instead, is, first, to *describe* this Kantian idea of the connections between reason, self-interest, and morality; then, to *contrast* it with the three classic models sketched above; and, finally, to draw attention to how well the Kantian model fits with (what I take to be) views widely shared among ordinary people without prior commitments to philosophical theories. That the Kantian view has striking affinities with the assumptions of "common sense," I concede, is no proof of the correctness of either the Kantian view or the common assumptions; but it is a fact, I suggest, that warrants giving the Kantian view on these matters more serious consideration than it usually receives in contemporary discussions.

For ease of exposition I will begin with *what I take to be* a "common-sense" view, relatively unencumbered with the technical terminology of philosophical theories. Although I will try to present this in a way that reveals it as a familiar and sensible perspective, I do not plan to defend it against skeptics or even to *argue* that it is a widely held view.[3] Instead, my aim is merely to call attention to ways in which the view I attribute to common sense is at odds with the three philosophical models sketched above, but not with the Kantian model that I shall sketch. In fact, I suggest, the common-sense view is just the practical result that the Kantian model, reasonably construed, supports and explains. Although this conclusion is modest, it is not insignificant; for, if I am right, the Kantian model, which is often dismissed because of its alien terminology or its (supposed) dubious metaphysical commitments, turns out to represent something closer to our ordinary, pretheoretical views than it is usually thought. This may help us to "make sense" of the Kantian view, even if we choose in the end to reject it; and, since widely shared views are at stake, it may lead us to question more seriously the background assumptions of the alternative, currently dominant models of practical rationality.

One brief caveat is needed before I proceed. Since my aim is to compare certain general "models," "perspectives," or background assumptions that characterize various debates about reason, self-interest, and morality, I will need to paint with a broad brush, leaving many matters of detail for later. Obviously, contemporary choice theorists give subtly different accounts of how efficiency, coherence, and information figure in instrumental

---

[3] These tasks are obviously too much to take on here. Defending what I call "the common-sense view" would by itself be a major philosophical project, and establishing its credentials as very widely held among many otherwise diverse peoples would be a very challenging sociological/historical task. Neither is necessary for my purposes, though admittedly my conclusions will be of less interest to those who deny the plausibility or the breadth of appeal of the view I attribute to common sense. The main point is that this view, sketched here in familiar, nontechnical language, seems to have more affinity with the Kantian model, despite the austere Kantian terminology, than with the self-interest model, the coherence-and-efficiency model, or the consequentialist model. Readers, I expect, will find this claim more striking and important the more they agree with my conjecture that what I call "the common-sense view" is plausible and widely held; but the extent to which they agree on this is a matter for each to judge.

reasoning; consequentialism comes in many varieties; and Kantians differ among themselves regarding which are the most "essential" features of Kant's philosophy. There are many "in house" debates over fine points among advocates of the same general "model," and these are not to be disparaged. My hope, however, is that we may gain some further understanding by taking, in addition, a broader "overview" of some major differences in approach. Too often, I suspect, those deeply committed to very different approaches fail to understand one another because they raise questions and look for answers in terms that make sense only within their background framework of thought. Objections that seem decisive to some, then, strike others as utterly without force, and larger issues about the merits and disadvantages of the alternative frameworks are too often ignored.

II. A COMMON-SENSE VIEW OF REASON, SELF-INTEREST, AND MORALITY

If we try to suspend our commitments to philosophical theories, I suspect, we will not find ourselves talking so much of "principles of rational choice," "practical reason," and the like, but rather about what we have "good reasons" to do, what is "reasonable," "makes sense," and so on.[4] Technical distinctions between empirical reason and pure reason, instrumental and noninstrumental reason, etc., will not appear, but of course we will make use of such common expressions as "a selfish reason," "a moral reason," "good as a means," "desirable as an end," "morally good," "good *for* me," etc., as well as metaphors such as "reason demands . . . ," "passion overcoming reason," "listening to reason," "reason surrendering to impulse," etc. What we are after is what a "reasonable" person would do, what we "have the best reasons" to do, what "makes most sense" to do; what we want to avoid is what is "unreasonable," "crazy," "makes no sense," "is unwise," "inadvisable," "against all good reason."

There are distinctions here to be noticed, even in the metaphors. For example, sometimes reason *demands*, but often it *permits* many choices, and sometimes it *advises without demanding*. In other words, there are some things it is utterly unreasonable to do; but there are many things such that one could as reasonably do them or something else, because

[4] In my discussion I will deliberately deviate from the philosophical practice of distinguishing "rational" from "reasonable," e.g., as explicitly done in John Rawls, *Political Liberalism* (New York: Columbia University Press, 1993), pp. 48–54. Ordinary language does not honor a sharp distinction here, though there are subtle differences in the various "reason" expressions we use. The Kantian view of reason, I shall suggest, is closer to a common-sense idea of the reasonable than the thinner and more technical idea of the rational in contemporary philosophy, but I continue to use "rational" in a broader sense (including the reasonable) as a reminder that (as I believe) philosophers have kidnapped that ordinary term for their own purposes. This was a well-meaning offense, no doubt, but it is a constant source of confusion at the intersection of technical and nontechnical discourse.

there is no better reason to do the one than the other; and, finally, there are other things such that one has, on balance, some good reason to do them, but one would not be properly criticizable as "unreasonable" for not doing them.[5] This last point, incidentally, contrasts with an assumption often shared by philosophers, especially those who work within the first three "classic" models, namely, that it is always irrational not to act on the very best reasons. On this view, it seems, reason *demands* when there is the slightest balance of reasons for an act; it *permits* an act only when there is an even balance of reasons for and against; and it never merely *advises without demanding*, that is, never asserts that there is some reason to do something even though not doing it would not be unreasonable.

A. Reasonable self-regard

To begin, let us try to set aside other-regarding reasons and to focus instead on the nonderivative reasons we have for taking an interest in ourselves, securing our own good, and so forth. One aspect of the common-sense view, I think, is that reasonable persons will place a very high priority on securing those conditions that are necessary for them to continue living as reasonable agents with adequate (or, ideally, full) possession of basic human capacities of body and mind. For example, to sacrifice one's sight or hearing, or an arm or leg, to satisfy a particular self-regarding desire unrelated to such a basic capacity would typically be regarded as utterly foolish and unreasonable. To preserve one's life, at least so long as one retains a certain minimum level of human capability, has long been regarded a paradigm of the concern for oneself that reason demands, at least when the interests of others are not at issue.[6] Quite often, I find, people regard it as morally objectionable, as well as foolish, to ignore these more stringent demands of reasonable self-interest, but the

[5] This idea fits well with Rudiger Bittner's suggestion that prudential reason does not "demand" but merely "advises." See his *What Reason Demands*, trans. Theodore Talbot (New York: Cambridge University Press, 1989), esp. chs. 6 and 7. The idea is, I believe, congenial with the position developed by Michael Slote in *Beyond Optimizing: A Study of Rational Choice* (Cambridge, MA: Harvard University Press, 1989).

[6] I pass over several matters of detail here, partly because I suspect that they may not be settled features of the overlapping views I call "common sense." For example, is it ever reasonable to sacrifice one's sight, or life, to complete some personal project that one has come to treasure above all, assuming (artificially) that others' interests are not involved? For our purposes, it is enough to say that common sense holds that reasonable people place *a very high priority* on life and basic human capacities. Questions can also arise, of course, about what the basic capacities are and what degree of maintenance is rationally required. That one should try to preserve one's sight and limbs is uncontroversial, but does reason demand that we train our bodies to the peaks of athletic fitness? It is generally conceded that to "fry one's brains" on drugs is foolish, regardless of the pleasures one might gain; but to what extent does reason demand that we develop our intellectual acuity, memory, etc.? More-theoretical issues that I pass over here concern how the "unreasonableness" of self-destructive behavior is to be explained. Some hold that it is inherently irrational; but one might argue that it merely reflects means-ends incoherence or cognitive confusion, given that the human desire to survive and thrive as human is in fact deep and virtually universal in us.

considerations most uncontroversially considered moral seem to be other-regarding ones.

If we can free ourselves from the influence of the various theoretical models, we will also recognize, I think, that the common-sense view is that reason does not dictate all or even most self-regarding choices. That is, for each person there is a wide range of options, most of the time, among which the person is "free" to choose, without being irrational or unreasonable. Often there will be no antecedent reason to choose one option over the other; neither choice would be more or less reasonable. What color clothes to wear on a given day, whether to have strawberry or chocolate ice-cream, and whether to vacation in the mountains or at the beach are familiar examples. A reasonable person may, and typically will, choose "whichever he or she prefers," we say. However, there is no *demand* to uncover some fact (the "preference") and then follow that, on pain of irrationality.[7] When we deliberate, a felt inclination to do something is not necessarily a good reason for doing it, and similarly the fact that one feels inclined to favor one option over another does not necessarily make that choice more reasonable.[8] Our inclinations may be destructive to ourselves as well as to others (e.g., jealous rage); but they may also simply be pointless, utterly unrewarding when indulged (e.g., an urge to hear or see something disgusting). In neither case do we *need* to conclude that they give us "some reason" to satisfy the inclination.[9] Of course, in the absence of any contrary reasons, we typically *will* choose to do what we feel more inclined to do; and so after acting we often cite such de facto "preferences" to explain what moved us to act as we did. If we understand "preferences" in this way, as *given* "leanings" or "feeling inclined," then our preferences are among the things we reasonably de-

---

[7] Here I am also supposing that common sense differs from the position of Richard Brandt and others who maintain, roughly, that the rational thing to do is to efficiently pursue maximum satisfaction of the desires one *would* have if fully informed, subjected to "cognitive psychotherapy," etc. See Richard B. Brandt, *A Theory of the Good and the Right* (Oxford: Clarendon Press, 1979), esp. pp. 110–29; and Brandt, "The Concept of Rational Action," *Social Theory and Practice,* vol. 9 (1983), pp. 143–64. For criticism of theories of this type, see, for example, Allan Gibbard, "A Noncognitivist Analysis of Rationality in Action," *Social Theory and Practice,* vol. 9 (1983), pp. 199–221; Don Loeb, "Full Information Theories of the Good," *Social Theory and Practice,* vol. 21, (1995); and Connie S. Rosati, "Persons, Perspectives, and Full Information Accounts of the Good," *Ethics,* vol. 105, no. 2 (1995), pp. 296–325. Some desires and preferences that common sense recognizes as quite foolish or crazy may be revealed as such by exposure to more information in cognitive psychotherapy, but it seems doubtful that common sense is committed to the *general* thesis that choices based on desires that would be extinguished under such a process are thereby irrational. (Brandt, I should note, introduces his definitions as stipulative and makes no claims that they conform to common sense.)

[8] I explain and try, informally, to make this view persuasive in my *Autonomy and Self-Respect* (Cambridge: Cambridge University Press, 1991), ch. 12.

[9] The same point, I believe, applies to the hypothetical inclinations that we would have with full information and cognitive psychotherapy, but this is more controversial. In any case, this more sophisticated controversy—whether members of a special class of hypothetical filtered, informed desires always give us reasons—involves technical complications about which we should not expect "common sense" to have an opinion.

liberate about and among the factors that move us to act, but they are not things we are rationally constrained to follow or maximally fulfill.

There is another sense of "preference," I think, but this again is not a sense that supports the idea that reason restricts our permissible self-regarding choices by demanding that we follow (or maximally fulfill) our preferences. When we seem to be citing "preferences" as *good reasons* for acting, I think, the preference is usually not a discovered fact of being inclined but rather a choice, a verdict, or an endorsement. In the absence of compelling reasons, in deliberation we review our options and their anticipated outcomes, etc., often feeling inclined one way and then another in the course of our reflections. The conclusion—what, for various reasons, we choose or endorse as our ranking of options—we commonly speak of as our "preference." Once one has deliberately formed a preference, this gives one "good reason" to make certain other appropriate choices; but, as a mere preference, it is seen as revisable. That is, again in the absence of compelling counter-reasons, one can typically reconsider and, if one likes, endorse a different ranking of options, thus deliberately reversing the order of previous preferences. In short, although reasonable people "do what they prefer," absent contrary other-regarding or self-regarding reasons, it is not a demand of reason that we make our self-regarding choices so that they fulfill some *given* set of inclinations or preferences. Mere inclinations are not in themselves good reasons to act, and we may reasonably alter our preferences.

So far I have suggested that, in common opinion, reason demands concern for preserving one's life and human capacities but permits a wide range of options for each person. Among the things permitted, however, there is a distinction between what is rationally indifferent and what is rationally advisable but not mandatory. Like "supererogatory" acts in the moral sphere, we think of some self-regarding acts as, from a rational deliberative point of view, good to do but not required. That is, there is some reason to do the act in question, but not a reason of the kind and strength to warrant thinking an agent "irrational" or "unreasonable" for not doing it. There is an ideal of being fully governed by relevant "good reasons," and one who fails to do what one judges to be supported by "the best reasons" falls short of this ideal; but I suspect this ideal is more honored in theory than in practice. An example of what reason "advises," in the sense I have in mind, might be choosing to exercise slightly harder and eat even less fat when one already maintains an above-average but not quite ideal dietary and exercise program.[10]

---

[10] Another possible example is the choice of a less expensive brand of food, judged equally as tasty and nourishing as another brand which has a more attractive package. If the cost difference "means" relatively little to one, it seems not unreasonable to choose the slightly more expensive brand even though one realizes that, on reflection, the pretty package "means" even less and thus one has slightly better reason to choose the less expensive

In each of the cases discussed above, I am supposing that common sense regards the conclusions as independent of other-regarding reasons. I mean not only that the conclusions about what reason demands, permits, and advises are *applicable* to situations where only self-regarding considerations are relevant, but also that the grounds for the claims do not stem indirectly from duties or rational requirements regarding others. It is unreasonable not to take steps to preserve oneself and one's human capacities, for example, and not just because we must be alive and fit to fulfill our other-regarding duties.

A final note here may help to avoid misunderstanding. My main concern has been to identify a common-sense view of the sorts of self-interested *ends* that any reasonable person is expected to have.[11] The central points were that, by common opinion, it would be unreasonable not to take an interest in one's survival and in maintenance of one's basic human capacities; but, beyond this (and perhaps a few other special concerns), we may reasonably choose among a variety of possible ends; and we are not rationally constrained to make particular choices of ends according to whether and how strongly we happen to feel inclined toward them. There are, of course, many further common-sense ideas about the *procedures* of rational deliberation and planning, once the ends have been fixed, that I have not discussed. One may have reasonable ends but plan and carry out their pursuit in quite irrational ways (e.g., relying on superstitions, failing to review options, wasting resources, ignoring conflicts with other ends, etc.). Common sense also recognizes another paradigm of irrationality, I think, namely, the weakness or incoherence of will shown by failing to take available means, which one knows are necessary, while nonetheless stubbornly refusing to "give up" the end.[12]

---

brand. This point that it is not always unreasonable not to act on the best reasons has been more thoroughly discussed by others and is not a major thesis on which I want to insist. I note, however, that common sense's apparent adoption of this idea may be subject to several different explanations. One may be that, in the case in question, the agent, on reflection, endorses the end of having the pretty package now, thus making it his or her "preference," despite realizing that he or she would not endorse this ranking as a general policy. That current preference, as a reflective endorsement, is itself a good reason for acting, absent compelling counter-reasons, and thus tips the scale of reasons in favor of now buying the more expensive and attractive package. We can say that the opposite choice also would not have been unreasonable, for, had the agent made it, he or she would no doubt have endorsed the end of saving a little money now over having the pretty package, and thus again would have been acting on the stronger reasons.

[11] I am referring here to the *content* of the ends that a person may reasonably be expected to have, as opposed to (further) constraints on the adoption of ends, which I count as *procedural*, having to do, for example, with ascertaining that they are attainable, compatible with one's other ends, internally consistent, etc.

[12] These controversial cases are treated more fully in my discussions of hypothetical imperatives, in *Dignity and Practical Reason in Kant's Moral Theory* (Ithaca, NY: Cornell University Press, 1992), chs. 1 and 7.

B. Reasonable concern for others

Let us now consider common opinion about what reason demands, permits, and advises with regard to the interests and concerns of others, insofar as our focus is exclusively on these (rather than, for example, on self-interest). Again, in real life, acts and policies that affect others almost always have an impact on the agents themselves, but we can still ask what reasons others' interests and concerns give us in themselves, i.e., considered apart from their impact on self-interest. The question is not about *how to rank* reasons of self-interest versus other-regarding reasons, but rather about what reasons an agent has, if any, that have their source in the interests of others without being grounded in the agent's self-interest.

The main point here, I believe, is quite obvious, though details may be controversial. That is, common sense holds that any reasonable person counts certain basic interests of others as providing him or her with reasons to do, or refrain from doing, various things, provided that various exception-making circumstances are not present. If, for example, I encounter someone severely injured and it costs me nothing very significant, on balance, to prevent his loss of life, intense suffering, etc., then I have some reason to do so, unless certain special circumstances obtain. Various exceptions have often been allowed, but are increasingly challenged in modern times: for example, the basic interests of persons have been discounted because they are enemies, defectives, racial inferiors, outlaws, immoral, despised by gods, etc. Even in these cases, it is not clear whether those who disregarded the interests of these persons did so because their interests do not "count" at all or rather because other interests (e.g., social order, one's own survival, pleasing the gods, etc.) were overriding. It is not easy to get our neighbors to acknowledge, *practically*, that the suffering in war-torn or famine-struck foreign countries gives us reason to contribute to relief, but almost all will grant that in principle we should help, provided we could do so effectively and at little cost.[13] All the more, most people in the contemporary world, I believe, acknowledge that, *absent any reason to the contrary*, one should refrain from killing, maiming, and severely harming other human beings. And, though urgent self-interest and "justice" are common excuses for overriding the basic interests of others, virtually no one would publicly affirm that whim, personal dislike, or minor financial gain are adequate "reasons" to override these interests. Putting out a small effort to save the lives of other nonthreatening, innocent human beings is just something reasonable people must do, whether they happen to feel like doing so or not.

[13] Most people, no doubt, think that it matters how many others are as well-situated to help, whether the victims are "remote" in distance and affiliation, etc. I am not supposing, then, that most people accept Peter Singer's demanding standards for sharing resources, but only that most would grant that, other things equal, one has "some reason" to help if one *can* help effectively and at very little cost. (See Peter Singer, *Practical Ethics*, 2d ed. [Cambridge: Cambridge University Press, 1993], ch. 8, esp. pp. 229–46).

The common-sense view, then, seems to be that reason demands that we treat the basic interests of others, in most cases at least, as potential reasons for us. What about their personal preferences—the innocent ends and activities they endorse for themselves? Here, I suggest, common sense is more permissive, but still gives some weight to the personal preferences of others, again provided certain conditions are met. Prominent among these conditions would be that their preferred ends and activities are not immoral, destructive of others, and the like. Assuming this condition is met, however, most would grant, I think, that one should refrain from interfering with another's preferred projects, and should perhaps even aid them, at least if there was virtually no cost to oneself to do so. That I have a preference for doing something (which is not in itself immoral or irrational) is a (revisable) reason for me to do it; but the fact that someone else prefers that I not do it is also some reason, at least worth considering, that I not do it. Since there are thousands, even millions, of people with whom one may come into contact, the reason we must acknowledge as arising from any random individual's personal preferences will be relatively small, compared to all other possible considerations (including the preferences of others). Thus, common sense takes the rather indefinite view that each permissible preference is "some (small) reason" in favor of acting to promote it, but there are so many other ways to act with as much reason that, in effect, reason permits a wide range of choice as to when and how one promotes the personal preferences of others. A practice of squelching or ignoring them for no reason at all, however, would be unreasonable.[14]

Finally, to draw out the parallel with self-regarding reasons, I suppose that common sense acknowledges that, from its regard for others, sometimes reason *advises* us to act in a certain way without demanding that we do so. The sort of case I have in mind is, say, where an option would apparently promote the personal preferences of quite a few people as opposed to an alternative that would promote the equally strong preferences of somewhat fewer, and contrary reasons of other kinds (e.g., self-interest, justice) are inapplicable. Here, I imagine, we might say that it is usually "better" to do the former, and even that there seems to be "somewhat more reason" to do so; but nonetheless, unless one has special responsibility for the larger group, one would not be criticizable as irrational or unreasonable if one did the latter. Common sense does not, I think, treat "reasons" in such cases in the quasi-mathematical way we sometimes think of "evidence" *weighing* in favor of a hypothesis. Others'

---

[14] We should note, however, that one's own preference, or reflectively endorsed inclination, not to do a particular favor for someone is also a reason that one may often take into account. When I really prefer not to do a favor, then, I am not ignoring the preferences of others "for no reason." This is not to say that my preference not to do favors is always, or even generally, a *sufficient* reason to make it reasonable to refuse the favor; but it is a reason, often relevant.

(permissible) preferences are various factors for a reasonable person to consider favorably, but they are not measurable factors that can be added up to yield a rational requirement.[15]

This brief review of reasons acknowledged by "common sense" is not meant to be exhaustive. For simplicity I have concentrated on just two types of self-regarding and other-regarding reasons—basic human interests and personal preferences—but for other purposes a fuller list and more subtle distinctions might be introduced.[16]

C. Weighing self-interest and concern for others

Clearly there are many differences of opinion about how a reasonable person weighs the various factors when self-interested and other-regarding concerns conflict. In very broad outline, however, I think there is considerable agreement. For example, most would agree, I think, that certain basic human interests (in life, limb, sight, etc.) are so important to each person that it is unreasonable, barring special explanation, to make someone sacrifice a basic interest so that another person can satisfy some nonbasic, minor preference. Thus, other things equal, it is unreasonable to expect elderly persons to terminate their lives early just to provide a few extra dollars for greedy heirs who prefer for them to die at once. Similarly, it would be unreasonable, other things equal, for me to let someone else die, when I could save the person at virtually no cost to me, just because his death would save me a few dollars or because I wish the person dead. To act in these ways would be not just immoral but quite unreasonable, for there are compellingly better reasons for preserving the life in each case than for the alternative. People may disagree to some extent on exactly which goods are basic and of high priority, relative to others; but that there are such differences that require placing strong other-regarding considerations above weak self-regarding ones is surely a widely shared belief.

When we ask where a reasonable person draws the line between self-regard and other-regard, there is, I suspect, no determinate common-sense answer. Most people, as Michael Slote notes, are not so "neutral" as to accept the basic utilitarian position—each person's welfare should count the same in our deliberations, *ceteris paribus*, as each other person's. Other quantitative alternatives, such as "Give about 50 percent regard for self

[15] I should note that I am thinking of cases where we only consider that *someone* has a personal preference, setting aside special relationships. For example, if I am legally appointed to be impartial executor of funds for underage heirs, then I might be explicitly obliged to satisfy more of their permissible preferences, other things equal, rather than fewer, in fulfilling my task; but that is a very special context. I might also note that the common-sense permissibility of not acting on the "best" other-regarding reasons stemming from others' preferences might be explained in terms of an overriding self-regarding permission to choose for oneself, without counting the numbers, where to invest one's "charity" efforts (in promoting the preferred ends and activities of others). But these matters go beyond my main concerns here.

[16] I leave aside, for example, the familiar view that the fact that an act would cause an animal extreme pain is a reason for anyone to refrain from it, whether they "prefer" to or not. See note 55.

and 50 percent regard for *all others*," seem odd to me, not because I am sure that common sense demands more—or less—but because they presuppose that ordinary opinion converges on some determinate quantitative division.[17]

The explanation of this, I suspect, lies in a second main point about the ranking of self-interest and concern for others: to a great extent, conflicts between the interests of different people already fall under moral and social rules, developed over time, and endorsed as reasonable by one's community and tradition. Thus, one does not need to confront all such conflicts with only a simple formula, like "50 percent for me, 50 percent for others," to guide one's decisions. We have many presumptions already in place: murder is wrong; self-defense is permissible if necessary, proportionate, etc.; one should aid others in need if it costs one little, but great risk and self-sacrifice are supererogatory; the fact that a person owns something is a reason to respect his consent as to its use; and so on.[18] Common sense treats most of these rules as open to exception and possibly revision, but as quite unreasonable to ignore, barring very special circumstances. Such rules, assumed to be mutually advantageous in a broad sense, determine for us in many types of cases when self-interest must yield and when it may take precedence. The rules, in effect, define for each agent an area of permissible choice and an area of responsibility, without imposing a need to think in terms of percentages of weight one must give to self-regarding and other-regarding considerations. Perhaps, for example, even though I am far from destitute, the $100 in your pocket would bring me more pleasure, or satisfy more intense preferences of mine, than it would for you; nonetheless, you may reasonably keep the money and even refuse to engage in such speculative cross-person comparisons because the money is *yours* and, on the common view, our property rules (regarding such cases, at least) are reasonable.

What makes these accepted rules reasonable, when they are—and by what criteria are they reasonably criticized and revised? Here we move

---

[17] See Michael Slote, *From Morality to Virtue* (New York and Oxford: Oxford University Press, 1992). Slote gives an extensive description of "common-sense morality" as he sees it, noting where it diverges from utilitarianism (pp. 31–84). He argues that common-sense *morality* is incoherent in various ways, but that common-sense views on *virtue* are more plausible. Regarding virtue, he suggests, common sense seems to give *roughly* equal regard to self and to all others:

> I am saying that our ordinary thinking about the virtues treats the category of trait-possessor and the category of "other people" (i.e. people other than the trait possessor) as of roughly equal importance, and this latter suggests (perhaps it does more than suggest, but I don't at this point want to claim any more than it suggests) an ideal of character and action that, for any given choice of agent/possessor, exemplifies roughly equal concern for the agent/possessor and for others treated as a class or category to which everyone other than the agent/possessor belongs. (p. 98)

[18] It is common now for philosophers to insist that the "shoulds" and "reasons" requiring concern for others be labeled "moral" in contrast to the "nonmoral" or "rational" "shoulds" and "reasons" pertaining to self-interest and efficient pursuit of one's ends; but common sense, I think, does not draw such a sharp line, and to insist on it here would beg questions that are at issue (e.g., what makes reasons "moral"?).

from the heart of pretheoretical common sense to the borders of *theory* of moral and practical reason. Insofar as there is an answer that can be attributed to most people, it will be complex, I suspect, acknowledging that many factors need to be taken into account to find the *most reasonable rules*, just as (most often) many factors were probably causally contributory in the development of the *actual rules* we find in our culture. Considerations of consequences in terms of pleasures and pains (a philosophical favorite) are relevant; but so too are considerations of distributive justice, of desert, of the value of special relationships, of needs for respect, peace, and room for autonomous choice. Virtually any theory that reduced the reasons for moral rules to one type of substantive value would inevitably, I think, leave out considerations commonly thought relevant. The rules are seen as constraints that reasonable people would agree on, if viewing the matter properly; but they serve to affirm and secure many different values.

III. COMMON SENSE AND SOME NON-KANTIAN IDEAS OF PRACTICAL REASON

Let us review, in broad outline, some familiar philosophical accounts of practical reason in order to compare and contrast these with the several ideas I have attributed to "common sense." The point, I should repeat, is not to refute or confirm these theories, as coincidence with ordinary thought is admittedly no proof of correctness. Rather, the point for now is simply to understand better some major ways in which distinct perspectives on reason, self-interest, and morality differ.

A. The self-interest model: Deliberative rationality as the intelligent pursuit of self-interest

Sometimes philosophers suggest that to deliberate well, using reason most appropriately, is to make full and good use of one's cognitive powers to determine what courses of action will best promote one's self-interest. One acts reasonably, then, by following the conclusion of such deliberation or, when time is limited, by following one's best estimate, in the circumstances, as to what the conclusion would be if one could deliberate more thoroughly, etc.[19] Views of self-interest vary of course, and so do the procedures of deliberation believed most effective in finding the

---

[19] The view I sketch here is akin to what is often called "ethical egoism," i.e., the view that what one *morally ought* to choose is just what maximizes one's self-interest. (Another version says that it is always *morally permissible* to do what maximizes one's self-interest.) By contrast, the view I sketch is about what it is *reasonable* to choose. The latter view, I suspect, is more common, but some philosophers apparently hold both the view I sketch and some form of ethical egoism. Uncontroversial historical examples are hard to find, but surely among the best candidates to illustrate the self-interest model of reasonable choice would include Epicurus, Thomas Hobbes, and Henry Sidgwick. See A. A. Long and D. N. Sedley, *The Hellenistic Philosophers* (Cambridge: Cambridge University Press, 1987), pp. 102–57; Thomas Hobbes,

means to promote it. Some try to reduce self-interest to a common denominator of pleasure, or pleasure/pain balance; others interpret it in terms
of satisfaction of desires, or of filtered "informed" desires and aversions;
some (G. E. Moore?) may treat it as obtaining the most "intrinsically valuable experiences" for oneself; others, more pluralistic, treat one's self-interest
in terms of expected "personal benefits," identified by enumeration.[20] There
are different ways of coping with different probabilities of costs and benefits, with better and worse "qualities" of experience, and with tensions
between how one conceives one's future good now and how one may conceive it later.[21] These differences, fortunately, do not matter for purposes
of the broad-stroke comparisons that concern me here.

What is important in order to avoid confusion, however, is to understand that, according to the self-interest standard I have in mind here,
"self-interest" is conceptually distinct from the interests of others. Many
have argued, of course, that *in fact* pursuit of self-interest and promoting
the interests of others coincide, yielding the same recommendations for
action.[22] But even to make this traditional argument is to suppose that the
ideas of self-interest and other-interest can be distinguished. In fact, your
happiness and welfare may be so dependent on the happiness and welfare of certain other people that what makes them unhappy will make
you unhappy, but presumably you can at least entertain the idea that this
might change and that you might thrive while they suffer. Or, if this is too
hard to imagine in your own case, you can no doubt conceive that others,
less loving, find themselves in that situation where they can distinguish
their self-interest from that of others.

Although my primary aim is not to evaluate the various perspectives
under review, I cannot resist saying in passing that, despite its notable
history, the self-interest model of rationality seems to me incredibly implausible. The theory, we must note, is not merely the theorist's affirma-
tion of a personal policy to pursue self-interest above all, together with
the claim that, for her or him, this is a rational policy. The theory is more
general than that, implying that anyone who deliberately pursues the
good of another without regard to whether it proves best for himself or

---

Leviathan, ed. C. B. Macpherson (Baltimore: Penguin Books, 1968), part I, esp. pp. 110–222;
Henry Sidgwick, *The Methods of Ethics*, 7th ed. (Chicago: University of Chicago Press, 1962),
pp. 119–95. See also Derek Parfit, *Reasons and Persons*, esp. chs. 1 and 6.

[20] The latter is proposed in Gregory Kavka, *Hobbesian Moral and Political Theory* (Princeton:
Princeton University Press, 1986), p. 42.

[21] Another variation worth noting is a view that while the "objectively rational thing to
do" is what best promotes self-interest, because self-interest is best served by not pursuing
it directly it is not rational for us, most of the time, actually to engage in deliberation about
what will best promote self-interest. The view is a response to the "paradox of egoism," the
alleged fact that it is not most in one's self-interest deliberately to pursue what is most in
one's self-interest.

[22] See, for example, Joseph Butler, *Five Sermons*, ed. Stephen Darwall (Indianapolis: Hackett Publishing Co., 1983). For a rather different strategy of argument, see Robert G. Olson,
The Morality of Self-Interest (New York and Chicago: Harcourt, Brace, and World, Inc., 1965).

herself is irrational in doing so.[23] Moreover, the theory implies that people are also irrational if they pursue other ends, say, intellectual or artistic goals, for their own sake, without explicit regard for (and not because of) any benefits that success might bring them. To declare irrational so much of what we apparently do would seem to require strong justification. But what reason can one give for the self-interest theory? Surely it is not a conceptual or "analytic" claim, because there are no grounds for supposing that the many theorists as well as nonphilosophers who deny the claim are thereby saying something self-contradictory. Nor would the claim that it is "intuitive" or "self-evident" be convincing, given how controversial it is. Historically, the case for it seems to turn on assertion of psychological egoism as an empirical generalization about human nature.[24] However, as Joseph Butler, David Hume, and others have argued, once the theory is separated from certain tautologies with which it has been confused, it is easily seen to be empirically false.[25] In any case, even if true, the fact that people always do pursue their own advantage would not show that it is somehow a requirement *of reason* to do so. If psychological egoism were true, then admittedly it would be futile to *preach* that we should take into account reasons other than self-interested ones. Again, however, that point is no support for the self-interest theory as a normative theory of rationality. In fact, it highlights the implausibility of the psychological egoism on which it was supposed to depend, for it seems obvious that preaching norms of rationality other than the self-interest theory has not been utterly futile, as a matter of fact.

That the self-interest theory conflicts with our common-sense assumptions should be obvious now. Although both agree that individuals, generally, have good reason to preserve themselves and maintain their basic

[23] Even the indirect self-interest theory mentioned above (in note 21) has implausible consequences, though less blatant ones. On that view, anyone who deliberately pursued the greater good of others at a slight sacrifice of his or her own good would be doing something "objectively irrational"; and any pursuit of the good of others as an end at all would be irrational unless *grounded somehow* (e.g., by prior policy decisions) in one's aim for one's own best self-interest. Although the theory is consistent, it involves the bizarre claim that people who deliberate and act well are in most cases doing so in order to pursue ends quite different from the egoistic end that, according to the theory, really justifies their acting as they do. See Michael Stocker, "The Schizophrenia of Modern Moral Theories," *Journal of Philosophy*, vol. 73 (August 12, 1976), pp. 453–66.

[24] Psychological egoism comes in many forms, but for now it may suffice to characterize it as the view that it is an unalterable law of human nature that every human being always aims ultimately for what he or she believes is in his/her best self-interest, and for nothing else. A somewhat weaker version, i.e., "each person is so constituted that he will look out only for his own interests," is well discussed in James Rachels, *The Elements of Moral Philosophy* (New York: Random House, 1986), pp. 53–64.

[25] See Butler, *Five Sermons*; David Hume, *Enquiries Concerning Human Understanding and Concerning the Principles of Morals*, 3d ed., ed. L. A. Selby-Bigge and P. H. Nidditch (Oxford: Clarendon Press, 1978), pp. 212–32; Joel Feinberg, "Psychological Egoism," in Feinberg, *Reason and Responsibility*, 4th ed. (Encino, CA: Dickenson Publishing Co., 1978), reprinted in *Moral Philosophy*, ed. George Sher (San Diego, New York, and Chicago: Harcourt Brace Jovanovich, 1987), pp. 1–15.

human capacities, the self-interest theory makes rationally mandatory many acts and policies that common sense sees as optional. First consider cases not involving others. If I choose to forgo a number of virtually cost-free pleasures or choose to indulge a minor short-term whim at the acknowledged cost of more (minor) future benefits, then the self-interest theory regards this as quite irrational.[26] Common sense, however, takes a more permissive view, so long as the benefits sacrificed were not vital human interests. An expression of that view, as I imagine it, would be this: "The future benefits, perhaps, give you some reason to resist the whim, but you would not be unreasonable to go for the alternative, if you like; as long as you realize what you are doing, do as you please." It is tempting to add, on behalf of common sense: "The choice to sacrifice virtually cost-free pleasures, though within the bounds of reason, is nonetheless quite unusual, not at all what one would expect." On reflection, however, it is not clear to me that this is true. Philosophical theories lead us to expect that no one knowingly turns down virtually cost-free pleasures, but in fact the phenomenon seems all too common.

Next consider cases involving the interests of others. Here the conflict with common sense is even more evident. The self-interest theory implies that to choose to give any benefit to another when one does not expect any benefit to oneself, not even the "pleasure of giving," would be contrary to reason. Any sacrifice of one's own perceived long-term self-interest, however slight, for the sake of the enormous benefit of many others, would be irrational, according to the theory. Many philosophers argue, of course, that in the long run a policy of immediate self-sacrifice in such cases tends to benefit the agent and thus is a good strategy for maximizing benefits for oneself. However, whether true or not, this thought will seem quite unnecessary to most common-sense deliberators; for the latter, I think, are quite ready to grant that they already have "good reason," even "sufficient reason," to make the minor self-sacrifice, and this is not because they expect to get a compensating personal "kick" from helping others. Again, when the choice falls under certain legal, social, or moral rules that are seen to be (for the most part) mutually advantageous, the self-interest theory would demand, on pain of irrationality, that we break such rules whenever we can achieve a long-term, on balance, personal benefit from doing so, no matter how slight this benefit might be or how great the losses others may suffer as a result of our violating the rule. But common

---

[26] When I refer to "virtually cost-free pleasures," I do not mean to deny that there may always be some costs in opportunities, time, effort, etc. What I have in mind (more strictly) are significant pleasures (not very-minor or barely discernable ones) that can be obtained at very small, insignificant costs so that, on balance, the costs are negligible for practical purposes. It is regrettable, I think, but not contrary to demands of practical reason that people often let the quality of their lives be somewhat diminished by minor but persistent habits of self-denial of pleasures of this sort. Perhaps fuller understanding of why they do this would help to free them from such habits, but the appropriate response, I suggest, is not a charge of irrationality of choice but sympathetic encouragement to "lighten up."

sense, as I have said, seems to grant in such cases that the rules give us a good, and usually sufficient, reason to conform, even when this is (to some degree) contrary to our long-term maximum self-interest.

B. The coherence-and-efficiency model: Deliberative rationality as seeking means-ends coherence and efficiency[27]

Currently a more common perspective on rational choice is the idea that rational deliberation is simply a process of working toward an appropriate fit between the ends one adopts and the means one uses to achieve them. The view accepts Hume's idea that our ends are not *in themselves* either rational or irrational, though they might be *called* "irrational" in a *derivative* sense if adopted because of irrationally formed beliefs about the factual background situation. What is practically irrational, in a straightforward sense, is to select inappropriate means, *given* the set of ends that the agent has in fact adopted.[28] Examples include violations of what John Rawls calls "the counting principles": using more resources than needed to achieve a set of ends; choosing means that achieve a less inclusive set of ends than one might with the same resources; choosing the means less likely than others to achieve the ends, where other things are equal; and so on.[29] These are "counting principles" because they enable us to determine what is unreasonable in some cases simply by "counting" up resources spent and ends achieved, without evaluating or ranking the ends themselves.

[27] A principle of efficiency, as I understand this, would direct us, given fixed goals, to take means that are least costly in terms of resources, or, given fixed resources, would direct us toward a higher degree of satisfaction of our ends. If all our values are commensurable and expressible in terms of some common denominator, then it might be possible (and many would say desirable) to dispense with "coherence" and reduce rational choice to efficiency, seen as choosing so as to bring about the greatest possible amount of that value (which might be, for example, "preference-satisfaction"). The model I call "coherence and efficiency" does not assume that all values are commensurable and thus introduces standards of informed reflection and coherence among means and ends, distinct from and beyond efficiency. For example, if certain means are necessary to an end, one must choose the means or else give up the end; to hold on to an end while refusing to take the necessary steps to achieve it is a form of practical incoherence. (We might be incapable of such incoherence if we were immune to self-deception.) Similarly, it is generally a mark of incoherent (though possible) practical thinking to pursue goals that undermine one's other goals or to employ means that violate the values that were the basis for choosing one's goals. Finding himself in such a situation, a reasonable person will make some adjustment in his set of goals to make them more "coherent," even if there is no quantitative measure of value to indicate *which* ends among his incoherent set of ends should be revised or abandoned.

[28] This point, incidentally, goes beyond Hume, as I understand him. For Hume, acts, choices, and preferences cannot be "contrary to reason," except in the derivative sense mentioned. If they involve wasting resources, taking unnecessary risks of failure, etc., they are foolish and imprudent but not, strictly speaking, irrational. But the coherence-and-efficiency model treats such inappropriate selection of means to fixed ends as a paradigm of practical irrationality.

[29] John Rawls, *A Theory of Justice* (Cambridge, MA: Harvard University Press, 1971), pp. 407–16.

Another familiar principle that remains neutral regarding the nature of the ends, and thus naturally suits the coherence-and-efficiency model, is the Hypothetical Imperative. In a version reconstructed from Kant, this says: If there are means available and necessary to achieve your end, then you (rationally) must take those means—*or give up the end*.[30] This last qualification is important, for there is nothing irrational about deliberately changing your ends. What is irrational, even incoherent, is to refuse to take known necessary means without at the same time revising the set of ends one professes and sees oneself as having. When we first will an end, we necessarily intend ("will") that at some time we will take some means to achieve the end. Typically, however, neither the end nor the "taking some means" is willed unrevisably. If we find out later that the only available means are too costly, in terms of other things we care about, then it is reasonable to drop the end, which takes away the reason to adopt the costly means. Rawls's counting principles presumably must be understood as similarly qualified. They tell us what to do if, but only so long as, we continue to affirm the initial set of ends; but under various conditions, revising one's ends is quite reasonable. The upshot of all these principles is that they demand that the deliberator seek efficiency and coherence in selecting means to his or her ends, a process which involves both apt selection of means and thoughtful adjustment of one's ends.

Virtually any sensible account of practical reason will *include* principles of efficiency and coherence between means and ends. What is distinctive about what I call "the coherence-and-efficiency model" is that it assumes that principles of this sort are *sufficient* for practical rationality. In particular, the model denies (with Hume) that reason tells us what specific ends we must adopt or what rules we must follow.

Now, how does this second model square with the common-sense view? Consider, first, self-regarding considerations. The coherence-and-efficiency standard is permissive in many ways that common sense would approve; for, by abstaining from evaluation of ends, the standard allows that reasonable people may adopt quite different ends, even ends that involve self-sacrifice and seem quite bizarre to others. Thus, while reason demands means-end coherence and efficiency, it permits, in principle, virtually any act one chooses, provided one can knowingly endorse a means-ends package that recommends the act. Only human nature, and one's individual character, limit the content of what one may reasonably do.

The permissiveness of the coherence-and-efficiency model, however, is too unlimited to accord with common-sense views. For example, unlike the common-sense view, it does not require that a person place a high priority on his or her own life and limb. Most people, most of the time, may in fact adopt these as high-priority ends; but if one chooses not to,

---

[30] I discuss this principle at some length in *Dignity and Practical Reason in Kant's Moral Theory*, chs. 1 and 7.

then, by the coherence-and-efficiency standard, there is nothing irrational in that, provided one makes the appropriate adjustments in one's set of ends and means.[31]

The conflict with ordinary opinion is even sharper in cases involving the vital interests of others. The coherence-and-efficiency standard, for example, agrees with Hume's dictum, which Hume no doubt knew would outrage "common sense," that it is not unreasonable to prefer the destruction of the whole world to the scratching of one's finger.[32] Even if by doing something easy, and of little or no cost to myself, I would prevent the imminent misery of many others, the coherence-and-efficiency model does not count that as "a good reason" *in itself* for me to do it. The model's advocates will quickly add that, *if* I care about others or about the rewards of their good opinion (as most people do), *then* I have good reason to take the preventive action. But this is not enough to square with common opinion, as I see it; for the latter holds that I would be unreasonable not to prevent the harm to others, *whether or not I happen to care for them or for my reputation.* Similarly, the coherence-and-efficiency model must recommend that a person break any conventional legal or moral rule if, all things considered, doing so is the best means to the ends he or she reflectively endorses (or "prefers" most). But with regard to murder, rape, torture, betrayal of friends, etc., common opinion seems firm in its view that it is unreasonable to do these things as means to one's ends, even if they are effective and coherent with one's other ends.

C. The consequentialist model: Deliberative rationality as seeking to maximize intrinsic value

Another way of looking at the aims of reasonable deliberation is an analogue of the moral principle of utilitarianism. Typically, utilitarianism is regarded as a basic normative principle that distinguishes between what is morally right and what is morally wrong to do. The root idea, which is subject to many refinements, is that acts are morally right or wrong depending solely on their consequences, and that consequences are better or worse depending upon whether they promote happiness or the reverse.[33] The starting point is the idea that happiness, or some al-

---

[31] According to the coherence-and-efficiency standard, it is not in itself irrational, for instance, to risk one's life for trifles, but if one has that attitude, it is unwise to invest much in long-term projects.

[32] David Hume, *A Treatise on Human Nature*, ed. L. A. Selby-Bigge (1888; reprint, Oxford: Clarendon Press, 1995), p. 416.

[33] There are many important distinctions that have emerged from the vast literature on utilitarianism and consequentialism, but I hope no harm is done by my oversimplifying here. For other purposes, for example, one might note that "consequences," as usually understood, are not all that counts in many versions, e.g., G. E. Moore's; for acts themselves, as distinct from their consequences, could have intrinsic value. See G. E. Moore, *Principia Ethica* (Cambridge: Cambridge University Press, 1902), pp. 1–21. The many subtle variations on "rule-utilitarianism," as well as "motive-utilitarianism," are also highly significant in many discussions, but not, I think, here.

ternative, is objectively an intrinsic value, regardless of whose happiness it is, and unhappiness, or perhaps something else, is intrinsically bad, no matter who has it. Then a course of action is recommended or proscribed according to whether or not it, or the general acceptance of a related moral code, promotes the most intrinsic value possible in the circumstances. Often this sort of theory is presented as a standard of "objective right" rather than as a deliberative guide; and it is usually treated as a *moral* standard, which leaves open the question of whether it is always *rational* to be moral.[34] But the analogue that I want to consider is an idea about what should guide reasonable deliberation in general, rather than a criterion of ("objective") moral rightness. Essentially, the idea is that the fact that doing something would promote an intrinsic value is a good reason for doing it, just as the fact that something would have an intrinsically bad effect (or hinder an intrinsic value) is a reason not to do it. The most reasonable course to take in deliberation, then, would in general be to seek sensibly and effectively to promote, on balance, the most intrinsic value possible.[35]

If we were dissatisfied with the other perspectives on deliberative rationality that we have considered because of their apparent conflicts with "common sense," then we might find some features of the current (consequentialist) perspective attractive. Notably, the latter derives both self-regarding reasons and other-regarding reasons from a common source, and thus it is not committed to the view that the good of others gives us reasons to act only indirectly when and because promoting the good of others also promotes our own good (or aids in the coherent-and-efficient satisfaction of our personal ends). Although empirical assumptions are needed, it seems one could argue plausibly from the consequentialist standard that virtually everyone has strong *presumptive* reasons to place a high priority on preservation of his or her own life and the maintenance of his or her basic human capacities; for these seem to be prerequisites for realizing intrinsic value in one's own life, if anything is.[36] If so, everyone would also have strong presumptive reasons to preserve the lives and basic capacities of others; for these are, to the same extent, prerequisites for realizing intrinsic value in the lives of others. This requirement to count the basic good of others as weighing heavily in our deliberations may also make the consequentialist standard closer than the self-interest

---

[34] Some argue that encouraging people to use the utilitarian principle as a deliberative guide would result in less than the most possible intrinsic value; and for this reason they recommend that, for the most part, we (or common folk) rely on familiar specific moral rules as our deliberative guides. See R. M. Hare, *Moral Thinking* (Oxford: Clarendon Press, 1981), pp. 44–64.

[35] Here I am thinking that "the most intrinsic value, on balance" is the result when negative intrinsic values are "subtracted" from positive ones. (That we can really perform such calculations is, of course, a fiction.)

[36] We need, in addition to empirical premises, also some account of intrinsic value, such as Mill's, which allows us to identify such value as happiness, or high-quality happiness, or Aristotelian thriving, or something similar. See J. S. Mill, *Utilitarianism* (Indianapolis: Hackett Publishing Co., 1988), pp. 7–11.

and coherence-and-efficiency models to common-sense views about how reasonable people rank self-interest and other-regard. At least it seems quite plausible to suppose that most consequentialist theories will uphold the common-sense idea that to be reasonable a person must be ready to sacrifice some minor interest of his or her own if necessary and sufficient to avert a major disaster to many other people. Moreover, consequentialists should also readily endorse the idea that, other things equal, it is unreasonable for a person to sacrifice his or her most intense and stable interests merely to satisfy the whims of others. Sophisticated consequentialism, such as Richard Brandt's rule-utilitarianism, can argue that reasonable legal, social, and moral rules will not dictate our every move but rather will leave each of us a considerable area of freedom within which we may do as we please.[37] Since, by definition, consequentialist theories justify rights-conferring rules only by reference to their expected long-term results, they cannot *start* from an antecedent right to liberty, and they will need to appeal to strong empirical premises, claiming the overall benefits of leaving people free within certain limits to do as they please.

In other ways, however, the consequentialist model seems far removed from common-sense views. It has often been argued, for example, that in various real and hypothetical cases *consequentialism as a moral theory* conflicts with common-sense opinion about what it is morally right to do;[38] and, since common sense supposes it is only reasonable to do the morally right thing, these conflicts translate into conflicts between common sense and our analogous *consequentialism as a theory of reasonable deliberation*. In my opinion, these conflicts are deep and serious, not to be dismissed ad hoc by conjuring up new consequences each time troublesome counterexamples appear or by inventing new epicycles in the definition of consequentialism. My view here, however, is admittedly controversial, and I shall not press it. Instead, I just want to point out something that should be less controversial, namely, that at least when considered *as a theory of reasonable deliberation*, consequentialism is at odds with how people actu-

[37] See, for example, Richard B. Brandt, "Toward a Credible Form of Utilitarianism," in *Morality and the Language of Conduct*, ed. Hector-Neri Castaneda and George Nakhnikian (Detroit: Wayne State University Press, 1965), pp. 107–43; and Brandt, *A Theory of the Good and the Right* (*supra* note 7), pp. 163–99. For the distinction between "act" and "rule" varieties of utilitarianism and consequentialism, see note 41 below.
[38] Many introductory texts and anthologies on ethics, as well as professional books and articles, offer such "counterexamples" to utilitarianism together with discussions of rule-utilitarian, or other consequentialist, devices to circumvent these problems. See, for example, Sir David Ross, *The Right and the Good* (Oxford: Clarendon Press, 1930), pp. 16–47; James Rachels, *The Elements of Moral Philosophy* (New York: Random House, 1986), pp. 90–113; William K. Frankena, *Ethics* (Englewood Cliffs, NJ: Prentice Hall, 1973), pp. 34–43; Alan Donagan, *The Theory of Morality* (Chicago: University of Chicago Press, 1977), pp. 172–99; Donagan, "Is There a Credible Form of Utilitarianism?" in *Contemporary Utilitarianism*, ed. Michael D. Bayles (New York: Doubleday Anchor Books, 1968); J. J. C. Smart and Bernard Williams, *Utilitarianism: For and Against* (Cambridge: Cambridge University Press, 1973); and David Lyons, *Forms and Limits of Utilitarianism* (Oxford: Clarendon Press, 1965).

ally think about choices in ordinary life. According to direct- or act-conse-quentialism, for example, in deliberation my concern should be entirely forward-looking, aimed at promoting the most (or best balance of) intrinsic value (e.g., happiness) that I possibly can. But common sense counts many backward-looking considerations as also relevant, and not just derivatively so: promises, past injustices, debts of gratitude, a history of friendship, etc. Moreover, people do not ordinarily think of it *as their responsibility* to consider and weigh impartially every (intrinsic) good and bad to every person, however remote. Consequentialists sometimes concede this point, claiming that we are justified, in most ordinary contexts, in restricting consideration of costs and benefits more locally because wider-ranging deliberations in those ordinary contexts prove counterproductive. Nonetheless, there is still a conflict, for the common-sense view is that no such justification is needed. That is, there is no reason to *presume* in the first place that my deliberations are reasonable only if I weigh every interest (or "intrinsic good") for every person equally with the comparable interest (or "intrinsic good") of every other, including myself, my family, and my friends. Since there is no such presumption, there is no need to try to "justify" all of our more narrowly focused deliberations from a remote, impartial God's-eye point of view.[39]

This is not to deny that impartial weighing of interests has its place: for example, in courts of law, in government policy making, in arbitration of family disputes, and the like. Even here, though, the range of interests to be impartially considered is limited by the decision maker's jurisdiction as well as various rules of relevance. Beyond this, common-sense morality also acknowledges a fundamental equal moral status for all human beings, and this means that in discussing the formulation and implications of basic moral principles, we must keep in mind that these are not designed to serve the special interests of any particular group as opposed to another, and therefore in applying the principles we must try not to be influenced *inappropriately* by our own special attachments and circumstances.[40] But even this general feature of common-sense morality does not amount to the sort of *impersonal* weighing of interests (or "intrinsic values") that consequentialists have prescribed for moral debates; and, even more obviously, it is not a plausible standard, or even a presumptive standard, that ordinary opinion endorses for all reasonable deliberation.

Since many other problems in direct- or act-consequentialism are ameliorated by a move to rule-consequentialism, one might initially expect

---

[39] On this point, the self-interest standard and the coherence-and-efficiency standard seem quite correct; the Kantian disagreement with them lies elsewhere, as should become evident later.

[40] The need for the qualification "inappropriately" here should be evident; for *some* attention to our actual circumstances, including our particular loves and hates, is often relevant to the reasonable application of general moral principles. What is needed now is more constructive effort to work out standards of appropriateness of particular concerns in various contexts and less rhetoric about the evils of impartialism (or the opposite).

that an analogous move might help square our *consequentialism as a standard of reasonable deliberation* with common sense.[41] Moving in this way to a dual standard for deliberation helps resolve the immediate problem, but it seems only a superficial improvement. That is, the rule-consequentialist can agree with common sense that in most everyday deliberations, agents can quite reasonably restrict the range of interests (or "intrinsic values") they consider, because doing so is a part of a policy that, in the long run, has the best consequences, when all interests (or "intrinsic values") are considered impartially. (Another part of that useful policy, presumably, is that ordinary deliberations be constrained by various substantive moral rules.)[42] But then the problem seems only removed a step. Assuming they could understand the philosophical move to rule-consequentialism, the representatives of common sense might respond as follows: "Why do you presume that our ordinary deliberations are reasonable only if they would be recommended from the alien perspective of consequentialist rule-makers, who (unlike us) debate and decide rules with intrinsic concern for *nothing but* maximizing (or at least impartially promoting) what they consider good *consequences*? Do we really suppose that reason requires us to submit to their principles and policies simply because these seem well-calculated (or estimated) to raise the relevant population's average or total level of 'good results,' no matter how the benefits and burdens are distributed? Their vantage point, however lofty, is not ours, nor are we committed to regarding it as authoritative. Even if such rule-makers were wonderfully well-informed and purely impartial, why should I suppose that, to be reasonable, *I* must submit all my life-projects, interests, and even my promptings of conscience to these legislators for approval or disapproval?" There are various responses that consequentialists can offer, and, though I remain skeptical, I acknowledge that they should eventually be examined respectfully and in detail.[43] For present purposes, it

---

[41] "Act-consequentialism" generally refers to any theory of normative ethics that affirms, perhaps with minor modifications, that one acts in the right (or best) way if and only if one does what will (or probably will) have the best results, compared to one's options, in the long run, considering all persons (or all sentient beings). "Rule-consequentialism" generally refers to any version of normative ethics that affirms, perhaps with minor modifications, that one does what is right (or best), among one's options, if one acts as directed by an ideal (or actual) moral code, or set of rules, such that general acceptance of that code (which is not the same as perfect conformity to it) by most people in the relevant community would have the best results in the long run, considering all persons (or sentient beings). Consequentialists differ among themselves as to what makes results "good" and whether there need always be a quantifiable "best." "Utilitarians" are often considered consequentialists who reduce "good results" to pleasure and pain, or at least benefits and setbacks to the welfare of individuals (but this usage does not fit G. E. Moore's "ideal utilitarianism"). See the citations in note 38.

[42] Endorsing this idea, a colleague of mine says that we should *be* utilitarians but *think like* Kantians.

[43] Strategies for showing the rationality of adopting rule-utilitarianism are discussed in Hare, *Moral Thinking*, ch. 12, and Brandt, *A Theory of the Good and the Right*, chs. XI and XVII. Ad-

should suffice to note that common sense does not initially acknowledge that reason demands submission of its deliberative practices to the rule-consequentialist standard; thus, even if a good argument for this is forthcoming, it would speak in favor of a *revision* of common sense, rather than a *reconciliation* between common sense and rule-consequentialism.

IV. A KANTIAN MODEL: DELIBERATIVE RATIONALITY AS COHERENT AND EFFICIENT PURSUIT OF ONE'S ENDS CONSTRAINED BY RESPECT FOR IDEAL CO-LEGISLATION

In this final section, I want to sketch an alternative idea of deliberative rationality that I draw from Kant. The sketch will admittedly have to leave many details open, and I will not be concerned to defend its credentials as Kantian.[44] My hope, however, is that the sketch is sufficient to suggest some interesting points of comparison with common sense and some contrasts with the three philosophical models reviewed above.

The Kantian model assumes that human beings have both self-interested and other-regarding desires, even if the self-regarding ones have a tendency to dominate in conflict situations. Viewed from a practical standpoint, however, human choices are not simply the result of whatever competing desires and aversions we have at the moment. We have a capacity to review options, consider consequences and precedents, develop norms, strategies, and personal values, and then to choose, in the light of all these, what ends we will adopt and what policies we will follow in pursuing them. We act according to *rationales*, or complexes of beliefs, policies, and deep normative commitments. Even when our motive is inclination, the explanation is not that the inclination caused the behavior (as if it were some inner force moving a machine). Rather, though we

---

vocates of either of our first two models of rational deliberation would need to argue from empirical evidence that it is, derivatively, rational to adopt rule-consequentialism as a moral philosophy. Also, I suspect confusion about "intrinsic value" sometimes gives a false appearance of supporting the thesis that trying to maximize intrinsic value, directly or by rules, is rationally necessary. If one defines "intrinsically valuable" as "having properties that provide good reasons for anyone to favor the thing," or something like this, then the move to justify maximizing intrinsic value could at least get started. But traditionally, from classic utilitarians to Moore and his successors, this has not been what is meant. Bentham, for example, identified intrinsic value with certain sensations, and Moore treated it as a metaphysical, simple, nonnatural, supervenient quality. In both cases, intrinsic value is conceptually independent of what we have reason to choose.

[44] My aim here is merely to reconstruct and summarize a Kantian position rather than to show how it is drawn from Kant's texts; but for purposes of comparing my sketch with Kant's writings, the main texts to consider are the following: Immanuel Kant, *Groundwork of the Metaphysic of Morals*, trans. H. J. Paton (New York: Harper and Row, 1964); *Critique of Practical Reason*, trans. Lewis White Beck (New York: Macmillan Library of Liberal Arts, 1985); *Religion within the Limits of Reason Alone*, trans. T. M. Greene and H. H. Hudson (New York: Harper and Row, 1990); and *The Metaphysics of Morals*, trans. Mary Gregor (Cambridge: Cambridge University Press, 1991). Page numbers in brackets following citations of Kant's texts refer to the standard Prussian Academy edition numbers, included in most translated editions.

might have done otherwise, we endorsed the end of satisfying that inclination (perhaps having seen no reason not to) and chose some means to
satisfy it, according to the general norm of the Hypothetical Imperative.[45]
Merely having an inclination is not in itself a reason for doing anything,
though naturally in the absence of any reason to the contrary, we commonly endorse satisfying our inclinations; i.e., we adopt doing so as an
end. Having adopted an end gives us some reason to take necessary
means to it, but not a *compelling* reason. This is because freely adopted
ends are also revisable, and they (rationally) must be revised if the only
means available to satisfy them conflict with some unconditional rational
norm.

As human beings who are adult and not severely defective, we are
rational beings in at least the *minimal sense* that we find ourselves ines-
capably committed to certain norms for deliberation and thought that
have certain features which have led Western tradition to identify them
with our "rational nature." Exactly what these features are is not easy to
say, but, very roughly, the dispositions of thought and deliberation that
we identify with our "rational nature" are those that especially reflect, for
example, our concerns for consistency, coherence, conceivability, wider
and wider explicability, discovery by methods of reflection, intersubjective justifiability, and having beliefs that are (in senses appropriate to the
context) universal and necessary. Perhaps, too, our "rational" dispositions
are seen as dispositions to submit to the standards, among those we find
in our own practices of thought and deliberation, that, even on persistent
reflection, we cannot help but see as authoritative, whether we like it
or not.

What are these rational norms which we are disposed to regard as
authoritative? Some are, of course, norms of logic and general principles
of empirical understanding, but our concern is with norms of practical
reason. Clearly the Hypothetical Imperative is part of the Kantian view,
and other principles of instrumental reasoning might well be added.[46]
Insofar as both the Hypothetical Imperative and other instrumental principles are understood so as to allow for the revision of ends, it is always
rational to respect those principles.[47] They cannot, by themselves, dictate
action against unconditional rational moral norms, if there are any.

What other practical standards of reasonable deliberation are there? Let
us consider the negative side of the Kantian position. First, the Hypo-

---

[45] This is not to suggest the silly view that we actually go through all these steps consciously every time we make significant choices. The elements are meant to reflect aspects
of what is involved, often as background beliefs and commitments, when, as we ordinarily
say, "his reason for doing that was . . . ," and the like.

[46] Other instrumental principles might be, for example, those that Rawls (in *A Theory of
Justice*, pp. 407–16) calls "counting principles."

[47] I develop this view of the Hypothetical Imperative in *Dignity and Practical Reason in
Kant's Moral Theory*, chs. 2 and 7.

thetical Imperative and other instrumental principles alone are insufficient to account for everything that, as human beings, we count as rationally mandatory. These principles, taken by themselves, allow that all sorts of murderous conduct would be rational, for example, for persons who adopt extremely inhumane ends; but on the Kantian view there are compelling reasons not to destroy human lives for cruel and sadistic purposes.

Second, Hume was right to criticize the previous rationalistic tradition that too readily pronounced all its favorite substantive values "self-evidently rational." Reason is not an intuitive access to a Platonic realm of values; and mere analysis of the concept of "rational beings" can establish neither that they are peace-loving, generous, and law-abiding nor that they are relentlessly power-hungry, exclusively self-interested, or, for that matter, committed to any other familiar set of substantive values. Such values are too variable and controversial to have a plausible claim to be overridingly authoritative and intersubjectively justifiable for all who share the dispositions we associate with our "rational" nature. Thus, the most *basic* universal norms of practical reason, if there are any, will not be expressible in terms of *substantive* ends that any rational person must pursue.[48] The basic norms will not include, for example, "Promote peace," "Increase pleasure and diminish pain," "Obey God's commands," "Maximize your power to survive," or even "Seek to flourish according to your *telos* as a human being." Instead, they will have more to do with a general *orientation* or *attitude*, and with *procedures* necessary for rational deliberation.[49]

Third, various attempts to identify a common denominator in all the different things that people have considered valuable as ends misconstrue the nature of value judgments. For example, theories that are "naturalistic," in the sense introduced by G. E. Moore and refined by others, commonly confuse descriptive claims about what people in fact take interest in and evaluative claims about what is worthy of interest.[50] This complaint would apply not only to simple theories, such as R. B. Perry's "value = any object of interest," but also to complex, sophisticated theories, such as Richard Brandt's, that identify value as the objects of desires

[48] The distinction between "substantive" and "nonsubstantive" is perhaps relative to context, just as the line between "specific" and "nonspecific" is. Thus, I am not claiming that the Kantian basic norms of rational deliberation are so "formal" as to have no action-guiding or deliberation-constraining content at all, but am only trying to contrast them with more specific and controversial substantive principles such as "Maximize your wealth and power," "Follow God's commands," "Choose the most pleasant life," and "Promote the greatest happiness of the greatest number."

[49] For example, the moral attitude is one that values humanity in each person and constrains an agent's choices by principles determined by trying to deliberate according to the procedural standards of the Kantian legislative perspective, to be sketched below.

[50] See, for example, Moore, *Principia Ethica*, pp. 1–21; William K. Frankena, "The Naturalistic Fallacy," *Mind*, vol. 48 (1939), pp. 464–77; and R. M. Hare, *The Language of Morals* (Oxford: Clarendon Press, 1952), pp. 79–93.

that are informed, stable, and capable of surviving a special cognitive scrutiny.[51] Kant's complaint is not that such views commit a "naturalistic fallacy," but that they confuse (1) that which it is conditionally and contingently reasonable to choose with (2) that which it is necessarily reasonable to choose. What is fundamentally valuable is that which it is necessarily rational to choose, and none of the natural properties that "naturalists" identify with value (being desired, pleasure, an object of interest, fitness for survival, etc.) have this characteristic. Nothing becomes valuable, for example, *simply* by virtue of being an object of interest, not even if the interest is informed, stable, and capable of surviving cognitive psychotherapy.[52] A similar point would apply to the idea of objective "intrinsic values," as conceived by Moore and others. Since these are allegedly real, simple, nonrelational "properties" of things in the natural world (especially "experiences"), the claim that doing something would produce intrinsic value does not in any way imply that we *have a reason* to do the act. It is logically possible to be perfectly rational and yet indifferent to intrinsic value, in Moore's metaphysical sense, just as one can be indifferent to various natural properties.

More constructively, Kant's positive account of norms of reason (beyond instrumental principles) is implicit in the progressive development of his idea of the Categorical Imperative. Although the idea has implications that can be expressed as positive prescriptions, the tone and guiding thought is perhaps better expressed in terms of reasonable *constraints* on our pursuit of personal projects. The first formula, roughly, tells us *not* to act on maxims that we could not *reasonably* choose for everyone;[53] but, for the most part, the criteria of reasonable choice (as well as identification of maxims) are left for later formulas. The humanity formula says that "rational nature" *in each person* is to be treated as an objective "end in itself," a special unconditional value setting limits on how any person may be treated.[54] On a thin reading, the central point is that, in determining what is permissible, it is not simply *your reason* (as the first formula might have suggested) but *reason in each person* that must be consulted and satisfied. The "practical reason" that we do and must regard as authoritative in our

[51] See Ralph Barton Perry, *Realms of Value* (Cambridge: Harvard University Press, 1954), pp. 3, 107, 109; and Brandt, *A Theory of the Good and the Right* (*supra* note 7), ch. 6.
[52] By "fundamentally valuable" here I mean only moral and nonmoral values as defined or characterized in the most general terms, not the more specific values that we might draw from such general characterizations in the light of empirical facts.
That persons have dignity for Kant was morally fundamental; that adultery is wrong was derivative. Similarly, that each person's "happiness" consistent with duty is good for that person would be a basic point about personal value, whereas that playing games is good for everyone, or any particular person, would be derivative (if true). The naturalists' error, from the Kantian perspective, was not in their (correct) recognition that empirical facts about what we want, find satisfying, etc., are crucially relevant to most of our value judgments; it was rather that they *identified* the value judgments with judgments about natural properties.
[53] Kant, *Groundwork*, pp. 88–92 [420–25].
[54] Kant, *Groundwork*, pp. 95–98 [427–30].

deliberations is a faculty that we *share*, and not merely in the weak sense in which we might "share" a desire for self-preservation, money, or domination of others in competition.[55] As in logic and science, reason is a capacity that enables all who use it properly to determine (or work more closely toward) conclusions justifiable to all, despite the fact that the world appears differently to individuals from their various perspectives, and despite the fact that their diverse desires often pull them toward conflicting policies and value judgments.[56] We treat persons as mere means when we blatantly ignore the need to obtain their consent in order to be able reasonably to do certain things to them.[57] More generally, we treat their rational nature as an end in itself only if we could justify our treatment *to them*, insofar as they are willing to consider the matter from the same shared perspective of common reason.

Later formulas of the Categorical Imperative begin to fill in some of the further conditions needed to make the Kantian idea of common practical reason workable. For example, each person with practical reason is to be seen as having "autonomy of will" and thus as being ready to acknowledge as finally authoritative those basic principles, and only those, of which one can identify oneself, together with others, as the "author" or "legislator" in a sense implying that one is committed to them as a legitimate standard for oneself.[58] That we will such principles as legislators with "autonomy" implies further that what moves us to accept them is not our attachment to the particular (rationally optional) personal goals and projects that our desires as individuals incline us toward, but rather some general concerns that all reasonable human beings have.[59] The model

[55] I distinguish the "thin" from the "thick" interpretation of the humanity formula of the Categorical Imperative in "Donagan's Kant," *Ethics*, vol. 104, no. 1 (1993), pp. 22–52. Neither interpretation, I should note, makes explicit any grounds for the decent treatment of animals, although neither denies that there are such grounds or implies that the ground is merely Kant's unsatisfactory argument that cruelty to animals creates habits of cruelty to people. A theory that, in the end, cannot convincingly articulate good grounds for the decent treatment of animals is woefully incomplete, as Kant's critics have often pointed out.

[56] Kant's aim is similar in some respects to Hobbes's, when Hobbes, after noting that in a state of nature we each call the objects of our diverse desires "good," insists that we need a common authoritative standard to determine a "good" that all will acknowledge. See Hobbes, *Leviathan*, pp. 120–21. For Hobbes, the standard, of course, was the Sovereign's voice, once the state was established—whereas Kant's standard, the voice of "practical reason" is a construct from ordinary reasonable deliberation, namely, an ideal of duly constrained joint deliberations of persons presumed to have certain general dispositions (traditionally associated with our "rational nature").

[57] This is meant as an example, with obvious gaps, not a general criterion of treating someone as a mere means. Sometimes, of course, coercion is justified and a person's failure to consent is not a barrier; to sort cases, we need, among other things, to appeal to the idea of hypothetical consent or justifiability to the person under specified ideal conditions.

[58] Kant, *Groundwork*, pp. 98–102 [431–34].

[59] Note that among these concerns would be the general concern with one's own happiness: that is, wanting, within the bounds of reason, to realize some large set of jointly possible ends that one endorses upon reviewing the many diverse things one feels inclined toward. This concern, of course, will be important, though not the only factor, in applying the abstract idea of reasonable deliberation to actual conditions.

of legislation from the perspective of legislators in a "kingdom of ends" brings together these, and some other, aspects of the Kantian ideal of reasonable deliberation. It is important, for example, that legislators take into account that each person has a set of "private ends," even though, as legislators, they must "abstract from the content" of those ends when they make laws.[60]

Moreover, for purposes of applying the Categorical Imperative, Kant introduces a thicker idea of "humanity as an end in itself," presumably an interim conclusion about what rational autonomous co-legislators would agree to. This is the idea that each person, qua rational agent and legislator, has dignity, an "unconditional and incomparable worth," without "equivalent."[61] Thus, there is, Kant thought, a rational presumption in favor not only of using one's rational powers, but of preserving them from harm (by avoiding drunkenness, gluttony, and suicide), developing them (by education and self-scrutiny), and honoring them (through self-respect and respect for others). The idea that dignity, unlike "price," admits no equivalents, amounts to an important constraint upon deliberation from the legislative perspective, namely, that legislators must not think of the value of *persons*, like that of *things*, as subject to rational trade-offs (for example, they must not reason, as they would about things, that two are worth twice as much as one).[62]

Pulling these ideas together, the main point is that reasonable deliberation, beyond instrumental reasoning, is deliberation *constrained by* this constructed ideal of joint legislation of rational agents with autonomy. An alleged consideration in favor of doing something is a "good reason" for doing it only if the consideration is compatible with what lawmakers, as defined by the model, would accept. What makes a concern or requirement "moral," rather than "nonmoral," is not whether it is other-regarding or self-regarding but, rather, whether it would be deemed "necessary" from the proper legislative perspective. Moral requirements are "categorical" in that, from that common perspective of shared reason, one must respect them regardless of whether or not they serve one's interests or inclinations.[63]

Kant himself seemed to have confidence, perhaps faith, that reasonable people with minimum effort could reach agreement on what rules would be approved and what policies would be ruled out by the proper use of

---

[60] Kant, *Groundwork*, pp. 100–102 [433–35].

[61] Kant, *Groundwork*, pp. 102–3 [435–36]. See also my "Donagan's Kant."

[62] My efforts to work out this legislative model (and to identify the problems with it) so far include mainly chapters 2, 3, 4, 10, and 11 in my *Dignity and Practical Reason in Kant's Moral Theory*; "A Kantian Perspective on Moral Rules," *Philosophical Perspectives*, vol. 6 (1992), pp. 285–304; and "Donagan's Kant." An application of the idea, independent of Kant, can be found in my *Autonomy and Self-Respect*, ch. 6.

[63] The supreme moral principle, what is supposedly expressed in the various forms of the Categorical Imperative, is "categorical" (indeed supposedly the only "categorical" imperative) in a further, stronger sense, implying that to show its rational necessity, unlike that of derivative principles, one does not need empirical premises. (Here I report the Kantian view without endorsing it.)

our shared practical reason; but contemporary readers, I suspect, will find this incredible, or at least an exaggeration.[64] In the face of acknowledged disagreement, a natural extension of Kant's idea, I suggest, would be the following. Each person's responsibility, as a reasonable and moral agent, is to do his or her best, so far as the seriousness of the issue warrants the effort, to judge what should be approved from the legislative perspective. That is, one needs to try to work out what "bills" the legislators have most reason to endorse. In doing so, one must rely on one's own honest, conscientious reflections guided by the conditions of the ideal perspective;[65] but since the outcome one seeks is justifiability to all who take up the perspective, one cannot reasonably avoid consulting others and taking their judgments into account when they differ from one's own. The regulative ideal, what we could call "the objectively right," is the point (if there is one) at which the best reflections of all reasonable deliberators would converge; but (despite what Kant himself thought) we can never be sure that there will be such convergence points on the various issues about which we deliberate. For practical purposes, then, when moral judgments of reasonable people differ, the best a conscientious agent can do is to *act on his or her own judgment*, after due consultation and weighing the judgments of others.[66] In doing so, without negligence, one would be blameless, but not necessarily objectively right. At best there is a workable standard for conscientious living, not for infallible conformity to moral "truth."

The details of this ideal perspective are underdetermined and controversial even among Kantians, but enough of a sketch has been given, I hope, to enable us to draw some general contrasts and comparisons with the views of reason, morals, and self-interest reviewed earlier.

First, the Kantian view, like the consequentialist one, does not give rational priority to self-interest or satisfaction of one's own preferences. There is, as it were, a common rational source for both self-regarding and

[64] The idea that reasonable Kantian legislators would reach agreement is more plausible, though perhaps still not guaranteed, when the principles are quite general and leave some room for possible exceptions—e.g., "Everyone should make some efforts to contribute to the happiness of others." Even specific, unqualified principles may be reasonably presumed to be agreeable to all who take up the legislative perspective (with its stipulated attitude and constraints)—e.g., "One should not torture and kill human beings solely for the amusement of oneself or others." Those who insist on the inevitability of disagreement are usually focusing on borderline "hard cases," are not heeding the Kantian constraints on moral deliberation, or both.

[65] It should be clear that this ideal construction of a legislative perspective makes no pretense at being describable, or defendable, entirely in "neutral," nonevaluative terms—although how various "evaluative" terms are to be analyzed remains a matter of controversy.

[66] There is a trivial sense, of course, in which one always acts, if one acts intentionally, on one's own judgment; but what I have in mind is something else. There is a possibility of judging (even after consultation with others) that one thing is best, but then doing instead what "most people" judge best *simply because they say so* (rather than because they have convincing reasons). It is this latter kind of "acting against one's judgment" that goes against the conscience of a responsible agent.

other-regarding requirements. Thus, on the Kantian view, though the question arises why it is really rational to follow the (self-regarding and other-regarding) norms we call "moral," the task of answering this question is not equated with showing that what is *obviously rational* (self-interest or preference-satisfaction maximization), despite appearances, really supports what was *dubiously rational* (moral regard for others). Whether the issue concerns one's own life or the life of another, the question to ask is whether reasonable, autonomous legislators, under the various Kantian constraints, can justify to each other the treatment that is proposed.[67] In effect, the Kantian idea of reasonable deliberation (like common sense) has built into it concern for the "voice" of every reasonable person.[68]

Second, Kant's conclusions about rational self-interest are, broadly speaking, coincident with two main points I attributed to common sense earlier. That is, one is rationally required to place a high priority in deliberation on self-preservation and the maintenance of one's human capacities; but otherwise, assuming compatibility with duties to others, what particular personal ends one adopts is rationally optional. When we are adequately fulfilling our moral duties to others and the basic self-regarding duties, reason does not *demand* further either that we pursue life-enriching, "higher-quality" pleasures or that we try to *maximize* (informed) preference-satisfaction. Coherence and consistency in one's set of means and ends is enough. For example, if we respect others' rights, help others to some extent, avoid suicide, drunkenness, neglect of our talents, etc., we are rationally and morally free to pursue our various diverse ways of life.[69]

Third, Kant agrees with the common-sense view that reason demands that we constrain our pursuit of self-interest by a mandatory regard for others. For example, reasonable moral deliberation, he thinks, favors at-

[67] Alternatively, if they cannot agree on the specific treatment, can they justify to each other some general principles governing institutions that might acceptably arbitrate residual disagreements on specific issues?

[68] Skeptics about the necessary rationality of morality should not feel cheated by this stipulation, for the stipulations are aspects of an *analysis* of deliberation from a moral point of view and *not* covert attempts to allay or circumvent skeptical doubts. Skeptical worries can still be raised at a different point: why accept the results of *what Kantians call "reasonable deliberation"* as authoritatively binding on ourselves? At this point, one might argue, Kant's *arguments* seem to run out and he must appeal to "the fact of reason," i.e., the supposedly inescapable sense of moral consciousness that we have some genuine moral duties. What Kant in the end defends is that, by analysis, we see that, if you accept the fact of reason, you must accept that rational deliberation goes beyond instrumental reason in the ways I have sketched. But if you really reject the "fact of reason," not just by saying that it is intellectually unproven but by freeing yourself (like a sociopath?) from the moral attitude and purging your dispositions to judge and act according to it, then probably neither Kant nor anyone else has an *argument* that will change you.

[69] The "etc." here refers to the rest of the various perfect and imperfect duties that Kant argues for in the *Groundwork*, *The Metaphysics of Morals*, and various political writings. For the latter, see *Kant: Political Writings*, ed. Hans Reiss (Cambridge: Cambridge University Press, 1992). The list includes more duties than I explicitly mentioned, but the main point is that both moral and nonmoral reason leave considerable leeway for individual choice of way of life.

titudes of gratitude, beneficence, and respect, as well as principles regarding contracts, property, and legal authority. The justification is not that in the long run such constraint will prove beneficial to oneself; on the contrary, these duties are binding even if opposed to self-interest. Here again, Kant's account is more like the consequentialist model of reason than the previous ones. Moreover, like the views of some consequentialists (but not all), Kant's conclusions accord with the common-sense view that, beyond our strict duties to others, there is much "playroom for free choice" regarding when, how, and how much we undertake efforts on behalf of others. There is room for the morally indifferent; Kant ridicules the denial of this as "strewing our steps with duties as if with man-traps."[70] Beneficence is a "wide, imperfect duty of virtue": unenforceable, flexible, not a response to "rights," and leaving a wide latitude for choice in when and how to fulfill it.[71] As in the common-sense view, what one owes to others is not measured in terms of percentages of time and effort for others versus for oneself, but is rather spelled out roughly in legal systems and traditional ethical principles that, like common sense, typically give priority to life and integrity of body and mind.

Finally, unlike consequentialist models, the Kantian view maintains the primary importance of the moral agent in ways that, I believe, accord with common sense. Thus, despite the ultimate appeal to a shared faculty of human reason, the Kantian view is arguably not as objectionably "impersonal" and "impartialist." Here, in conclusion, are a few reflections that may suggest what I have in mind.

The starting point of Kantian reflection on reason, self-interest, and morality is supposed to be the perspective of an ordinary reasonable and conscientious person, deliberating about what he or she ought to do (but prepared to follow the philosophical argument wherever it leads). It is by analyzing the ordinary consciousness of being under duties, supposedly, that one is able to articulate the ideal of co-legislation by reasonable, autonomous agents; and it is the fact that the latter is (supposedly) merely an extension of the former that explains why we regard the latter to be authoritative for us. Thus, the moral point of view is not a "view from nowhere," nor is it the alien idea of detached utility-maximizers. It is supposed to be the abstractly articulated presuppositions of ordinary conscientious agents.

Further, although the model of co-legislation requires us to consult and take seriously the moral opinions and arguments of others, in using it one is not expected to suspend or subordinate one's own conscientious judgments. Where there is disagreement among apparently reasonable conscientious agents, one must try, after due consultation and listening, to

---

[70] Kant, *The Metaphysics of Morals*, p. 209 [409].
[71] See Kant, *The Metaphysics of Morals*, pp. 192–94 [387–91] and 243–54 [448–61]. Interpretation here is somewhat controversial. My interpretation and evidence can be found in *Dignity and Practical Reason in Kant's Moral Theory*, ch. 8.

judge what ("bills") to propose as the most reasonable and thus most justifiable to all (under the constraints of the legislative perspective). Unlike in Brandt's theory of value, empirical facts about everyone's hypothetical preferences (even if known) would not by themselves fix determinate answers to value questions; and as with Rawls's initial "original position," stipulated features of the choosing parties fix determinate answers only at a certain very general level. As a would-be Kantian legislator, one is aiming at justifi*ability* to all who try to take up the proper perspective. But the fact that most others firmly persist in disagreeing with me does not force me, on pain of irrationality, to grant that their majority judgment is better than mine. The Kantian model is not so tightly defined as to permit, regarding most issues, the simple deduction that all legislators would agree on certain results. And the differences between real people trying to adopt the perspective and the ideal of legislators who fully instantiate it are so great that one cannot simply infer from the fact that one differs from (or agrees with) most other people that one's own judgment is mistaken (or correct). In using the Kantian model as a guide, there will always remain a need to make one's own conscientious judgments.

In the face of real moral disagreement with others, in fact, the Kantian position (as I see it) is that each person has the responsibility *to act on* his or her own best moral judgment. Due consultation with others, weighing their arguments, etc., are necessary if one is to take seriously that one is looking for what can be justified to all; but to follow majority judgments just because more people share them would be to deny one's responsibility as an autonomous agent.

Another way in which the moral agent has priority in Kantian ethics is that most, if not all, duties are *agent-relative*, in a certain sense. They do not say, for example, "Murders ought to be prevented," but rather "You ought not to commit murder." Typically they direct each agent not to commit certain acts (murder, theft, lying, promise-breaking, adultery, etc.) and to perform others (debt-paying, aiding those in dire need, etc.), rather than putting forward a goal (such as general happiness) as worthy of pursuit, the more the better. Each agent is thus especially "responsible" for his or her own conduct within a defined sphere, and whether others act likewise in comparable circumstances is typically "not one's business." Individual law-abiding agents are to be trusted, when possible, to carry out their specific and limited responsibilities; and beyond this they are largely free to do as they please. A conscientious person, then, can usually plan a course of life for him- or herself that is both morally sound and individually satisfying. At least, we do not face a general, ever-present, and all-encompassing responsibility to maximize good outcomes, or minimize wrongdoing, throughout the world.

Similarly, we have agent-relative rights. That is, each person, Kant thought, has a sphere of reasonably protected liberty to pursue his or her own ends without interference from others. Each has a permissible space, the boundaries of which may be legitimately crossed only with that agent's consent. Thus, just as I am not under an all-encompassing responsibility to promote good outcomes or prevent wrongdoing in the world, I am not *subject* to an all-encompassing moral authority of others to treat me in any manner that would minimize crime and immorality or otherwise promote the best states of the world. In this respect, in a Kantian world one's life is *more one's own* than in a consequentialist world, at least more so than in an act-consequentialist world.

Even if rule-consequentialists should argue for just the same boundary rules as Kant endorses, their mode of argument for them, I suspect, would involve both questionable empirical premises (that respecting the "boundaries" always maximizes good results) and an impersonal, alien point of view. Most ordinary conscientious people, I believe, are deeply disposed and publicly committed to some limited form of *reciprocity* with others. Roughly, they are prepared to constrain their self-interested pursuits, within some limits, provided that others will do likewise. They are willing to treat the most vital interests of others as worthy of mutual protection insofar as they are assured similar protection for their own vital interests. They will even count nonvital personal preferences of others as worthy of *some* consideration for noninterference or aid, provided that others will do likewise and that sufficient liberty for one's own projects is ensured. Even those free-riders who refuse such minimal cooperation, I imagine, often tend to acknowledge as reasonable the complaints of those whose restraint they exploit. Though naturally and reasonably reluctant to give up their freedom, most people are prepared to listen to good reasons offered by others as to why, in limited ways, everyone's yielding such freedom makes sense from their common-sense perspective. Now, my thought is just that the Kantian legislative perspective is essentially an abstract expression and refinement of such basic commitments as these, and that these, in turn, are dispositions that we associate with being "reasonable" in everyday life, not outbursts from a hidden noumenal realm. By contrast, the rule-utilitarian legislator is more than an extension of common reasonable commitments. It may be, as some suggest, an "angelic" disposition, this willingness to devote oneself to rules, whatever they may be, that would best satisfy an overriding desire for maximum human welfare, impartially distributed.[72] But the Kantian, like anyone of common sense, cannot help but wonder, "Why is it reasonable for *me*, or *you*, to count the rules so derived as authoritative for *us*?"

Philosophy, The University of North Carolina at Chapel Hill

---

[72] See Hare, *Moral Thinking*, pp. 44–64.

THE RING OF GYGES: OVERRIDINGNESS AND THE UNITY OF REASON*

By David Copp

I. Introduction

Does morality override self-interest? Or does self-interest override morality? These questions become important in situations where there is conflict between the overall verdicts of morality and self-interest, situations where morality on balance requires an action that is contrary to our self-interest, or where considerations of self-interest on balance call for an action that is forbidden by morality. In situations of this kind, we want to know what we ought *simpliciter* to do. If one of these standpoints overrides the other, then there is a straightforward answer. We ought *simpliciter* to act on the verdict of the overriding standpoint.

For purposes of this essay, I assume that there are possible cases in which the overall verdicts of morality and self-interest conflict. I will call cases of this kind "conflict cases." The verdict of morality in a conflict case would be a proposition as to what we ought morally to do, or as to what we have the most moral reason to do; the verdict of self-interest would be a proposition as to what we ought to do in our self-interest, or as to what action is best supported by reasons or considerations of self-interest.[1] These propositions are action-guiding or normative in a familiar sense.[2] The conflict between morality and self-interest in conflict cases is therefore a normative conflict; it is a conflict between the overall verdicts of different normative standpoints. I take it that the question of whether morality overrides self-interest is the question of whether the verdicts of morality are *normatively more important* than the verdicts of self-interest. In due course, I will explain the idea of normative importance as well as the ideas of a normative proposition and of a reason.

I will be defending the position that neither morality nor self-interest overrides the other, that there simply are verdicts and reasons of these

* For helpful discussion of the issues addressed in this essay, I am grateful to Philip Clark, James Drier, Ishtiyaque Haji, Dale Jamieson, Michael Jubien, Jeffrey C. King, the other contributors to this volume, and its editors.

[1] I do not assume that the overall verdicts of morality and self-interest are always that some particular action is required. For all that I say, quite different verdicts are possible, including the verdict that a situation is a moral dilemma. For simplicity, I limit attention to cases in which morality and self-interest require a particular action.

[2] Nothing of importance to my argument turns on the questions that divide realists from antirealists or cognitivists from noncognitivists in ethics.

different kinds, and that there is never an overall verdict as to which action is required *simpliciter* in situations where moral reasons and reasons of self-interest conflict. Accordingly, I reject the position that, in each situation, all the reasons there are determine one overall verdict, the verdict we might call the verdict of "Reason" or "Reason-as-such."[3] In my view, there is no standpoint that can claim normative priority over all other normative standpoints and render a definitive verdict on the relative significance of moral and self-interested reasons. That is, in cases of conflict between kinds of reasons, there is no fact as to what a person ought *simpliciter* to do. I will explain these claims. I will be defending a kind of skepticism about the unity of practical reason.

From one point of view, it will seem that my position threatens the rational significance of morality, and its significance in guiding our actions. From this point of view, morality purports to be the final arbiter of how to act. Morality purports to tell us what we ought to do, period, and without qualification. If moral reasons do not override all others, however, then these appearances are illusory. For if moral reasons are not overriding, there might not be sufficient reason for a person to act morally in situations where the morally required action would be contrary to her self-interest. A person may not be guilty of any failure of rationality if she always acts in her self-interest in such situations.

From a second point of view, however, my position may seem to offer liberation from morality rather than to threaten to discredit it. From this standpoint, the demands of morality are sometimes excessive, for it is sometimes impossible to comply with these demands while also living a worthwhile life.[4] If morality were overriding, the demands of morality could not rationally be escaped. It may therefore seem liberating to recognize that moral reasons are not actually overriding.

I reject both of these points of view. As for the first, I will argue that morality is not discredited by its failure to override self-interest, for it is also the case that self-interest fails to override morality. As for the second, I will argue that there is no privileged standpoint from which to assess whether the demands of morality are "excessive." It is true that moral demands may appear excessive from the standpoint of self-interest, assuming, of course, that morality can demand actions contrary to one's self-interest. This is not a telling point in my view, however, since self-interest does not override morality. Moral demands may appear excessive from other standpoints as well, standpoints that assess our lives as worthwhile, appealing, or excellent. I will argue, however, that these stand-

---

[3] The overall verdict of "Reason" could be complex. For example, it could be that several options are equally acceptable overall.

[4] See Bernard Williams, "Moral Luck," in his *Moral Luck* (Cambridge: Cambridge University Press, 1981), pp. 22–24, 36–39. See also Michael Slote, *Goods and Virtues* (Oxford: Oxford University Press, 1983), pp. 77–107; and Susan Wolf, "Moral Saints," *Journal of Philosophy*, vol. 79 (1982), pp. 419–39.

points also do not override morality. It is never the case that we ought *simpliciter* to violate the demands of morality.

Before I can begin to explain and defend my view, I need to clear the ground of obstructions. I begin in Section II by discussing my assumption that there can be conflict cases. In Section III, I distinguish two conceptions of self-interested reasons, a conception of self-grounded reasons and a conception of reasons to promote personal excellence. Section IV defines the notion of overridingness in terms of normative importance. It also introduces the idea of "Reason-as-such," the idea of a standard for comparing the normative importance of morality and self-interest. Sections V and VI argue that neither morality, nor self-grounded reason, nor a standpoint of personal excellence is to be identified with Reason-as-such. Section VII argues that the idea of Reason-as-such is incoherent and that practical reason is disunified in a fundamental way. In Section VIII, I discuss whether this result discredits morality in any interesting way.

II. CONFLICT BETWEEN MORALITY AND SELF-INTEREST

Consider the myth of Gyges, as told by Plato in the *Republic*.[5] Gyges is a shepherd in the service of the king of Lydia. One day he discovers a magic ring that makes him invisible when he twists it a certain way on his finger. Using the ring to become invisible at crucial times, Gyges commits adultery with the queen, attacks the king with her help, kills the king, and takes over the kingdom.

Plato's description of Gyges' situation is sketchy, but we can adjust the details as we like so that, for almost any moral theory and theory of self-interest, Gyges' situation was a case of conflict. To begin, imagine that Gyges did what he did because he believed that it would be in his self-interest. Now add details so that his belief was true. As a result of killing the king and winning the queen and the kingdom, he achieved a position in which he felt content with his life in a way that he had never felt before. With the queen, he enjoyed a fulfilling relationship of a kind he had never achieved before. As king, he developed talents of leadership and statecraft that he would not otherwise have developed. He valued his achievements. Given these details, which I hereby stipulate to be part of the story, I believe there is no room to deny that killing the king and winning the queen were in Gyges' self-interest, unless one accepts a highly implausible account of the nature of self-interest.

Next, we add details so that what Gyges did would count as morally wrong on almost anyone's account. Killing a person and violating a trust are at least prima facie wrong. Assume that the overall consequences of Gyges' actions were worse than the consequences would have been if he had remained a shepherd. Gyges was a good king, but not as good as the

[5] Plato, *Republic*, 359d–360b.

king he deposed and killed. The former king was benevolent, kind, and just. Gyges' intentions were morally indefensible; his plan made no room for the good of the king, the queen, or the kingdom, and considered only his own good. We can assume that Gyges realized he was in the wrong. Finally, Gyges' action expressed the vices of envy, greed, lust, and the desire for power. Again, I stipulate all of this, and thus I believe there is no room to deny that Gyges' actions were morally wrong unless one has an implausible view about morality.

To be sure, some philosophers, including Plato, would argue that morality and self-interest must necessarily coincide. If these philosophers are correct, then, of course, unless Gyges' situation in the story is not possible, my assessment of it in terms of morality and self-interest must in some way be mistaken.

It might be argued, for example, that it is in one's self-interest to be as good as one can be, and that Gyges would have been a better person if he had remained a shepherd. I believe that arguments of this kind turn on an equivocation. It is in one's self-interest to achieve the best *for oneself*, but it does not follow that it is in one's self-interest to be as *good* as one can be. It certainly does not follow that it is in one's self-interest to be as *morally* good as one can be. It would not have been better *for Gyges* if he had chosen to stay with his sheep.

Ethical egoism is the doctrine that a person is morally required to perform a given action just in case, of all the alternatives, the action would be most in the person's interest. Egoism implies that morality and self-interest cannot possibly conflict; it implies that Gyges did not do anything wrong, given that he acted in his self-interest. Egoism is quite implausible, however, and I assume it is false.

We surely do believe that it is possible for morality and self-interest to diverge. Otherwise, for example, we would not bother to teach morality to our children as a system of norms distinct from self-interest.[6] Of course, morality and self-interest may coincide in certain circumstances, but whether they do coincide is a contingent matter. It may be a fortunate truth that the pursuit of advantage never leads one morally astray. The Gyges example shows merely that this is not a necessary truth.

On my view, conflict situations involve conflict between normative verdicts. Some philosophers might deny this. They might claim that, to count as normative, a verdict would have to entail the existence of a reason, and they might deny that morality and self-interest are both sources of reasons. They might claim that there is a single basis for all reasons. On a Kantian approach, one might hold that reasons are considerations that would move fully autonomous agents. Moral considerations and considerations of self-interest are reasons only if they would move fully autono-

---

[6] This point is made by Samuel Scheffler in his *Human Morality* (New York: Oxford University Press, 1992).

mous agents.[7] On this view, conflict between reasons of these kinds would entail the existence of conflict in the motivations of fully autonomous agents, which one might argue to be impossible. On a Hobbesian approach, one might claim that all reasons are grounded in self-interest. One might infer from this that there are no reasons that conflict with reasons of self-interest.

It would take me too far afield were I to attempt to discuss these views in detail. There are, however, two things I would like to point out.

First, I do not need to insist that cases of conflict involve conflict between different kinds of *reasons*. All that I need to insist is that cases of conflict involve conflict between different overall verdicts as to what an agent *ought* to do, verdicts that are normative, or action-guiding. I merely assume the following: it is possible for the overall verdicts of morality and self-interest to conflict, where these verdicts are normative verdicts as to what an agent ought to do.[8] As I will explain, my understanding of the problem of overridingness depends on this assumption.

The second thing I need to point out is that, intuitively, morality and self-interest are both sources of reasons. I added details to Gyges' story to make it plausible that Gyges' killing the king was both morally wrong and in his self-interest. Given that Gyges' actions were in his self-interest, it is intuitively plausible that there were self-interested *reasons* for him to act as he did. And given that Gyges' actions were morally wrong, it is intuitively plausible that there were moral *reasons* for him not to do what he did. Gyges' situation illustrates the intuitive plausibility of the idea that there are moral reasons as well as reasons of self-interest and that there can be conflict between them.

III. REASONS, NORMATIVITY, AND SELF-INTEREST

The issue about overridingness is an issue about the relative normative significance of overall verdicts delivered by morality and self-interest. People can differ about what these overall verdicts would be in given cases, of course, and there are different theories about this. It is for this reason, in part, that the case of Gyges is so useful. We can agree that the case is a conflict case even if we do not agree in general about the notions of morality and self-interest.

Despite this, however, I cannot ignore the disagreement there is about the notion of self-interest. There are basically two views. These views agree that something is in a person's self-interest just in case it would be good for the person. They disagree about the content of the standards for assessing how well a person's life is going for her. A "subjectivist" view

---

[7] A view of this kind was suggested by Thomas Hill, Jr., in discussion.

[8] Strictly speaking, I may not need to assume the possibility of cases of conflict. For even if cases of conflict are not possible, there would still be the two kinds of verdict, and we could ask whether one kind overrides the other.

might propose that a person's life is going well for her to the extent that her desires are being satisfied or her values are being fulfilled. More generally, a subjectivist view proposes a standard that evaluates a person's life on the basis of its relation to certain subjective psychological states of the person, such as the person's values, desires, or feelings of pleasure. An "objectivist" view proposes certain other characteristics that contribute to how well a life is going, characteristics that are not matters of the relation between the life and the person's subjective states. For example, an objectivist view might judge a person's life on the basis of whether the person is developing her talents. An objectivist view can be mixed, of course. For example, an objectivist view could give great weight in evaluating a person's life to whether the person is content with her life.[9]

It is possible to accept both subjective and objective standards without taking a position on the notion of self-interest. Indeed, standards of both kinds could be sources of reasons, although presumably reasons of different kinds.

In order to explain what I mean, I need to sketch an account of the nature of reasons. Nothing in my argument depends on the details of the account, but my formulation of the argument will make use of a central intuition about normativity.

The intuition is that if something has a normative property, such as the property of being right or wrong or good or bad, there are criteria that it meets or fails to meet; furthermore, a standard or a norm could in principle be formulated that calls for things of the relevant kind to meet the criteria at issue. For example, if an action is morally required, then it meets certain relevant moral criteria, and there is a moral standard or norm that calls on us to perform actions meeting these criteria. Of course, we can imagine various arbitrary standards, such as one calling on us to stand on our heads before eating any meal. Because of this, we need to add that the standards in question are not arbitrary. They are "authoritative," or "justified."

Elsewhere, I have proposed a model of the truth conditions of normative propositions that makes use of this idea.[10] I assume that there are true propositions regarding what we are morally required to do and regarding what we ought to do in our self-interest. On my account, the truth of such a proposition depends on the existence of a relevant "justified" standard.

I think there are reasons of many different kinds, including moral reasons, aesthetic reasons, and, presumably, reasons of self-interest. If there is a warranted, authoritative, or justified normative standard of a certain kind, and if this standard calls on people to choose in a certain way, then,

[9] Richard Kraut discusses the idea of the good for a person in his essay "Desire and the Human Good," *Proceedings and Addresses of the American Philosophical Association*, vol. 68, no. 2 (November 1994), pp. 39–54.

[10] See my *Morality, Normativity, and Society* (New York: Oxford University Press, 1995).

I say, there are reasons of that kind for people to choose in that way.[11] If an agent is morally required to do something, my view implies that there is an authoritative moral standard that calls on her to do the thing. Given what I said about reasons, it follows that there is a moral reason for her to do it. Similarly, if an agent ought to do something because it would be in her self-interest, my view implies that there is an authoritative standard that calls on her to do things that are in her self-interest. It follows, in turn, that there is a self-interested reason for her to do the thing.

The source of the authority of standards of the various kinds is a substantive issue that is beyond the scope of this essay. Given what I have said, it should be plain that a theory of moral judgment requires an account of the circumstances under which moral standards are relevantly authoritative.[12] Similarly, a theory of judgments of self-interest must provide a justification of the standard that calls on each of us to seek what is most in her interest; that is, it must provide an account of that in virtue of which the standard is relevantly authoritative.

Recall that I distinguished objectivist as well as subjectivist views about the content of standards of self-interest, standards as to how well a life is going for the person whose life it is. It is quite possible that some standards of both kinds are suitably justified, although presumably standards of the different kinds would be justified on different grounds. For simplicity, I will assume that this is so. Given the view I sketched about reasons, it follows that there are reasons of both kinds. I will assume, in particular, that each of us has reason to pursue a life in which his talents are fully developed and about which he feels content. I will call reasons of this kind "reasons of personal excellence." I will assume, moreover, that each of us has reason to pursue a life in which his desires or values are satisfied. I will call certain reasons of this kind "reasons of self-interest." Reasons of self-interest are a subclass of "self-grounded" reasons. This is the next idea that I need to explain.

"Self-grounded" reasons are reasons grounded in a person's own standpoint. I propose that the best life for a person, as assessed from her own standpoint, is the life that best meets her basic needs while also satisfying her values without frustrating her mere desires. A person's basic needs, values, and desires together determine what reasons she has that are grounded in her own standpoint. I have developed this proposal elsewhere.[13]

[11] This is an account of "normative reasons." For a similar view, see Michael Smith, *The Moral Problem* (Oxford: Basil Blackwell, 1994), p. 95.
[12] Elsewhere, I have argued that moral standards are relevantly authoritative just when, roughly speaking, society needs their currency among its members in order to flourish. That is, their currency would be in the interest of the society as a whole. See my *Morality, Normativity, and Society*.
[13] See my *Morality, Normativity, and Society*, ch. 9. The standard calling on me to satisfy my basic needs is not subjective in the sense I explained before. I cannot take the space to explain this here.

This is not exactly an account of self-interest. It allows that *any* of a person's values or desires can give her reasons, provided they do not conflict with her needs, even though some of her values may not concern her own good. A person may have moral values, for example, and if so, my account implies that she has self-grounded reasons to realize these values. Hence, if Gyges had attached more value to keeping trust with the king, he might have had sufficient self-grounded reason to stay with his sheep rather than to try to take over the kingdom. This would not, however, have made it in his *self-interest* to stay with his sheep. Despite this, it seems to me that if a person has self-interested reasons grounded in the fact that she values or desires things for her own life, then her other values and desires must also ground reasons of the same kind. That is, a person's self-interested reasons are *among* the reasons she has that are grounded in her needs, values, and desires. I call this larger class of reasons *self-grounded*.

A person's values can be bizarre or self-destructive. It might be objected on this basis that the mere fact that a person values something gives her no reason to achieve it. Fortunately, nothing in my argument turns on the issue raised by this objection. Those who disagree with me will likely find that their view is addressed when I discuss reasons of excellence.

I assume, then, that there are both self-grounded reasons and reasons to pursue excellence. I submit that the question as to which of these kinds of reasons is more properly thought to be, or to include, "self-interested" reasons is neither interesting nor substantive.

IV. Overridingness

Let us return, then, to the questions about overridingness. What is a person to do when there is conflict between the action called for from the moral standpoint and the action called for from the self-grounded standpoint? Before we can begin to deal with these questions, we need to clarify the notion of overridingness. I interpret the notion as follows.

The claim that morality overrides self-grounded reason would be the claim that morality is *normatively more important* than self-grounded reason. We are assuming that Gyges morally ought not to have killed the king and yet that killing the king was best for Gyges in light of his needs, values, and desires. The claim that morality overrides self-grounded reason would imply that Gyges ought *simpliciter* to have done what he morally ought to have done.

To make sense of such a claim, we must suppose that there is a justified standard in terms of which to judge the relative normative significance of normative standpoints. This standard would specify criteria bearing on the normative importance of morality and self-grounded reason, or on the importance of their verdicts. The fact that morality is normatively more important than self-grounded reason, if it is a fact, would be the fact that morality meets the criteria specified by the standard in question, or that it meets the criteria more completely than does self-grounded reason.

This standard must of course be justified or authoritative. In addition, it must be *normatively more important* than any other standard that specifies criteria bearing on the comparative importance of morality and self-grounded reason. We want to know whether moral reasons override self-grounded reasons *period*, not merely whether moral reasons are overriding as assessed by some standard or other. We therefore need to know whether morality overrides self-grounded reason when assessed in terms of criteria specified by the normatively most important standard bearing on the comparison of standards. This standard must also bear on the choice of actions, for if morality overrides self-grounded reason when assessed in terms specified by this standard, then we ought *simpliciter* to act morally in every case of conflict.

If we ought *simpliciter* to act morally in every situation, then, on my view, there is a relevant authoritative standard that calls on us, in every situation, to act morally. I introduced this idea before. Now this standard could not simply be one among many. In order for its assessment of what we ought to do to be definitive and final, in order for it to settle what we ought to do *simpliciter*, it would have to be normatively the most important standard. We are not interested merely in whether, when a person is morally required to do something, she is required to do it by some standard or other.

In summary, then, the fact that morality overrides self-grounded reason, if it is a fact, would consist in the fact that morality is *normatively more important* than self-grounded reason as assessed in terms of the *normatively most important* standard bearing on the comparison of standards and the choice of actions. We could call this standpoint or standard, if it exists, *Reason*, or *Reason-as-such*. Then we could say that morality overrides self-grounded reason just in case it is never Rational (knowingly) to do otherwise than act morally in situations of conflict.[14]

The standard of Reason-as-such would have the following properties, which, for future reference, I will call "comprehensiveness" and "supremacy": First, there are various special standpoints or standards for choice—standpoints such as that of morality, self-interest, prudence, etiquette, law, aesthetics, and so on. The standard of Reason would take the verdicts given by all the special standpoints regarding any situation where an agent needs to choose; it would evaluate these verdicts without any question-begging; and it would produce an overall verdict as to what the agent is to do. As I will say, it would be "comprehensive." Second, the standard of Reason would be the normatively most important standard for assessing such verdicts and choosing how to act. Hence, an agent *ought simpliciter* to comply with its overall verdict. Reason-as-such would

---

[14] Samuel Scheffler says that the "claim of overridingness" is "the claim that it can never be rational knowingly to do what morality forbids" (*Human Morality*, p. 52).

not be merely another standpoint alongside the special standpoints. As I will say, it would be "supreme."

The issue of whether there is such a thing as Reason-as-such is not the same as the issue of whether morality overrides self-grounded reason. For Reason-as-such might fail to align necessarily with either morality or self-grounded reason. It could be that although it sometimes aligns with morality, and sometimes aligns with self-grounded reason, it sometimes aligns with neither. If I am correct, however, the existence of Reason-as-such is a necessary condition of its being the case that morality overrides self-grounded reason. For if morality overrides self-grounded reason, there is a comprehensive and supreme standard such that, necessarily, in every case of conflict, it yields the verdict that each agent is to comply with the overall verdict of morality. It would follow that each agent ought *simpliciter* to do the morally right thing.

V. MORALITY, SELF-GROUNDED REASON, AND REASON-AS-SUCH

Assuming that there is a standard of Reason-as-such, there are three possibilities. First, it may be that the verdicts of morality are verdicts of Reason-as-such, and the standpoint of Reason includes morality. Second, it may be that self-grounded verdicts are verdicts of Reason-as-such, and Reason includes the self-grounded standpoint. On either of these views, Reason-as-such is seen as simply a wider standpoint than the moral standpoint or the self-grounded standpoint, respectively. The third possibility is that the standpoint of Reason is different in character from both of these other standpoints. This possibility leaves open whether Reason necessarily agrees with morality or with self-grounded reason.

There is something to be said for each of the first two possibilities. Consider the idea that the moral standpoint is the supreme standpoint in cases where morality renders a verdict. One might claim it is analytic, or conceptually guaranteed, that if morality requires Gyges not to kill the king, all things considered, then Gyges ought *simpliciter* not to kill the king, and there is no further question as to what he ought to do. One might add that it is analytic, or conceptually guaranteed, that if morality requires Gyges not to kill the king all things considered, then since Gyges ought *simpliciter* not to kill the king, he *would* refrain from the killing if he were *fully rational*. On this view, in cases where morality yields an overall verdict, its verdict is identical with that of Reason-as-such. Call this view "moral rationalism."[15]

Consider now the idea that the self-grounded standpoint is the supreme standpoint, the standpoint of Reason-as-such, in cases where self-grounded reason renders a verdict. One might claim that it is analytic, or conceptually guaranteed, that if Gyges' needs, values, and desires argue

[15] Michael Smith defends a similar view in *The Moral Problem*, pp. 85–91, 130–202, esp. pp. 182–84.

that it is best for Gyges to kill the king, then it is *rational* of Gyges to do so, and there is no further question. He simply ought to kill the king. On this view, in cases where the standpoint of self-grounded reason yields an overall verdict, it is identical with that of Reason-as-such. Call this view "self-grounded rationalism."

The reply to these suggestions is essentially that although they purport to answer the question about overridingness, in fact they do not. For, in each case, the question could be reformulated. Let me explain.

Moral rationalism contends that it is analytic that if one morally ought to do something all things considered, then one ought to do the thing *simpliciter*, and there is no further question as to what one ought to do. I agree, of course, that when a person ought morally to do something, we often speak simply of what the person "ought" to do, without mentioning the qualification that this is what she ought *morally* to do. But the fact that this qualification is not mentioned hardly settles what an agent ought to do in a case of conflict between morality and self-grounded reason. We can ask: What is the thing that the person ought to do from a standpoint that provides a definitive assessment of the relative normative priority of morality and self-grounded reason? Or is there no such standpoint?

Moral rationalism also claims that it is analytic or conceptually guaranteed that if one morally ought to do something, all things considered, then one will do it if one is "fully rational." But in the absence of an argument that the "fully rational" person in this context is the person who does exactly what is required by Reason-as-such, this claim merely sidesteps our question. Our question could be reformulated as follows: Consider a case where there is conflict between what a person would do if she were "fully rational" (i.e., what she morally ought to do) and what she ought to do from the self-grounded standpoint. What is the thing she ought to do *simpliciter*, from a standpoint that provides a definitive assessment of the relative normative priority of morality and self-grounded reason?

It might be replied that no requirement counts as a *moral* requirement unless it is overriding. On this view, of course, there is no problem of whether morality is overriding. However, for any *putative* moral requirement, or "schmoral" requirement, there is a problem of whether it is in fact a moral requirement. On this view, there may be no moral requirements since "schmoral" requirements may not be overriding. The question we are interested in could be expressed as follows: In a case where there is conflict between what a person ought "schmorally" to do and what she ought to do in light of her needs, values, and desires, is her "schmoral" requirement a moral requirement? What is the thing she ought to do from a standpoint that provides a definitive assessment of the relative normative priority of these two verdicts?

Self-grounded rationalism claims that the thing that a person ought to do in light of her needs, values, and desires is the "rational" thing to do. I agree, of course, that this is a common way of speaking. We do at least frequently express verdicts as to what would be in our self-interest as verdicts about what it would be "rational" to do. This does not settle the question about overridingness, however, for the question could be reformulated: Consider a case where there is conflict between what a person morally ought to do and what she would be "rational" to do, given her needs, values, and desires. What is the thing she ought to do from a standpoint that provides a definitive assessment of the relative normative priority of these two verdicts?

There is a substantive question we want to ask, and the views I have been considering do not answer it. They may appear to answer it, but in each case the question arises again, even if in different terminology.

Here is a way to think of the problem. Morality consists of a particular system of justified standards. These standards call for certain things; they call for Gyges not to kill the king. Similarly, the norm of self-grounded reason calls for agents to pursue the satisfaction of their needs, values, and desires. This norm calls for Gyges to kill the king. The question about overridingness is about the relative normative importance of these two systems of norms. It cannot be answered on the basis of either system. Each of these systems is concerned to evaluate our actions, traits of character, and the like; neither is concerned with the issue about the relative significance of normative standpoints. Moreover, although each system can yield a verdict about verdicts of the other system, these verdicts do not settle the relative normative significance of the systems. Morality would prescribe that we comply with our moral duty rather than act on our self-grounded reasons in cases of conflict, but self-grounded reason would prescribe that we act on our self-grounded reasons in such cases. These verdicts leave unanswered the key question as to which of these verdicts is normatively the more important.

I conclude, then, that in order for morality to override self-interest, or vice versa, there would have to be some other normative standpoint that ranked one as normatively more significant than the other. And this standpoint would have to be normatively more significant than either morality or self-grounded reason; it could not be merely another standard for choice alongside morality and self-grounded reason that gives rise to merely another special kind of reasons. This supreme and comprehensive standard, if it exists, would be the standard of "Reason," or "Reason-as-such."

I believe there is no such thing. Before I attempt to show this, however, let me explore the credentials of the standpoint of personal "excellence." Some philosophers would identify this standpoint with self-interest. I want to consider whether it can be identified with Reason-as-such.

VI. The Standpoint of Personal Excellence

Several recent discussions of the issue of whether morality is overriding, and of the related issue of whether morality is "too demanding," have invoked ideas about the admirable, desirable, or excellent life. Bernard Williams discusses the importance of our "projects" to the "rational justification" of our choices. In discussing a fictionalized Gauguin, who wrongfully abandoned his family in order to go to the South Pacific to pursue his career as a painter, Williams appears to say that Gauguin made the best choice.[16] Williams's thought may be that morality asked too much of Gauguin, for Gauguin could not reasonably have been expected to sacrifice success in the central project of his life in order to take care of his family. Michael Slote argues that Gauguin receives our *admiration* even though the central choice of his life was morally wrong.[17] Perhaps Gauguin deserved our admiration because his choice to pursue his painting made his life more fulfilling and successful than it would otherwise have been. Susan Wolf discusses the desirability of living an *interesting* and *appealing* life, and she argues that a morally flawless life would not generally be an especially appealing one to others.[18] She might therefore say that even though Gauguin's life was *morally* flawed as a result of his decision to abandon his family, he lived a more appealing or interesting life than he would have if he had decided otherwise. Similar things could perhaps be said about Gyges, for he too had a "project" that morality asked him to abandon, and he lived a more interesting life than he would have, if he had complied with his moral duty. One might admire him for his success in his project.

Williams, Slote, and Wolf appear to be invoking a standard that is distinct from morality, a standard concerned with the choice of the best life — the life that would be best *for* the person whose life it is. Let me simplify by assuming that they have the same fundamental idea in mind, a standard of "personal excellence." Each of them appears to be suggesting that morality deserves equivocal support at best from this standpoint of personal excellence.[19]

An Aristotelian view of personal excellences is a familiar one, and I will suppose, for the sake of argument, that an Aristotelian view is at work in the thinking of Williams, Slote, and Wolf. In particular, I will assume that the following standard is at work: We are to pursue projects that, if pursued, would develop our most valuable talents as fully as they could be developed while also giving us enjoyment. The best life for a person is a life of success in enjoyable self-developing projects.

Given this framework, we see immediately that the standard of excellence is distinct both from the familiar standards of morality and from the standard of self-grounded reason. Moreover, it is arguable that the pur-

---

[16] Williams, "Moral Luck," pp. 22–24, 36–39. Williams's discussion is difficult to follow, so I cannot claim to have the only or the best interpretation.

[17] Michael Slote discusses "admirable immorality" in his *Goods and Virtues*, pp. 77–107.

[18] See Wolf, "Moral Saints."

[19] The idea of the good for a person is discussed by Richard Kraut in "Desire and the Human Good." Thomas Hurka has developed an account of personal excellences in *Perfectionism* (New York: Oxford University Press, 1994).

suit of excellence does not necessarily align either with morality or with self-grounded reason.

It is plausible, for example, that although Gauguin's choice was morally wrong, it was recommended by the standard of excellence. Painting was the central project of Gauguin's life, and his talent for painting was arguably the most valuable of his talents. As for Gyges, I stipulated that his action of taking over the kingdom enabled him to develop talents of leadership and statecraft that he would not have been able to develop as a shepherd. It is arguable that these talents are more valuable than the talents a shepherd could develop, and, in any case, Gyges had already developed the latter talents. Arguably, then, the standard of excellence supported the actions of both Gauguin and Gyges despite their being morally wrong. Apparently, then, excellence does not necessarily align with morality.

Self-grounded reason calls on a person to choose what would be best for her from her own standpoint, in light of her needs, values, and desires. The standard of excellence, however, calls on a person to choose what would most facilitate a life of enjoying self-developing projects. Such a life is not necessarily best from the person's own standpoint, given her own values. The projects she values may not be projects that would best develop her talents. If Gyges had most valued his work as a shepherd, then continuing to work as a shepherd would have been recommended by self-grounded reason even if the pursuit of political power would have been recommended by the standard of excellence. It is certainly arguable, then, that the best choice from the standpoint of self-grounded reason is not necessarily the same as the best choice from the standpoint of personal excellence.

These claims about personal excellence would of course be debated by some philosophers. Some would argue that a person living the most excellent life would necessarily be living a morally virtuous life. For our purposes, however, the crucial issue is whether the standard of excellence can be identified with that of Reason-as-such. Does this standard have the two properties of comprehensiveness and supremacy?

The standpoint of excellence does yield verdicts about at least some of the verdicts of morality and self-interest. It may therefore be comprehensive. The key question, however, is whether it is supreme. Is the standpoint of excellence normatively the most important standpoint? Unless this is so, it is not the case, when a person is required to do something by the standard of excellence, that she ought to do it *simpliciter* and without qualification. And unless this latter thing is so, then the fact, if it is a fact, that the standard of excellence aligns in Gyges' case with self-grounded reason would have no tendency to show that morality is overridden in this case by self-grounded reason. It would have no tendency to show that Gyges ought *simpliciter* to kill the king.

Intuitively, the standpoint of excellence is merely a special standpoint of evaluation. What we ought to do in order to best develop our talents is not what we simply ought to do, without any qualification. If this is correct, the standpoint of excellence is not supreme among all special standpoints in the way that Reason-as-such would be, if it existed.

The claim that the standpoint of excellence has the property of supremacy is the claim that it is supreme over other standpoints as assessed in terms of certain relevant criteria. Let these criteria be specified by a standard S. The first point I want to establish is that the standard of excellence is not itself this standard S. The standard of excellence speaks to the relative excellence of our choices, not to the relative normative importance of various standards for choice. In some cases it does yield verdicts about the verdicts of other standards; it prescribes that we pursue excellence in cases of conflict, rather than that we comply with either our moral duty or self-grounded reason. But morality also delivers a verdict in such cases; it prescribes that we comply with our moral duty rather than pursue excellence. The verdict of the standard of excellence in favor of the pursuit of excellence leaves unanswered the key question of whether this verdict is normatively superior to the (perhaps) contrary verdict of morality. This question cannot be answered by the standard of excellence. To suppose otherwise would be to argue in a circle. Hence, the standard of excellence is not standard S.

It follows that the standard of excellence does not have the property of supremacy. For in order to yield definitive assessments of the relative importance of normative standpoints, S must be supreme. It must take the verdicts of the various standpoints and yield verdicts about them, and these verdicts must be definitive in the way that only the verdicts of the normatively most important standpoint could be. Hence, the claim that the standard of excellence is supreme has led to the conclusion that it is *not* supreme, that S is supreme. It follows that we must deny the claim and conclude that the standard of excellence is not the standard of Reason.

VII. Skepticism about the Unity of Reason

When we deliberate about what to do, we may try to take into account all relevant considerations and to make the best or the right decision. We may not want to make a decision that is merely right or best from one standpoint. We may want to make the decision that is best *period*.[20] This would be the decision required by Reason-as-such.

To be sure, a morally virtuous person wants to do what would be morally best, but she then presumably thinks that to do what is morally best *is* to do what is best, period. At least, she does not think that something else would be best, period. This is part of what it is for her to be morally virtuous. Similarly, a self-interested person wants to do what would be best for herself, from her own standpoint. But she presumably thinks that what would be best for her from her own standpoint *is* the

[20] Philip Clark has stressed this point, in discussion.

best thing for her to do. At least, she does not think that something else would be the best thing for her to do, period. Otherwise, she would not be wholly self-interested, for she might think she could do better than pursue her self-interest.

I have claimed that there is no standard of Reason, no supreme and comprehensive standpoint. If we accepted this position, we would have to give up the thought that when we deliberate, we can make the best or right decision, period. For this thought presupposes that there is a standard for the evaluation of choices that is normatively the most important. This would be the standard I have been calling the standard of Reason or Reason-as-such, the standard that yields verdicts as to what we ought to do *simpliciter*, and without any qualification.

To be sure, I have not *shown* that there is no such supreme and comprehensive standard; for all I have argued, then, it is possible that one does exist. But I have argued that morality is not identical with Reason, nor is self-grounded reason, nor is the standard of excellence. These standards are all warranted in their own ways, and they give rise to reasons of their respective kinds, or so I assume, but they are not normatively supreme.

I believe that there is no such thing as Reason-as-such. First, I do not believe we have any clear conception of what such a thing would be. Consider any candidate for the standard of Reason. Call it "S." It is quite unclear what status S could have that would give it the kind of supremacy it would need in order to qualify as the standard of Reason. It is also unclear what status it could have that would give it authority, such that it would indeed be a source of reasons, without giving it a special perspective on the facts of situations where choices must be made. We would then see S as simply another special standard rather than as the one standard qualified to appraise the significance of the verdicts of all of the special standpoints.

Second, there is the following *reductio* of the idea that our candidate S has the property of supremacy. The claim that a standpoint has the property of supremacy is the claim that it is the *normatively most important* standpoint. I argued before that comparisons of the relative normative importance of standpoints must be made in terms of criteria specified by some relevant authoritative normative standpoint. Hence, the claim that the candidate S has the property of supremacy is the claim that it is normatively more important than any other standpoint, as assessed from a relevant authoritative standpoint. That is, if S is normatively the most important, then there is some authoritative standard R that yields the verdict that S is normatively the most important standpoint. R assesses the relative significance of S's verdicts and the verdicts of all the special standpoints, and R determines that the verdicts of S are definitive as to what we ought to do *simpliciter*. Now, either standard R is identical to S, or it is not.

We cannot suppose that R is identical to S. For a standard cannot be normatively the most important in virtue of its meeting criteria that it *itself* specifies as criteria to be met by standards. The standard of Reason is to be normatively the most important *simpliciter*, not merely normatively the most important from its own standpoint. Morality prescribes that we ought to do our moral duty, and it judges that standards that prescribe otherwise are morally wanting by comparison with itself. But this fact about morality does not suffice to make it the case that morality is the normatively most important standpoint *simpliciter*; at best it shows that morality is the *morally* most respectable standpoint. Similarly, the standard of self-grounded reason is presumably the most respectable from the standpoint of self-grounded reason. And for any candidate *S*, there is presumably a sense in which *S* assesses the significance of its own verdicts by comparison with the verdicts of other standpoints; for it prescribes, I assume, that we ought to perform exactly the actions it prescribes. But this does not suffice to make it the case that *S* is normatively the most important standpoint *simpliciter*; it merely shows that *S* is the most acceptable standpoint from its own standpoint. This verdict of standard *S* leaves unanswered the key question as to whether the verdict of *S* is normatively more important than all other verdicts. To suppose otherwise would be to argue in a circle. Therefore, if *S* is normatively the most important standpoint, then it meets criteria specified by some authoritative standpoint *R* that is distinct from *S*. This is what constitutes *S* as normatively the most important.

This standard *R* must be normatively the most important standard. Otherwise, its verdict would not settle definitively the relative normative status of *S* and the special standpoints. Otherwise, there would be some standpoint superior to *R*, and *its* assessment of the relative importance of *S* and the special standpoints would be the definitive one. But then, if *R* is normatively more important than *S*, it follows that *S* is not in fact the normatively most important standpoint.[21] Moreover, although we ought *simpliciter* to do what *S* prescribes, this is a judgment made from the standpoint of *R*, not a judgment made from the standpoint of *S* itself. Hence, *S* itself is not to be identified with the standard of Reason-as-such, which contradicts the assumption with which we began.

[21] Let me briefly discuss two possible objections to the conclusion that *R* must be normatively more important than *S*. (1) Perhaps *R* is exactly as important normatively as *S*. But then, what would constitute them as exactly equally important? It could not be the assessment of *R* by *S* and vice versa. This is simply to argue in a larger circle than we argue if we suppose that *R* is identical to *S*. There would then have to be some additional standard *T* that specifies criteria such that *R* and *S* are equally important. Now there is the problem of the relative status of *R*, *S*, and *T*, which raises the very issues that were supposed to be escaped by supposing that *R* and *S* are equally important. (2) Perhaps *R* and *S* are normatively "incomparable." But then all we have is that a standard of indeterminate significance ranks *S* as superior to all other standpoints. This is not sufficient to constitute *S* as normatively superior *simpliciter*; at most it shows that *S* is superior from the standpoint of *R*. Moreover, there might be some other standpoint *T* that is superior to *R* and that assesses *S* as normatively inferior to some other standpoint. To eliminate this possibility, we would have to suppose that no standpoint is superior to either *R* or *S*. But then there must be some other standard that specifies criteria of evaluation according to which no standard is superior to *R* or to *S*. This begins the regress anew. I see no way to avoid a regress problem.

The same *reductio* can be run on the assumption that *R* is the standard of Reason-as-such. It appears, then, that the idea of a standard of Reason-as-such is incoherent.

The incoherence can be displayed in two sentences: The claim that a standard *S* has the property of supremacy is the claim that it is normatively the most important standard as assessed in terms of some other standard, *R*, which is the normatively most important standard. But only one standard could be normatively the most important.

When we are trying to decide how to act, we do sometimes manifestly have the thought that there is something that it would be best to choose, period. This thought commits us to the existence of a standard that determines the proper weight of all the reasons that bear on a decision and that therefore determines what would be best or right *simpliciter*. If I am correct, this thought is false.[22] There are only the various reasons of the various special kinds, and in weighing them we are simply choosing which to act on. Our choice may be *guided* by the reasons there are, but it is not *determined* by the reasons. That is, again, the reasons do not balance out from a standpoint that determines their correct weight and the right choice, period and without qualification.

My position is a kind of skepticism about the unity of practical reason— "skepticism" seems the appropriate term, for although I deny that practical reason is unified, I concede that I have not proven this. My argument depends on the assumption that there are various special kinds of normative considerations, including those of morality and self-grounded reason, and that it is possible for such considerations to conflict. It also depends on the intuitions about normativity and reasons that I introduced earlier in the essay.

Henry Sidgwick also doubted the unity of practical reason. He thought it unlikely "that the performance of duty will be adequately rewarded and its violation punished." In consequence, he said, there is a "vital need that our Practical Reason feels of proving or postulating this connexion of Virtue and self-interest, if it is to be made consistent with itself. For the

---

[22] Hence, in *most* situations of deliberation it is false that there is something we could choose that would be best, period. There may be *some* situations in which this thought is true, however; for if all the special reasons speak in favor of the same option, then any plausible candidate for the standard of Reason would select that option as best, period. Compare the problem of social choice that was explored by Kenneth Arrow in his *Social Choice and Individual Values*, 2d ed. (New Haven, CT: Yale University Press, 1963). Arrow argued that there is no function that takes individual preference rankings over social options and yields a social preference ranking over those options—no function that meets certain theoretically desirable conditions. I am arguing that there is no standard that takes the rankings over sets of options given by the various special standards for choice and yields a supreme ranking over these sets of options—no standard that meets certain theoretically desirable conditions, including especially that it be comprehensive and supreme. In this note, I am pointing out that in certain special circumstances only one ranking could plausibly be accepted. In particular, if all the special standards rank the options the same way, then that is the only way that the supreme standard or Reason could rank the options.

negation of the connexion must force us to admit . . . that the apparently intuitive operation of the Practical Reason . . . is after all illusory."[23]

It may seem that matters are different when it comes to the choice of what to believe. It may seem that reasons of the kind that ground our knowledge, which we may call "epistemic" reasons, simply do override all other reasons that bear on what to believe. I doubt that this is correct. From the "epistemic" standpoint, we have reason to believe a proposition if it is more likely to be true than its negation, given the available information. But there are other kinds of reasons to believe things. In some cases, for instance, there may be self-grounded reasons to believe something, and these reasons may conflict with the epistemic reasons. Suppose, for example, that a person has certain values about the kind of person she wants to be. She values being a "God-fearing" person with traditional moral standards. Or she values having faith that God exists. In either case, her values give her reason to believe that God exists; they give her a self-grounded reason to believe that God exists. Reasons of this kind may conflict with epistemic reasons. It is not obvious in such cases what a person ought *simpliciter* to believe, even though it may be obvious what she ought *epistemically* to believe.

Epistemic reasons override self-grounded reasons only if there is some third standard for deciding how to believe, a standard that is comprehensive and supreme. It is not obvious that there is such a standard. We should not restrict our skepticism about the unity of reason to so-called "practical reason."

To be sure, conflicts between kinds of reasons to believe are not generally a problem. To believe something is to accept it as true. Because of this, the epistemic reasons for believing a proposition are central to the question of whether to believe it, for they speak to the issue of whether the proposition is more likely to be true or false. Normally a person simply *does* believe a proposition if she believes it is most likely to be true given the available information; for if she believes this about the proposition, it is a small step to accept the proposition as true. It *is* a step, however; and it is not necessarily the case that a person takes the step.

Notice that it is not paradoxical for a person to believe a proposition even though she concedes its negation is more likely to be true given the available information. She may suspect that the evidence is misleading, for example. Or she may be moved by some nonepistemic reason, such as a self-grounded reason. She may believe that God exists because she sees this belief as an expression of the virtue of faith, even though she concedes that it is not likely that God exists given the evidence. She may see the absence of evidence as a test of her faith.

[23] See Henry Sidgwick, *The Methods of Ethics*, 7th ed. (1907; New York: Dover Publications, 1966), pp. 496–509; the quoted passages are on pp. 508 and 509.

Therefore, the plurality of kinds of reasons that have a bearing on our decisions as to how to act is mirrored in a plurality of kinds of reasons for belief that have a bearing on our decisions as to what to believe. There is no supreme comprehensive standard of Reason-as-such in either case—or, at least, I believe there is no such standard.

VIII. The Standing of Morality and Self-Interest

What does the denial that reason is unified imply about the relative standing of morality and self-interest? If neither morality nor self-interest overrides the other, does it follow, for example, that there is no reason to be moral? Does it follow that there is no answer to the question "Why be moral?"

To begin with, my view does not challenge either the facts as to what we ought morally to do or their normativity, their bearing on our choices of how to act. Indeed, the question of whether morality overrides self-interest presupposes that morality yields verdicts as to what we ought morally to do. The correct moral verdicts, whatever they are, have a bearing on our choices of how to act because they are verdicts as to what we *ought* to do. They imply that there are reasons to act as we morally ought.

Moral reasons can of course be given for choosing to do the morally required thing. In cases of conflict, however, self-interested reasons can be given for choosing *not* to do the morally required thing, and I believe that there is no well-grounded answer to the question "What ought we to do *simpliciter*?" If this is correct, we might ask ourselves: Why should we be moral?

This question is normally understood as the question of whether we have sufficient self-interested reason to be moral. It may seem that if morality were overriding, morality would not need the support of self-interest, and the question "Why be moral?" would not be interesting. But, on the contrary, even if morality did override self-interest, it would still be important to determine whether there are good self-interested reasons to be moral, simply because people are typically moved to act in their self-interest. The question "Why be moral?" has an importance that is independent of the issue of overridingness.

It is part of my view that morality and self-interest are in similar positions. The question "Why act as self-interest requires?" is just as pressing, theoretically, as the question "Why be moral?" The "Why be moral?" question is the more pressing given the facts of human psychology, however; and the important standpoint from which to answer it is the standpoint I have called "self-grounded" reason, as I will explain.

A person normally does the thing that would be recommended by self-grounded reason, given the agent's own perception of her needs, values, or desires. This is a thing she perceives she needs to do, or it is a thing that she thinks would best promote satisfaction of her values or desires. Hence, typically, although not necessarily, when a person does what she is morally required to do, her action is recommended by self-grounded reason. Indeed, a person who acts morally acts on her moral values. That is, she subscribes to the moral standards that correspond to the overall moral verdict as to what she ought to do, and this explains her action. In such cases, a person may in fact be acting in the way that is best supported by her self-grounded reasons. I earlier explained that, in my view, reasons of self-interest are a subset of self-grounded reasons. A person who acts morally may be acting on the balance of *self-grounded* reasons, even if her action is not in her self-interest, narrowly construed.

Given all of this, and given our interest in having people act morally, it is in our interest that people subscribe to moral standards, and in particular, that they subscribe to justified moral standards. Moral education and the informal moral sanctions that reinforce our moral values are therefore of central importance to us all. For if people have the proper moral values, if they subscribe to justified moral standards, they thereby have self-grounded reasons to act morally. And from a person's own perspective, self-grounded reasons are as compelling, and they are compelling on the same basis, as self-interested reasons narrowly conceived.

If, therefore, we can create social conditions in which people have the proper moral values, we can thereby contribute to bringing about a situation in which there is less conflict between morality and self-interest than would otherwise be the case, and in which the remaining conflict is less important. For we can thereby help bring it about that people have self-grounded reasons to act morally. Of course, if there is conflict between people's ability to meet their basic needs and the demands of morality, then the balance of self-grounded reasons may still speak against morality. But this is no reason to despair of the place of morality in rational decision-making. It is rather a reason to favor creating a society in which people are enabled to meet their basic needs. A society in which people are enabled to meet their needs while also being encouraged to have proper or justified moral values would be one in which people on the whole would have self-grounded reasons to act morally. In such a society, morality and self-interest would walk the same road.

Philosophy, University of California, Davis

SELF-INTEREST: WHAT'S IN IT FOR ME?*

By David Schmidtz

I. Introduction

We have taken the "why be moral?" question so seriously for so long. It suggests that we lack faith in the rationality of morality. The relative infrequency with which we ask "why be prudent?" suggests that we have no corresponding lack of faith in the rationality of prudence. Indeed, we have so much faith in the rationality of prudence that to question it by asking "why be prudent?" sounds like a joke. Nevertheless, our reasons and motives to be prudent are every bit as contingent as our reasons and motives to be moral—or so I argue in Sections II and III.

A second theme of this essay is that *conflict* between morality and self-interest is contingent as well. The moral perspective, as characterized in Section IV, does not require a universal regard for others, whereas the kind of self-interested perspective characterized in Section III does not require a wholesale disregard for others. Both perspectives make room for a deep although not universal other-regard—or so I argue in Section V.

A third and related theme is that it is simplistic to use self-interest as an all-purpose scapegoat for our failures to be moral. Often, the problem lies elsewhere. Consider that peer pressure often leads people to do things that are not only immoral but imprudent as well. Many people insist that we can be motivated to be moral even when being moral is not in our interest. I agree, but I also believe the other side of the coin—that our motivation to be moral can fail us even when morality and self-interest coincide. I argue the point in Section VI.

II. Why Be Prudent?

Julia Annas remarks that "[i]t is often taken for granted that there is a problem in showing that it is rational for the agent to take the moral point of view, in a way in which there is no problem in showing that it is rational for the agent to take the prudential point of view."[1] One reason for this is that we tend to read "why be moral?" as asking why people should have other-regarding goals, when their having such goals is not

* I thank Neera Badhwar, Stephen Darwall, Ned McClennen, Don Scherer, Doran Smolkin, David Sobel, and especially Elizabeth Willott for helpful comments. And I thank William Nelson for whatever role his book *Morality: What's in It for Me?* (Boulder: Westview Press, 1990) may have played in inspiring this essay's title.
[1] Julia Annas, "Prudence and Morality in Ancient and Modern Ethics," *Ethics*, vol. 105 (1995), p. 242.

taken for granted. In contrast, we read "why be prudent?" as asking why
people should have self-regarding goals, when their having such goals
normally is taken for granted. From that perspective, the question "why
be prudent?" seems moot. The cost of being moral is obvious, possible
benefits notwithstanding, which makes "why be moral?" a serious question. In turn, the benefits of prudence are altogether too obvious, which
makes "why be prudent?" seem less than serious.

In the real world, though, we cannot take prudence for granted, for the
connection between prudence and motivation is as contingent as the
connection between morality and motivation. That we have reason to be
prudent does not entail that we will be sufficiently motivated by our
prudential concerns, for some people are not strongly motivated by anything. If they want to keep their jobs and they know that the only way to
keep their jobs is to drag themselves out of bed, then they have reason to
drag themselves out of bed. They know that failing to do so is not in their
interest. But that does not entail that they will succeed in dragging themselves out of bed. Thus, one could (and, I think, should) be an externalist
about prudence in the same way many philosophers are externalists about
morality.

Similarly, we might consider it paradigmatically prudent to avoid vitamin deficiency. Even so, there is nothing incoherent in asking why I
should care about whether I have a vitamin deficiency. We can say I
should care because it would affect my health. Nevertheless, when we say
that avoiding vitamin deficiency is prudent, we leave room to ask, "If that
is what prudence is all about—if to be prudent presupposes substantive
concerns that I am not sure I share with paradigmatically prudent people—
then why should I be prudent?" And if such questions sound so odd in
connection with an end like being healthy that we might fear for anyone
who asked them seriously, there are versions of such questions that even
the most well-balanced of us might ask. For example, why should I aspire
to be in the kind of condition that my doctor calls normal health? Why
should I seek one level of financial security rather than another? Is there
anything particularly rational about having a statistically normal degree
of self-concern?

The lesson seems to be that "why be prudent?" is as real a question as
"why be moral?" Hobbes told us that "[t]he Foole hath said in his heart,
there is no such thing as justice."[2] We have been worrying about how to
answer Hobbes's Foole ever since. There is an existentialist "Foole," though,
who says in his heart that there is no good reason to care about anything,
and it is by no means clear which of the two Fooles is easier to answer.
Thus, Annas is right to doubt that the rationality of prudence goes without saying.[3] Nevertheless, I argue in the next section, there are good

---

[2] See chapter 15 of Thomas Hobbes's *Leviathan*.
[3] Annas, "Prudence and Morality," p. 257.

reasons to be moral; one reason is that being moral gives us reason to be prudent.

III. EUDAIMONISM

Is being moral worth the price? It depends on what being moral is like, and there are different theories about that. Eudaimonism is one such theory, and this section considers the extent to which a eudaimonist interpretation of self-interest and of morality points the way to their reconciliation. For present purposes, the best way to characterize eudaimonism is to contrast it with more modern theories. Thus, eudaimonism is the theory that the central task of ethics is not to say which acts are right but rather to say which ways of life are good. It is a theory about the nature of the good life for human beings. Modern moral theories seem primarily to range over the subject matter of interpersonal constraints, but eudaimonism is a theory that is at least as much about goals as about constraints, and intensely personal goals at that. It involves realizing that we are the outcomes as well as the makers of our choices, taking shape over time as a result of a continual interplay between character and conduct. In that sense, eudaimonism is about rational personhood, not rational choice.

Annas defends eudaimonism against the charge that it reduces morality to prudence.[4] Her defense may be correct as historical exegesis. But is eudaimonism, so construed, interesting? What is interesting about eudaimonism, I have always thought, is that it plausibly represents a sophisticated kind of self-concern as the core of morality.[5] Obviously, this is not to say that eudaimonism finds no place for concern for others. However, it has a distinctive way of explaining how and why concern for others is part of being moral. Concern for others is nonbasic; that is, it enters the theory in terms of the role it plays in a good life.

I myself reject the idea that morality is reducible to prudence. It would be a mistake, however, to say that if morality is not reducible to prudence, then it must also be true that morality cannot be justified in prudential terms. To see why, suppose we could show that authentic concern for others as ends in themselves tends to make a person better off. (It seems to me perfectly obvious that it does.) This does not entail (or even suggest, really) that other-regard reduces to a sophisticated kind of self-regard. Indeed, the whole point is that it does not. The kind of concern for others that plays a central role in a good life is a nonreducible concern for others as ends in themselves. Concern for others is derivative, on this view, only in the sense that its derivation is possible; that is, it can be justified on something other than its own terms.

---

[4] *Ibid.*, p. 245ff.

[5] I do not subscribe to eudaimonism as such. My own view is that morality has more than one core and that something like eudaimonism is one of them. The next section elaborates.

In any case, eudaimonism suggests that there is nothing intrinsically wrong with self-interest.[6] On its face, caring about oneself (or one's family or corporation or country) is not wrong at all. Normally, the problem is not too much concern for oneself (or one's country, etc.) but rather too little concern for others: failing to have due concern or respect for those one identifies as "other" in contrast to those one defines as "self." This is not the only thing that could ever possibly be wrong with self-interest. Narcissism, for example, is an unhealthy and unseemly kind of self-interest quite apart from how narcissists treat others. Still, the thing that normally worries us about self-interest, when it worries us, is that regard for oneself can crowd out regard for others. This can be a tragedy for oneself, not just for others. The self-obsessed person misses out on the good of true friendship, and that is an objective fact. Whether that can be proven to the self-obsessed person is beside the point.

This problem—that regard for oneself can crowd out regard for others—is a real risk, of course, but such crowding out is hardly inevitable. Healthy self-regard and healthy regard for others can go hand in hand. The amount of caring a person can do is not fixed. In fact, some ways and degrees of caring for ourselves can help us develop our capacity to feel genuine concern for others[7]—and vice versa.

Caring about other people gives us more to live for (and thus more reason to care about our lives as goal-directed agents) than we would have if we cared only about ourselves. For the same reason, caring about myself in ways that go beyond securing bare survival gives me more to live for. If I care only about literal survival, I literally risk boring myself to death. Therefore, even in terms of the most narrowly construed end of bare survival, means-end reasoning can lead people to conclude that broadening their base of concerns is pro-survival. By this route, people can, and some people do, arrive at reasons to aspire to a kind of other-regard and a kind of high-minded regard for one's own character that together constitute (what I think of as) *eudaimonia*. In my case, prudence dictates a quest for *eudaimonia*, because setting my sights any lower would constitute so wasteful a use of my natural talents and positional advantages as to be imprudent. I can already see how bitterly disappointed I would be with myself in years to come if I were to set my sights any lower. When I dedicate myself to projects that require me to use my natural talents to full advantage, I thereby confer instrumental value

---

[6] Note that self-interest need not be viewed as inherently individualistic. We sometimes speak in terms of corporate self-interest or national self-interest. Likewise, in economic models that assume all agents are purely self-interested, it sometimes turns out that "self-interest" allows for concern for the well-being of one's household or family as well as oneself.

[7] For more on this theme, see Neera Kapur Badhwar, "Altruism versus Self-Interest: Sometimes a False Dichotomy," *Social Philosophy and Policy*, vol. 10, no. 1 (Winter 1993), pp. 90–117.

upon my life, health, financial solvency, and so on, thereby bolstering and justifying my inclination to be prudent.

It is hardly difficult, though, to imagine Hobbes's Foole asking whether there is any good reason to be so concerned about one's character development. "Looking deep into my soul," the Foole might say, "it seems to me that the only things I really care about are looking clever and crushing people in philosophical debate. And it strikes me that I'll probably win more debates and look more clever if I don't bother nurturing within myself a tendency to be scrupulously constructive and fair. So, given that I don't currently embrace the sort of ends you describe under the label of eudaimonic self-interest, what would be the point of trying to embrace such ends as my own?"[8]

In "Can One Justify Morality to Fooles?"[9] Debra DeBruin criticizes what she calls the rationalist project in ethics—the project of showing that all rational beings, in virtue of being rational, have reason to be moral. Suppose she is right to think morality cannot be justified to Fooles. (I think she is.) Why try? Even if, contra DeBruin, we could demonstrate that all rational beings have reason to be moral, would there be any point? Presumably we do not think it would induce the Fooles of the world to change their ways. Evidently, we would find the demonstration comforting somehow, but why? If I want to verify that the package of goals and goal-directed activities emerging from my deliberations is indeed rational, it makes little sense to ask whether embracing that package would be rational for the Foole.

Perhaps instead we should simply accept that morality is not for everyone. Not everyone has self-interested reasons to be moral. (If Fooles act immorally, we can still berate them for being immoral, of course, but not for failing to act in their own interest.) Moreover, not everyone who has self-interested reasons to be moral has the same reasons. That being moral is worth the price for most of us is a contingent truth. It depends on facts about our natures and on circumstances that are not universal. But then, something like that is true of prudence as well. At least, the kind of high-minded prudence that we find within eudaimonist moral theory is a form of prudence whose motivational power cannot be taken for granted. It is only human to be imperfectly committed to, and imperfectly skilled at, being eudaimonically self-interested.

Still, if we accept that Fooles need not be irrational, then are we wrong to call them fools? Not necessarily. Suppose Fooles have shaped their characters in such a way that morality cannot be justified to them, but they would have been better off if they had not done so. Suppose morality

---

[8] A rough draft of this essay had the skeptic caring only about money, but then it struck me that money is too easy—too self-congratulating—a target for philosophers. Better, I thought, to try for an example that hits a bit closer to home.
[9] Debra DeBruin, "Can One Justify Morality to Fooles?" *Canadian Journal of Philosophy*, vol. 25 (1995), pp. 1–31.

fails to motivate Fooles the way it motivates us because we have reflective intellectual and sympathetic emotional capacities that Fooles lack. If having those capacities gives us more to live for, then we have good reasons to be glad we are not like Fooles, even if Fooles can see no reason to wish they were more like us. Further, if it is the Foole's own fault that he lacks those capacities, then the Foole is truly a fool.

That may be some comfort to those who need it, but it does not change the basic conclusion. Some people simply are not interested in themselves in that high-brow fashion.[10] The reconciliation of morality with eudaimonic self-interest will have no motivational bite with people like that. From their perspective, why should it? If we try too hard to refute Fooles by arguing that refusing to be moral entails failing to act in their own self-interest, it probably will turn out that all we have done is retreat to a definition of self-interest that Fooles do not care about. So a Foole who comes back to us and says, "Self-interest: what's in it for me?" will be asking a reasonable question, given that what actually interests the Foole is something other than what we insist on calling true self-interest.

IV. WHAT WE CALL MORAL

I have discussed prospects for reconciling morality and self-interest along eudaimonistic lines. This section characterizes the moral perspective in more general terms. I describe a role that eudaimonism can play within a more general moral theory, setting the stage for a moral and prudential defense of limited self-regard, and limited other-regard as well.

Introductory philosophy textbooks generally offer one or two withering critiques of ethical egoism, yet many philosophers persist in believing that healthy self-interest has an important place in a moral life. Perhaps the problem with ethical egoism is its implication that one ought to be interested in nothing beyond oneself.[11] Another and more subtle reason why friends and foes of self-interest pass each other like ships in the night is that they have different conceptions of self-interest. Self-interest, to its philosophical critics, is a kind of low-brow hedonism, centered around maximizing one's own pleasure. To its philosophical friends, self-interest is a kind of high-minded eudaimonism, centered around concern with one's character, or concern with living a good life, where "good" is defined in nonhedonic and even moralized (principled) terms. In short,

[10] Such people need not be Fooles. They will, as the text explains, have no reason to care whether morality can be grounded in eudaimonic self-interest, but that does not mean they will have no reason to be moral. They may be compassionate by nature, they may want to be faithful to the teachings of their parents, they may believe that accounts will be settled in the next life, and so on.

[11] I doubt that any professional philosopher has ever defended ethical egoism so construed, but in any case that seems to be the theory that the textbooks attack.

self-interest's friends defend Aristotle's self-actualizing citizen while its foes attack Hobbes's Foole.

We know that morality is not merely a matter of "looking out for number one." But how much (or what kind of) regard for others is it morally obligatory to have? Is it enough to have a healthy respect for others, or are we also supposed to embrace their hopes and dreams as our own? Is it obligatory to have equal regard for everyone? Or can it be moral to be what Simon Blackburn has referred to as Family Man, that is, a person (not necessarily a man, of course) who cares a lot about friends, family, and neighbors, but relatively little about strangers in faraway places?[12] Family Man's regard for others is deep and genuine but nevertheless parochial.

I think parochial other-regard is morally defensible, but defending it requires me to set out the theoretical context in terms of which I shall defend it. I realize that there is a risk in trying to see all this in terms of a theoretical framework. A theory can function like a set of blinkers on a horse, blinding a theorist to anything that does not fit neatly within the manifold of the theory. It has happened before; it could happen to me. Moral theory often seems pretty primitive compared to the inarticulate subtlety of common sense. Still, despite the risks, I think we need some theory here.[13]

What would it mean to call a theory a good theory?[14] What I look for in a theory is not something that tells me what to do, but rather something that helps me understand what to take into account when trying to make decisions. In my view, morality is a cluster of things with different origins and different purposes, and there is no good reason to presume (or worse, stipulate) that the parts of the cluster will never come into conflict. Simplifying the truth is a theoretical virtue, insofar as it helps us understand, but there is a fine line between simplifying the truth and covering it up.

Typically, when we call something moral we will be understood as (in some sense) endorsing the person, behavior, or attitude so described.[15] If we look at the various things we call moral, though, is there any reason to think they warrant endorsement? That they do is hardly analytic. On

---

[12] Simon Blackburn, "Kant versus Hume on Practical Reasoning," manuscript.

[13] I will be borrowing and trying to develop points from my book *Rational Choice and Moral Agency* (Princeton: Princeton University Press, 1995).

[14] I do not think the idea is as puzzling as referring to a corpse as a "good corpse," but it is a bit puzzling, and "good moral theory" is more puzzling still. "If someone says of a thing that it's a good swimmer or a good hammer, we know what is being predicated of the thing; if someone says of a thing that it's a good pebble or a good molecule or a good corpse, we find ourselves at a loss—what *does* the speaker have in mind?" See Judith Jarvis Thomson, "Goodness and Utilitarianism," *Proceedings and Addresses of the American Philosophical Association*, vol. 67 (1994), p. 9.

[15] The suggestion that we focus on the act of calling something moral rather than on morality per se is inspired by Allan Gibbard, *Wise Choices, Apt Feelings* (Cambridge: Harvard University Press, 1990).

the contrary, we call many things moral, which implies that we *think* they warrant endorsement; however, we sometimes make mistakes. We sometimes change our minds.

On what basis, then, would something truly warrant the endorsement implicit in our calling it moral? There seems to be more than one answer. Different parts of morality have different kinds of normative force. If the endorsement implicit in our calling things moral is a genus with more than one species, what makes the different kinds of normative force relatives? The genus, I would say, is not defined in terms of a particular reason for endorsement to which all the others ultimately reduce. Instead, it is defined in terms of a particular perspective from which we offer the various reasons for endorsement within the genus.

What, then, is that perspective? Could it be a perspective of naked self-interest? If something would be good for me (increasing my income or helping me crush an opponent, say), is that a good reason for me or anyone else to endorse it as moral? Generally not. When we call something moral, we take ourselves to be endorsing it on grounds that our listeners ought to share. In other words, when I tell you something is moral, I am not just saying that I approve of it, or even that I have *reason* to approve of it; I am saying that *we* have reason to approve of it. I speak from a plural perspective. I speak from what I take to be the perspective of you and me as a group. Or if I know that you disagree with me about the issue at hand, then I speak from a perspective that I think we as a group ought to have. I am implying that, although you may not realize it, we as a group have reason to endorse the thing I am calling moral.[16] That, in essence, is what listeners typically will understand me to be implying.

Thus, different reasons for endorsement belong to the same genus in the sense that they all are meant to be reasons we openly can accept as reasons for endorsement from a plural perspective. Whereas the genus of reasons for moral endorsement is defined in terms of the plural perspective, species within the genus consist of particular considerations that count as reasons for endorsement from that perspective. When we call something moral, listeners will infer that we believe we have reasons for endorsement that can withstand scrutiny by, and indeed should be shared by, the other members of the group.

I am tempted to say that space limitations preclude further elaboration of the precise nature of the moral perspective. The truth is that I see no easy way to be more precise. In the end, characterizing the moral perspective in impressionistic terms may be the best we can do. Part of the

---

[16] Perhaps this begs the question against those who say that the moral point of view is essentially self-effacing, taking other people's interests into account while ignoring one's own. I allow that things we might endorse from such a perspective often would be moral, but I do not think we can safely say such a perspective defines the moral perspective. For a powerful argument that failing to take one's own interests seriously can be a moral failure, see Jean Hampton, "Selflessness and the Loss of Self," *Social Philosophy and Policy*, vol. 10, no. 1 (Winter 1993), pp. 135–65.

reason why it is so difficult to characterize the moral point of view, perhaps, is that there may be no such thing as *the* moral point of view. There may be more than one.

Or perhaps the moral point of view comes in degrees. The logical limit of the plural perspective is the perspective that encompasses literally everyone (or every living creature, as the case may be). This logical limit of the moral perspective is what many moral philosophers identify as the moral perspective.

There are reasons for this. One nice thing about characterizing the moral perspective in terms of its logical limit is that the logical limit is a relatively precise notion. For example, it would be simpler and more precise to say that X is not moral unless all perspectives converge on the conclusion that X is moral, or unless everyone agrees that X is in his or her self-interest. When a Foole joins the group, though, does morality scale down its demands so as to make them more acceptable, either in moral or self-interested terms, to the group's lowest common denominator?[17] I doubt it. We could try to simulate the plural perspective's logical limit while at the same time cutting ostensible Fooles out of the picture by saying that X is not moral unless it is acceptable to all of the "reasonable" people concerned. I do not believe that either, for I think such a theory too conveniently soothes the consciences of people who want to dictate the terms of association. Theoretical attractions notwithstanding, identifying the moral perspective with the plural perspective's logical limit appears to be at odds with common sense. When I am out on the street honestly trying to get through the day without doing anyone wrong, I do not take quite so expansive a perspective, and it just seems fantastic to suppose my somewhat narrower perspective is necessarily a less than moral perspective.

If universalistic impartiality is not the essence of the moral point of view, though, then what is? The plural perspective can be parochial (and any perspective achievable by human beings can hardly avoid being parochial), but to be a moral perspective, I would say, it must not be deliberately exclusive. It does not require expanding one's perspective to include all living things, but it does require us not to deliberately ignore those whose interests we know to be at stake. So, suppose I endorse policy X as moral, and you observe that X works to a certain subgroup's disadvantage, and I say, "Oh, them. Truth is, I don't care about them." In that case, whatever I was doing when I referred to policy X as moral, it was something other than honestly trying to figure out whether policy X is moral. When I say I simply do not care about an affected subgroup, that comes pretty close to saying that I do not care about what is moral.

---

[17] Insofar as the Foole openly proclaims his rejection of obligations that the rest of us endorse from a plural perspective, we could argue that the Foole is not part of the group in the way the rest of us are.

In contrast, if I believe that my reason for endorsing X would stand as a reason for endorsement even when the interests of all affected parties are taken into account, then it stands as a reason for me to call X moral. The idea is not that I must believe that everyone affected will be *pleased* by X. (That would amount to saying that X must appeal to other people's naked self-interest in order for me to have grounds for calling it moral, which is barely an improvement over saying that X must appeal to my own.) Instead, the idea is roughly this: I have to believe that if I cared sincerely and equally about everyone affected by X, my reason for endorsing X would still be a good reason.[18]

What counts, then, as a good reason for thinking that something warrants endorsement from a plural perspective, and thus warrants being called moral? First, my grounds for endorsing something cannot be the bare fact that I call it moral. When we ask which considerations give us grounds for the endorsement implicit in our calling something moral, we are asking for grounds for introducing the term 'moral' in the first place. Thus, to avoid circularity, the considerations in virtue of which something warrants such endorsement have to be expressible without using the language of morals.

Second, as already noted, listeners would be unimpressed if a speaker were to offer his or her own naked self-interest as grounds for general endorsement. And indeed, speakers rarely do so. Still, naked self-interest is in one key respect the sort of thing we are looking for: it can be expressed as a reason without using the language of morals. And there are more-refined kinds of self-interest that have the same theoretical virtue and that do count as grounds for endorsement from a plural perspective. Hobbes's Foole is not the sort of person whom we have reason to approve of from a plural perspective, but Aristotle's self-actualizing citizen is.

Let me qualify that. From a plural perspective, we approve of people taking care of themselves, trying to be very good at what they do for a living, and so on. When the subject matter at issue is a person's goals and how they shape that person's character, the property of being reflectively rational in the eudaimonist sense is a reason for endorsement from the plural perspective. But that is only one of the subject matters that we ponder from a plural perspective. We also evaluate and sometimes endorse interpersonal constraints. That is, we endorse some laws and some customs but not others. We endorse some rights-claims and not others. We endorse constraints against making a living as a mugger, but not because being a mugger is bad for one's character. We have other sorts of reasons for endorsing interpersonal constraints. In particular, we have good reason to endorse interpersonal constraints if, when they are em-

---

[18] If this is what taking a moral perspective is like, then it is easy to see why different people, honestly trying to do what they believe (and believe with some justification) is right, could end up bitterly opposed to each other. There is nothing about taking the moral perspective that can guarantee convergence on substantive conclusions.

bedded in and work through social structure, they are collectively rational in the sense that they make it easier for people in general to live peaceful and productive lives in the manner of Aristotle's self-actualizing citizen. This is not the only sort of reason for endorsement we might have, but it is a reason for endorsement.

Insofar as we can cash out both self-interest and morality in eudaimonist terms, one might infer that there is no conflict between them. I do not think that conclusion would be warranted, though; at the very least, it has to be qualified in two ways. First, that is not all there is to morality, and the reconciliation of morality's eudaimonist strand with self-interest leaves open a real possibility of residual conflict with morality's other strands. Second, that is not all there is to self-interest, either. The concern we can have for our characters is but one of the forms that an interest in ourselves can take. People have other interests as well, interests that do not necessarily coincide with eudaimonic self-interest or with eudaimonic morality or with morality's other strands. We have to live with conflict, but the problem is not just that we live in sporadic conflict with knaves; we also live in sporadic conflict with ourselves and with our loved ones. The people we trust never to let us down are people who have moments of weakness just like everyone else.

Note, though, that if high-minded eudaimonic self-interest is a kind of morality as well as a kind of self-interest, then it can also be a perspective from which non-question-begging adjudication of residual conflict is feasible. When I ask myself whether I should keep this particular promise given that keeping it has this particular and unexpectedly high cost, I can ask myself what kind of person I want to be. If I then decide to keep the promise, it would be reasonable enough to interpret it as a case of letting morality override self-interest. It would be at least as reasonable, though, to say that I was weighing this particular promise against this particular cost and making a decision from a single perspective that is at once a perspective of morality and of self-interest. It is a perspective from which I ask myself what kind of person I want to be.

V. PAROCHIAL OTHER-REGARD IS MORALLY AND PRUDENTIALLY JUSTIFIABLE

That should be enough of a theoretical framework to get us started in assessing the morality of Family Man's parochial brand of other-regard. Julia Annas says that "although we naturally care more for ourselves than for others, and for those who are personally known to us than for those we have no knowledge of, these differences are not given importance from a moral point of view."[19] There is something to this, of course, but it does not entail that we are obliged to have equal concern for everyone. We can approach the justification of parochial other-regard from two directions.

---

[19] Annas, "Prudence and Morality," p. 253.

First, there are limits, grounded in self-interest, to how exclusively self-interested we should be. When we start from eudaimonic self-interest, we have a justification for expanding the scope of our concern to include family, friends, and community. An expanded scope of concern straight-forwardly gives us more to live for. A more expansive set of concerns also constitutes a set of concerns that we have no reason to hide from the people around us. (In contrast, if the people around us meant nothing to us, that *would* be something to hide.) For better or worse, the harmony we want to have with each other is not mere absence of war; we also seek a harmony of opinion. We want accord.[20] Developing an ability to see things from a plural perspective puts us in a better position to live with integrity in a social setting, and to have the kind of peace of mind that comes with having companions and having nothing to hide from them. Thus, eudaimonic self-interest provides a rationale for cultivating a deep if not necessarily universal regard for others.[21]

There are also limits, grounded in impartial concern for the common good, to how impartial we should ask people to be. As Geoffrey Sayre-McCord puts it: "In some cases, at least, remaining in one's position of partiality, say with respect to one's family or friends or oneself, is appro-priate and would itself secure the approval of those who do occupy the general point of view."[22] I cannot claim that we as a group have reason to give special attention to my interests merely in virtue of the fact that my

[20] Christine Korsgaard notes that, on Hume's account of sympathy, the sentiments of others are contagious. The sentiments that others have about us tend to "get under our skins." So when people show disdain for knaves, it will be hard for knaves not to feel disdain for themselves. Even when the knave does not get caught, knowing that others would feel disdain if they understood his true nature will be enough to make it hard for the knave not to feel disdain for himself. See Korsgaard's *The Sources of Normativity* (New York: Cambridge University Press, forthcoming), lecture 2.

[21] This is not to deny that a gap may remain between morality and self-interest. Self-interest, perhaps even the eudaimonistic form of self-interest that focuses on developing a socially and psychologically integrated character, can weigh in favor of respect and concern for one's inner circle to the exclusion of those outside the circle. Morality cannot. Morality need not counsel concern for outsiders, but it certainly counsels a measure of respect. This gap is a problem for any theory that tries to reduce all of morality to eudaimonic self-interest. It is less of a problem for my theory, since my theory does not try to ground the obligation to respect others in self-interest. My theory's eudaimonistic strand pertains to a different issue: the choice of personal goals to pursue within the constraints set by morality's interpersonal strand. See my *Rational Choice and Moral Agency*, ch. 8.

[22] Geoffrey Sayre-McCord, "On Why Hume's 'General Point of View' Isn't Ideal—and Shouldn't Be," *Social Philosophy and Policy*, vol. 11, no. 1 (Winter 1994), p. 222. In this difficult but fascinating and important essay, Sayre-McCord argues that the point of moral senti-ments and moral discourse, for Hume, is to help people achieve harmonious social life. Sympathy is part of the key to harmony, but uncorrected sympathy cannot deliver on the promise to help us achieve harmony (p. 217). It does not produce accord. Thus, we need to correct for biases and idiosyncrasies in our sympathetic reactions and attachments. We need a general point of view that is mutually accessible and thus constitutes a common ground on which we can come to an accord. However, Sayre-McCord insists that this general point of view is not and should not be the view of an Ideal Observer. The perspective of an Ideal Observer is a perspective to which no one has access. Those who affect the stance of an Ideal Observer just end up projecting their own uncorrected sympathies onto the Ideal Observer. Their resulting misguided smugness makes it harder rather than easier for them to achieve accord with anyone, especially each other.

interests are a special concern to me. However, I could claim that we as a group have reason to endorse people in general paying attention to their own interests and the interests of their loved ones. On the one hand, we do not endorse money managers using their clients' money to do special favors for family members. After all, the role of money manager has built into it a fiduciary obligation to make investment decisions on behalf of one's clients rather than oneself. On the other hand, we do endorse devoting special attention to family members when one is doing so on one's own time. The moral point of view can endorse a personal point of view from which a person without apology cultivates differential concerns.

Further, whether or not we approve of certain forms of partiality from an impartial perspective, partiality is in any case something we have to live with, and there are better and worse ways of doing that. Certain social constraints which are actually in place make us better off by helping us to pursue our own projects in peace and by creating conditions in which our efforts are mutually supportive. We have no reason to endorse structures that *would be* collectively rational if all people were altruists or practicing utilitarians or cosmopolitan liberals. We have reasons to endorse social structures only if they actually make people better off when tried in the real world. In the real world, Family Man is ubiquitous, and therefore a moral institution is one that responds to his virtues and vices (or hers, as the case may be) in such a way as to lead him to act in ways that enable the Family Men of the world to prosper in peace, and to create conditions under which Family Men sometimes transcend that parochial mindset and become something more inspiring. On my theory, good institutions are not oblivious to human nature, but neither do they passively accept it as it is. Rather, moral institutions (like good teachers, I suppose) respond to people as they are on behalf of what they could be.

When it comes to institutional design, if we want a result that is collectively rational, then we must try to see beyond a utilitarian perspective in the following sense. To grasp how an institution will function, we need to ask not how it looks from a utilitarian perspective but how it will look from a nonutilitarian perspective. In particular, we need to ask how it will look to people who are self-interested, for their reactions to the institution largely determine how it actually functions. (Some ostensibly consequentialist theories say that if only everyone would obey the principle of utility, the institution would have good consequences. To me, this is stunningly insensitive to actual consequences.) Therefore, a theorist who cares about consequences will want institutions that induce self-interested people to make themselves better off in peaceful and constructive ways, ways that make the people around them better off as well. That is how institutions have good consequences, if and when they do.

Because the connection between prudence and morality is contingent, it becomes the job of moral institutions to encourage people to be moral as well as prudent. Institutions can do this by setting up structures of opportunity and incentive that minimize the contingent conflict between

prudence and morality. That is, the essence of collectively rational institutions is that they make it individually rational for people to act in
collectively rational ways.

From an impartial perspective, then, there is reason to condone and
sometimes even encourage various kinds of partiality. Insofar as we evaluate laws and customs and rights-claims in terms of how they serve the
common good, we have reason to respect laws and customs and rights-
claims that make room for special concern for family, friends, and community. The existence of, and toleration of, such special concern makes
people in general better off. Special care for oneself and one's family can
be morally admirable, not merely permissible. In any case, trying to stamp
out this special concern or trying to prevent people from acting on it
would not serve the common good. In effect, on egoism's own ground we
have reason to nurture limited altruism, whereas on utilitarianism's own
ground we have reason to endorse or at the very least condone limited
parochialism.

VI. Conclusion

Sometimes, being moral requires being careful not to be presumptuous
in taking the plural perspective. Identifying too closely with others—
presuming to make decisions on their behalf in virtue of their being
members of the group whom one takes oneself to be representing—can be
immoral. It can blind us to the extent to which the costs and benefits of
our actions are external to ourselves. Part of the art of being moral is
being sensitive to other people while at the same time remaining keenly
aware of their separate personhood. The last part is sometimes the hard
part when it comes to giving our loved ones their due.[23]

At other times, being moral requires one to be self-centered enough to
resist pressure to bend to the group's collective will. I took a couple of
undergraduate philosophy courses in a Catholic college. The college was
part of the university I was attending and its courses were available to the
student body in general. Near the end of my time there, the college had
a faculty meeting at which a motion was made that the college's course
syllabi would no longer include material that was contrary to the teachings of the Catholic Church. The motion was carried, with one person, a
tenured philosophy professor, voting against. At the conclusion of the
vote, the dissenting professor stood up, announced his resignation effective that day, then left the meeting to clean out his office.

---

[23] David Brink, in his essay in this volume, develops the view that proper self-love
requires a concern for others proportional to the degree of "interpersonal psychological
continuity" that exists between oneself and others. This seems plausible. My point here is
only that it can be immoral to be led by a close identification with others to treat their
interests as being on a par with one's own. The degree of psychological continuity between
my wife and me (having lived with her since we were teenagers) is substantial; nevertheless,
there are things I get to do to myself that I do not get to do to her, notwithstanding our close
identification with each other.

Suppose the lone dissenter did what was right. (I believe he did. In my view, the college had no right to secretly censor its syllabi while pretending to be an institution whose mission was to contribute to a liberal-arts education.) Voting against the motion (to say nothing of resigning in the aftermath) was not easy. However, it would be an oversimplification to say that conflict with self-interest is what made it hard. What made it hard was peer pressure. At least a few of the people in that room thought the motion was disgusting and were ashamed to find themselves going along with it. What drove them to vote for it was not self-interest so much as an inability to resist peer pressure.[24]

The episode reminds me of Stanley Milgram's experiments on obedience to authority. Milgram found that normal people, faced with a choice either to inflict (apparently) life-threatening electric shocks on an (apparently) innocent victim or to disobey an order to administer said shocks, more often than not will administer the shocks. It is not that they *prefer* to administer the shocks. On the contrary, they would rather disobey the order, but they obey nonetheless, for disobeying requires a kind of strength that they do not have. Milgram concludes that "few people have the resources needed to resist authority. A variety of inhibitions against disobeying authority come into play and successfully keep the person in his place."[25] The fact that it can be hard to be moral is, I infer, not always self-interest's fault. Doing the right thing in the face of social pressure to do otherwise is not easy. It is an act of courage.

Moreover, people are no better at resisting peer pressure on behalf of prudence than they are at resisting peer pressure on behalf of morality. I still recall how much pressure there was to smoke cigarettes in the eighth grade—yet another real-life Milgram experiment, except that obedient subjects inflict the damage on themselves rather than on a third party. Which shows that acting in one's own interest requires courage, too— sometimes more than we can muster.

Philosophy, University of Arizona

---

[24] I concede that going along with social pressure sometimes is a matter of calculated self-interest. Most people's political opinions seem to depend a lot on what they think their current audience wants to hear, for example. Thus, giving in to pressure is sometimes like trying to catch the social wind in one's sails. At other times, though, the social wind blows people away. We should not ignore the difference. Those who feel a need to insist that all action is self-interested may want to say that caving in to pressure to do what is not in our interest is (psychologically) impossible, in the same way that genuine altruism is (psychologically) impossible. What looks like altruism, or like caving in to pressure, must—no matter what—be thought of as a subtle manifestation of self-interest. Suffice it to say that the eudaimonistic notion of self-interest I am using here is not vacuous. It leaves conceptual and psychological room for action driven by something other than self-interest so conceived.

[25] Stanley Milgram, *Obedience to Authority: An Experimental View* (New York: Harper and Row, 1974), p. 6.

SELF-LOVE AND ALTRUISM*

By David O. Brink

I. Introduction

Whether morality has rational authority is an open question insofar as we can seriously entertain conceptions of morality and practical reason according to which it need not be contrary to reason to fail to conform to moral requirements. Doubts about the authority of morality are especially likely to arise for those who hold a broadly prudential view of rationality.[1] It is common to think of morality as including various other-regarding duties of cooperation, forbearance, and aid. Most of us also regard moral obligations as authoritative practical considerations. But heeding these obligations appears sometimes to constrain the agent's pursuit of his own interests or aims. If we think of rationality in prudential terms—as what would promote the agent's own interests—we may wonder whether moral conduct is always rationally justifiable. Indeed, we do not need to think of rationality in exclusively prudential terms to raise this worry. The worry can arise even if there are impartial reasons—that is, nonderivative reasons to promote the welfare of others. For as long as there are prudential reasons, a conflict between impartial reason and prudential reason appears possible. Without some reason to treat impartial reasons as superior, the supremacy of other-regarding morality must remain doubtful.[2] These worries about the authority of other-regarding morality provide some incentive for those who want to defend the rational authority of

* I am indebted to Richard Arneson, Neera Badhwar, David Copp, Stephen Darwall, Thomas Hurka, Terry Irwin, Diane Jeske, Philip Kitcher, Christopher Morris, Bruce Russell, Gerasimos Santas, Alan Sidelle, Michael Slote, Ed Stein, Nicholas Sturgeon, Virginia Warren, Gary Watson, the Los Angeles area Moral and Political Philosophy Society (MAPPS), the other contributors to this volume, and its editors, for helpful discussion of issues in this essay.

[1] I have discussed some of these issues elsewhere, for instance, in "Rational Egoism, Self, and Others," in *Identity, Character, and Morality*, ed. O. Flanagan and A. Rorty (Cambridge: MIT Press, 1990). Here, I focus on developing a nonstrategic form of egoism; I try to give a fuller sense of the historical traditions on which my own account draws so heavily and to present the principal systematic claims, worries, and resources more clearly than I have before.

[2] For a discussion of one version of this second form of the worry, see my "Kantian Rationalism: Inescapability, Authority, and Supremacy," in *Ethics and Practical Reason*, ed. Garrett Cullity and Berys Gaut (Oxford: Oxford University Press, 1997).

morality to try to reconcile the demands of self-interest and other-regarding morality.[3]

One form of reconciliation assumes that different people's interests are conceptually distinct but argues that they are in fact causally interdependent. This view might be called *strategic egoism*. On this view, it is in the long-term interest of agents to develop, maintain, and act on other-regarding attitudes, because compliance with familiar other-regarding moral norms of restraint, cooperation, and aid is mutually advantageous. Though each would be better off if others comply while she does not, the compliance of others is generally conditional on her own. If so, the way to enjoy the benefits of others' compliance is to be compliant oneself.

I have discussed the limitations of this view elsewhere.[4] The main problems with strategic egoism have to do with the scope and stability of its justification of other-regarding norms. The strategic egoist can justify other-regarding duties only toward partners in systems of mutual advantage. But it is a common view that morality has a wider scope than this; it imposes obligations of restraint and aid where the agent stands to gain nothing strategically from the cooperation or restraint of the beneficiary. So, for instance, on this view (1) a person can apparently have no reason to be concerned about future generations, and (2) if the wealthy and talented have sufficient strength and resources so as to gain nothing by participating with the weak and handicapped in a system of mutual cooperation and forbearance, the former can have no reason, however modest, to assist the latter. If practical reason is interpreted in terms of strategic egoism but morality is not, then these are limitations in the scope of the rational authority of morality. If morality itself is interpreted in terms of strategic egoism, then these are counterintuitive limitations in the scope of morality itself. Even where the strategic egoist does justify other-regarding norms, the justification is unstable. For on this view, compliance with moral norms is always a second-best option behind undetected noncompliance. So as Glaucon and Adeimantus point out in Plato's *Republic*, if only I were able to enjoy the benefits of the compliance of others without the costs of my own compliance, then I would have no reason to comply (359b8–360d8). But moral norms seem counterfactually stable—they would continue to apply in these counterfactual circumstances—as other-regarding norms that the strategic egoist can justify are not. This counterfactual instability represents a further limitation of the strategic-egoist account of morality or its authority.

---

[3] Because I do not assume that moral requirements must be rationally authoritative, I do not assume that doubts about the authority of morality imply skepticism or relativism. Moral requirements can be objective and important even if immoral conduct is not always irrational. Nonetheless, I have rationalist ambitions; I would like to see how far we can go in the direction of reconciling the demands of morality and the demands of practical reason, without distorting our views of morality or practical reason.

[4] See my "Rational Egoism, Self, and Others" (*supra* note 1) and "Objectivity, Motivation, and Authority in Ethics" (unpublished).

As long as we rely on pretheoretical understandings of self-interest, it is difficult to avoid the conclusion that the coincidence between other-regarding morality and enlightened self-interest is at best imperfect and certainly counterfactually unstable.[5] But there is an important philosophical tradition that insists that we ought to modify our pretheoretical understanding of self-interest on metaphysical grounds. According to this tradition, people's interests, properly understood, are metaphysically, and not just causally, interdependent such that acting on other-regarding moral requirements is a counterfactually reliable way for an agent to promote his own interests. Insofar as this sort of view rests on metaphysical claims about persons, we might call it *metaphysical egoism*. This sort of view is familiar from the Greek eudaimonist tradition, especially the work of Plato and Aristotle, and from the British idealist tradition, especially the work of T. H. Green. The version of metaphysical egoism that I find most promising draws on claims in these two traditions—in particular, Plato's discussions of love in the *Symposium* and the *Phaedrus*, Aristotle's discussions of friendship and political community in the *Nicomachean Ethics* (*NE*) and the *Politics*, and Green's discussion of self-realization and the extension of the common good in the *Prolegomena to Ethics*.[6] It develops these claims, in part, by appeal to some familiar, though not uncontroversial, claims about persons and personal identity. Because my own view draws so heavily on work in these two traditions, I want to sketch the principal context and features of these three historical discussions. I hope that the value of seeing their relations to each other and my own view will compensate for the fact that I must ignore or oversimplify a number of complex interpretive issues.

II. Eudaimonism and Other-Regarding Virtue

Socrates, Plato, and Aristotle are all eudaimonists; they think that an agent's practical reasoning should be regulated by a correct conception of his own happiness or *eudaimonia*. In the *Euthydemus*, Socrates assumes that we all aim at happiness (278e, 280b); the only issue is how to achieve it (279a, 282a). In the *Crito*, he believes that his practical deliberations about whether to escape his death sentence should be guided only by whether that would be a just course of action (48c–d), because he thinks a good life just is a life of justice (48b). In both the *Laches* and the *Charmides*, the investigations begin with the assumption that the virtues in question (courage and temperance) are important because they would improve and benefit young men if they were to acquire them, and at the end of the *Charmides*, Socrates assumes that if one had reason to be temperate it must be because temperance promotes the happiness of the person who has it

---

[5] Cf. Henry Sidgwick, *The Methods of Ethics*, 7th ed. (Indianapolis: Hackett, 1981), pp. 164–70, 499–503; and Gregory Kavka, "The Reconciliation Project," in *Morality, Reason, and Truth*, ed. David Copp and David Zimmerman (Totowa, NJ: Rowman and Allanheld, 1984).
[6] References to these works will be given parenthetically in the text.

(175d–176a). In later dialogues, Plato also appears to accept eudaimonism. In response to doubts about justice in the *Republic*, he defends the claim that justice is a virtue, to be admired and practiced, by arguing that justice contributes constitutively to the *eudaimonia* of the agent who is just. And in the *Symposium*, Diotima takes the pursuit of one's own *eudaimonia* to be beyond the need for justification (205a). Aristotle too appears to be a eudaimonist. Though people have different conceptions of *eudaimonia*, he thinks we all treat *eudaimonia* as the final good (*NE* 1095a16–21). *Eudaimonia* is the only unconditionally complete good; all other things are choiceworthy for the sake of their contribution to *eudaimonia* (1097a27–b6). In Book I, Aristotle makes clear that it is the agent's own *eudaimonia* that should regulate his practical reasoning. But this is also brought out when he insists that one would rightly resist undergoing a substantial change—for instance, one by which one was transformed into a god—even if this new being led a better life (1159a6–12, 1166a1–23).

Eudaimonism implies that if practical virtues are to be worth having and acting on then they must be beneficial to the agent. But then eudaimonism poses a clear threat to the recognition of moral or other-regarding virtues; insofar as virtues are traits of character whose exercise contributes to the agent's own *eudaimonia*, it may appear doubtful that other-regarding traits that are conventionally regarded as virtues are genuine virtues. This doubt is explored most fully in connection with justice in Plato's *Gorgias* and *Republic*. The basic problem is that the following four claims are inconsistent:

(1) Justice is a virtue.
(2) Virtues benefit their possessor.
(3) Conventional justice often requires the agent to benefit others at his own expense.
(4) Conventional justice = justice.

Claim (2) expresses the eudaimonist assumption on which Socrates (the character) and his interlocutors all agree. In the *Gorgias*, Callicles appeals to claims (1) through (3) to deny (4). He distinguishes between genuine or natural justice and conventional justice (483a) and argues that real or natural justice does not require the agent to help others or forbear from harming them, as conventional morality supposes (482d–e, 483a–b, 488b–490a). The naturally just person satisfies his own unrestrained desires (488b). In the *Republic*, Thrasymachus appeals to claims (2) through (4) to deny (1). He accepts the assumption that justice is other-regarding and denies that justice is really a virtue. By contrast, Socrates and Plato are committed to (1), (2), and (4); they deny (3). Though they believe justice is other-regarding, they insist that it also benefits the agent. In the *Republic*, Glaucon and Adeimantus recognize one way in which justice is mutually beneficial, but they insist that this does not afford an adequate eudaimonist defense of justice. Glaucon describes the origin and nature of

justice in terms of a social contract designed to secure mutual nonaggression and advantage (358e–359b). If justice involves conformity to such
norms, the real benefit comes from another's justice, not one's own; if one
does benefit from one's own justice, this is only because the justice of
others is conditional on one's own. When justice is understood this way,
it becomes clear why people practice it "as something necessary, not as
something good" (358c). If one's own injustice could go undetected, this
would apparently be best; one would enjoy the benefits of the justice of
others without the costs of one's own. If so, justice is the second-best
option, whereas undetected injustice is the first-best (359a). This is illustrated by the ring of Gyges, which enables the person wearing it to
become invisible (359b–360d); if I could maintain the appearance of justice, and so secure the benefits of other people's justice, without incurring
the costs of actually being just, I would have no reason to be just. Adeimantus and Glaucon claim that it follows that it is the appearance of
justice, rather than justice itself, that is valuable (360e–362c, 362e–363e,
365b–367e). They demand that Socrates show that justice is not merely an
instrumental good but that it is good "in and by itself" and "for its own
sake" (367b4–5, c8–9, e2–4). In so doing, they are rejecting appeal to the
purely strategic value of justice and insisting that the eudaimonist defense of justice be counterfactually stable.[7]

Unlike Plato, Aristotle does not explicitly confront eudaimonist doubts
about the other-regarding virtues. But he cannot avoid them. Because he
also accepts eudaimonist assumptions about the virtues, this raises for
him the question of how other-regarding traits such as courage, friendship, and justice, which he treats as virtues, can be genuine virtues.

III. Platonic Love

One way to look at the Platonic view of love (*eros*) is as a resource for
addressing a natural objection to the eudaimonist defense of justice in the
Republic. In response to eudaimonist doubts about justice from Thrasym-

---

[7] Some might deny the relevance of counterfactual instability. It has been suggested that
the Epicureans thought that they did not need to consider merely counterfactual challenges
to justice. See Cicero, *De Officiis* iii 39, and *De Re Publica* iii 27; cf. A. A. Long and D. N.
Sedley, *The Hellenistic Philosophers* (Cambridge: Cambridge University Press, 1987), p. 135. If
my commitment to other-regarding norms would collapse in radically different circumstances, does this show that there is anything wrong with my commitment to them in actual
circumstances? Even if one's commitments in some counterfactual circumstances—for instance, those in which everyone was self-sufficient and invulnerable—seem irrelevant to
one's commitments in actual circumstances, other forms of counterfactual stability are more
difficult to ignore. The story of Gyges, though fictional, merely makes vivid considerations
that are often at work in real-life situations. Often I can fail to observe norms of cooperation,
aid, and nonaggression with assurance of impunity. In these cases, it is as if I had a ring of
Gyges. If Gyges has no reason to honor these norms, neither do I in such cases. And even
in circumstances in which compliance with other-regarding norms is rational, the accessi-
bility of Gyges' circumstances suggests that my commitment in actual circumstances is to
my own self-interest, not to other-regarding morality. Cf. Terence Irwin, *Plato's Ethics* (New
York: Oxford University Press, 1995), section 130.

achus, Glaucon, and Adeimantus, Plato defends the claim that justice is a genuine eudaimonic virtue by arguing that justice contributes constitutively to the *eudaimonia* of the agent who is just. The value of justice depends on Plato's conception of justice as a psychic state in which one's appetites and emotions are regulated by practical deliberation about one's overall good. It is reasonably clear why this sort of psychic justice contributes to the agent's own eudaimonia. What is not clear is what psychic justice has to do with the conventional other-regarding justice about which eudaimonist doubts were expressed in the first place. Indeed, we seem to be back where we started. For it is unclear why someone whose actions are regulated by a concern for his own overall good should take anything more than a strategic interest in the well-being of others. If there is no systematic connection between psychic justice and other-regarding justice, then Plato's defense of justice is fallacious.[8]

Plato's account of love in the *Symposium* and the *Phaedrus* suggests such a connection.[9] The best sort of love, Plato thinks, aims at what is good or fine (*Symposium* 201a, 204d, 205d, 206b–e), in particular, at *producing* what is good or fine (206c–208b). Plato believes that virtue is fine, and that virtue, conceived of as a psychic state in which one's appetites and emotions are regulated by practical deliberation about one's overall good, is the controlling ingredient in a good life. So when A loves B, Plato concludes, A will aim to make B virtuous (*Symposium* 209a, 212a). Such love benefits the beloved, because one benefits by becoming virtuous precisely insofar as one is better off being regulated by a correct conception of one's overall good. Plato also believes, however, that the lover benefits from loving another (*Phaedrus* 245b), as he must if he is to reconcile love of another with his eudaimonism. The key to seeing how Plato can reconcile interpersonal love with self-love is to appreciate the way in which he thinks that reproducing one's virtuous traits in another is an approximation to immortality (*Symposium* 206c–208b).

According to Plato, my own persistence requires intrapersonal reproduction. My own continued existence, despite both compositional and qualitative change, is a matter of reproducing my traits into the future.

> Now although we speak of an individual as being the same so long as he continues to exist in the same form, and therefore assume that a man is the same person in his dotage as in his infancy, yet, for all we call him the same, every bit of him is different, and every day he is becoming a new man, while the old man is ceasing to exist, as you can see from his hair, his flesh, his bones, his blood, and all the rest

---

[8] Cf. David Sachs, "A Fallacy in the *Republic*," in *Plato II*, ed. Gregory Vlastos (Notre Dame: University of Notre Dame Press, 1971).

[9] This perspective on Platonic love is suggested and explored in Terence Irwin, *Plato's Moral Theory* (Oxford: Clarendon Press, 1977), pp. 241–42, 267–73, and Irwin, *Plato's Ethics*, ch. 18.

of his body. And not only his body, for the same thing happens to his soul. And neither his manners, nor his disposition, nor his thoughts, nor his desires, nor his sufferings, nor his fears are the same throughout his life, for some of them grow, while others disappear. . . . In this way every mortal creature is perpetuated, not by always being the same in every way, as a divine being is, but by what goes away and gets old leaving behind and in its place some other new thing that is of the same sort as it was. (*Symposium* 207d3–208b12)[10]

To persist I must reproduce my existing traits into the future. But if my own continued existence is to be good for me, then I must reproduce my valuable traits into the future, and this requires me to reproduce my virtuous traits into the future. Though Plato mentions both physical and psychological persistence, it is clear that his real concern is with psychological persistence. For he regards the soul essentially as a capacity for deliberation, decision, and action (*Phaedrus* 245c–e), and he regards the dominant component of *eudaimonia* as consisting in the proper psychic ordering of the agent's soul. My persistence, then, requires my psychological reproduction into the future, and if this is to be good for me, it should involve the reproduction of those parts of my psychology that contribute to my virtuousness. But interpersonal love involves the reproduction of my virtuous traits in another, who can live beyond me; this is why interpersonal love is correctly viewed as the next best thing to immortality (*Symposium* 206c1–209e5). It also explains why spiritual intercourse and love are better than bodily intercourse and love; spiritual love begets greater and more valuable progeny (*Symposium* 209a1–e4). This allows us to regard someone like Socrates or Solon as more fecund and closer to immortality than someone like the old woman who lived in the shoe (who had so many children she didn't know what to do).

On Plato's view, then, intrapersonal and interpersonal love are parallel; indeed, love of another is really just a special case of self-love. I extend myself into the future by reproducing my traits into the future. When I reproduce myself systematically I persist; when I don't, I do not. But I can also reproduce myself somewhat less systematically in others by sharing thought and discussion with them, in particular, about how best to live (*Apology* 38a). On this view, the interests of those whom I love become part of my interests in just the sort of way that the interests of my future self are part of my overall interests. On this view, my concern for my beloved's good, as for my own future good, is not unconditional; it is choiceworthy as a constituent part of my overall good. As such, however, it is choiceworthy in itself.

---

[10] This translation from the *Symposium* is adapted from that of Michael Joyce in *The Collected Dialogues of Plato*, ed. Edith Hamilton and Huntington Cairns (Princeton: Princeton University Press, 1961).

IV. Aristotelian Friendship

Aristotle assumes that virtues must contribute to the agent's own *eudaimonia*. But then he owes us an explanation of how the other-regarding traits such as courage, friendship, and justice, which he recognizes as virtues, are genuine virtues.

Aristotle links virtue with what is fine (*kalon*) (*NE* 1103a10, 1120a24, 1122b6–8). In the *Rhetoric*, he links what is fine with what is beneficial to others.[11]

> Virtue is, according to the usual view, ... a faculty of conferring many great benefits. ... The parts of virtue are justice, courage, temperance, magnificence, magnanimity, liberality, gentleness, prudence, wisdom. If virtue is a faculty of beneficence, the highest kinds of it must be those which are most useful to others, and for this reason men honor most the just and the courageous. ... (1366a36–b6)

> [Also fine are] all those actions done for the sake of others, since these less than other actions are done for one's own sake; and all successes which benefit others and not oneself; and services done to one's benefactors, for this is just; and good deeds generally, since they are not directed to one's own profit. (1367a4–6)

Insofar as this conception of virtue is tied to the good of others, it is recognizably a moral conception of virtue. The obvious question is whether the moral virtues are eudaimonic virtues.

Though Aristotle's own ethical views in the *Nicomachean Ethics* begin from reflection on common beliefs, his views sometimes revise common sense, even a reconstructed common sense of the sort presented in the *Rhetoric*. Significantly, Aristotle's own account of the relation among virtue, the fine, and the good of others is different from that found in the *Rhetoric*. For in the *Nicomachean Ethics* he links virtue with what is fine and what is fine with a *common good* (1122b21, 1123a5, 1129b15–18). He brings this out in his discussion of proper self-love:[12] "And when everyone competes to achieve what is fine and strains to do the finest actions, everything that is right will be done for the common good, and each person individually will receive the greatest of goods, since that is the character of virtue" (*NE* 1169a8–12). In linking virtue with a common good, Aristotle is rejecting the popular contrast, noted in the *Rhetoric*, between other-regarding concern and the agent's own good, and is attempting to link eudaimonic virtue with moral virtue. For Aristotle, as for Socrates and Plato, the real test case for this claim would seem to be

---

[11] Translations of passages from the *Rhetoric* are from the revised Oxford translation in *The Complete Works of Aristotle*, ed. Jonathan Barnes (Princeton: Princeton University Press, 1984).

[12] Translations of passages from the *Nicomachean Ethics* (*NE*) are from *Nicomachean Ethics*, trans. Terence Irwin (Indianapolis: Hackett, 1985).

justice, because justice is perhaps the most clearly other-regarding virtue (*Rhetoric* 1366a36–b6); in fact, general justice is complete virtue in relation to another (*NE* 1129b20–30).

Aristotle's insistence on the connection between justice and a common good suggests that we look to his account of friendship for help in constructing a eudaimonist defense of justice, because friendship is the virtue appropriate to communities or associations in general and includes the perfection of justice (1155a22–28, 1159b25–1160a8).[13] If so, this gives a special importance to his discussion of friendship that could explain why he devotes what might otherwise seem to be disproportionate attention (two whole books) to friendship.[14]

Initially, Aristotle suggests that all forms of friendship involve reciprocal concern for the other's own sake (1155b28–33). He then identifies three different kinds of friendship: friendship for *advantage*, friendship for *pleasure*, and the *best* kind of friendship (*NE* VIII 3–8). Both advantage-friendship and pleasure-friendship, Aristotle then claims, involve something less than concern for the other's own sake (1156a11–13). Advantage-friendship typically involves the concern one develops for other members of mutually beneficial cooperative schemes; such friends last as long as they share common and mutually advantageous goals. Pleasure-friendship involves strong and intense emotions among friends that reflect the pleasure each takes in the qualities and company of the other; these friendships involve a strong attachment and concern for the other, but these attachments are not stable insofar as they are based on transient emotional intensity. Both kinds of friendship are to be contrasted with virtue-friendship. This is friendship among people similarly virtuous in which each cares about the other for the other's own sake.

Aristotle anticipates some of his claims about the justification of virtue-friendship (which begins at IX 4) in VIII 12, where he suggests that we should take parental friendship as our model of friendship. The parent is concerned with the child's welfare for the child's own sake. This concern is appropriate on eudaimonist grounds, because the parent can regard the child as "another-self" (1161b19, 28). The child can be regarded as another-self of the parent, because the child owes its existence and physical and psychological nature in significant part to the parent; this both echoes and helps explain the common view that a parent's interests are *extended* by the life of the child.[15] Aristotle suggests that similar claims can be made

[13] My understanding of Aristotle's account of friendship and its role in his ethical theory has been influenced by Terence Irwin, *Aristotle's First Principles* (Oxford: Clarendon Press, 1988), esp. ch. 18.
[14] Even justice gets only one book (*NE* V), and it is not uncommon to regard friendship, unlike justice, as a comparatively minor virtue.
[15] Insofar as this is true, Aristotle can provide further justification for his assumption that there are posthumous benefits and harms and that the welfare of one's loved ones and the success of one's projects, after one is dead, are part of a complete good (*NE* 1100a10–31, 1101a23–30).

about friendship between siblings. In virtue of living together, siblings causally interact in important ways and share many things in common, and thus can regard each other as other-selves (1161b30–35).

Despite important differences between familial friendship and virtue-friendship, Aristotle's account of familial friendship brings out clearly what is crucial to his justification of the other-regarding concern of virtue-friendship. Aristotle explains the justification of virtue-friendship in terms of proper self-love (1166a1–2, 10, 1166a30–32, 1168b1–1169a12). "The excellent person is related to his friend in the same way as he is related to himself, since a friend is another self; and therefore, just as his own being is choiceworthy for him, the friend's being is choiceworthy for him in the same or a similar way" (1170b6–9). One plausible interpretation of Aristotle's claims about the relation between friendship and self-love is reminiscent of Plato's analogy between intrapersonal and interpersonal reproduction in his account of philosophical *eros*. Aristotle believes that proper self-love requires a proper conception of the self and of what is beneficial for the self. After insisting that the important features of interpersonal friendship are to be found in intrapersonal friendship, Aristotle writes:

> Hence he [the virtuous person] wishes goods and apparent goods to himself. . . . He wishes and does them for his own sake, since he does them for the sake of his thinking part, and that is what each person seems to be. He wishes himself to live and to be preserved. And he wishes this for the part by which he has intelligence more than any other part. For being is a good for the good person, and each person wishes for goods for himself. And no one chooses to be another person even if that other will have every good when he has come into being. . . . Rather [each of us chooses goods] on condition that he remains whatever he is; and each person would seem to be the understanding part, or that most of all. (1166a15–23)

Later, in distinguishing proper from vulgar self-love, Aristotle makes a similar claim:

> However, it is this [the virtuous person] more than any other sort of person who seems to be a self-lover. At any rate, he awards himself what is finest and best of all, and gratifies the most controlling part of himself, obeying it in everything. And just as a city and every other composite system seems to be above all its most controlling part, the same is true of a human being; hence someone loves himself most if he likes and gratifies this part. (1168b28–34)

In these passages Aristotle wants, in part, to identify a person with the controlling part of his soul or his understanding. We know that Aristotle thinks a human is essentially a psycho-physical compound in which reason can regulate thought and action (1097b24–1098a16, 1102b13–1103a3).

If so, it would be reasonable for him to think that the persistence of an individual consists in the continuous employment of his rational faculties to regulate his thought and action. Moreover, we know that the virtues of character involve the rational part of the soul regulating the nonrational part of the soul in such a way that the nonrational part of the soul harmonizes with the exercise of practical reason (1102b25–28) and that the correct exercise of practical reason—the proper realization of an individual's essence—is the controlling ingredient in his *eudaimonia* (1098b15–16, 1099b17–27, 1100b1–11, 1100b31–34). This would explain why Aristotle thinks that proper love for oneself involves a concern for one's practical reason and its virtuous exercise.

If this is what underlies Aristotle's account of proper intrapersonal love, we can see how he thinks interpersonal love or friendship might be modeled on it. I preserve or extend myself by exercising my practical reason—forming beliefs and desires, deliberating about them, and acting as the result of deliberate choice. But the same sort of psychological interaction and interdependence can be found, presumably to a lesser extent, between two different persons. On Aristotle's view, friends share similar psychological states, such as aims and goals (1170b16–17), and live together (1159b25–33, 1166a1–12, 1171b30–1172a6). Even if psychological similarity is necessary for friendship, it is clearly insufficient; it should be produced and sustained by living together and sharing thought and discussion (1157b5–12, 18–21, 1170b10–14). This account of interpersonal psychological dependence among friends allows us to see how Aristotle thinks we can view a friend as another-self and thus how he can view the justification of friendship in terms of self-love. So, for example, Aristotle thinks that the way in which a (decent) parent nurtures, educates, and provides opportunities for her child establishes psychological relations between them that justify us in claiming that the child's well-being extends the well-being of the parent (1161b17–29). It is this same sort of psychological interdependence that exists between friends who share thought and discussion that justifies each in seeing the other as extending his interests and, hence, as another-self. But then we can see how Aristotle can think that friendship involves concern for the friend's own sake and yet admits of eudaimonist justification. If B extends A's interests, then B's interests are a part of A's. This is true when A and B are the same person and when they are different people. My friend's good is a part of my own overall good in just the way that the well-being of my future self is part of my overall good. On this view, my friend's good, like my own future good, is not unconditionally complete; it is choiceworthy as a constituent part of my overall good. As such, however, it is a complete good, choiceworthy in itself.

Indeed, Aristotle can extend the scope of his eudaimonist justification of interpersonal concern from friends to other members of a just political community. It is true that he recognizes that virtue-friendship cannot hold on the scale of a political community that is just (*NE* 1158a11–12,

1170b29–1171a20; *Politics* 1262b3–20) and that political communities are associations for mutual advantage and do not involve the best sort of friendship (*NE* 1160a11–15). Nonetheless, political communities that are just have to a significant degree the two features that are crucial to the justification of virtue-friendship and familial friendship: there is commonality of aims and aspirations among members of the political association, and this commonality is produced by members of the association living together in the right way, in particular, by defining their aims and goals consensually (1167a25–28, 1155a24–28). Insofar as this is true, members of such a political association can see the interests of other members implicated in their own interests. And members of such a community can aim at justice for its own sake, because justice, Aristotle believes, promotes the *common* good, which is presumably the good common to them insofar as they are members of an interdependent political community (1129b15–18). This begins to explain Aristotle's reasons for his well-known belief that we are essentially political animals (*NE* 1097b9–12; *Politics* 1253a2) and that, as a result, the complete good for an individual can only be realized in a political community.

V. Green on Self-Realization and the Common Good

Green belongs to the nineteenth-century tradition of British idealism, but his own ethical views are in some ways similar to important strands in the Greek eudaimonist tradition and were in fact heavily influenced by his study of Plato and Aristotle. These aspects of his views are clearest in his principal ethical work, the *Prolegomena to Ethics*.[16] Whereas he thought that Plato and Aristotle had too narrow a conception of various virtues and the common good (*PE* 257, 261–62, 265–66, 270, 279–80), he thought they were right to ground an agent's duties in an account of *eudaimonia* whose principal ingredient is a conception of practical virtue regulated by the common good (253, 256, 263, 271, 279).

Like other idealists, such as F. H. Bradley, Green thinks that the proper conception of self-realization involves the good of others as a constituent part. For Bradley, this kind of reconciliation is a direct consequence of a fundamentally anti-individualist metaphysics that treats persons as aspects of an interpersonal organic unity.[17] From my perspective, this risks assuming something too close to what one wanted to see proved. By contrast, Green argues for reconciliation and any collectivist metaphysical claims from recognizably individualist premises.[18]

---

[16] T. H. Green, *Prolegomena to Ethics*, ed. A. C. Bradley (New York: Thomas Crowell, 1969); references to specific sections of this work will be given parenthetically in the text.

[17] See F. H. Bradley, *Ethical Studies*, 2d ed. (Oxford: Clarendon Press, 1927), esp. essay V.

[18] To my mind, Green's ethical theory is vastly superior to Bradley's; it is not only better informed as to the history of ethics and less dogmatic, but also much more subtle and resourceful.

Green thinks that moral responsibility requires capacities for practical deliberation and that practical deliberation requires self-consciousness. Nonresponsible agents, such as brutes and small children, appear to act on their strongest desires or, if they deliberate, to deliberate only about the instrumental means to the satisfaction of their desires (86, 92, 96). By contrast, responsible agents must be able to distinguish between the *intensity* and *authority* of their desires and deliberate about the appropriateness of their desires and aims (92, 96, 103, 107, 220).[19] But this requires one to be able to distinguish oneself from particular desires and impulses and to be able to frame the question about what it would be best on the whole for one to do (85–86).[20] Green thinks that the process of forming and acting on a conception of what it is best on the whole for me to do is a process of forming and acting on a conception of my own overall good (91–92, 128).

> A man, we will suppose, is acted on at once by an impulse to revenge an affront, by a bodily want, by a call of duty, and by fear of certain results incidental to his avenging the affront or obeying the call of duty. We will suppose further that each passion . . . suggests a different line of action. So long as he is undecided how to act, all are, in a way, external to him. He presents them to himself as influences by which he is consciously affected but which are not he, and with none of which he yet identifies himself. . . . So long as this state of things continues, no moral effect ensues. It ensues when the man's relation to these influences is altered by his identifying himself with one of them, by his taking the object of one of them as for the time his good. This is to *will*, and is in itself moral action. . . . (146)

To be a moral agent, Green thinks, requires distinguishing oneself from one's beliefs and desires, deliberating about them, and acting on those deliberations. He concludes that an agent should see his own good as consisting in the full realization of these deliberative faculties (172, 180–81, 192, 234, 239, 254).

Moreover, Green believes that full self-realization can take place only in a community of ends (183–84, 190–91, 199, 232) in which no one can "contemplate himself as in a better state, or on the way to the best, without contemplating others, not merely as a means to that better state, but as sharing it with him" (199). I must view others as my "alter egos"

[19] Here, as elsewhere, Green shows the influence of both Butler and Kant. Cf. Bishop Butler, *Fifteen Sermons Preached at the Rolls Chapel*, abridged as *Five Sermons*, ed. Stephen Darwall (Indianapolis: Hackett, 1983), sermon II, paragraphs 13–14; Immanuel Kant, *Grounding for the Metaphysics of Morals*, trans. J. Ellington (Indianapolis: Hackett, 1981), pp. 446–48, 457, 459–60 (Academy pagination); and Kant, *The Critique of Practical Reason*, trans. L. W. Beck (Indianapolis: Library of Liberal Arts, 1956), pp. 61–62, 72, 87 (Academy pagination).
[20] Cf. Terence Irwin, "Morality and Personality: Kant and Green," in *Self and Nature in Kant's Philosophy*, ed. Allen W. Wood (Ithaca: Cornell University Press, 1984).

(191, 200) and aim at a common good (202, 236). But why? Green thinks that capacities for practical deliberation require self-consciousness and ground self-realization. *Self*-realization involves aiming at a "permanent" or overall good. But an agent's interactions with others extend the effects of his deliberations more widely and, hence, make his own life more permanent and complete (229–32).

> That determination of an animal organism by a self-conscious principle, which makes a man and is presupposed by the interest in permanent good, carries with it a certain appropriation by the man to himself of the beings with whom he is connected by natural ties, so that they become him as himself and in providing for himself he provides for them. Projecting himself into the future as a permanent subject of possible well-being or ill-being—and he must so project himself in seeking for a permanent good—he associates his kindred with himself. It is this association that neutralises the effect which the anticipation of death must otherwise have on the demand for a permanent good. (231)

Green is not explicit about how family members or others with whom I associate make my good more permanent. The interest he thinks an agent is justified in taking in others seems to depend on the shared life of the agent and others (232). Practical reason relies on self-consciousness and thus aims at a life that realizes well one's deliberative capacities. These capacities are exercised in the reflective pursuit of activities that involve judgment, planning, and control. But cooperation with others on common ends allows one to participate in larger and more complex projects that affect others and have more lasting significance (191, 232). Insofar as I enter into such relationships and contribute to such projects, I extend my deliberative control and thus extend my own good. But as my deliberations and those of others become interdependent, so do our interests. Though Green thinks small, intimate associations make for a fuller realization of our moral capacities than a solitary existence does, he thinks that we achieve still fuller self-realization when we participate in more-inclusive political communities regulated by liberal principles.

Green concludes that if proper self-realization implies that the good of each includes in part the good of others, then this undermines the popular contrast between self-love and benevolence (232). We should view those with whom we participate in such associations as "alter egos," for whom we care as we care about ourselves (191, 200). We should weight their interests with our own, and see ourselves as compensated when we make what would otherwise be sacrifices to them and to our common projects (376). Indeed, Green goes so far as to claim that when each is engaged in proper self-realization, there can be no conflict or competition of interests (244).

VI. Persons, Persistence, and Deliberative Control

Like Plato, Aristotle, and Green, I want to explore the resources for a eudaimonist defense of other-regarding concern that models interpersonal relations and concern on intrapersonal relations and concern. My version of metaphysical egoism, like theirs, relies on certain assumptions about persons and personal identity.

Locke distinguished between persons and men (or, as we might say, human beings) and claimed that the concept of a person is a normative or "forensic" concept.[21] In both morality and law, persons are responsible agents; it is only persons who can properly be praised and blamed, because it is only persons who can properly be held accountable for their actions.[22] Plato, Aristotle, and Green all see nonresponsible agents, such as brutes and small children, as acting on their strongest desires. By contrast, responsible agents can distinguish between the intensity and authority of their desires. For Plato, Aristotle, and Green, this requires being able to deliberate about one's overall good and to regulate one's appetites and emotions and, ultimately, one's actions in accord with these deliberations (*Republic* 437e–442c; *De Anima* II 2, and *NE* 1102b13–1103a3, 1111b5–1113a14; *PE* 91–92, 96, 103, 107, 128, 146, 220). If so, capacities for practical deliberation—formulating, assessing, revising, choosing, and implementing projects and goals in light of a conception about what is best—are essential to being a person.

Deliberative capacities may be essential to being a person, but this does not itself tell us what the persistence of a particular person consists in. Persons appear to survive some physical and psychological changes, but not others. If we distinguish sameness of person from sameness of human being, it is arguable that what personal identity consists in, and what distinguishes substantial from nonsubstantial change for a person, is some kind of continuity of mental life.

For it is arguable that it is only those physical changes that destroy continuity of mental life that destroy a person; other physical changes are alterations in a persisting person. For instance, brain damage that preserves important elements of a continued mental life is nonsubstantial change and harm; but destruction of the brain is (normally) substantial change, in particular, death, because it terminates a heretofore continuous stream of consciousness.

Moreover, it seems clear that certain psychological changes and incapacities do or would produce substantial change, regardless of the sort of

---

[21] John Locke, *An Essay Concerning Human Understanding*, ed. P. H. Nidditch (Oxford: Clarendon Press, 1975), book II, chapter xxvii, sections 8, 15, 17–21, 23, 26.

[22] Nonresponsible agents might usefully be praised or blamed for forward-looking (e.g., deterrent) reasons; but they do not *deserve* praise or blame. Moreover, in claiming that 'person' is a "forensic" concept, Locke means not only that only persons can be held responsible but also that holding P2 responsible for P1's actions only makes sense if P2 = P1. I am here appealing to the former claim. I doubt the latter claim is true; I suspect responsibility presupposes deliberative control, rather than identity.

physical change involved in this mental change and regardless of the physical continuity that might exist through this psychological change. So, for example, if I enter an irreversible and complete vegetative state, then, other things being equal, this is a substantial change that destroys me, regardless of how this psychological change is realized physically and whether my body continues to function.

Furthermore, there are thought experiments in which important kinds of mental and physical continuity, which normally go together, come apart, and in which our intuitions about personal identity seem to track psychological relations. Locke imagines that the same person might inhabit different bodies at different points in time, as when the person of a prince might come to occupy the body of a cobbler if the consciousness of the prince is somehow transferred to the body of the cobbler.[23] But Locke leaves the mechanism by which such a transference might occur unspecified. Sydney Shoemaker describes a more satisfactory case of body switch that involves brain transplant.[24] In Shoemaker's case, surgical techniques have advanced so that brains may be surgically removed, reconnected, and transplanted in ways that preserve psychological continuity. Two patients, Brown and Robinson, have fairly similar bodies, and each undergoes brain surgery in which the brain is removed; however, during the procedures, their brains are inadvertently put into the wrong bodies. The person with Robinson's brain and Brown's body dies on the operating table due to complications. The surviving patient—call him Brownson— has Brown's brain and Robinson's body. Though Brownson has Robinson's body, all of his intentional states (e.g., his beliefs, desires, and intentions) are similar to and causally dependent on Brown's, rather than Robinson's, intentional states. Is Brownson Robinson or Brown (or neither)? If we were to enter Brownson's hospital room without knowing what had transpired in the operating room, presumably we would initially identify Brownson as Robinson. But as we talked to Brownson, our views would likely change. Brownson has apparent memories of Brown's life, not Robinson's. He intends to finish writing a book like Brown's book, not Robinson's. And he is eager to return to Brown's wife and children, whereas Robinson had no wife or children. When we learned what had transpired in the operating room, it would seem natural to view the inadvertent brain-transplant as a body switch. People receive artificial limbs or organ transplants; a body switch is just an extreme case of this. If so, Brown is the surviving recipient and Robinson is the dead donor. That is, Brownson is Brown. Our intuitions about Brownson seem to support a mentalistic, rather than a bodily, view of personal identity.[25]

---

[23] Locke, *An Essay Concerning Human Understanding*, sections 14, 15, and 19.

[24] Sydney Shoemaker, *Self-Knowledge and Self-Identity* (Ithaca: Cornell University Press, 1963), p. 23.

[25] However, Brownson does have one very important part of Brown's body, viz., his brain. There is, therefore, a kind of physical criterion of identity—one that defines personal iden-

On one such mentalistic view, what makes persons at different times the same person and, hence, what unites different parts of a single life is psychological continuity.[26] A series of persons is psychologically *continuous* insofar as contiguous members in the series are psychologically well connected. A pair of persons are psychologically *connected* insofar as the intentional states (e.g., beliefs, desires, and intentions) and actions of one are causally dependent upon those of the other. Of particular importance, given our views about persons, are *deliberative* connections that hold among actions, intentions, and prior deliberations in the deliberate maintenance and modification of intentional states and in the performance of actions that reflect these prior deliberations. Connectedness is a matter of degree; it is a function of the strength and centrality of individual connections and the number of connections.[27] Continuity can also be a matter of degree; given two chains A and B, if the links in A are better connected than the links in B, then any points in A will be more continuous than any points in B. On this view, personal identity consists in maximal psychological continuity.

VII. Interpersonal Self-Extension

But personal identity cannot consist in psychological continuity alone, as is demonstrated in fission cases in which a single stream of consciousness divides into two equal branches.[28] Consider the following case. Tom, Zeke, and Zach are identical triplets and get in a serious car accident. Zeke and Zach are brain-dead; Tom is not, but his body is hopelessly mangled. Assume that it is possible to transplant Tom's brain into Zeke's body and that this preserves Tom's psychological continuity. If we do this (case 1),

---

tity in terms of continuity of the brain—that can accommodate the kind of body swap in Brownson's case. But this is an implausible form of the physical criterion. The obvious question is "*Why* is the brain especially important?" No one thinks that the foot, the nose, or even the heart is necessary or sufficient for personal identity. The brain is a candidate only because in this case, and most others, continuity of the brain is what secures continuity of mental life. But then the reason for focusing on the brain is psychological, not physical. This supports a psychological criterion, however, not a physical one.

[26] Similar mentalistic views are defended by Derek Parfit, *Reasons and Persons* (Oxford: Clarendon Press, 1984), part III; and Sydney Shoemaker, "Personal Identity: A Materialist's Account," in Sydney Shoemaker and Richard Swinburne, *Personal Identity* (Oxford: Blackwell, 1984).

[27] Some kinds of psychological connections may seem more central or important than others. For instance, my career goals and plans and the actions that depend upon them seem more central to my psychological profile than my preference about what shirt to wear on a particular morning and the actions that depend on that preference. But my career aims seem more central than my fashion preferences largely because more of my beliefs, desires, intentions, and actions depend on the former than on the latter. If so, perhaps qualitative differences among psychological connections can be cashed out in purely quantitative terms.

[28] The problem of fission for mentalistic views about personal identity was first raised, I believe, by Thomas Reid; see Reid, *Essays on the Intellectual Powers of Man*, ed. Baruch Brody (Cambridge: MIT Press, 1969), p. 357. Fission and its significance are discussed by David Wiggins, *Identity and Spatio-Temporal Continuity* (Oxford: Blackwell, 1967); Robert Nozick, *Philosophical Explanations* (Cambridge: Harvard University Press, 1981), ch. 1; Parfit, *Reasons and Persons*, ch. 12; and Shoemaker, "Personal Identity," sections 12–13.

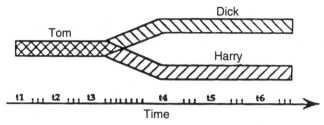

FIGURE 1. Fission and psychological continuity.

we regard Tom as the surviving recipient and Zeke as the dead donor (Zach is simply dead). Now assume that half the brain is sufficient to sustain psychological continuity.[29] If half of Tom's brain is seriously damaged and we transplant the healthy half into Zeke's body (case 2), Tom again survives. If, however, Tom's entire brain is healthy and we transplant half of it into Zeke's body and half into Zach's (case 3), then we have a case of fission. Call the recuperating patient in Zeke's body Dick and the one in Zach's body Harry. There is just as much psychological continuity between Tom and Dick and between Tom and Harry as there was between Tom and the recuperating patient—that is, Tom—in cases 1 and 2. (See Figure 1.) There seem to be five main options about how to describe what happens to Tom during fission and his relationship to Dick and Harry.

   (i) Tom does not survive fission; in particular, he does not survive as Dick or as Harry.

  (ii) Tom survives as Dick, rather than Harry.

 (iii) Tom survives as Harry, rather than Dick.

 (iv) Tom survives as Dick and as Harry.

  (v) Tom survives as the scattered person consisting of Dick and Harry.

Each answer is initially hard to believe.

[29] There is clinical evidence that suggests that severing the corpus callosum can produce two distinct spheres of consciousness, corresponding to the right and left hemispheres of the brain. See, for example, R. W. Perry, "The Great Cerebral Commissure," *Scientific American*, vol. 210 (1964); and Thomas Nagel, "Brain Bisection and the Unity of Consciousness," in *Personal Identity*, ed. John Perry (Los Angeles: University of California Press, 1975). When hemispheres are severed, dividing consciousness, each hemisphere can "learn" to perform some functions that the other had performed for the united brain, and in some patients various capacities usually found in only one hemisphere are found in both. Insofar as this is true, the possibility of dividing the brain and preserving two qualitatively identical but distinct streams of consciousness is not so fantastic. A residual empirical obstacle is that the functionality of a single hemisphere of the brain seems to depend upon the integrity of the brain stem, which does not admit of division. But these empirical obstacles to dividing the brain are not important, I think. What we would or should say about personal identity in merely counterfactual circumstances can constrain what we think personal identity consists in and what its significance is, and this can affect what we can or should say about personal identity and its significance in actual circumstances.

Against (i), we might note that there is just as much psychological continuity between Tom and Dick and between Tom and Harry as there was between Tom and the recuperating patient—that is, Tom—in cases 1 and 2. If Tom survives in cases 1 and 2, how can he fail to survive fission? Surely, he has the same reasons to be concerned about Dick and about Harry in case 3 as he did to be concerned about himself in cases 1 and 2. As Derek Parfit says in his discussion of fission, how can a double success be counted a failure?[30]

Moreover, neither (ii) nor (iii) seems plausible. Dick and Harry have exactly equal claims to being Tom. It is true that one, but not the other, could nonetheless be Tom. But in virtue of what facts would one of them, rather than the other, be Tom? If we believe that personal identity must consist in facts about the relations among the physical and/or psychological states of persons, their claims to be identical to Tom must stand or fall together.

But they cannot each be Tom; (iv) must be false. Identity is a transitive relation (if A = B and B = C, then it must be true that A = C). And it seems clear that Dick is not the same person as Harry; they wake up in different hospital beds, have distinct streams of consciousness, and go on to lead different lives. But if Dick is not identical to Harry, then Tom cannot be identical with Dick and with Harry (if B ≠ C, then it cannot be the case both that A = B and that A = C).

Nor can Tom survive as a scattered person, viz., the sum of Dick and Harry. In part because persons are normatively significant entities—the bearers of rights and responsibilities—persons must be functionally integrated systems; if one is to be held responsible for one's actions, then one's actions must be caused in the right way by one's beliefs, desires, deliberations, and choices. But Dick and Harry are not functionally integrated. For instance, other things being equal, Dick's deliberations and intentions do not cause Harry to act, and Harry's pain does not cause Dick to engage in pain-avoidance behavior. Tom must be identical to a person. Dick and Harry are each persons; they do not together constitute a person.

The best response, I believe, is to accept (i) and claim that Tom does not survive fission. The transitivity of identity requires that any account of the relation of identity must be one-one, rather than one-many. But psychological continuity is a one-many relation. Thus, whereas fission preserves psychological continuity, it cannot preserve identity. To preserve identity, psychological continuity must take a nonbranching form. Our view about personal identity would then be something like this:

> P2 is identical with P1 just in case P2 is (sufficiently) psychologically continuous with P1 and there is no other continuer of P1 that is as continuous with P1.

[30] Parfit, *Reasons and Persons*, p. 256.

But fission seems to preserve what justifies concern; Tom seems to have as much reason to be concerned about Dick and about Harry as he did to be concerned about himself in cases 1 and 2. If this is true, we should conclude that what principally matters with respect to the rationality of concern is psychological continuity, rather than personal identity per se.[31]

Fission is a case of *interpersonal psychological continuity*. It is an exotic case. Though exotic, it is the limiting case of a very common phenomenon. Though I am normally most strongly continuous with myself in the future, I can be psychologically continuous with others with whom I interact psychologically. Interpersonal, as well as intrapersonal, psychological continuity is quite common. Interpersonal connections and continuity can be found among intimates who interact on a regular basis and help shape each other's mental life; in such relationships, the experiences, beliefs, desires, ideals, and actions of each depend in significant part upon those of the others. We can see this in the familial friendships that Plato, Aristotle, and Green all take as their model. Parents make plans for their children that affect the children's actions, opportunities, and experiences; they impart information and teach skills; they make suggestions, act as sounding boards, and set limits. In these and countless other ways, parents help shape their children's faculties, experiences, beliefs, desires, values, opportunities, and goals. Similar relations hold among spouses and friends who share experiences, conversation, and plans. They can also be found, to a lesser extent, among partners in cooperative ventures where the deliberations, desires, plans, and expectations of each are formed together and conditioned by each other. More generally, membership in various sorts of associations will affect the beliefs, desires, expectations, and plans of members so as to establish significant interpersonal psychological continuity among the association's members. In these ways, interpersonal psychological connectedness and continuity can extend broadly, even if the degree of connectedness (and sometimes continuity) often weakens as these relations extend further.

In more normal (nonbranching) interpersonal cases, what distinguishes intrapersonal continuity and interpersonal continuity is the *degree* of continuity. There are more numerous and more direct psychological connections—between actions and intentions and among beliefs, desires, and values—in the intrapersonal case. And where the connections among links in a chain are all weaker, continuity between any points in the chain will also be weaker. If so, we can see how I am more weakly continuous with my intimates than I am with myself. We can also see how I might be continuous with others, besides my intimates, even if more weakly so. I

[31] If so, Parfit is wrong to claim (as he does in *Reasons and Persons*, pp. 259-60, 278-79) that it is an "empty question" which answer is right because they all describe the same outcome. I am unsure myself whether psychological continuity, rather than identity, is all that matters; if it can matter, in the relevant way, that psychological continuity takes a unique or nonbranching form, then identity will have some independent value. However, it is enough for present purposes that psychological continuity has significant independent value.

interact directly with others, such as colleagues and neighbors, and this interaction shapes my mental life in certain ways, even if the interaction in such cases is less regular than is my interaction with intimates and even if the effect of such interactions on my mental life is less profound than is the effect produced by interaction with my intimates. Moreover, I interact with a much larger net of people indirectly, when our psychological influence on each other is mediated by other people and complex social institutions, though the continuity thus established is, as a result, weaker. Indeed, the nature of my relationship to others and of the bonds among us is a function of the degree of interpersonal psychological continuity among us. In branching cases, such as fission, there is no intrinsic psychological difference between intrapersonal and interpersonal relations, not even one of degree. Tom bears the same intrinsic psychological relations to Dick and Harry in case 3 as he does to his recuperating self in cases 1 and 2. What makes fission an interpersonal case is simply that continuity takes a one-many form.

If so, the separateness or diversity of persons is not so fundamental.[32] Insofar as distinct individuals are psychologically connected and continuous, each can and should view the other as one who extends her own interests in the same sort of way that her own future self extends her interests. Precisely because it is the limiting interpersonal case, fission brings this out most clearly. In nonbranching cases, such as cases 1 and 2, psychological continuity extends Tom's interests in the sense that later selves inherit, carry on, and carry out the projects and plans of earlier selves. In nonbranching cases, it also extends Tom's life. In the fission case, however, continuity does not literally extend Tom's life, only because it takes a one-many form. But, by virtue of being fully psychologically continuous with Tom, Dick and Harry will each inherit, carry on, and carry out Tom's projects and plans (though presumably in somewhat different directions over time). This seems to be a good ground for claiming that Dick and Harry extend Tom's interests, in the very same way that his own future self would normally extend his interests, even if they do not literally extend his life. This helps us better understand the common claim, which Plato, Aristotle, and Green all endorse, that in more conventional interpersonal cases there is interpersonal extension of interests. Among intimates, they claim, B's good can be regarded as a part or component of A's good. The ground they offer for this claim is that A and B interact and help shape each other's mental life; the experiences, beliefs,

---

[32] In this way, I agree with Parfit, who thinks that personal identity is "less deep" and normatively less significant on the psychological reductionist view; see *Reasons and Persons*, chs. 14 and 15. Unlike Parfit, however, I do not think that this follows from considerations about the metaphysical depth of a reductionist view per se; it follows from seeing that there is interpersonal, as well as intrapersonal, psychological continuity and that the difference between the two is at most a matter of degree. I discuss this issue somewhat more fully in "Rational Egoism and the Separateness of Persons," in *Parfit and His Critics*, ed. Jonathan Dancy (Oxford; Blackwell, forthcoming).

desires, ideals, and actions of each depend in significant part upon those of the other. These are the sorts of conditions of psychological continuity and connectedness that are maximally realized in normal intrapersonal cases and in fission cases. Here they are realized to a very large extent in familiar interpersonal cases. This means that each should regard the good of those to whom she stands in such relationships as a constituent part of her overall good, just as she should regard the good of her own future self as a constituent part of her overall good. This allows us to agree with Aristotle and Green that insofar as A and B are psychologically connected and continuous, each is justified in regarding the other as "another-self" (*NE* 1161b19, 28, 1169b6, 1170b7) or an "alter ego" (*PE* 191, 200).

On this view, interpersonal psychological interaction and dependence provide a metaphysical-egoist justification of other-regarding conduct and concern. Of course, concern itself is an ingredient in many associations, especially intimate associations. For instance, concern is part of what it is to be a friend to someone, whether the friendship is toward another or toward oneself. But this does not mean that our justification of concern is circular. For we can justify concern for associates in terms of other associative relations. Typically, concern is preceded by other kinds of associative relations. For instance, people interact with each other before they display the special concern for each other characteristic of friends or neighbors.[33] The development and expression of this concern arises from and is justified by these past interactions and shared history. Moreover, it is significant for the purposes of my argument, that people often have these associative reasons for concern without having and expressing (proportionate) concern. Concern takes the form of a cluster of dispositions, among other things, to share the other's joys and sorrows, to keep abreast of developments in the other's life, to protect the other against certain sorts of harms and risks, and to advance the other's plans and prospects in certain ways. If so, concern for oneself or another clearly contributes to *further* psychological interdependence. In this way, associative relations justify concern, which can strengthen associative relations, which then justifies further concern, and so on. There is no circularity here.

However, even if we accept this much of the metaphysical-egoist justification of other-regarding concern, a number of foundational worries remain. It is worth raising these worries and exploring resources for reply.

VIII. The Good of Self-Extension

What is the *value* of interpersonal self-extension? We might agree that proper self-love requires a concern for others proportional to the amount of interpersonal psychological interaction and dependence that already exists between oneself and others. But presumably the amount of inter-

---

[33] Even parental concern for a newborn is preceded by decisions, plans, and actions on the parent's part on which the newborn's existence and condition depend.

action one has with others, as well as the form it takes, is often under one's control. Why should one cultivate interpersonal psychological relations? It seems a circuitous way to benefit oneself. Why not just spend my financial, emotional, and intellectual resources directly on myself, rather than cultivating relationships through which I can then benefit myself?

The metaphysical egoist should claim that interpersonal self-extension promotes my *eudaimonia* in distinctively valuable ways. As Aristotle makes most clear, it is in my interest to exercise those capacities that are central to the sort of being I essentially am (*NE* I 7). If I am essentially a person, then a principal ingredient in my welfare must be the exercise of my deliberative capacities. Indeed, if we endorse a deliberative conception of welfare or *eudaimonia*, we can begin to explain how prudence can be a requirement of practical reason. For when prudence is understood in deliberative terms, it aims at the exercise of the very deliberative capacities that make one a responsible agent, capable of having and acting on reasons for action. Moreover, if my persistence depends upon the extension of my deliberative control into the future, we can see how the exercise of my deliberative capacities is part of my welfare. But then it can be claimed that interpersonal psychological dependence of the sort discussed can extend my interests in important ways.

The central premise of the argument is that I am not self-sufficient at producing a complete deliberative good.[34] Again, Aristotle's claims are especially instructive (*NE* 1162a20–24, 1170a5–7; *Politics* 1253a25–27, 1261b10–15). "For it is said that the blessedly happy and self-sufficient people have no need of friends. For they already have [all] the goods, and hence, being self-sufficient, need nothing added. But your friend, since he is another yourself, supplies what your own efforts cannot supply" (*NE* 1169b4–6). Part of what Aristotle may have in mind is that cooperative interaction with others is mutually beneficial and that family, friends, and neighbors protect each other from misfortune by sharing their resources (1170a5). Important as these benefits are, however, they appear to give interpersonal interaction only strategic or instrumental value.

Aristotle can and does have something more in mind. He focuses on the sharing of thought and discussion, especially about how best to live, as well as cooperative interaction. Sharing thought and discussion with another diversifies my experiences by providing me with additional perspectives on the world. By enlarging my perspective, it gives me a more objective picture of the world, its possibilities, and my place in it. This both

[34] Insofar as the metaphysical-egoist attempt to reconcile self-interest and other-regarding moral demands depends upon the fact that people are not individually sufficient for a complete deliberative good, the reconciliation depends upon contingent facts, and the resulting defense of the authority of other-regarding demands will not hold in all possible worlds. But this sort of counterfactual instability is very different from that which afflicts strategic egoism (cf. note 7); for the worlds in which strategic egoism fails are very similar to the actual world (indeed, they include the actual world), whereas the worlds in which metaphysical egoism fails are very different from the actual world. As a result, it is not clear that the sort of counterfactual instability that afflicts metaphysical egoism is a problem.

explains and qualifies how we should understand Plato's and Aristotle's suggestion that part of the value of intimates, with whom one shares thought and conversation, consists in their providing a "mirror" on the self (*Phaedrus* 255d5, and *NE* 1169b34–35). Insofar as we regard the exercise of deliberative capacities as the chief ingredient in *eudaimonia*, we can see how self-understanding and self-criticism are both parts of *eudaimonia*. Interaction between those who are psychologically similar provides a kind of mirror on the self. Insofar as my friend is like me, I can appreciate my own qualities from a different perspective; this promotes my self-understanding. One need only think of the familiar way in which parents experience pride and sometimes chagrin when they see various habits and traits of their own manifested in their children. But interaction with another just like me does not itself contribute to self-criticism. This is why there is deliberative value in interaction with diverse sorts of people many of whom are not mirror images of myself. This suggests another way in which I am not deliberatively self-sufficient. Sharing thought and discussion with others, especially about how to live, improves my own practical deliberations; it enlarges my menu of options, by identifying new options, and helps me better assess the merits of these options, by forcing on my attention new considerations and arguments about the comparative merits of the options. Here we might appeal to Socratic and Millian claims about the deliberative value of open and vigorous discussion with diverse interlocutors.[35] Moreover, cooperative interaction with others allows me to participate in larger, more complex projects and thus to extend the scope of my deliberative control over my environment. In this way, I spread my interests more widely than I could acting on my own. Here too diversity can be helpful; cooperation among people is improved and extends the interests of each person further when it draws on diverse talents and skills. This, I think, is part of what Green has in mind in claiming that cooperation with others on common ends contributes to a more permanent good for the agent (*PE* 191, 232). In these ways, interpersonal psychological relations arguably make for fuller realization of my deliberative capacities.

IX. Noninstrumental Concern

Is egoistic concern too *instrumental*? Morality seems to require not just that we perform the actions it demands of us but also that we fulfill its demands from the right sort of motives, and sometimes morality seems to require not just that we benefit another but that we do so out of a concern

[35] This is a latent theme in Plato's early and transitional dialogues; it comes closer to the surface in the *Gorgias*, where greater probative value is attached to discussion with diverse and more radical interlocutors. Cf. Terence Irwin, "Objectivity and Coercion in Plato's Dialectic," *Revue Internationale de Philosophie*, no. 156/157 (1986), pp. 49–74. The deliberative value of freedom of expression and diversity of opinion and lifestyle is an important strand in John Stuart Mill's arguments against censorship, moral legislation, and paternalism, especially in *On Liberty*; see my "Mill's Deliberative Utilitarianism," *Philosophy and Public Affairs*, vol. 21 (1992), pp. 67–103.

for the other for her own sake. This is certainly true about the concern owed to intimates. If justified concern for another is, as the metaphysical egoist claims, a special case of self-love, then mustn't such concern be at bottom instrumental? If so, this is objectionable because it fails to justify concern for others for their own sakes and because it threatens to make the justification of other-regarding concern insufficiently stable.

In assessing this complaint, it is instructive to look at the Socratic view of love and friendship and compare it with Platonic and Aristotelian views. In Plato's *Lysis*, Socrates maintains that one who had a complete good would have no need of love or friendship and that friendship can only exist between people who stand to gain from association with each other (215a–b). In this way, friendship is predicated on mutual benefit (214c). This view of love and friendship fits nicely with Socrates' eudaimonism, which implies that I have reason to care for another insofar as this contributes to my own *eudaimonia*. For Socrates, however, such concern must be instrumental. For he believes that only an unconditionally complete good is intrinsically valuable: "All such value as this is set not on those things that are procured for the sake of another thing, but on that for the sake of which all things are procured" (219e9–11).[36] Those things desired for the sake of something else are not intrinsically, but only instrumentally, valuable (219c–220b). But a lover, according to Socrates, values his beloved for the sake of the lover's own *eudaimonia*. It follows that a lover can love his beloved only instrumentally, and this is incompatible with caring about one's beloved for his own sake.

However, Platonic and Aristotelian eudaimonism do not require purely instrumental concern for the beloved. Whereas Socrates assumes that valuing something for the sake of another always reflects purely instrumental concern, Plato and Aristotle reject this assumption.

In the *Republic*, Glaucon and Adeimantus demand that Socrates show justice to be beneficial *in itself* and not simply for its normal causal consequences (357a–367e). Plato subsequently defends justice by arguing that justice secures the right ordering of the agent's soul and thus contributes to his *eudaimonia*. If we are to make sense of Plato's defense of justice as a response to the challenge that Glaucon and Adeimantus pose, we must interpret him as arguing that justice is valuable for its *intrinsic*, as well as its extrinsic, consequences. If justice contributes to the agent's happiness, because justice is a part of the agent's happiness, then Plato will have shown that justice is valuable "in and by itself" (367b4, e2–4). Plato does regard justice as the controlling part of *eudaimonia*; he hopes to show that one is always better off being just than being unjust, no matter what the extrinsic consequences of justice and injustice turn out to be (360e–362c). But this *comparative* claim does not assume that justice is sufficient for a

---

[36] This translation from the *Lysis* is by J. Wright in *The Collected Dialogues of Plato* (*supra* note 10).

complete good. In particular, the comparative claim allows Plato to recognize the value of external goods, independent of virtue (361e4–362a2). But then Plato's view seems to be that *eudaimonia* is a whole of which justice (and virtue generally) is a proper part. Justice is desirable for the sake of something else, namely, *eudaimonia*. But being desirable for the sake of *eudaimonia* does not imply that justice is only instrumentally valuable; it is valuable in itself for its constitutive contribution to happiness. If Plato can make this claim about justice, he can make this claim about friendship and love. The lover can love his beloved for the contribution this makes to the lover's own *eudaimonia* and for the beloved's own sake if the good of the beloved is a constituent part of the lover's own *eudaimonia*.

On Aristotle's view, a good is complete if it is chosen for its own sake, and a good is unconditionally complete if all other things are chosen for its sake and it is not chosen for the sake of something else (*NE* 1094a18–19, 1097a27–b6). Aristotle believes that *eudaimonia* is the only unconditionally complete good; all other goods are chosen for its sake. Some goods chosen for the sake of *eudaimonia*, though not choiceworthy in themselves, are choiceworthy as causal means to some ingredient of *eudaimonia*; these goods are incomplete, instrumental goods. But other goods—such as the virtues—that are chosen for the sake of *eudaimonia* are also choiceworthy in themselves. They are chosen for the sake of *eudaimonia* in the sense that they are constituent parts of *eudaimonia*; they are valuable in their own right for their constitutive contribution to a valuable life. Such goods are complete or intrinsic goods, not mere instrumental goods, though they are not unconditionally complete goods. Here Aristotle is making explicit the sort of assumptions Plato must make about justice in *Republic* II–IV; in Aristotle's terms, Plato thinks justice is a complete good, but not an unconditionally complete good. If the lover treats the good of his beloved as a complete good that is also choiceworthy for the sake of his own *eudaimonia*, the lover is concerned for the other's own sake while valuing his beloved's well-being for the constitutive contribution this makes to his own *eudaimonia*.

Thus, both Plato and Aristotle have the analytic resources to provide a eudaimonist justification of interpersonal concern that is derivative but not instrumental. When I undergo a present sacrifice for a future benefit, I do so because the interests of my future self are interests of mine. The on-balance rationality of the sacrifice depends upon its promoting my overall good. But because the good of my future self is part of this overall good, concern for my overall good requires, as a constituent part, a concern for the good of my future self. In this way, concern for my future self for its own sake seems compatible with and, indeed, essential to self-love. If psychological relations extend an agent's interests, then the good of others can be part of my overall good just as my own future good can be. Though the on-balance rationality of other-regarding action depends upon its promoting my overall good, concern for my overall good requires, as a constituent part, concern for the welfare of those to whom I am appropriately psychologically related. This is why Plato and Green view interpersonal love as the next best thing to immortality (*Symposium* 206c1–209e5; *PE* 231) and why Aristotle and Green claim that a proper conception of how others figure in self-love undermines the popular contrast between self-love and altruism (*NE* IX 8; *PE* 232).[37]

X. SCOPE

Another worry concerns the *scope* of the metaphysical-egoist justification of other-regarding concern. If its justification of other-regarding conduct and concern is limited to those to whom one is already psychologically related, then the scope of this egoist account of the authority of morality may seem disturbingly narrow. The scope of egoistic concern will be especially narrow if the relevant relations obtain only among intimates and like-minded members of small associations. But the metaphysical egoist can claim that the relevant interpersonal relations do and should extend quite widely.

Psychological connectedness does not require like-mindedness. Though Aristotle sometimes speaks as if the relevant relations among friends must involve similar beliefs and values (*NE* 1159b3–5, 1161b35, 1162a13, 1165b17, 1166a7, 1167a23–b10, 1170b16), it is not clear that this is or should be an essential feature of his position, at least insofar as he seeks to model interpersonal concern on intrapersonal concern. For within my own life, I exercise deliberative control and establish psychological connections with my future self when I intentionally modify beliefs, desires, or values, as well as when I maintain them unchanged. Now it may be that my successive selves will typically be fairly similar; perhaps wholesale and instantaneous psychological change is impossible or at least would involve a substantial change, which I would not survive. But intrapersonal psychological dependence is compatible with significant qualitative change. This allows us to explain how it is that we have prudential reason to undertake changes in our characters that count as improvements; our persistence requires only deliberative control, not fixity, of character.[38] If so, it seems that, in the interpersonal case, Aristotle should allow for friends to be psychologically dissimilar, provided the mental states and actions of each friend exert significant influence on those of the other.[39]

[37] Jennifer Whiting objects to the colonial or imperial perspective that she thinks the egoist must impose on interpersonal concern; see Whiting, "Impersonal Friends," *The Monist*, vol. 74 (1991), pp. 9–10. Purely instrumental concern for another, of the sort to which Socrates seems to be committed, is colonial or imperial in some straightforwardly objectionable way. But where the egoist can justify derivative but noninstrumental concern for others, it is unclear what the moral objection to the egocentric perspective is.

[38] For more discussion of these issues, see my "Rational Egoism and the Separateness of Persons" (*supra* note 32).

[39] In discussing the puzzle about whether to wish one's friend the good of divinity, Aristotle claims that one who cares about the friend for the friend's own sake would not wish this

Indeed, if others are to extend my interests by diversifying my experiences, by providing me with resources for self-criticism as well as self-understanding, by broadening my deliberative menu and improving my deliberations, and by allowing me to engage in more complex and varied activities, it is important that we be different and not too like-minded (*Politics* 1281a42–b15). Moreover, psychological influence can be exerted between people, on each other, even when they have not had direct interactions, as when two people influence each other through their conversations with a common third party. The ripple-effects on others of our conversations, plans, actions, and relationships can extend quite widely.

Moreover, continuous selves need not be connected. Any elements in a series are continuous just in case contiguous members in the series are well connected; this implies that noncontiguous members (e.g., the endpoints) of such a series are continuous even if they are not well-connected or connected at all. If so, people can be psychologically continuous who are not at all connected, provided they are members of a series of persons each of whom is connected to some degree with his neighbor in the series. There is room for debate about the comparative roles of continuity and connectedness within a suitable mentalistic view of personal identity.[40] Perhaps both relations matter and extend one's interests, but I think it is clear that continuity must matter.[41] If so, then the relations that justify other-regarding concern can extend far beyond the circle of those with whom one regularly interacts.

In thinking about the proper scope of eudaimonistic concern, it is worth thinking about differences between Aristotle and Green with respect to the scope of the common good. I noted that despite differences between virtue-friendship, which serves as his principal model for friendship, and political association, Aristotle can extend the central elements of his eudaimonist defense of friendship to political association, because political communities that are just have to a significant degree the two features that are crucial to the justification of virtue-friendship and familial friendship: there is commonality of aims among members of the political association, and this commonality is produced by members of the association living together in the right way, in particular, by defining their aims and goals consensually (*NE* 1167a25–28, 1155a24–28). This establishes a common good among citizens, each of whom has a share in judging and

---

good on the friend, because the friend would not survive the transformation (*NE* 1159a5–11). This seems right. But persistence does not require fixity of character over time. Thus, while it is plausible that one should not wish on oneself or others the good of divinity, it is not plausible that one should not wish on oneself or others significant improvement of character; rather, this is just what friendship toward oneself and others requires. If so, then concern for someone, whether oneself or another, for his own sake requires neither similarity nor fixity of character. Insofar as Aristotle disagrees (esp. 1165b17–30), his claims seem problematic.

[40] For a brief discussion, see my "Rational Egoism and the Separateness of Persons."

[41] Continuity must figure in a mentalistic account of identity if only to meet Reid's demand that any criterion of identity be transitive; see Reid, *Essays on the Intellectual Powers of Man* (*supra* note 28), p. 358.

ruling (*Politics* 1275a22–33). Justice aims at a common good (*NE* 1129b15–18), and this, we said, is how Aristotle can construct a eudaimonist defense of justice. But this conception of the common good is still quite limited. Restricted as it is to those whom Aristotle thinks are fit for citizenship, it excludes women, barbarians, slaves, and manual laborers (*Politics* 1278a3–9); indeed, he thinks that manual laborers ought to be drawn exclusively from a pool of barbarians and natural inferiors (1329a24–26). It is these restrictions on the common good that Green finds unacceptable:

> The idea of a society of free and law-abiding persons, each his own master yet each his brother's keeper, was first definitely formed among the Greeks, and its formation was the condition of all subsequent progress in the direction described; but with them . . . it was limited in its application to select groups of men surrounded by populations of aliens and slaves. In its universality, as capable of application to the whole human race, an attempt has first been made to act upon it in modern Christendom. (*PE* 271)

As the last part of this passage suggests, Green's own conception of the common good is universal; full self-realization and the securing of a really permanent good occurs only when each respects the claims made by other members of a maximally inclusive community of ends (214, 216, 244, 332).[42]

There are good eudaimonist reasons for recognizing a more inclusive common good than Aristotle does. First, there already are significant forms of personal, social, and economic interaction and interdependence between Aristotle's citizens, on the one hand, and women, slaves, manual laborers, and resident aliens, on the other. The arguments for recognizing a common good based on interpersonal self-extension require including them in the common good. Perhaps Aristotle's view is that they are part of a common good, but not of a political common good, because they are unfit for sharing in political rule. He thinks that some—such as slaves and, to a lesser extent, women—are naturally inferior (*Politics* II 4–7, 12–13). They are, he thinks, like the nonrational part of the soul; they can apprehend and follow the reason of another but they are incapable of the sort of deliberation involved in ruling and necessary for human happiness (1254b20–24, 1260a12–22). If so, these natural inferiors, even if part of a common good, are better suited to manual labor than to citizenship.[43]

---

[42] Insofar as he conceives the common good universally, Green's view is perhaps closer to the Stoic than to the Aristotelian view. See Cicero, *De Finibus* iii 63. This aspect of the Stoic view is emphasized in Julia Annas, *The Morality of Happiness* (New York: Oxford University Press, 1993), ch. 12.

[43] Part of Aristotle's justification for restricting citizenship assumes that manual labor is inimical to deliberation and virtue (*Politics* 1329a35–38). Dull and repetitive labor over which the worker has no control is menial and can only be instrumentally valuable to the extent that it furnishes life's necessities. But manual labor need not be menial in this way. As long as the farmer or artisan has responsibility for and control over production, distri-

This argument clearly rests on the assumption of natural inferiority. Aristotle might think that he has empirical support for his position. His observations about women and slaves might lead him to suppose not simply that they had achieved less by way of individual and civic accomplishments than full-fledged citizens, but also that they were, in one sense, capable of less. But this sort of incapacity is presumably the *product*, rather than the cause, of being denied citizenship. Aristotle realizes that capacities must be properly cultivated and stimulated in order to develop properly. If I have not been given a proper education and training or suitable deliberative opportunities and responsibilities at various points in my development, I will not be prepared for proper deliberation about the management of my own affairs or those of the community. Use it, or lose it. Thus, even if everyone had equal innate capacities, we should expect the unequal development of deliberative capacities in systems where education and deliberative opportunities and responsibilities are distributed unequally. But then the unequal capacities that discriminatory practices and institutions produce cannot be appealed to as justification for those practices and institutions. So there appears to be no good reason for Aristotle not to recognize the claims to citizenship that existing patterns of interaction justify. This provides a backward-looking justification for recognizing a more inclusive conception of the common good. Moreover, as we have seen, interaction with others contributes to the full realization of my deliberative powers by diversifying my experiences, by providing me with resources for self-criticism as well as self-understanding, by broadening my deliberative menu and improving my deliberations, and by allowing me to engage in more complex and varied activities. Moreover, the deliberative value of this interaction is enhanced when others have diverse perspectives and talents. This provides a forward-looking justification for recognizing a more inclusive conception of the common good.

Because this push toward a more inclusive conception of the common good is motivated by Aristotelian considerations, it is a friendly amendment to Aristotle. But can the common good be genuinely universal in scope, as Green wants it to be, if it is the result of interpersonal interaction? For then there must be someone—the proverbial remotest Mysian (Plato, *Theaetetus* 209b8)—with whom one has no previous relation, however indirect.[44] Should it somehow come within my power to help the remotest Mysian, at little or no cost to myself, it might seem that the eudaimonist cannot explain justified concern for him. This might seem like a defect in an account of the scope of morality or its authority.

If the remotest Mysian and I stand in no relations of connection or continuity, then his good is not already part of mine. Thus, I can have no

---

bution, and the organization of his labor process, manual labor can and will involve the exercise of important deliberative capacities. By Aristotelian criteria, meaningful manual labor ought to be an intrinsic good.

[44] The introduction of the proverbial remotest Mysian into discussions of the scope of ethical concern is discussed by Annas, *The Morality of Happiness*, ch. 12.

backward-looking eudaimonistic reason to be concerned about him. But I can have forward-looking reasons. For it is now within my power to interact with him, and all the reasons for cultivating interpersonal self-extension (see Section VIII above) apply and provide a forward-looking rationale for concern. Even when the remotest Mysian and I have no prospect of further interaction, my assistance will enable or facilitate his pursuit of his own projects, and this will make his subsequent actions and mental states dependent upon my assistance. Indeed, other things being equal, the greater the assistance I provide, the greater is my involvement in his life. To the extent that another's actions and mental states are dependent upon my assistance, I can view the assistance as making his good a part of my own. Assistance to the remotest Mysian earns me a share, however small, of his happiness, much the way care and nurture of my children grounds posthumous interests I have in their continued well-being. This is why Green thinks that self-realization involves contributing to a larger, more permanent and comprehensive good (*PE* 229–32). If so, it seems a eudaimonist can legitimately seek a universal common good, of the sort Green contemplates.

XI. WEIGHT

A final worry concerns the *weight* of the reasons for other-regarding concern. Both connectedness and continuity are matters of degree. Normally, there are more numerous and direct psychological connections among successive stages within a single life than between lives. And where the connections among links in a chain are all weaker, continuity between any points in the chain will also be weaker. If so, we can see how I am more weakly continuous with my intimates than I am with myself. We can also see how I might be continuous with others, besides my intimates. I interact directly with others, such as colleagues and neighbors, and this interaction shapes my mental life in certain ways, even if the interaction in such cases is less regular than is my interaction with intimates, and even if the effect of such interactions on my mental life is less profound than is the effect produced by interaction with my intimates. Moreover, I interact with a much larger net of people indirectly, when our psychological influence on each is other is mediated by other people and complex social institutions. We can think of the degrees of connectedness and continuity in terms of a set of concentric circles, with myself occupying the inner circle and the remotest Mysian occupying the outer circle. As we extend the scope of psychological interdependence, the strength of the relevant psychological relations appears to weaken and the weight of one's reasons to give aid and refrain from harm presumably weakens proportionately. Despite the wide scope of justified concern, it must apparently have variable weight. Is such an *interpersonal discount rate* acceptable?

This depends, in part, on the precise shape of the interpersonal discount rate. As long as psychological connectedness is itself one of the psychological relations that matter, then there will be an interpersonal discount rate, because an agent will be differentially psychologically connected to others. But as long as psychological continuity is also one of the relations that matter, a significant level of concern can be justified for anyone with whom one is psychologically continuous. Suppose A is friends only with B, whereas B is also friends with C. All else being equal, A is as continuous with his friend's friend, C, as he is with his friend, B. Insofar as continuity is one of the relations that matter, then, A has as much reason to be concerned about his friend's friend as about his friend. He will have reason to give greater weight to the interests of his friend insofar as connectedness also matters. These points generalize beyond friendship. So the importance of psychological continuity ensures that a significant threshold of concern can be justified well out into outer circles. There will nonetheless be significant differences in the degree of concern that can be justified, above this threshold, in different circles if connectedness has independent significance.

This kind of interpersonal discount rate need not be a threat to our understanding of other-regarding morality or its authority. For it is commonly thought that, even if morality has universal scope, the demands that it imposes are a function not simply of the amount of benefit that one can confer but also of the nature of the relationship in which one stands to potential beneficiaries. Common-sense morality recognizes more stringent obligations toward those to whom one stands in special relationships— for instance, toward family and friends and toward partners in cooperative schemes—than toward others.[45] Aristotle, for one, clearly accepts this sort of *moral discount rate*; he thinks that, all else being equal, it is better to help and worse to harm those to whom one stands in special relations than it is to do these things to others (*NE* 1160a1–6, 1169b12; *Politics* 1262a27–30). It seems a reasonable hypothesis that the interpersonal relationships that have special moral significance are just those relationships of psychological interaction and interdependence that extend one's interests. If so, then there will be a moral discount rate that is isomorphic to the egoist interpersonal discount rate. Indeed, it would be a virtue, rather than a defect, of this justification of other-regarding concern that it embodies an interpersonal discount rate.

XII. THE BALANCE OF REASONS

The metaphysical egoist models interpersonal relations and concern on intrapersonal relations and concern and thereby extends the boundaries

---

[45] C. D. Broad calls this interpretation of common-sense morality "self-referential altruism"; see Broad, "Self and Others," in *Broad's Critical Essays in Moral Philosophy*, ed. David R. Cheney (London: George Allen and Unwin, 1971).

of self-interest and self-love so as to include the good of others. This view figures importantly in Platonic and Aristotelian eudaimonism and in Green's ethics of self-realization. I have tried to articulate one conception of metaphysical egoism that draws on these traditions and appeals to plausible claims about persons and their persistence. This view implies a conception of interpersonal relations that should lead us to see people's interests as metaphysically, and not just strategically, interdependent. Moreover, this egoist justification of other-regarding conduct is robust. We can explain how each should view this interdependence as good; interpersonal self-extension makes possible the fuller realization of the deliberative powers of each. We can also explain how the justification of other-regarding concern is derivative but noninstrumental. We can defend an inclusive conception of the common good and thereby offer a defense of other-regarding conduct with wide scope. Finally, we can see how differences in the very relations that, on this view, justify concern appear also to be morally significant differences. Metaphysical egoism implies that complying with other-regarding duties is a counterfactually reliable way of advancing the agent's own overall good, properly conceived. This is a significant result, whether we understand practical rationality in exclusively prudential terms or not.

However, my argument, even if successful, does not itself imply that the authority of other-regarding moral demands is overriding or supreme. Unlike Green, I do not see these claims as establishing the strong thesis that there can be no conflict or competition of interests among people (*PE* 244).[46] I have argued that the good of others is a necessary and distinctively valuable part of an agent's overall good. But it is one aspect of an agent's overall good that must interact and may compete with more self-confined aspects. When I expend intellectual, emotional, and financial resources on meeting the legitimate claims of others, this contributes to my overall good in distinctive ways; but it also consumes resources that might have been spent on my education, my vocation, or my avocations. There are opportunity costs to every commitment, even especially important commitments, and sometimes the opportunity costs of important commitments are themselves important. If so, other-regarding and more self-confined aspects of an agent's overall good are distinct and at least potentially conflicting.

The only prospect I see for a principled and largely noncompetitive accommodation of these two aspects of self-interest requires that we focus our prudential evaluation not on individual actions or types of action but on comprehensive modes of life. There are familiar ways of partitioning our lives and regulating these parts so that they are directed at different

[46] I am not sure that this strong thesis can be reached from recognizably individualist premises; it may require fundamentally anti-individualist metaphysical claims, according to which persons are merely parts of an interpersonal organic whole and must view their own well-being in terms of the proper functioning of the whole of which they are a part.

aspects of prudence. For instance, we go some way toward meeting other-regarding demands of those with whom we are not in regular contact by channeling resources through community and international charitable organizations. This can be done in predictable and comparatively nonintrusive ways. We divide the rest of our time, energies, and resources into various spheres, involving work, friends, family, and personal activities. Of course, there are better and worse ways of allocating one's time, energies, and resources both within and among these spheres. But the idea is that there are ways of conceiving of these spheres and dividing one's energies among them so that even if many of one's actions contribute disproportionately to distinct components of self-interest, one's actions as a package might promote well all the different components of one's good.

Arguably, the best prospects for accommodation can be found in circumstances of *democratic equality*, in which democratic institutions operate against a background of personal and civic liberties and opportunities and comparative social and economic equality that establishes a decent minimum standard of living. Democratic decision-making affords the opportunity for widespread participation by people with diverse perspectives in a process of mutual discussion and articulation of ideals and priorities. As a result, democratic processes establish psychological interdependence more widely, make possible participation in public deliberations, and improve the quality of the personal deliberations of members of such a society. A background of personal and civic liberties with comparative social and economic equality makes possible more widespread development of individual talents and capacities, and this will expand the range of experiences, values, and perspectives that individuals can enjoy vicariously and draw on in their own deliberations. Democratic equality would not only exercise the deliberative powers of each but also would provide a background against which one might be able to accommodate other-regarding and more self-confined aspects of self-interest. For one division of moral and political labor that might make accommodation possible would be for individuals largely to be free to express partial commitments to themselves, their intimates, and their immediate associates, provided the political community they live in ensures each the resources, education, and opportunities necessary to realize his own deliberative good effectively. This kind of partiality would be legitimate in systems of democratic equality, once an individual had met his responsibilities of democratic citizenship.

But then the legitimacy of this kind of partiality requires a certain level of material and economic prosperity and institutions of democratic equality. Even when we are dealing with local political communities, these conditions are infrequently met. But if, as Green and I believe, the proper conception of the common good is maximally inclusive, then it seems that the political condition of partiality that is metaphysically prudent is very hard to satisfy. Many local political communities lack requisite material and economic prosperity or otherwise fail to produce democratic equality, and there is no global community that is able or willing to establish democratic equality within and among local communities. Until such time as these local and global political conditions are met, significant partiality may be difficult to justify even from the point of view of prudence. This suggests that the accommodation of self-regarding and other-regarding aspects of self-interest is a political good and achievement, not fully within any one person's control.[47]

Whether and to what extent there can be a successful accommodation of other-regarding and self-confined aspects of self-interest is an important issue that requires further study. But this does not simply leave us where we started. For I have argued that the good of others forms a distinctive part of the agent's overall good, a part whose importance must be reckoned with in the balance of reasons. This is an important claim. Even if practical reason is exclusively prudential, it vindicates the weak rationalist thesis that there is always reason to act on other-regarding demands, such that failure to do so is *pro tanto* irrational. It is less clear whether it helps vindicate the strong rationalist thesis that there is always overriding reason to act on other-regarding demands, such that failure to do so is on balance irrational. This depends upon the resolution of other issues. If practical reason is exclusively prudential, the plausibility of the strong rationalist thesis will depend upon whether self-confined and other-regarding aspects of an agent's overall good can be accommodated in noncompetitive ways. As I have suggested, there may be possible circumstances of democratic equality that allow this accommodation, but it is unlikely that they already obtain generally. If democratic equality does not obtain generally, it will be hard to maintain the strong rationalist thesis on purely prudential grounds. If, however, as I am inclined to believe, practical reason has impartial as well as prudential dimensions, then the prospects for a reasonably strong rationalist thesis look better.[48]

---

[47] The claims I sketch in this section for a principled accommodation of self-confined and other-regarding aspects of self-interest bear some resemblance (I'm not sure how much) to claims that Thomas Nagel and Samuel Scheffler make about the reconciliation of personal and impersonal moral demands; see Nagel, *Equality and Partiality* (New York: Oxford University Press, 1991), and Scheffler, *Human Morality* (New York: Oxford University Press, 1992), esp. ch. 8. One difference is that whereas Nagel and Scheffler are concerned about the accommodation of different aspects of morality, I am concerned about the accommodation of different aspects of self-interest. It is also worth noting apparent similarities between my claims and claims Hegel makes in *The Philosophy of Right*, trans. T. M. Knox (Oxford: Clarendon Press, 1952), and *Introduction to the Philosophy of History*, trans. Leo Rauch (Indianapolis: Hackett, 1988). My claim that proper self-realization requires partitioning one's life into differentially regulated spheres is like the Hegelian claim that it is only by participating in the three very differently organized spheres of family, civil society, and the state that one is able fully to realize oneself in the modern world. My claim that accommodation of these two aspects of self-interest is not always possible and would be a political accomplishment is like the Hegelian claim that reconciliation is a possibility only in the modern world. Unlike Hegel, however, I am not confident that full accommodation is yet possible.

[48] Cf. my "Kantian Rationalism: Inescapability, Authority, and Supremacy" (*supra* note 2).

For then both impartial reason and prudence, in one voice, will speak in favor of other-regarding morality, and only prudence, in another voice, might speak against it. How often the balance of reasons will tip toward other-regarding morality will depend upon the details of metaphysical egoism, impartial reason, and other-regarding morality. Nonetheless, I hope to have said enough about the nature and resources of metaphysical egoism to show that it has an important role to play in our understanding of the rational authority of morality.

Philosophy, University of California, San Diego

SELF-INTEREST AND SELF-CONCERN*

By Stephen Darwall

I. Introduction

In what follows I consider whether the idea of a person's interest or good might be better understood through that of care or concern for that person for her sake, rather than conversely, as is ordinarily assumed. Contrary to (informed) desire-satisfaction theories of interest, such an account can explain why not everything a person rationally desires is part of her good, since what a person sensibly wants is not necessarily what we (and she) would sensibly want, insofar as we care about *her*.

First, however, a tale:

> There was no other explanation which seemed reasonable. . . . [W]as it not reasonable to assume that he meant never to claim his birthright? If this were so, what right had he, William Cecil Clayton, to thwart the wishes, to balk the self-sacrifice of this strange man? If Tarzan of the Apes could do this thing to save Jane Porter from unhappiness, why should he, to whose care she was intrusting her whole future, do aught to jeopardize her interests?
>
> And so he reasoned until the first generous impulse to proclaim the truth and relinquish his titles and his estates to their rightful owner was forgotten beneath the mass of sophistries which self-interest had advanced.[1]

Having found a telegram addressed to Tarzan with the news that Tarzan rather than he is the rightful Lord Greystoke, William Cecil Clayton ponders his future and the recent actions of "this strange man," Tarzan. Tarzan despairs, notwithstanding this recent news, of providing his beloved Jane

* I am indebted to the other contributors to this volume for helpful comments and discussion of an earlier version of this essay, and to Ellen Frankel Paul for editorial advice. I owe much as well to David Sobel, David Velleman, and Elizabeth Anderson for discussion of the issues with which this essay is concerned, and to Anderson's *Value in Ethics and Economics* (Cambridge: Harvard University Press, 1993) and Sobel's "Preferences, Well-Being, and Taking a Person into Account Morally" (unpublished), from which I have learned much.

Finally, I am indebted to the growing literature on the "ethics of care," including the work of Lawrence Blum, Carol Gilligan, Annette Baier, and Robin Dillon, among many others. This essay may be viewed, in part, as an attempt to work out more fully an idea I first broached in *Impartial Reason*, namely, that to care about someone, whether oneself or another, is to have a conception of his or her good as giving reasons to anyone (capable of similar concern). What I did not there consider, and what I here suggest, is that the idea of a person's good or interest is itself to be understood in terms of such concern. (See my *Impartial Reason* [Ithaca, NY: Cornell University Press, 1983], pp. 160–63.)

[1] Edgar Rice Burroughs, *The Return of Tarzan* (New York: Grosset and Dunlap, 1941).

the social place he believes her happiness requires. Worse, Jane is already promised to Clayton and would not permit herself to leave him, or, at least, to do so happily. So Tarzan decides to leave Jane with Clayton, thereby clearing her way to a happy life, although at the cost of his own happiness.[2]

As he marvels at Tarzan's self-sacrificing altruism, Clayton's own deliberations are a mass of self-serving "sophistries." *He* believes that Jane can never really be happy with him, since she loves Tarzan, and that he can assure Jane's happiness by relinquishing his social place to Tarzan, its rightful occupant, and releasing her from her promise. Since, however, he also believes that he would himself be better off with Jane, he persuades himself that it is only fitting that he live out the role Tarzan evidently intends for him.

The point of Burroughs's heavy-handed contrast is obvious enough. Clayton's self-deceit is a creature of civilized society, which demands that self-interested motivation be masked and indirect, laying low under rationalizations through which we self-servingly squelch naturally generous human motives. The ubiquity of masks, moreover, breeds cynicism about the very possibility of genuine other-concern, at least in polite society. Clayton can see Tarzan's leaving as self-sacrificial only because he regards Tarzan as a naïf, incapable of civilized sophistries. This gives Burroughs his final irony. In his admiration for Tarzan's noble self-sacrifice, Clayton finds the materials for his own self-serving rationalization.

But what is self-interest?[3] And what claim does it make on us? I shall argue that these questions are interrelated. So long as the concept of a person's interest is seen as having its natural home in a theory of *rational* action—as, roughly, whatever it makes sense for a person to want and, therefore, to attempt to realize—a wide view of self-interest will seem attractive, if not inevitable. To a first approximation, self-interest will seem to consist in whatever an agent (rationally) *takes* an interest in. I shall argue, however, that such views are too wide. They make self-sacrificial acts such as Tarzan's impossible, since anything worth some apparent sacrifice thereby becomes part of the agent's interest, and therefore no real sacrifice at all.[4] My contrary suggestion will be that self-interest and the desire to promote it are most naturally seen as expressions of self-*concern*. A person's interest is not the set, or weighted sum, of things in which he takes an interest. These, we might say, are his interests. The idea of a person's good or *interest*, I will propose, is one we need insofar as we (or he) can care about *him*.

To care about a person is not to care about whatever that person cares about, or would rationally care about, even if the person in question is

---

[2] Not to worry: Tarzan and Jane are happily reunited at the end of the novel.

[3] "Self-interest" is ambiguous as between a person's good or *interest*, on the one hand, and her desire to promote it (the interest she takes in her interest) on the other. Unless context makes clear otherwise, I will generally use "self-interest" in the former sense.

[4] On this point, see Mark Overvold, "Self-Interest and the Concept of Self-Sacrifice," *Canadian Journal of Philosophy*, vol. 10 (1980), pp. 105–18.

oneself. This will lead us to a narrower view of self-interest and moreover will link it, I shall suggest, less to a theory of rational desire and action than to something like morality, since in caring about someone (another or ourselves) we see that person's good as giving reasons to anyone, or at least to anyone who can care.

Perhaps ironically, if there is a natural home for the concept of interest (and therefore self-interest), it will likelier be one defined, like morality, by attitudes of concern and respect that have individual persons as objects. And this brings the interrelation between our two questions back into view. If self-interest is the object of a desire spawned by self-concern, and if self-concern is, as I shall argue, only incidentally egocentric—its object being, unlike that of attitudes *de se*, the individual one is, rather than oneself as such—then self-concern will be an instance, in one's own case, of an attitude one can have in principle toward any individual, a concern that the moral point of view is thought to express equally toward everyone.[5] It will follow, then, that only what can engage us from that perspective can be counted as part of a person's interest.

This reinforces the disconnection between interest and preference-satisfaction from a different direction. Thomas Scanlon and others have argued that the mere fact that something would further the satisfaction of someone's preference, even her rational preference, makes in itself no moral claim.[6] I may prefer some outcome both sensibly and strongly, but without some showing that it will make a difference to my (or someone else's) good or interest, or to our moral relations, it is hard to see what relevance this fact can have from a perspective that is rooted in equal concern and respect. Similarly, Amartya Sen has argued that the mere fact that someone prefers, even rationally, to suffer self-sacrificingly for some ideal does not lessen the moral reason to refrain from causing him suffering, even if in causing him suffering one does no harm to his ideal.[7] If the moral point of view is one of equal concern for everyone's good or interest, either actual or qua moral agent, these phenomena can be explained by the proposal that a person's good or interest consists, not in the realization of what that person (rationally) wants, but in what anyone would rationally want, insofar as he cares about that person.

II. SELF-INTEREST: THE SCOPE PROBLEM

I shall take it that a person's interest is no different from any of the following: her welfare, benefit, well-being, good, happiness, or what, in a

[5] A person's attitude is *de se* if it includes an ineliminable reference to him- or herself, as in: "He believes *he* is always being persecuted." See David Lewis, "Attitudes *De Dicto* and *De Se*," *Philosophical Review*, vol. 88 (1979), pp. 513–43.

[6] T. M. Scanlon, "Preference and Urgency," *Journal of Philosophy*, vol. 72 (1975), pp. 655–69. See also Thomas Nagel, *The View from Nowhere* (New York: Oxford University Press, 1986), pp. 166–71. Scanlon argues that preferences make, in themselves, no moral claim—not that considerations of interest do make such a claim.

[7] Amartya Sen, *Inequality Re-examined* (Oxford: Oxford University Press, 1992). I am grateful to David Sobel for this reference.

sense that I will explain shortly, would make her life go best. Philosophers sometimes distinguish within this set, but, as far as I can see, nothing ever dictates drawing the lines just where they do. For example, someone who holds an "objective" theory of a person's good or welfare, such as some version of what Derek Parfit calls an "objective-list" theory, might distinguish it from a theory of the person's happiness, reserving the latter term for some subjective state.[8] But this seems a semantic decision more than anything else. He might as well have included happiness along with welfare and good, and used some other term, say, "satisfaction," to refer to the subjective state.

There is, however, one distinction between different things that are meant by "a good life" that I do take seriously; and that is the distinction between a person's good, well-being, or interest, on the one hand, and the *worth* of her life, or parts of it, on the other. "A good life" may refer to the life that *benefits* the person most, in which her life goes best *for her*. This is the sense, I believe, that connects with self-interest (and with the person's well-being or good). Or it may refer to a *worthy* life for the person. Goodness as well-being is a life's being *desirable for* a person, in the sense that it is a life it would make sense to *desire for that person*, that is, would make sense for someone who cares for her (perhaps she herself) to desire for her. Whether a life is worthy, on the other hand, is a matter of its being *estimable* or admirable, rather than desirable.[9] Of course, any plausible theory of interest or well-being for human beings cannot ultimately be independent of considerations of worth. I shall return to these issues in Section VI.

I take it that the very idea of interest, benefit, or a person's good, therefore, contrasts with that of worth in referring to a value that *accrues to* a person and *exists in appreciation by* the person to whom it accrues. Doubtless, this is the source of hedonism's perennial attraction as a theory of interest or well-being. Although "appreciate" need not be taken subjectively, it can seem hard to see how else plausibly to take it.

What, then, is a person's interest, well-being, or good? In the past twenty-five years a number of philosophers have followed what they have taken to be Henry Sidgwick's lead in identifying it as the (ideal) object of the person's informed desires.[10] Sidgwick's own normative theory

---

[8] Derek Parfit, *Reasons and Persons* (Oxford: Clarendon Press, 1984), esp. appendix I.

[9] This distinction is sometimes put as that between prudential value and perfectionist value. As near as I can tell, the term "prudential value" derives from James Griffin, *Well-Being: Its Meaning, Measurement, and Moral Importance* (Oxford: Oxford University Press, 1986). On the distinction between prudential and perfectionist value, see L. Wayne Sumner, "The Subjectivity of Welfare," *Ethics*, vol. 105 (1995), pp. 764–90.

[10] Henry Sidgwick, *The Methods of Ethics*, 7th ed. (1907; reprint, London: Macmillan, 1967), pp. 111–12; further references will be noted parenthetically in the text as *ME*. Richard Brandt offered a similar definition of welfare in "Rationality, Egoism, and Morality," *Journal of Philosophy*, vol. 69 (1972), p. 686. John Rawls relies on Sidgwick's formulation in defining a rational life plan for a person in *A Theory of Justice* (Cambridge: Harvard University Press, 1971), p. 408. Peter Railton offers an account of a person's good in Sidgwick's manner, but with an important revision. For Railton, what is for a person's good is not what that person would want if he were fully informed, but what a fully informed version of himself would

of good was hedonistic, but there seems little doubt that a significant attraction of informed-desire accounts has been their ability to vindicate the widespread sense that much of what is valuable in our lives goes beyond subjective experience while preserving the subjectivity of value (for a person) as what is valuable *to him*. If, on reflection, it matters to us that our lives be real rather than the output of an experience machine, for example, informed-desire accounts can underwrite our sense that the former really is better (for us). As in James Griffin's example of Freud, who, appreciating what each would be like, preferred to spend his last days in torment rather than in a drug-induced euphoric confusion, it seems quite plausible that enduring even painful reality can sometimes be better for a person.[11] An informed-desire theory can explain why this is so.

At the same time, it seems unacceptably broad to include within a person's interest whatever he wants when fully informed, as the example of Tarzan shows. Call this the "scope problem." Tarzan believes that leaving Jane with Clayton is what he would informedly prefer, but Burroughs clearly does not want us to infer that Tarzan should therefore think this would be best *for him*. If that were so, leaving Jane would not be self-sacrificial. It would be doing what (Tarzan thinks) would most advance *his* good, as well as Jane's. An example from Parfit makes the point even more strikingly.[12] If, after an affecting conversation with a stranger whom you will never hear of again, you form a desire for her welfare, the satisfaction of that desire years later and unbeknownst to you does not add to *your* welfare.

Informed-desire accounts face objections on other fronts as well. One problem concerns temporal perspective. The time of something whose value for the person is in question may be well enough fixed, but what point in the person's life do we fix on to idealize her desires in order to determine the thing's value for her? If I want to know whether it would be in my interest to go to a concert a year from now, do I ask: What, if I were to know everything (including how it will then seem to me), would

---

want for himself as he actually is; see Peter Railton, "Moral Realism," *Philosophical Review*, vol. 95 (1986), pp. 163–207. This avoids what Robert K. Shope called the "conditional fallacy"; see Robert K. Shope, "The Conditional Fallacy in Contemporary Philosophy," *Journal of Philosophy*, vol. 75 (1978), pp. 397–413. See also Robert K. Shope, "Rawls, Brandt, and the Definition of Rational Desires," *Canadian Journal of Philosophy*, vol. 8 (1978), pp. 329–40. Railton, however, distinguishes between a person's good and her welfare; see note 24 below. James Griffin also defends a kind of informed-desire account in *Well-Being*. In *Impartial Reason*, I followed Sidgwick's formulation as an account of a rational conception of the good life, but distinguished it from an account of the person's good for reasons I hope to clarify and develop here. See *Impartial Reason*, p. 105.

For criticisms of full-information accounts of a person's good, see J. David Velleman, "Brandt's Definition of 'Good'," *Philosophical Review*, vol. 97 (1988), pp. 353–71; David Sobel, "Full Information Accounts of Well-Being," *Ethics*, vol. 104 (1994), pp. 784–810; and Connie S. Rosati, "Persons, Perspectives, and Full Information Accounts of the Good," *Ethics*, vol. 105 (1995), pp. 296–325.

[11] James Griffin, "Are There Incommensurable Values?" *Philosophy and Public Affairs*, vol. 7 (1977), pp. 59–79.

[12] Parfit, *Reasons and Persons*, p. 494.

I want now for then? Or do I ask: What would I then want for then? Or are facts about interest somehow relative to the temporal perspective of an agent deliberating about how to promote it?

A second issue concerns the difference between what a fully knowledgeable me would want in my circumstances and what a fully knowledgeable me would want for me in my circumstances as I actually am. How can it be in my interest to do what I *would* want were I to be fully knowledgeable and experienced if my relatively benighted state prevents me from appreciating the benefits that a fully knowledgeable and experienced me would realize?[13] I propose to set these two problems and others aside for the moment, however, to focus on the issue we have just raised concerning the scope of (informed) desires, the satisfaction of which a person's good or interest might be held to consist in.

Mark Overvold has suggested a restriction to deal with the scope problem: in order for the satisfaction of a(n informed) desire to add to a person's good, the person must himself be an "essential constituent" of the desired state of affairs. More specifically, in order for a desired outcome (at time t) to constitute a benefit to that person, the person's own existence (at t) must be a logically necessary condition of the outcome's obtaining (at t).[14] This restricts outcomes that can positively or negatively affect someone's interest to those within her own life. Since the object of Tarzan's desire that Jane be happy does not essentially involve him, its satisfaction does not count toward his welfare—and similarly for the desire for the once-met stranger's welfare in Parfit's example.

Gregory Kavka has argued against Overvold's restriction, saying that it would exclude such self-interested desires as the desire for posthumous fame. Were someone to neglect her duties in order to advance such an aim, Kavka points out, "we wouldn't hesitate to characterize it as selfish."[15] But desires may be selfish without being self-interested or such that their satisfaction contributes to self-interest.[16] For example, an action may be both selfish *and* self-destructive.[17] The all-too-familiar cases of men who kill their partners and children and then themselves would seem to be such instances. So from the fact that the desire for posthumous fame can motivate selfish behavior, we should not conclude that its satisfaction, even if informed, adds to a person's welfare.

[13] See the references to Robert K. Shope and Peter Railton in note 10.

[14] Overvold, "Self-Interest and the Concept of Self-Sacrifice," 117–18n. Overvold formulates this restriction to deal with a "self-sacrifice" objection to the sort of informed-desire account of self-interest that Richard Brandt proposes in "Rationality, Egoism, and Morality."

[15] Gregory S. Kavka, *Hobbesian Moral and Political Theory* (Princeton: Princeton University Press, 1986), p. 41.

[16] In fairness to Kavka, we should note that his primary interest is to fashion a category of "self-interested desire" for a workable formulation of psychological egoism, in order to evaluate whether Hobbes was a psychological egoist. A conception of self-interested desires broader than desires for self-interest might well be preferable for that purpose.

[17] So what makes a motive selfish? Good question. If selfishness is not always an (excessive) form of self-concern, it must include other forms of self-obsession (arrogance, for example) as well.

Of course, there might be other reasons for objecting to Overvold's restriction. Although a desire for posthumous fame might be selfish without being self-interested, it might be self-interested nonetheless. Perhaps posthumous fame can make an intrinsic addition to a person's welfare. We must remember, however, that the issue is not whether posthumous fame is something it can make sense for a person to care about, but whether its realization *benefits the person*. Self-sacrificial cases such as Tarzan's show that we must distinguish these two issues. Once we separate them, I think it is hard to see how things entirely beyond the boundaries of a person's life *can* benefit or harm that person intrinsically, how they can make an intrinsic difference in the value of life *for that person*.[18]

Let us take it provisionally, therefore, that any plausible informed-desire account of a person's interest would have to accept something like Overvold's restriction as a necessary condition. Combining the two as a putative sufficient condition generates an informed-desire version of what Parfit has called the *success theory*: something is in a person's interest if it advances what that person would (informedly) desire *for her life*.[19] How plausible is this theory? Again, the question is not whether it would make sense for a person to *take an interest* in whatever she would informedly desire for her life, but whether whatever satisfies this condition is thereby *in* her interest in the sense of being something that *benefits her* or makes her life go better *for her*.[20]

To see that it is not, consider Jane's situation. As Burroughs represents her, Jane's greatest desire is to do her duty. Having promised to marry Clayton, she believes she must ultimately do so (although she allows herself to believe that she may put him off for a while). Of course, Jane wishes desperately that she hadn't promised herself to Clayton and gotten into this situation—but there it is; she has. And what she wants most to do in her situation as she sees it (on what she takes to be good evidence) is to do her duty and marry Clayton. Moreover, her desire to do

---

[18] As Parfit points out, however, this does not entail that things outside the boundaries of a person's life cannot be part of something that does make an intrinsic difference to the person's welfare. Being a good parent and giving my children upbringings suitable to their futures may be an important constituent of my welfare—it may be part of what I want for *my* sake as well as for theirs—and its success conditions will depend on occurrences beyond my life's boundaries. (See Parfit, *Reasons and Persons*, p. 495.)

[19] Parfit, *Reasons and Persons*, p. 494.

[20] The success theory should also be understood to include a restriction to intrinsic desires. To see this, consider Tarzan's situation. Tarzan desires (informedly, we may suppose) that Jane be happy; but the satisfaction of this desire does not advance his interest according to the success theory, since its object (Jane's happiness) is not itself part of his life. To use Overvold's formulation, it is not a logically necessary condition of Jane's being happy that Tarzan exist. But consider Tarzan's (derived) desire that he live the rest of his life without Jane. This *is* a desire that satisfies Overvold's restriction. Suppose that Tarzan's view of things is correct, that Jane really would be happier if he were never to see her again. It will then be true that this is what Tarzan would want most with full information and experience. But if the satisfaction of his desire for Jane's happiness is not in his interest, then the satisfaction of his desire to live the rest of his life without her can hardly be so if the only reason he has the latter desire is because he has the former.

her duty is both intrinsic and one whose object concerns her own life. But that hardly makes it in her interest to marry Clayton. Of course, it may be in her interest nonetheless. For example, maybe (as Tarzan believes) she would be so miserable if she broke her promise that, in the circumstances, duty and interest coincide. But that would not be simply because her duty matters to her more than other things, but because of what her life would be like were she to break, or keep, her promise. What is true, of course, is that her duty matters to her more than her own interest.

This is only one example of a wide variety of desires that are intrinsic and that satisfy the Overvold restriction, but whose realization is not related in any principled way to the person's interest. In many such cases, it seems certain that the desire's satisfaction does not contribute to the person's good to a degree proportional to its strength, and it seems arguable that its satisfaction is not in the person's interest at all. Consider a consuming passion for fame during one's lifetime. A person may know what such fame would be like, and still desire it wildly out of proportion to any real benefit. The object of his desire unquestionably matters a great deal *to* him, but may nonetheless not be particularly good *for* him, although, of course, it may be. In such cases, I am inclined to think, what matters most to the person is not what *would* matter most to him *if he cared more about himself* and the quality of his own life.

I believe that the key to understanding the concept of interest or a person's good, is to see its connection to caring and concern. A person's interest is what we want promoted insofar as we care about that person.[21] If, consequently, any informed-desire standard can serve as a plausible criterion of interest, I think it is likely to be closer to something like the following. Something is in a person's interest if it is what that person would want for herself, as she actually is, insofar as she is fully knowledgeable and experienced *and* unreservedly concerned for herself.

III. Sidgwick's Account

I shall consider some consequences of this suggestion in Sections V and VI. At this point, however, I want to approach our problem anew from a different angle, by investigating Sidgwick's influential account of a person's good. Actually, Sidgwick gives several different formulations, and it is instructive to compare these. He begins with:

(1) [Something is desirable for a person if it is] what would be desired [by that person], with strength proportioned to the degree of desirability, if it were judged attainable by voluntary action,

---

[21] I do not, of course, mean that if my concern for someone makes me want something for her then this is sufficient for that thing to be something that would actually be good for her. It must be something it makes sense for someone who cares about her to want for her for her own sake.

supposing the desirer to have a perfect forecast, emotional as
well as intellectual, of the state of attainment or fruition. (*ME* 111)

A consequence of (1), Sidgwick believes, is:

(1') [M]y good on the whole is what I should actually desire and
seek if all the consequences of seeking it could be foreknown
and adequately realised by me in imagination at the time of
making the choice. (*ME* 111)

Sidgwick argues that (1) and (1') are inadequate because they are insufficiently attentive to comparisons and opportunity costs. Someone may
be well enough satisfied with something without its being for his good on
the whole, since it may make him relatively impervious to alternatives
which he might have preferred. So Sidgwick substitutes:

(2) [A] man's good on the whole is what he would now desire and
seek on the whole if all the consequences of all the different lines
of conduct open to him were accurately seen and adequately
realised in imagination at the present point in time. (*ME* 111–12)

With this classic formulation of Sidgwick's in hand, we may now return
to the "time of desire" issue we previously set aside. Notably, (1') and (2)
consider the question of what is for a person's good from the perspective
of an agent in a position to make choices that can affect its realization. To
determine whether it is for my good to attend a concert a year from now,
I am to consider what I would want *now for then* if I were fully informed,
including being informed about what it would be like to attend the concert then.[22] This has a number of interesting consequences. Most strikingly, it appears to make facts about a person's good relative to the
standpoint of an agent considering whether to seek it. It is logically possible, for example, that even when preceded by fully informed and imaginatively vivid consideration of the same facts and features, my desires
with respect to the impending concert could change. And if so, then either
there is no enduring fact of the matter about the contribution going to the
concert on that date would make to my good, or any such facts are
relative to an agent's choice context.

But why should the contribution going to a concert a year from now
would actually make to my good depend in any way on what I would
want *now*, even were I to take fully into account what it would be like for
me then? If we distinguish the issue of whether going to the concert
would be *in* my interest from the question of whether it would make

---

[22] For the distinction between "now for then" and "then for then" preferences, see R. M.
Hare, *Moral Thinking* (Oxford: Oxford University Press, 1981), pp. 101–6.

sense for me now to *take* an interest in going to the concert a year from now, it seems fairly clear that while what I would informedly want is arguably relevant to the latter question, it has no evident relevance to the former. Formulation (2) conflates these two issues.

We can see this more clearly by noting how Sidgwick goes on. He says of (2) that it proposes a deliberative ideal that "is entirely interpretable in terms of *fact*, actual or hypothetical, and does not introduce any judgment of value . . . still less any 'dictate of Reason'" (*ME* 112). Consequently, it leaves out a central aspect of the idea of a person's good as he understands it, namely, that it is an end the person *ought* to seek. So Sidgwick suggests a substitute for (2), albeit one that "keep[s] the notion of 'dictate' or 'imperative' merely implicit and latent":

(3) "Ultimate good on the whole for me" [means] what I should practically desire if my desires were in harmony with reason, assuming my own existence alone to be considered. (*ME* 112)

The relative clause, "assuming my own existence alone to be considered," is a fascinating addition, to which I shall return presently. The point I wish to make now is that Sidgwick evidently treats it as an adequacy condition on an account of a person's good that it secure what he takes to be its necessary practical relevance to the agent's deliberative standpoint at earlier times. To count as an adequate account of a person's good, a theory must ensure that what it reckons to be *in* a person's interest is something in which reason dictates that he should *take* an interest (including that he should do so at any time at which that thing might be promoted).

Something like this movement of thought, I believe, lies behind the acceptance of informed-desire theories of a person's good or interest, generally. What an agent can herself be brought to desire through improved knowledge, experience, or imagination offers an "internal reason" in Bernard Williams's sense.[23] Informed-desire theories thus promise an account of interest that guarantees that if something is in our interest, we have reason to take an interest in it.

However, while informed-desire theories may be plausible as theories of rational choice—theories of what it is rational for an agent to take an interest in—their plausibility may not be preserved when we consider them as accounts of what is in a person's interest. While it is plausible that in order to establish that going to a concert a year from now is something it is rational for me to take an interest in now, some practical connection to my current deliberative standpoint must be shown, it is simply not obvious why this should be necessary for something in the future to be in my interest. Whether it would benefit me to go to a concert a year from

---

[23] Bernard Williams, "Internal and External Reasons," in Williams, *Moral Luck* (Cambridge: Cambridge University Press, 1981), pp. 101–13.

now seems not to depend on anything about my deliberative perspective now. So far as I can see, when we have established that some future action would be in my interest, it is still very much an open question whether that is something it is rational for me to take an interest in now.

Of course, we might, as a semantic matter, simply use 'in the agent's interest' to refer to whatever is useful in promoting the agent's (current) interests, her rational interests, or some subset of these. If we do, however, we lose the conceptual connection between interest, on the one hand, and benefit, well-being, or welfare, on the other, which are not deliberation-relative.[24] The benefits of going to a concert a year hence do not accrue to me now (or to some present "stage" of me), no matter how much I now care about going then.[25]

Sidgwick is a hedonist; he believes, therefore, that the best life for a person is the one that offers her the most pleasure in the long run. But whether my going to a concert a year from now would be hedonistically optimal may depend only minimally on my current choice context.[26] Why, then, does Sidgwick think that what I would ideally want now is whatever would turn out to be hedonistically optimal for me overall? Formulation (3) provides the key. My good is what I would desire "if my desires were *in harmony with reason*" (*ME* 112, emphasis added). Sidgwick believes that it never makes sense for someone to want something other than a pleasurable experience.[27] If, consequently, my desires with respect to future experiences are out of proportion to the pleasure I expect from them—for example, if I care less now about the pleasures of a concert a year in the future than I do about other, more proximate things—then either my proximate desires take things other than pleasurable consciousness as objects, which Sidgwick believes they cannot rationally do, or they conflict with "an equal regard for all the moments of our conscious experience . . . [that] is an essential characteristic of rational conduct" (*ME* 111).

In earlier editions of the *Methods*, Sidgwick brings hedonism more directly into his definition of a person's good:

[24] Something like this may be at work in Peter Railton's remark that his distinctive informed-desire account of a person's good should not be regarded as an account of that person's "welfare." See Railton, "Facts and Values," *Philosophical Topics*, vol. 14 (1986), p. 30, n. 9.
[25] Of course, some of the benefits may accrue to me now, like the pleasure of knowing that I will be going. I take it for granted that it is the (enduring) person who benefits, not a "person-stage." On this point, see David Brink, "Sidgwick and the Rationale for Rational Egoism," in *Essays on Henry Sidgwick*, ed. Bart Schultz (Cambridge: Cambridge University Press, 1992), pp. 199-240.
[26] That is, it would depend on my current choice context only insofar as there are current pleasures and pains that are relevant to a decision to do now what would be necessary to go to the concert a year from now.
[27] That is, a pleasurable experience for someone or other. See Sidgwick, *The Methods of Ethics*, book III, ch. XIV, "Ultimate Good." I am not sure if this is precisely what Derek Parfit has in mind when he cites the "in harmony with reason" formulation to show that Sidgwick holds what he (Parfit) calls a "critical present-aim theory," but it supports that conclusion. See Parfit, *Reasons and Persons*, p. 500.

(2') [W]hat he would desire on the whole if all the consequences of all the different lines of conduct open to him were *actually exercising on him an impulsive force proportioned to the desires or aversions which they would excite if actually experienced.*[28]

From Sidgwick's account of pleasure as desirable consciousness, together with his belief that we would desire nothing on reflection except (desirable) consciousness, it will follow that a person's good lies along the "line of conduct" that promises the most pleasure. Formulation (2') is effectively a procedural version of the "equal regard" constraint referred to in the previous paragraph, interpreted in the light of hedonism.

To conclude our investigation of Sidgwick's account, I want to note two important elements that those who draw from him frequently ignore. First, as I observed briefly before, in addition to including an explicit restriction to *rational* desires, Sidgwick's definition of a person's good is also restricted to desires that concern only the person herself. A person's good is what that person would desire were her desires "in harmony with reason, *assuming [her] own existence alone to be considered*" (*ME* 112, emphasis added). Second, even before he states formulation (1), Sidgwick restricts it to what a person desires both *intrinsically* ("for itself") and *"for himself—not benevolently for others"* (*ME* 109, emphasis added).

Both restrictions are important, the second, especially so, in view of the connection I have suggested between self-interest and self-concern. If we take Sidgwick literally here, we have to interpret a desire *for oneself* as not simply a desire *with respect to oneself* but as a self-analog of benevolence, something that could motivate action *for one's own sake*. This effectively restricts Sidgwick's informed-desire theory of a person's good to desires whose objects are desired out of a self-concern that is the analog in one's own case of benevolence.

As should be evident from Section II, I regard this restriction as well-motivated. If the notion of rational or informed desire is to enter into an account of a person's interest, it will not be through the idea of what that person would sensibly desire, or even what he would sensibly desire with respect to himself and his own life, but through some notion of what someone who cared for him (perhaps he himself) would sensibly desire *for him(self)*.

Now it is central to the way Sidgwick sees things that a person's own good necessarily makes a rational claim on that person. Nothing can count as an adequate account of a person's interest or good unless it secures the rational dictate to promote it. So far as I can see, though, practical reason includes no intrinsic requirement that we care either about others or about ourselves, since rational agency seems possible

[28] Henry Sidgwick, *The Methods of Ethics*, 3d ed. (London: Macmillan, 1884), p. 108, emphasis added. This passage is quoted and usefully discussed in Roger Crisp, "Sidgwick and Self-Interest," *Utilitas*, vol. 2 (1990), pp. 267–80.

without even the capacity to care about a person, oneself or another, for that person's sake.[29] Because I regard the self-concern restriction as well-motivated, however, I draw the conclusion that there is no fundamental rational requirement to promote one's own interest or good on the whole.[30] Others may agree with me that practical reason does not dictate either self-concern or benevolence, but want to preserve a basic connection between a person's good and what that person has reason to do. This will require them to reject a connection between self-interest and self-concern and to move toward a wider view of self-interest. I turn next, therefore, to the question of whether there is some rational requirement to pursue one's good on the whole.

IV. SELF-INTEREST AND RATIONAL CHOICE

Sidgwick is a hedonist about a person's good or interest *and* about what it makes sense for a person to desire and take an interest in. I believe that is why he thinks that a person's good must make a rational claim on her.

But why must these two views go together? Why couldn't hedonism be true as a theory of interest, welfare, or benefit, but false as a theory of rational desire and choice? I am not suggesting that hedonism *is* true as a theory of interest or welfare, but it seems more plausible to think of it in that way than as an account of rational desire and choice. The very idea of interest or welfare, as I have said, is of a value that accrues to and exists in being appreciated by some individual. And if, like Sidgwick, one thinks of pleasures as experiences or feelings that are "apprehended as desirable by the sentient individual at the time of feeling [them]," then a welfare or interest hedonism may seem a natural conclusion (*ME* 129). But this progression of thought requires no view whatsoever concerning whether a person's (future) good or interest, so conceived, makes a rational claim on an agent deliberating about what she should take an interest in or do. One could be led to a hedonism of welfare or interest on these grounds while holding steadfastly to some version of what Parfit calls a "present-aim theory" of rational choice, for example. Thus, I might simultaneously think that it would be in my interest to go to a concert a year from now, because it would give me pleasure, but also believe that this makes no

[29] Of course, Sidgwick does not really think that reason dictates that we care about ourselves or others in the sense I have in mind either. Rather, he thinks that among the self-evident axioms are rational dictates such as "a smaller present good is not to be preferred to a greater future good," "a rational being is bound to aim at good generally . . . not merely a particular part of it," and so on (*ME* 381, 382). However, to arrive at the principles of rational prudence and benevolence, these must themselves be interpreted in terms (indeed, solely in terms) of persons' goods, of what is good *for persons*. That is, it must be true that what is good for persons (either for oneself or for persons generally) should matter to a rational agent. And I cannot see how that could be true unless practical reason could somehow dictate that one care for oneself (and for others).

[30] It is consistent with this that there could be a derivative rational requirement for agents with a certain kind of psychology (maybe ours) to care about themselves or others, if rational deliberation would give rise, given their psychology, to such concern.

significant rational claim on my current deliberations if, on reflection, I care relatively little about my overall interest.

Moreover, not all objections to a hedonist theory of rational choice obviously apply to a hedonism of interest or welfare. For example, Jane thinks she should marry Clayton because she has promised to do so. She thinks not just that it would be morally wrong, in some externalist sense, to fail to marry him, but that there is decisive reason for her to do so. We can imagine that she also thinks that this has nothing to do with considerations of anyone's pleasure, and, therefore, that she would reject a hedonist theory of rational choice. But this would not commit her to rejecting a hedonist theory of welfare or interest. Indeed, one could be a hedonist about welfare or interest while holding that there are all sorts of things—ideals, norms, moral principles, projects, aesthetic or religious conceptions, and so on—which cannot be understood hedonistically but which nonetheless make a rational claim in deliberation.

The fact that hedonism can have an appeal as a theory of interest that does not transfer to a hedonist theory of rational choice shows that we do well to separate these two matters. We should not follow Sidgwick's lead in supposing that something cannot count as an adequate theory of interest or good unless it secures a rational claim to promote it.

One thing that separates the question of what it is rational for a person to choose or do from the issue of what is in her interest is the "internalism requirement." Philosophers of very different fundamental commitments— both Humeans and Kantians, for instance—find it plausible to assume that in order for something to make a rational claim on an agent, it must be something that can engage her practically in deliberation.[31] Unless a consideration is one by which an agent would be motivated were she to take account of it rationally, it can provide her no reason to act. To be a reason for her, a consideration must be something *on* which she could (autonomously) act.

What makes the internalist requirement a plausible constraint on a theory of rational choice has to do with the nature of reasons for acting and their essential connection to deliberation from the agent's point of view. When it comes to the question of a person's welfare or interest, however, these features are not in play. Indeed, a being can have an interest or welfare without being an agent at all. Doubtless it is true, as Peter Railton has argued, that a plausible theory of a person's good or interest must be tied *somehow* to what can interest or motivate that person,

---

[31] Compare, for example, Williams, "Internal and External Reasons" with Christine Korsgaard, "Skepticism about Practical Reason," *Journal of Philosophy*, vol. 83 (1986), pp. 5–26. The term "internalist requirement" derives from Korsgaard's article. I discuss the intuitive ideas underlying empirical naturalist internalism, on the one hand, and autonomist internalism, on the other, in "Internalism and Agency," *Philosophical Perspectives*, vol. 6 (1992), pp. 155–74. I discuss the development of these two traditions among the seventeenth- and eighteenth-century British Moralists in my book *The British Moralists and the Internal 'Ought': 1640–1740* (Cambridge: Cambridge University Press, 1995).

on pain of his being "intolerably alienated."[32] But, Sidgwick to the contrary, there seems to be nothing in the very idea of self-interest that guarantees any rational dictate to promote it.

Parfit has argued, partly along similar lines, that some version of a present-aim theory provides a more plausible theory of rational choice than does a self-interest theory.[33] This may not cut against Sidgwick, however, since what Parfit calls a "critical" present-aim theory *could* hold that the only desires that survive *rational* reflection (that are "in harmony with reason") are those for one's own good on the whole (or for pleasure more generally).[34] To put it another way, there is a way of interpreting the internalism requirement, such that a proponent of the self-interest theory can claim his theory satisfies it just by virtue of claiming that the desire for one's greatest good is inherently rational. But interpreted this way, the internalism requirement has no teeth. Any considerations put forward as reasons can be held to satisfy it, since it can always be said that an agent would be motivated by them *if rational* (that is, if she were adequately responsive to reasons).

To interpret the internalism requirement in the proper spirit, we need to distinguish dependent from independent variables. Once we allow a substantive view about reasons to drive our standard of rational reflection, we risk a toothless internalism. The internalism requirement should therefore be understood to hold that in order to be a reason for someone to act, a consideration must be something she would be moved by on rational reflection, where what counts as rational reflection is not itself determined by some prior theory of reasons (such as the self-interest theory). For this reason, I think internalists should favor what Parfit calls a "deliberative" rather than a critical version of the present-aim theory.[35]

One thing at issue between present-aim and self-interest theories of rational choice concerns temporal context. According to deliberative present-aim theories, whatever makes a rational claim must have some practical relevance to the agent's deliberation at the time of choice. Again, however, there seems to be no reason to suppose that what is in a person's interest must meet such a condition. Whether it would be to my benefit to attend a concert a year hence seems to be one question. And, if it would, whether that gives me a reason now to take an interest in doing so seems to be another. Only the second question, it seems, requires practical connection to the agent's deliberative perspective.

Now Sidgwick allows that one might sensibly ask, from the present perspective, whether there is reason to do what would be for one's good

---

[32] Railton, "Facts and Values," p. 9.

[33] Parfit, *Reasons and Persons*, pp. 117–94.

[34] See note 27.

[35] Note that internalists are by no means restricted to anything like Richard Brandt's notion of cognitive psychotherapy as a deliberative ideal. I argue for a more Kantian ideal in *Impartial Reason*, pp. 201–39.

on the whole. But he formulates the challenge this way: "Why should I sacrifice a present pleasure for a greater one in the future?" (*ME* 418). And he evidently thinks it a serious challenge only for those who hold Humean views of the self and personal identity (*ME* 419). But this way of posing the challenge already assumes (better, insinuates) a form of egoism, namely, what Parfit calls "hedonistic egoism of the present."[36] Rather than asking what necessarily connects long-run self-interest to an agent's rational concerns (as required by a present-aim theory), it seeks to determine the relation of long-run self-interest to a particular concern (to have pleasure now), whose rational standing it insinuates. Posed in this way, the challenge can reasonably be met.[37] If the problem is simply to justify a *sacrifice* of some present good to oneself, then it is surely enough to say that it is to procure some greater good to oneself in the future, which will more than compensate the sacrifice. Only temporally extended beings can be benefited or harmed, so the present and the future are merely different times at which one can be benefited, not the locations of different beneficiaries, me-now versus me-then.[38] The real challenge to the self-interest theory comes, as Parfit argues, not from an egoism of the present moment, but from the present-aim theory.

V. Self-Interest and Self-Concern

Let us return now to viewing self-interest from the perspective of self-concern. We can begin with an example to illustrate that although concern for a person gives rise to a desire for her interest or welfare, it is not similarly related to a desire for outcomes in which she takes an interest, even a rational interest. Suppose your friend Sheila is in the following situation. By donating all her disposable wealth she can realize an outcome she cares very much about, say, the rebuilding to a certain degree, D, of a city ravaged by war. But there is a catch. Sheila also has a degenerative disease, which, if it is not checked, will create memory loss and confusion severe enough so that she will be unsure where her money has gone and unable even to hold stable beliefs about the state of rebuilding in the war-ravaged city. Happily, there is a relatively inexpensive drug that can arrest the symptoms of Sheila's disease without side effects. However, the drug is not free, Sheila will not accept donations, and she cares so much about rebuilding the city that, even though the difference the cost of the drug would make in the rebuilding effort is quite small (call it d), she nonetheless wants (and would continue to want on reflection) to forgo the drug and donate all she has to the rebuilding effort.

Sheila ranks the outcome of the city's being rebuilt to degree D, together with her advanced disease, memory loss, and uncertainty about

---

[36] Parfit, *Reasons and Persons*, pp. 141–42.
[37] As David Brink has argued in "Sidgwick and the Rationale for Rational Egoism."
[38] On this point, see *ibid.*

the city's actual state (call this outcome O_1), higher than the outcome of the city's being rebuilt to degree D *minus* d but with her knowing about the rebuilding and her role in it, and a generally improved mental state (call this outcome O_2). You are convinced that Sheila prefers O_1 to O_2, and that this ordering of outcomes would survive reflection. You care about Sheila and thus desire what is in her interest (for her good). Does caring about her and wanting what is in her interest dictate your ordering these outcomes in the same way Sheila does, even on reflection? It seems obvious that it does not. Although Sheila prefers O_1 to O_2, this in no way directs your concern for her to the same ordering. On the contrary, insofar as you care about Sheila and what is in *her* interest, wouldn't your ordering be the opposite of hers? Wouldn't you prefer O_2 to O_1? (Notice, by the way, that while the quality of Sheila's experience in these two outcomes probably plays a significant role in your ordering of them, insofar as you care about her, it is not the only factor. In O_2, Sheila would *know* about the city's improved state and her role in it. We shall return to these matters in Section VI.)

Of course, even if you would prefer O_2 to O_1, insofar as you care about Sheila, this would not necessarily give you reason to subvert her wishes. In addition to being concerned for her and her well-being, you may also think that you should respect her wishes. Your concern for her for her sake may be in tension with your respect and concern for her as an autonomous moral agent.[39] One strategy, which would make clear both your concern and your respect for Sheila would be to offer to care for her during her illness. This would communicate to her the seriousness of your estimate of the costs she is imposing on herself (and on people who care about her) as well as your respect.[40]

The sense that informed-preference views of interest face a scope problem arises independently of any thought that the idea of interest depends on that of concern for a person for her sake. The example of Tarzan shows that. We sense a gap between options Tarzan rationally prefers and what is in his interest. What Sheila's example shows is that the proposal that interest depends on concern can explain why such a gap should exist. If what it is for something to be in Sheila's interest is for it to make sense for someone who cares about her to desire it for her sake, it follows that if Sheila's ranking and that of someone who cares for her were to diverge in this way, this would explain why even though Sheila rationally prefers O_1 to O_2, O_2 is nonetheless more in her interest (better *for her*) than O_1.

Of course, this is not the only hypothesis that can explain why a gap exists between a person's interest and what he (rationally) takes an interest in. But a "rational-care theory" of interest has virtues that other theories that can also explain the gap do not. For example, meta-ethical

---

[39] I owe this point to Tom Hill.
[40] I thank Jennifer Roback Morse for this suggestion.

hedonisms and objective-list accounts, which hold that being in a person's interest is the same thing as being, or being a means to, pleasure or something on a list of goods, also entail that what is in a person's interest can diverge from what he takes an interest in, perhaps even a rational interest. But they seem unable to capture the *normativity* or recommending power that is intrinsic to the very idea of a person's interest or good. We can know that something will give pleasure or that it is on the list and still ask why this creates normative reasons. If, however, a person's interest just consists in whatever it makes sense for someone who cares about that person to want for her for her sake, then normativity is built in.

The idea is not that a person's interest makes a (rational) claim on any agent, or even, necessarily, on the agent herself. As I argued in Section IV, that it does not is an objection to rational-preference theories of interest. The normative claim of a person's interest is rather on any person who cares about that person for her own sake.[41] The proposal is thus able to explain all three of the following: (i) why a person's interest does not make the kind of normative claim on her that rational-preference theories of interest suppose; (ii) why a gap exists between what is in a person's interest and what he takes a rational interest in; and (iii) why being in a person's interest includes an essential normative component nonetheless, making a rational claim on anyone who cares about the person.

Despite these virtues, a rational-care theory of interest may still seem problematic. Don't we need to understand the idea of interest first before we can understand what care is? I don't think so. This might be true if caring for someone were the same thing as desiring the promotion of his good or interest, but it is not. We can see this by noting that while the fact that a person cares for someone can explain why that person desires the promotion of his interest, the reverse is not true. We cannot explain the person's concern for someone by pointing to the person's desire for his good. There can be desires for the promotion of someone's interest for *its sake*, moreover, that are entirely unrelated to care or a desire to benefit him for *his sake*. It is entirely conceivable that someone might find the idea of promoting someone's benefit an intrinsically attractive option without really caring about him at all. Whatever their more specific structure, care and concern seem related to a whole complex of forms of emotional engagement, sensitivity, and attention in ways that a simple desire that another be benefited need not be.

When we care about someone, we desire things for her *for her sake*. The object of care is the person *herself*, not some state or property involving her. In caring for her, we, of course, want certain states and properties

---

[41] That is, the normative claim that is intrinsic to the concept of interest. It may follow from a theory of rationality, together with facts about an agent's psychological makeup, that rational deliberation (including, say, vivid consideration of a person's plight) would trigger psychological mechanisms leading that agent to care. And if that were so, then a person's interest would have a normative claim on such an agent. Maybe each of us is such an agent.

involving her to be realized. When they derive from care, however, such desires also have an "indirect object" in addition to these direct objects. In caring for her, we want these things *for her*.[42] This does not mean just that we want the properties and states to involve her, as opposed to someone else—or even that the desires are to be understood *de re* rather than *de dicto*. We want them for her *for her sake*.

There is, of course, much to be learned about the nature of care, but the phenomenon is familiar enough, as are many of its parameters. We know, for example, that we are likelier to care about someone when we engage her and her situation empathically, and that the reverse process holds as well. And even if we do not know very much about what care is, we may know it when we see it. As far as a rational-care theory of interest goes, it is enough that there be facts of the matter about whether someone cares for a person that are independent of any fact about interest. And it is enough for us to be able to put the theory to use that we can recognize instances of caring.

A rational-care theory of interest will not, of course, hold that someone who cares for another can make it true that something is in that person's interest just by desiring it for him for his sake. In order for a thing to be in a person's interest, it must be something which someone who cared about the person would *rationally* want for him for his sake.

Rational-care theories can be neutral regarding which theory of rationality and rational desire is correct, but they do hold that the existence of nonrelative facts about a person's interest depends on the existence of facts about what anyone who cares for that person would rationally want for him, insofar as she cares. There is thus no conceptual guarantee that self-interest makes any normative claim on the agent which it does not make on others. On the contrary, what is guaranteed is that if something is in someone's interest, then it is something which anyone who cares for that person (the agent himself or someone else) has reason to want for his sake.

On a rational-care theory, self-interest is simply a person's interest, viewed as his own, and its normative claim is independent of its being his own. In caring about oneself in the way that gives rise to the desire to promote one's good *for one's own sake*, one sees one's good as worth promoting in seeing oneself as care-worthy. This is not an attitude *de se*. One values oneself, and one's interest, from a perspective one can share with anyone who can care.

If self-interest is related in this way to self-concern, its natural home seems likelier to be in a realm of practical thought that is conceptually tied to regard for individual persons than, as is ordinarily supposed, in a theory of rational choice. A natural way of thinking about *morality* is as involving a way of viewing our lives from the perspective of an equal

---

[42] On this point, see Anderson, *Value in Ethics and Economics*, pp. 26–30. I am indebted to David Velleman for the term "indirect object" in this context. Thanks also to Tom Hurka for pressing me on the distinction between caring about someone and caring about her states.

concern and respect for all persons. Here again, it seems relatively clear that a concern for the interest of a person—whether as a moral agent, à la Kant, or on some thicker conception of human interest—does not translate into some desire for whatever outcomes the person herself takes a (rational) interest in. The ironic upshot of viewing self-interest through the lens of self-concern, then, is that the kind of normative claim self-interest makes on a person is likely to seem more like a moral claim than a *de se* rational claim.

VI. INTEREST AND WORTH

Finally, what does viewing self-interest from the perspective of self-concern tell us about the relation between welfare and worth, and about whether the conditions of a person's interest being realized are subjective or objective? In closing, I want to make some brief remarks about these questions.

As I mentioned at the outset, I believe that the question of what makes for a good human life is ambiguous. We could be asking: What makes for a life that is best for the person leading it? That is, what life most benefits a person or is most in her interest? Or we might be asking: What sort of life has greatest worth? Here, we are asking about what is admirable or estimable. And we appeal to a form of value that is quite different from that of a person's good or interest and that is not person-relative in any obvious way. Welfare or self-interest is what is good *for a person*. But worth or worthiness is not a form of welfare or goodness *for* anyone.[43] When we think of value as what is meaningful and significant, or as what can inspire and elevate, it is worth rather than welfare that we have in mind.[44]

This suggests that perfectionist theories may be most naturally viewed as theories of worth. Even if this is their most straightforward interpretation, however, it would be a mistake to think that perfectionists do not also frequently make claims about welfare or interest. Worth may not be the same thing as interest but may still be, for human beings, an essential element of any life that can be good *for them*. Surely this is a natural way of taking Aristotle's claim that human flourishing consists in a life of excellent distinctively human activity.

The question of how welfare interacts with worth is but one aspect of the more general question of how subjective features of a life (its felt qualities, for instance) and other, objective features interact in determin-

---

[43] Nonetheless, I have argued that they can be seen as a kind of *intersubjective value* (*Impartial Reason*, pp. 130–67). For a general theory of plural kinds or forms of value, grounded in a variety of distinctive evaluative emotions and attitudes, see Anderson, *Value in Ethics and Economics*.

[44] Compare Charles Taylor on "strong evaluation" in Taylor, "The Diversity of Goods," in his *Philosophy and the Human Sciences* (Cambridge: Cambridge University Press, 1985), pp. 23–47.

ing a person's interest. As experience-machine examples show, we clearly care very much about things other than the subjective quality of experience. To what extent, then, and in what ways does the welfare or interest of a person depend on his own subjective states, and to what extent does it depend on objective factors?

Although there is nothing simple to be said about this, I believe that viewing this question from the perspective of care and concern is helpful. What we want to know is: What should we wish for a person for his sake? Or, if it is a question of self-interest: What should we wish for ourselves for our own sake? From this standpoint, it seems inevitable that some mix of subjective and objective factors will be relevant. In caring for someone, we naturally enough want for him a life that includes worthy human activity, such as mutual love and creative expression, but we also want the person himself to value (esteem) these activities, and to derive pleasure and satisfaction from them. What we want for those we care about is the right match between the subjective and the objective. We want lives for them that are genuinely meaningful and significant, that they can themselves affirm and accurately grasp in their relation to others and to the world, and that they can fully enjoy and relish.[45] And if self-interest is what we want when we care about ourselves, that is the kind of life that will be in our own interest as well.

Philosophy, University of Michigan

---

[45] Derek Parfit suggests something like this:

> What is good for someone is neither just what Hedonists claim, nor just what is claimed by Objective List Theorists. We might believe that if we had *either* of these, *without the other*, what we had would have little or no value. We might claim, for example, that what is good or bad for someone is to have knowledge, to be engaged in rational activity, to experience mutual love, and to be aware of beauty, while strongly wanting just these things. (Parfit, *Reasons and Persons*, p. 502)

WHO IS RATIONAL ECONOMIC MAN?*

By Jennifer Roback Morse

I. Introduction

There is, in Sarajevo, a man who comes out into the streets each day and plays his cello on the sidewalk. He does this at the same time each day, no matter how much shooting or shelling is going on, no matter how great the danger to himself. He describes himself as having decided to take a stand for beauty in the face of horror. Can the rational choice paradigm, as currently practiced in the various disciplines of economics, philosophy, political science, and law, offer an account of this man's decision and his behavior?

This admirable man seems to be a rebuke to the philosophies of calculated self-interest. Can we offer some account of his behavior, without descending into the tautological claim that he did what he did because he wanted to? Can we offer some insight into his wants that will make him intelligible? And not only intelligible, but can we account for him in a way that highlights his admirability, rather than suggesting that he is in some way an aberration, or perhaps even a fool?

There is a deep disorder within the human condition. All of the essays in the present volume point to this fact in one way or another. Some characterize the disorder as a conflict between virtue and self-interest. Others point to the dichotomy between the individual and other persons as being the source of the tension between morality and self-interest. Some of the essays attempt to resolve the tension by collapsing the two categories into each other. Moral or virtuous behavior then becomes a variety of self-interest, because the concept of the self and the self's interests has been expanded.

Even when this redefinition of the self is successfully articulated and defended, however, the disorder in the human condition continues to emerge. For we do not always do what is good for us, even when we

* I am grateful to the many people who discussed the material in this essay with me. These people include George Ainsle, Don Boudreaux, Margaret Brinig, Father Mark Broski, OSB, Nicholas Capaldi, Del Gardner, David Levy, Loren Lomasky, Robert Morse, Sam Pappenfuss, Ellen Paul, Steven Rhoads, Father James V. Schall, S.J., Barbara Bennett Woodhouse, and the students in my doctoral level course in microeconomics. I am also grateful to the other contributors to this volume, and to Luis Ravina, Dean of the University of Navarra School of Economics and Business Administration, for the opportunity to present this work there. The Lynde and Harry Bradley Foundation provided financial support. Father Mark Broski, OSB, produced the final versions of the graphs.

know the good. Animals instinctively do what is good for them. They are seldom observed in self-defeating behaviors. On the other hand, sentient beings who were perfect would always choose rightly.

Human beings are more than animals, but less than perfect sentient beings. We have an animal component to our nature. We have instincts that lead us toward pleasure and away from pain. But those very same instincts for the preservation of the body can sometimes mislead us. As thinking beings, we have deep longings for the good, the true, and the beautiful. Yet we very often take steps that lead us away from these ultimate goods. Thus, we can observe the frightening and unpalatable fact that disorder is deeply rooted within the human person, and in the human condition. And we must admit that, sometimes, this disorder is bigger than we are, and is more than we can manage.

In the course of this ongoing dialogue, one fact becomes evident: We cannot have a coherent theory about self-interest unless we correctly understand the self. That is, we must have a coherent theory about the nature of the human person. In this volume composed predominantly of work by philosophers, I, a lowly economist, will venture to offer an account of the human person.

This might seem odd; for the economist's view of the person contains numerous controversial points. Economists use as a working hypothesis the claim that people act consistently in their own self-interest. The economist finds the person already in possession of full knowledge of his preferences over goods, services, and activities. The economist then claims that persons behave consistently with those preferences, and that persons respond to incentives in a systematic way. This behavior is described by economists as rational.

In this essay, I argue that the economist's view is incomplete. But I also argue that this vision can be expanded to encompass important elements that are currently omitted. The technical modifications I offer are quite modest: they can be readily accommodated within the paradigm as currently practiced. However, the philosophical leap that I propose to economics seems to be more profound. And I hope that some of the economic approach that I bring to bear on these questions will offer some insight to the philosophers among the readers.

II. THE PROBLEM: THE ECONOMIST'S VIEW OF HUMAN NATURE

My modifications to consumer theory offer an account of several observed behaviors that are not readily explained within the current paradigm. I offer a model that allows the rational person to be at war with himself, some of the time. I offer an account of why the rational person might want to constrain himself. I also show how a rational person could face temptations: that prices could be too low or incomes could be too high.[1]

Currently, the economist's view of the person is that a person is a utility function. This utility function summarizes all the person's orderings or comparisons among various goods. Once the economist knows these pref- erence rankings as summarized by the utility function, the economist knows all that he needs to know about the person. The person is perfectly defined by the content of his preferences. The economic analysis proceeds as follows: the person's utility function confronts the relative prices of various choices that are given to him from outside of himself. The person calculates which of the options maximizes his utility. The person moves instantly to act in accordance with the calculation he has performed.

Thus, Homo economicus, rational economic man, is not really a choos- ing person in any meaningful sense. There is only calculation, no real choice. For under the standard assumptions about preference orderings, there is only one possible outcome to the confrontation of a given utility function with a given set of relative prices. There is no room for delib- eration, regret, or indecision, experiences that are familiar to everyone.

We might say that the utility function as envisioned by economists subsumes these considerations. The analysis proceeds as if the person instantly called up his utility function, immediately calculated his mar- ginal rate of substitution, or internal price ratio, compared it with the market price ratio, and moved directly to act in accordance with his calculations. Economists are aware, of course, that this model is not de- scriptively accurate; but they have argued that because the predictive power of the model is both deep and broad, the descriptive inaccuracy can be safely overlooked.

Economics did not always have this rather truncated vision of the human person and of human rationality. The father of economics, Adam Smith, was, of course, a professor of moral philosophy and of jurispru- dence. Smith's analysis of sympathy, or the connection between persons, is an important complement to his analysis of self-interested individuals acting in the market. In the nineteenth century, however, economics came to be dominated by utilitarian thought, which had a tendency to reduce moral as well as economic decision-making to a simple calculation, over a simple dimension, happiness. In the early twentieth century, the mar- ginalist revolution in economics also promoted an emphasis on calcula- tion, rather than reflection. And by now, the late twentieth century, economics as practiced in many universities is practically a branch of mathematics. Over time, economics has come to define itself as the sci-

---

[1] The literature on rational self-restraint is relevant to my analysis. See, for example, Jon Elster, *Ulysses and the Sirens* (New York: Cambridge University Press, 1982); and Richard Thaler and H. M. Shefrin, "An Economic Theory of Self-Control," *Journal of Political Economy*, vol. 89 (1981), pp. 392–406.

ence of allocating scarce resources among competing ends, or as the science of constrained maximization.[2]

My purpose in the present essay is to expand the economic model. In particular, I try to open up the black box that lies behind the utility function. We might say that the economic model currently in use is a reduced form model, behind which lies a complex structure. In the present essay, I examine parts of this underlying structure, parts that are not usually examined directly.

The key feature that I try to capture is the human person as a genuine acting agent. The economist's view of the person, as it now stands, is that the person is a pure stimulus-response machine. The preferences are given; the relative prices are given. The person is completely reactive. We might say that the person's behavior is perfectly predetermined, or predestined, once the utility function has been formed, however it might have been formed. There presently is no scope within economics for the genuinely creative act, for the uniquely personal contribution. These things flow from deep within the person, and have an impact on the external world. The present model tries to show how the person can have the capacity to be an initiator, as well as a reactor.

III. The Two Components of the Rational Person

For analytical purposes, I separate the person into two components: the rational person as calculator and the rational person as philosopher. The first component, the rational person as calculator, corresponds roughly to Homo economicus as traditionally understood. The rational person as calculator acts on the basis of given preferences. That is, the person acts as if he knows how much pleasure and pain he will receive from each possible action. The second component of the rational person realizes that his knowledge of his own preferences is incomplete, in that he may inaccurately anticipate how a good or activity will make him feel. Because of this imperfect knowledge, the person must periodically reconsider his conception of his own preferences. The person must do more than calculate: the person must reflect upon his own experience, and upon the experience of others. This is the rational person as philosopher.

A. The calculating person

Calculating man acts as if his preferences are given, and then confronts relative prices in the environment. These prices include the components

---

[2] Adam Smith, *The Theory of Moral Sentiments*, ed. D. D. Raphael and A. L. Macfie (Indianapolis: Liberty Fund, 1982). John Stuart Mill, *Principles of Political Economy, with Some of Their Applications to Social Philosophy* (1848; 7th ed., 1871), ed. Sir W. J. Ashley (London: Longmans, Green, and Co., 1909); cited in Joseph A. Schumpeter, *History of Economic Analysis* (New York: Oxford University Press, 1954), pp. 527–43. Alfred Marshall, *Principles of Economics* (1890), 8th ed. (London: Macmillan, 1964).

customarily considered in economic analysis: monetary prices of market goods, the cost of time, the opportunity cost of forgone alternatives. The rational person as calculator acts as if he knows what will give him pleasure and pain, that is, as if he knows his utility function. The rational person as calculator also acts as if he knows the relative prices of his actions. Of course, he may be mistaken on both counts. That is, he may not have accurately anticipated the direct impact of the good or activity on his own feelings of pleasure and pain; and he may have miscalculated the external costs and benefits that he would face as a result of his actions.

The possibility of these kinds of mistakes, especially about relative prices, is always present in the current paradigm of economics. In the expanded model I present below, there is scope for at least two other kinds of mistaken expectations. First, the person might have a perfectly sound notion of what would bring him pleasure and pain, but might nonetheless be mistaken about how to go about producing the goods he values. To borrow the terminology of economics, the person may have imperfect information about the technology for producing the goods that he knows will truly bring him pleasure. Second, the person may be mistaken in his expectation of which goods actually provide satisfaction. The person may know the technology, and the relative prices; but, based on experience, he may come to decide that the weights he initially placed upon the various goods were not appropriate.

Because of these different types of mistakes, the person could experience some confusion about the sources of his disappointment. The mere fact of not receiving the anticipated outcome will not necessarily lead the person to an instantaneous or costless adjustment. Indeed, it may take many iterations for a person to work out the details of how he needs to change.[3]

B. The reflecting person

At this point, the second component of the rational person comes into play. The person periodically ceases the usual process of calculating costs and benefits, in order to reassess the internal relative prices. Economists use the notion of internal relative prices to refer to the marginal rates of substitution among various goods and activities. And the person periodically adjusts those relative prices to reflect new data.

[3] The confusion among types of errors is reminiscent of other information problems studied in economics. In macroeconomics, the confusion between changes in the real, underlying conditions of the economy can be confused with mere changes in the money supply. The theory of rational expectations explains business cycles as the results of this confusion on the part of otherwise well-informed people. Among the standard references are Robert Lucas, "Expectations and the Neutrality of Money," *Journal of Economic Theory*, vol. 4 (April 1972), pp. 103–24; and Robert Barro, "Unanticipated Money, Output, and the Price Level in the United States," *Journal of Political Economy*, vol. 86 (1978), pp. 549–80.

During this period of adjusting the prices, the person is doing something other than calculating. The person is doing something that might be called "meta-processing."[4] The person is reflecting upon his previous actions and their consequences. He is considering whether his relative valuations on activities have really met his deeper needs. In short, the person is reflecting.

This is the process that makes us most fully human. We reflect upon what we in fact value, what kinds of persons we want to be, and how we might become those persons. This is the rational person as philosopher, rather than as calculator.

This division of the person into a calculating part and a reflecting part corresponds roughly to a division made by constitutional economic analysis, a division of politics into ordinary political play, in which the rules of the game are taken as constraints, and constitutional choice, in which the rules of the game are selected. In this analytical division, people first choose the rules of the political process under which all future political activity will take place; this is the constitutional choice phase. In the second phase, people actually play out the political game, according to the rules chosen in the constitutional phase.[5]

My framework is in some ways analogous to the constitutional economics framework. Calculating man is conducting business as usual, operating under a given set of preferences, assumptions about technology, and information about prices. But reflecting man is deciding whether these preferences and assumptions are truly the ones he wants to operate under. If he does not obtain the results he expected, he may want to alter some of the ways in which he makes decisions.

The framework I am proposing places no external constraints on the person's choice process. It simply notes that he may, by his own standards, believe that he needs to make some adjustments. Like the actors in the political game, an individual may come to believe that he can do better under a different decision-making regime. And, in that spirit, he will alter his own internal, relative valuations of goods and activities.

In the next section, I present a simple model of individual behavior that has some scope for inner conflict, frustration, and disappointment. This expanded model thus has room within it for reflection. That is, when people experience these inner conflicts, frustrations, and disappointments frequently and intensely enough, they have some motivation to question their own initial assumptions about the contents of their own preference ordering.

---

[4] See Robert H. Frank, *Passions within Reason* (New York: Norton, 1988); and Amartya Sen, "Rational Fools," *Philosophy and Public Affairs*, vol. 6, no. 4 (Summer 1977), pp. 317–44, reprinted in Sen, *Choice, Welfare, and Measurement* (Cambridge, MA: MIT Press, 1982).

[5] See James M. Buchanan and Gordon Tullock, *The Calculus of Consent: Logical Foundations of Constitutional Democracy* (Ann Arbor: University of Michigan Press, 1962); and James M. Buchanan, *The Limits of Liberty: Between Anarchy and Leviathan* (Chicago: University of Chicago Press, 1975).

IV. The Appetites and the Longings

My initial assumption is that every human person is born with both Appetites and Longings. We might generalize by saying that the Appetites are common to many animals, while the Longings distinguish us from animals. The Longings are the desires for the ultimate goods, such as truth, beauty, goodness, and love. The Appetites correspond to the bodily goods, nourishment, physical comfort, sleep, amusements, sexual gratification, and the like. These are pleasurable in themselves, and may also be instrumental in achieving the Longings.

A more accurate description would be "Appetitive Goods" and "Transcendental Goods" or "Ultimate Goods." We might say that the person has preference orderings or preference rankings among the Appetitive Goods, and that the person has Longings for the satisfaction of the Transcendental Goods. That is, each person has both preferences for the Appetitive Goods, and Longings for the Transcendental Goods. But the person may not be in full possession of the commodities, the knowledge, or the personal attributes necessary to satisfy either the preferences or the Longings.

I assume, as is customary in economics, that there is a direct connection between the consumption of material goods, and the satisfaction of the desires for Appetitive Goods. Indeed, the connection is so direct that consumption is essentially identical with the satisfaction of the desires for Appetitive Goods. By contrast, the connection between the consumption of material objects and the satisfaction of the Longings for the Transcendental Goods involves a greater number of steps. For a person to be in possession of the Transcendental Goods may require some combination of reflection upon experience, adjustment of dispositions, and gathering of information, as well as the simple consumption of material objects.

For the sake of brevity in expression, I use the terms "achieving the Longings" and "producing the Longings," as shorthand expressions for this process of satisfying the Longings for the Transcendental Goods — using some combination of material goods purchased on the market, and reflection taking place in the privacy of the person's mind.[6]

I assume that utility is a function of the Appetites and the Longings. The Longings have a greater intrinsic weight than the Appetites; but the Appetites have some value as instruments in achieving the Longings. At the same time, I assume that the Appetites may sometimes hinder the achievement of the Longings. Examples would include excessive indulgence in most any of the Appetites. For instance, the seven deadly sins delineated by the medieval scholastics are all excesses of things that are surely acceptable in some context: anger, pride, lust, gluttony, sloth, envy, and greed.

---

[6] For a fuller discussion of the content of the Longings, see Jennifer Roback Morse, *Putting the Self into Self-Interest: An Economist Looks at Values* (manuscript in progress).

We assume that people value the same things in that everyone has the same set of Appetites, and the same set of Longings. People differ among themselves in the relative weights they place on the various goods within each category, and the relative weights they place on Appetites versus Longings generally. Not only do people have a desire for both Appetites and Longings, but people also have some idea about how to obtain them. They have some notion of the method by which they can obtain the Longings. To use economists' language, they have at least a provisional understanding of the production technology for the Longings.

Some readers might object to the assumption that everyone has the same set of Longings, since many people do not seem to care at all about the higher goods. I respond as follows: It is true that we observe some people with very low levels of the higher goods in their lives. This does not, by itself, prove that these people do not place any value on them. The standard economist's response would be to observe that perhaps the price of the Longings was too high, relative to their budget set. I would amplify that remark by observing that one aspect of price that is often too high is that persons do not fully understand how to go about creating truth and beauty in their lives. Large portions of the educated classes deny the existence of such things as truth and beauty. The cost of discovering truth and beauty is likely to be rather high for ordinary people, when educators and opinion-makers so frequently claim that these concepts are either unknowable or arbitrary.

The key part of my claim is not that everyone in fact consumes these ultimate goods. Rather, my claim is that everyone has the capacity for the enjoyment of truth and beauty. And, once these things have been somehow discovered, anyone would place enough value on them to be willing to accept them if given as a gift. Moreover, people would be willing to sacrifice something, that is, to pay some price, to obtain more of the ultimate goods. Even a person of ordinary means and intellectual capacity can recognize that a life of truth, goodness, beauty, and love is preferable to a life of self-deception, evil, ugliness, and loneliness.

While we might list truth, goodness, beauty, and love as the ultimate goods among the Longings, we can observe a hierarchy of goods for many situations. In the examples that follow, I will contrast the desire for food with the desire for good health. We can easily see that food could be an Appetite, while health could be the associated Longing. The consumption of food is pleasurable in itself, and also instrumental in producing good health. We can consume more food than is good for our health. Many other examples will come to mind in the course of the analysis.

People can satisfy their Longings by using their time and some of their goods. A person might pursue beauty, for instance, by using some of his own time, together with purchased goods such as art classes, music lessons, concert tickets, and the like. It is in this sense that we may say that the Appetites can be inputs into the Longings. For it is necessary to remain alive in order to enjoy the Longings; thus, the bodily needs for food and sustenance and good health must be met. And beyond this most basic requirement, the person needs some material goods with which to pursue beauty, so that the Appetite for money may become an instrument by which the Longing is met.

The pursuit of the Appetites can, however, become a hindrance to the pursuit of the Longings. While a moderate amount of material goods might be necessary for the pursuit of the Longings, we can readily conceive of the possibility that one can detract from the pursuit of the higher goods by overindulging the Appetites. If we conceive of the Appetites as inputs into the production of the Longings, we may say that there is an optimal amount of the Appetites. Consumption of the Appetites beyond this amount will actually decrease the amount of the Longings produced.

Traditional consumer theory is entirely subjective, in the sense that values are whatever the consumer chooses. Economic analysis typically draws no distinction between good or bad preferences, between virtuous or vicious actions. The present model departs from this custom in one important particular: the preferences remain subjective, but the production of the Longings is objective. That is, there is a specific method or technology for achieving the Longings, that exists independently of anyone's choice. If a person wants friendship, there are things that must be done and other things that must be avoided. If one wants truth, whether in the sense of knowledge of facts, or in the sense of reliability, trustworthiness, and integrity, there are things to do and things to refrain from doing.

The model I am proposing retains the assumption of subjective preferences, which means that people may assign different relative values to the Longings and the Appetites; and people may assign different relative values to some of the Longings over others. This assumption allows a wide scope for individual variation, and for individual choice and self-expression, just as in the usual economic analysis. The two innovations of the present model are that everyone is born with the Longings and that the Longings can only be produced in specific ways.

We can make the following comparison between the present model and the traditional economic analysis of consumer behavior. The standard model takes the entire set of preferences as given, and can offer no reasonable account of how a person might go about changing it. The consumer's utility function is the fundamental parameter of the problem, and the analysis cannot proceed any more deeply than that. The utility maps or sets of preference orderings of the individual consumers can be viewed as the Archimedean fixed points, from which the economist can survey the problem and conduct his analysis.

The consumer's problem is to conform his behavior to that given utility map. Rational behavior becomes an exercise in resource allocation, because the ends of the person are taken as the givens, as the fixed points. There is no room in the analysis for a radical reordering of preferences. We know, of course, that people sometimes do restructure their preferences; but economists do not currently have a vantage point from which to view this process.

The present modification of consumer theory proposes a different fixed point. The person is not born with a complete set of preference orderings. Rather, the person is born with some Longings, which can be satisfied well or poorly. The person does not know the entire technology for producing the Longings. Neither does the person know how the Longings ought to be ordered, relative to each other, and relative to the lesser goods. The fixed point is the Longings, not the preference ordering among the observable consumer goods.

Therefore, a significant aspect of rational behavior will be to discover the proper means of obtaining the Longings, and the proper ordering of the Longings. As in the traditional model of consumer behavior, the person does have some fixed objective to which he must order himself. That objective is not entirely arbitrary, however. It is not entirely chosen by the person himself. There is some deeper, underlying reality inherent in the human condition, to which he must conform himself, if he is ever to be truly satisfied.

The person faces binding constraints, both in the traditional consumer calculus, and in my modified version. This attentiveness to constraints is one of the refreshing, and entirely wholesome, aspects of economic analysis. Economists are usually among the first to point out that the various experiments designed to save the world by changing human nature are doomed to failure. Economists were among the few who criticized the attempts to create the "New Socialist Paradise," in which scarcity had disappeared, peopled by "New Socialist Men," who had forgotten they had ever experienced pride in ownership. Most economists would agree that we cannot click our heels together and wish real hard, and thereby be magically transported into a world in which price controls do not create shortages. Economists have been successful to the extent that they have focused on something in human nature that is true, and to the extent that they have honored those truths about human nature.

But economics has traditionally limited its attention to constraints that are exterior to the person: budget constraints, technology and resource constraints, and the like. My extensions of consumer theory take this tradition one step deeper. I try to capture the fact that there are real constraints on what will make people happy. There are real constraints on a person's preference ordering, even though there is some scope for individual variation within those constraints. The person will be happier if he conforms himself to these constraints. These constraints are not arbitrary, not changeable, not entirely culturally determined. Most importantly, the technology of producing the Longings, and the right ordering of the Longings, are potentially knowable. The person will never experience truth by living a life of self-deception; the person will never experience love through self-centeredness; and the person will never experience happiness through self-indulgence.

The technical modifications of standard consumer demand theory are relatively modest. Including self-produced goods called truth and beauty is a simple application of the theory of household production. Hypothesizing a range over which more of an input actually reduces the output is not an extraordinary assumption either. But with these modest modifications of consumer theory, we introduce a considerable range of new complexities into the consumer's choice problem. These new complexities expand our understanding of what it means to be rational.

V. Indulgent and Reflective Indifference Curves

Denote by A* the consumption level of the Appetite that produces the maximum quantity of the Longing. At consumption levels higher than A*, the production of the Longing is decreased. However, because the person still obtains some pleasure from the indulgence of the Appetite, the loss of the Longing is partially offset by the increased pleasure of the Appetite. Denote by A− the level of the Appetite at which the lost production of the Longing is so great that it overwhelms the consumption value of the Appetite.[7]

The consumption of food provides a straightforward illustration of the idea. Eating produces pleasure in itself, and also contributes to the production of good health. It is possible, however, for a person to eat more than is healthy. Excess food consumption can lead to a variety of health problems. For some range of consumption, these health problems will be adjudged to be worth enduring, because of the pleasure of indulging the Appetite for eating; but, beyond a certain point, additional consumption of food creates such losses in the production of health that these losses exceed the benefits from the pleasure of eating.

With this small modification of consumer theory, we have introduced a large realm of new complexities into the consumer's problem. For there is now an objective element to the problem, as well as a subjective element. That is, the production function for the Longings will not necessarily be known immediately to the person. Indeed, a large part of the process of maturing is exactly about discovering how to attain the most valuable things in life. Moreover, the person will not know instantly what relative values he ought to place on the various Longings.

---

[7] The utility function associated with this problem is:

$$U = U(L, A, X)$$

where

$$L = f(A)$$

This is an example of the home production model, pioneered by Gary Becker in "A Theory of the Allocation of Time," *Economic Journal*, September 1965, pp. 493–517; and Gilbert R. Ghez and Gary S. Becker, *The Allocation of Time and Goods over the Life Cycle* (New York and London: Columbia University Press, 1975).

Finally, the Appetites and the Longings are potentially in conflict with one another. Therefore, at least some of the time, the person may experience some interior conflict. Do I really want to eat that second helping of dessert? Do I really want to stop at the bar on the way home from work? Do I really want to slightly exaggerate my accomplishments on my job application? And how much is a slight exaggeration?

By asking himself these questions, the consumer is in the process of deciding what the trade-off between the Appetites and the Longings will be. And, as he lives with the consequences of those decisions, he will discover something about what the trade-offs ought to be, about how he ought to make future decisions.

Economists use indifference curves to analyze consumer choice among goods available for purchase on the market. For instance, in Figure 1, the horizontal axis measures consumption of the Appetitive Goods, labeled on the graph as A, while the vertical axis measures consumption of all other market goods, labeled on the graph as X. In drawing this graph, I am implicitly assuming that all goods available for purchase can be classified as either Appetitive Goods, or as goods with no particular moral significance. I realize that it is possible that all goods potentially have some moral significance. In a later section of this essay, I consider this possibility more systematically.

The heavy straight line whose endpoints are labeled as B and B', represents the budget set. The budget set is delimited by the person's available income and the market prices of the goods A and X. Every combination of A and X lying between the budget line and the origin of the graph is financially feasible for the consumer to purchase if he so chooses. Indeed, sometimes the budget set is called the feasible set. The consumer's problem is to choose one of the feasible alternative combinations of A and X that gives him the highest level of utility.

Indifference curves are used to show the person's rankings among alternative combinations of goods. An indifference curve shows combinations of goods, among which the consumer would be indifferent. Most typically, indifference curves are shown as downward sloping curves that are convex to the origin. The downward slope captures the fact that the person prefers more of any good to less. A consumption bundle with larger amounts of both goods is preferable to one with less. So the set of points among which a person is indifferent must have trade-offs between the commodities built into it. The person is indifferent between consuming a bundle with a large amount of A and a small amount of X on the one hand, and a bundle with a small amount of A and a large amount of X on the other. In principle, the person can rank every alternative combination of goods relative to every other alternative. Therefore, every point on the graph could, in principle, be placed on one and only one indifference curve.

In Figure 1, the indifference curves labeled U_i and U_i' represent two levels of utility for a consumer. Because more consumption is assumed to

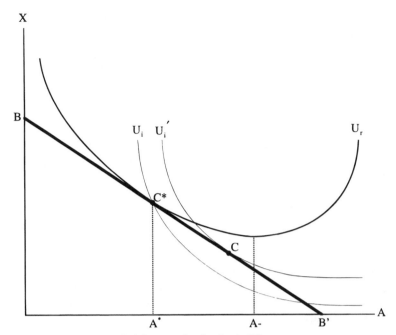

FIGURE 1. Indulgent and reflective indifference curves

A represents consumption of the Appetitive Goods. X represents consumption of all other market goods.

The line with endpoints of B and B' represents the budget set. (B shows the maximum quantity of X that could be purchased at a given income level and prices. If all income I were spent on X, at price p_x, the person could purchase I/p_x units of X. Likewise, the point B' shows the quantity of A that could be purchased if all income were spent on A: I/p_A.)

U_i and U_i' represent two levels of utility for a consumer. (All points along U_i give the consumer identical levels of utility. All points along U_i' give the consumer a higher level of utility than those points along U_i.) U_i and U_i' represent the "indulgent indifference curves." U_r represents the "reflective indifference curve."

A* represents the level of consumption of A that maximizes production of the Longings. A− represents the level of consumption of A at which the utility gained from the Appetites is outweighed by the losses of the Longings.

C represents the consumer's optimal choice using the indulgent indifference curves. C* represents the consumer's optimal choice using the reflective indifference curve.

be preferred to less, U_i' represents a higher level of utility than U_i. The point labeled C represents the consumer's optimal choice, because this is the highest level of utility attainable with the budget set implied by the person's income and the market prices.

In traditional consumer theory, the person would be shown as having a single set of downward-sloping indifference curves, with U_i and U_i' being representative members. I modify the standard theory in two respects. First, I illustrate two sets of indifference curves for the same person. The indifference curves labeled U_i and U_i' can be called the "indulgent indifference curves," while the one labeled U_r can be called the "reflective indifference curve."

The second modification is that, while the indulgent indifference curves have the usual convex curvature, the reflective indifference curve has an upward-sloping portion. The segment beyond A^* corresponds to the region in which production of the Longing begins to diminish. In the segment beyond $A-$, the production of the Longing has fallen off so dramatically that these losses outweigh the direct consumption pleasure of indulging the Appetite. A person who operates along the reflective indifference curve will choose A^* at these prices. If, on the other hand, the person uses the indulgent indifference curves, his optimal choice will be at point C, with a greater consumption of the Appetite than the technologically optimal amount, A^*.

In this essay, these indulgent and reflective indifference curves will be used to illustrate two distinct situations. In the first case, the person does not know how the Longing is produced, or does not know that a Longing is produced at all. The person acts upon the information contained in the indulgent indifference curves. That is, he acts as if the indifference curves had no upward sloping region. In this situation, the person acts on the indulgent indifference curves because he is ignorant of the true costs of overconsumption. This person indulges, and discovers a set of costs he did not accurately anticipate.

The second case is that the person knows how to produce the Longings, but puts no weight on the Longings. He acts as if the Longings have no weight in his utility function. By acting in this way, he accumulates a whole series of costs. If the Longing is good health, and the Appetite is for food, he may gain weight, get high blood pressure, have heart attacks, strokes, and so on. Perhaps the Longing is for friendship, and the Appetite is for career advancement and financial gain. If he acts as if he places no value on his friends, he may end up rich, old, and lonely. In the ordinary economic way of thinking, this person is perfectly rational. He is not ill-informed in any way. He is getting exactly what he wants, what he asks for, what he pays for.

VI. The Problem of Disappointment

Suppose the person places appropriate or reasonable weights on the Longings relative to the Appetites, but has imperfect information about how to produce the Longings. In Figure 2, $U_i(C^*)$ and $U_i(C)$ are representative of the indifference curves as the person imagines them to be, while $U_r(C)$ and $U_r(C^*)$ are representative of the indifference curves as they really are, given the objective technology of the production of the Longings. The person will act as if $U_i(C)$ and $U_i(C^*)$ are the correct indifference curves, and will choose to consume at point C. This person expects to enjoy $U_i(C)$.

Since he is mistaken about the technology, however, he will not actually receive $U_i(C)$, but rather $U_r(C)$. This person may come to realize that he

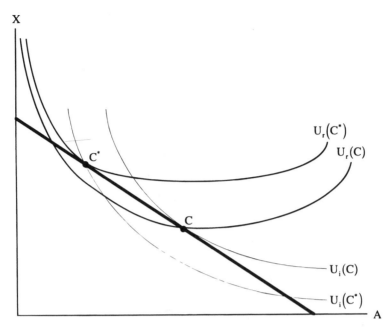

FIGURE 2. The alcoholic dilemma

$U_i(C^*)$ and $U_i(C)$ are representative of the indifference curves as the person imagines them to be. $U_r(C)$ and $U_r(C^*)$ are representative of the indifference curves as they really are.

C^* represents the optimal consumption choice using the reflective or real indifference curves. C represents the optimal consumption choice using the indulgent or imaginary indifferent curves.

has not received what he expected. He will look at the stream of results flowing from his choice, and realize that he had somehow been mistaken. Perhaps this is a first-year college student, away from home for the first time. Perhaps he did not realize, until the first midterm exam, how much effort would be required, and hence how little partying he could indulge in. The first midterm provides him with some disappointment, and some new data. He adjusts his belief about the technology of producing good grades, and this belief about technology is incorporated into the indifference curve.

Or perhaps these curves represent the situation of an alcoholic. Perhaps the Longing the person expects to achieve is happiness, or perhaps even peace. Perhaps he believes that a drink will calm him, or allow him to face the problems of his life. Using the indulgent indifference curve, he imagines himself to be better off consuming at C than at C^*, since $U_i(C) > U_i(C^*)$.

After a time of consuming in this region, however, reality sets in. He notices that he is not really better off. $U_r(C^*)$ is the utility he could have had, if he had consumed at a moderate, nontoxic level. This is the utility he could have had if he had been sober during his years of active alcoholism. This is the utility level associated with things like the job he lost, the friends he no longer has, the shame of his family, the loss of his self-respect. $U_r(C)$ is the utility he has in fact experienced during his years of active alcoholism. He comes to see that he would have been better off if he had been consuming steadily at C^*, instead of C, since $U_r(C^*) > U_r(C)$.

It is clear that his lack of understanding could be quite profound. Our hypothesis is that he begins the process with a certain conception of his utility function, based on his beliefs about technology, and the actual pleasure he will get from both the Appetites and the Longings. But when he experiences an outcome that differs from his expectation, he does not automatically know the correct, alternative indifference curve. I have drawn two sets of indifference curves on the graph, but the person may not have that much actual information about the problem. He might know nothing more than the level of utility he received. He may not know the entire indifference map associated with the alternative way of understanding the production of the Longings.

VII. Resources for Discovering the Technology of the Production of the Longings

What resources do we have to help us with the problems that arise from our lack of knowledge of how to produce the Longings? We have the assistance of other people. For it is not reasonable to suppose that each person can or ought to discover everything for himself, as if he were the first person to ever face these problems. Tradition, that is, the experience of past persons, can be of help to persons presently living. Older, more experienced persons can also be of help. The knowledge of other people is one entire class of resources available to the person facing these problems.

The person cannot automatically know which goods fulfill the deepest longings of the human heart, nor can he automatically know how to attain them. The person can be educated to some of them; and rather than such education being viewed as the suppression of the values the person naturally holds, it could instead be viewed as something of great assistance and value to the person. The philosophical questions about which goods bring true happiness can be viewed as informational problems. The questions about how to achieve these highest goods can be viewed as technological issues.

To a person trained in philosophy, this transformation of the discipline's traditional subject matter into economic jargon might seem strange, perhaps forced, or even offensive. I do not mean to give offense to philosophy as it has traditionally understood itself. On the contrary, my intention is to open up philosophy to some of my more mathematical colleagues in economics.

Many of the most rigorous practitioners of economic science have been unable to see the point of philosophical discussions about the good life. Because economic value is whatever the consumers say it is, some economists conclude that value more generally is whatever people say it is. The subjectivism of modern utility theory has left economists with nothing to say about the content of preferences. Some economists have concluded from this that there is nothing that can be said, by anyone.

But surely we can say that some things, like truth and beauty, are of value to everyone. The economist can, if he likes, if he must, simply observe the fact that it is these deeper things that finally satisfy. The advertisers of a new pair of Nikes, or a bottle of Coca-Cola, may promise a profound satisfaction, on the level of truth and beauty; but of course everyone knows, or can know, that these products cannot finally deliver. We can know from experience the disappointment that so often follows after ripping open the packages on Christmas morning. Even when we have received everything we thought we wanted, we find that we had placed too much hope in those presents, in those material objects. And surely the economist, along with everyone else, can understand that a person can never achieve the good of truth by plagiarism, or by falsifying data; nor can one achieve friendship by excessive preoccupation with oneself.

Certainly, then, one component of rationality must be the search for accurate information about the production of the highest goods. It is reasonable to expend time and effort discovering this information. It is not reasonable to accept uncritically the claims of others, either advertisers or philosophy professors. Thus, each person must develop some skills at distinguishing the reasonable advice from the unreasonable. Indeed, it seems that it would be rational to have a set of such skills, as well as a set of trusted persons or institutions to whom one could turn.

For instance, we have already noted that the disappointed person will not necessarily know the entire shape of an alternative set of indifference curves. If another person is giving him some guidance, however, that person may reveal the whole map to him. That is, his parents or peers may explain what happened to him in a way that accounts for the data he has. If so, then their conception of the entire indifference map may well be credible to him. Thus, he may be willing to accept, at least provisionally, their indifference map. He can act on it, observe the results of acting in accordance with it, and modify it accordingly.

VIII. THE MORAL PROBLEM: WHAT BELONGS
IN THE UTILITY FUNCTION?

Let me begin this section with the stories of three people personally known to me. Mr. X died of lung cancer, after a lifetime of smoking. Not only did he smoke throughout his life, he continued to do so even after he had been diagnosed with lung cancer. Indeed, in the last stages of his illness, his breath was so weak that he could not inhale enough to light the cigarettes himself. He asked other people to do this for him, and he continued to smoke down to his very last day.

Mr. Y was extremely obese. Toward the end of his life, he was confined to bed, because he was so heavy he was unable to walk. He would induce other people to go to the kitchen, and bring him food. During a stay at a treatment center for obese people, he ordered take-out pizza delivered to his room. He died in his early forties, at a weight of over four hundred pounds.

Ms. Z's husband took steps to end their marriage. Ms. Z could not accept this. She tried everything she could think of to "get him back." She pleaded with him, she tried in various ways to make herself more attractive to him. At the same time, she attempted to indirectly coerce him into coming back by trying to make him feel guilty, or otherwise uncomfortable. She hired detectives to follow him. She bought a gun and threatened to commit suicide. Finally, she did commit suicide, in such a way that her estranged husband would be certain to find her.

In a macabre way, the economic model is descriptively accurate with regard to the life choices of these three persons. Each of them was fully informed about the costs and benefits of his actions. The man dying of lung cancer knew perfectly well that smoking was ending his life. The man ordering pizza while at the obesity treatment center knew that this food choice was not conducive to his greater health. The woman knew as she pulled the trigger that she would die.

Each of them behaved in a purposeful fashion toward the ends they had chosen for themselves. Mr. X had decided that satisfying his Appetite for smoking was more valuable than his continued existence. Likewise, Mr. Y had decided that his Appetite for food consumption gave him more utility than the Longing of good health. And Ms. Z had decided that the benefit to her of knowing she had imposed large costs on her husband was worth the price of her life. Satisfying her Appetite for revenge had become more valuable to her than life itself.

I do not dispute the descriptive accuracy of the economists' model of behavior. These people were fully informed; they behaved purposefully; they got what they paid for. I just have trouble describing them as rational. Many adjectives come to mind as I reflect on these three friends: stubborn, even bullheaded; foolish; pitiful, perhaps even pathetic. I can even describe them as consistent. But I cannot bring myself to call them "rational."

To behave rationally means to behave in accordance with reason. Economists have used the word to refer exclusively to internal consistency. In the economists' sense, people behave rationally when they achieve their objectives at minimal cost. But the choice of objective is thought to be outside the realm of the rational choice model, or even outside the realm of reasoned discourse.

To be sure, economists are not alone in positing this value-neutrality, or in forwarding the claim that value is whatever people say it is. Philosophers and even theologians have done their share to remove the bridges between reason and value, between rationality and virtue. But economists have contributed to the construction of elaborate intellectual edifices that support the claim that nothing can be known about ultimate value, except to observe what people in fact value.

The model presented here allows us to make this distinction between the pursuit of given ends, and the choice of the ends themselves. A person who places no weight on the Longings may certainly pursue the Appetites in a manner that is both internally consistent and cost-effective (in a limited sense). But the deeper costs will accumulate around him. Whether they are the direct costs of visible harms to the body, or less visible costs to the person's inner life, or even more subtle opportunity costs of the love he never knew, and the friends he never had, these costs are real. They can be observed, both by the individual himself, and by those around him. I would argue that a person who continues to place no weight on the Longings, in spite of an accumulation of human wreckage around him, ought not be called rational.

Something can be known about the ultimate ends, about what people truly and most deeply want. The fact that the Longings are experienced internally, individually, and personally does not mean that people cannot have any evidence about what those Longings are. We can discern a happy person from a miserable one. We can even perceive that a person is superficially content, but is headed for disaster. We have the capacity to reflect upon ourselves, and, at times, realize that we are kidding ourselves in some basic way. It is these kinds of realizations that allow us to change.

The question of what to value is a major part of the human problem, and needs to be present as part of the economists' problem as well. Although it is not directly a resource-allocation problem, it will have resource-allocation consequences. If the choice of ends is not part of the problem, then we are describing as rational, people who could clearly change for the better but refuse to do so. These people could have changed their ends, and hence their behavior. They were not stupid people. They were not without resources. They were not, in some subtle way, coerced into doing as they did.

The examples I have presented so far illustrate disordered preferences in the most dramatic way. The people I have described are dead because of skewed thinking. I would like to turn now to a more subtle example of a person who places insufficient weight on the Longings. The example is more subtle because the harms the person experiences need not be immediate harms to the body or to one's continued existence. The model illustrates a person who can accumulate harms of a more interior sort, and yet the harms can be observed, both by himself and by others close to him.

IX. All Goods as Inputs into the Longings

In the model considered so far, two goods (represented in the figures by A and X) can be purchased in the market, but only one of these goods (A) is an input into the production of the Longings. There exists a good (X) that is not an input into the Longings. The indifference curves between these two market goods have an upward slope at some point. With positive prices, and an accurate understanding of the production technology for the Longings, no one, at any income level, would ever choose to consume beyond A−. For no matter how much income the person has, he can always spend that income on the good that has no potential to create disutility. In other words, the person can always substitute away from the consumption of the Appetites.

We now consider a slight variation in our model, a variation in which every market good is an input into the Longings.[8] In this case, the indifference curves between two such goods, A_1 and A_2, have a circular or oval shape, as shown in Figure 3. At the center of the indifference map is a "bliss point": that is, there is a point of maximal utility. Any movements away from this point, whether in the direction of higher consumption or lower consumption, will actually decrease the person's utility.

In this case, it is possible to overconsume in all dimensions. We can imagine a person with these indifference curves receiving too much income. In this situation, the person can only dispose of his excess income, since there is no other market good, by assumption, which can be consumed without detracting from the Longings.

We can interpret these indifference curves in two different ways. First, we may consider the behavior of a person who places no weight upon the Longings. This person ignores the technology of producing the Longings and simply consumes in accordance with the relative values of A_1 and A_2. The second way to interpret these indifference curves is to ask about people who place a very strong weight on the Longings. Since, by assumption, every good is an input into the production of some Longing, we might imagine that these people would have consumption patterns that would look rather different from those of other people.

A. No weight on the Longings

The person who places no weight on the Longings will go roaring past the bliss point. With every increase in income, this person's utility

---

[8] The utility function associated with this problem is:

$$U = U(L_1, L_2, A_1, A_2)$$

where

$$L_1 = f(A_1) \text{ and}$$
$$L_2 = g(A_2)$$

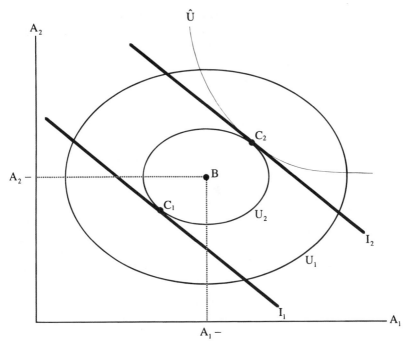

FIGURE 3. Roaring past the bliss point

A_1 and A_2 represent consumption levels of two different Appetitive Goods. A_1- and A_2- represent the levels of consumption at which the gains from the Appetites are outweighed by the losses of the associated Longings.

The oval shaped indifference curves U_1 and U_2 represent reflective indifference curves. $\hat{U}$ represents an indulgent indifference curve, with no weight on the Longings.

B represents the bliss point: the point of maximum utility, using the reflective indifference curves.

C_1 represents the optimal consumption given income level I_1. C_2 represents the optimal consumption given income level I_2, using the indulgent indifference curve $\hat{U}$.

level will deteriorate, rather than improve. He may find that his utility level is not what he expected, as his income level increases. He expected to receive something like $\hat{U}$ at income level I_2, but instead he received U_2.

In the initial experiences of incomes that increase past the bliss point, the person may not realize what is going on. If his income increases from I_1 to I_2, his consumption will change from C_1 to C_2. He will expect his utility to increase from something like U_2 to $\hat{U}$, but in fact he will experience no change in his utility at all. He will stay at utility level U_2, while simply shifting his expenditure and consumption pattern. He may believe that he has somehow not optimized properly. Or he may just continue to ignore the impact of his consumption of market goods on his enjoyment of the Longings. He may continue to place no weight on the Longings.

If he does not change the way in which he orders his choices, then his life, as measured by reference to the higher goods, can never improve. Indeed, with every increase in income, the person's life will actually deteriorate, rather than improve.

An example of a person in this condition might be the successful and acquisitive middle-aged man, who feels empty. Perhaps he has achieved everything that he hoped for in his career. Perhaps he has acquired everything that he thought would bring him pleasure. But he is still unhappy and empty. He has given little or no weight to the higher goods, what we have called the Longings, and thus, he has attained virtually none of them.

If he continues to order his consumption as he has, he will continue to get less, rather than more. He may decide that he needs a newer, younger, and prettier wife. He will destroy the deepest and most genuine values as he divorces his wife, devastates his children, and causes destruction from which it will take his family years to recover. And far from being the object of envy that he supposes himself to be with his trophy wife on his arm, he becomes the object of pity and ridicule. He subjectively placed no value on the higher goods, and, objectively, he has none of the higher goods. And this fact is readily observable to everyone around him, and to him as well, if he troubled to look.

Why might he look? He might find that even the newer, more expensive goods do nothing for him. He might miss his children, and thereby realize that he has missed some greater values than those he has acted upon. He might realize that he is surrounded by gold diggers and flatterers, people who give nothing of value to him, unless they calculate that he will give something to them. He might realize that some of the people he respects no longer respect him, and may even pity him. He may realize that there is no love in his life, because he has placed no priority upon it. He has not done the things required to create love in his life. And regardless of the relative priorities he thought he placed upon love and material goods, he will still find a longing for love; and that longing will go unsatisfied for as long as he continues to behave as he has.

Part of this person's problem is that he has too much wealth, relative to his bliss point. Our very stark analytical model is based on the premise that every good is an input into the Longings, and thus every good has the potential to be overconsumed. We might observe that while this claim need not be true at all levels of income, it is surely true that at some level of income it could become true. That is, if there is any potential for overconsumption at all, then a person with a very large income will eventually face the temptation to overconsume.

At the same time, the accumulation of wealth may not be independent of the person's choices. This fact works in favor of the creation of temptation, if the accumulation of wealth is itself a process which demands the sacrifice of higher values.

Perhaps the accumulation of wealth requires the person to spend long hours away from his loved ones, and perhaps this is the sacrifice he willingly makes. His willingness to sacrifice time with his family for higher monetary income creates the trade-off between the production of the higher goods and the accumulation of ordinary goods. If this is the case, then those with higher levels of wealth will, other things equal, tend to have less of the higher values.

On the other hand, the person might actually cultivate the higher values in the process of earning and accumulating. For instance, a person's reputation for honesty may be the essential ingredient for his business success. A person's ability to cultivate the talents of other workers in his field might be his key to fame and fortune. A person's devotion to truth might be a central motivation for his intellectual life, and this may in turn be the key to his economic security. In any of these cases, there is a complementarity between the consumption of ordinary goods and the production of the higher goods. The model I am proposing allows us to discuss this possibility.

When a person chooses his means of making a living, he is also making choices about the production of the higher goods. If he ignores the higher goods at this stage of the decision, he is likely to build his career without them. He may get lucky and select a career that actively requires the cultivation of the higher goods. In this case, he may find that more of his satisfaction than he expected is being generated not by the status and money of the job, but rather by the development of the higher goods. If he realizes this, he may, in one of his reflective moments, realize that this dimension is worth cultivating further, far more than he could have known initially. He has discovered virtue by accident, as it were.

B. Large weights on the Longings

Thus far, we have focused upon people who initially place little weight on the Longings relative to their Appetites. We might inquire about people who place a very high weight upon the Longings. These people may find any material goods at all to be a distraction from the cultivation of virtue. Their perception of the bliss point is not that more is better all the way out to infinity. Rather, their perception of the bliss point is that less is better, all the way down to the origin. These people believe that every Appetite must be suppressed in every dimension and in every context.

People with no weight on the Appetites may starve themselves. They may convince themselves that sexuality is wrong in all contexts. They may cut themselves off from all human contact and become hermits. They may conclude that the body itself, and all of the material world, is a source of temptation, and therefore intrinsically evil. They may destroy their material existence, in the pursuit of the higher goods. And this fact about them is an objective fact, in that it is readily observable to other people.

Some readers might conclude that my description of the person who undervalues the Appetites corresponds to members of certain religious sects and religious orders. One might therefore conclude that analysis of this particular extreme is uninteresting for the ordinary person, and that this analysis is only included for analytical symmetry. But there is more that needs to be said about the tendency to undervalue the Appetites and the body itself.

The first thing to be said about it is that the belief that the body is somehow suspect, and that all of its Appetites are to be suppressed, is a very old belief. We can see it in certain strands of Greek thought—for instance, the Stoics. The belief resurfaces in extreme form with the Manichees and the Albigensians. In every age, there always seem to be people who argue that the body and all its Appetites are evil, or that only the things of the mind and the spirit matter.

We should also understand the relationship between monasticism in the Western Catholic tradition, and this type of person who undervalues the Appetites. One might think that cloistered monks and nuns would correspond to such people, but that is not quite accurate. It is true that these monastics renounce the world outside their enclosures. It is true that their monastic lifestyle involves far less consumption of material goods than most people would be willing to accept. It is true that these monks and nuns place more weight on the Longings than most people do. Finally, it must be admitted that many people observing the choice of renunciation find it incomprehensible.

It is not true, however, that the people living in this tradition place no weight at all on the Appetites. Indeed, the Western monastic tradition came about partly in response to the problems created by this very excess.

In the period immediately following the end of the persecution of Christianity by the Roman Empire, many Christians sought holiness through the renunciation of the world. People went out into the deserts of Egypt to become hermits and live an ascetic life. Many of these people who were out on their own, pursuing their own path to the higher goods, developed their own personal theories about how much should be renounced, and how one ought to live.[9]

Early Church leaders became concerned about these developments in the desert for several reasons. First, the extreme renunciation practiced by some of these hermits led rather readily to the conclusion that the body itself, and the material world, were evils. This view is not an authentic Church doctrine, and therefore early Church leaders could not allow it to be presented as if it were. Second, these extreme practices, while conducive to certain kinds of virtues, led to the development of certain vices as well. In particular, these extreme sacrifices of the body very easily fed the

[9] Philip Hughes, *A History of the Church*, vol. 1 (New York: Sheed and Ward, 1952), pp. 136–44.

ego, and thus could lead to a kind of spiritual vanity. Thus, the man living in the desert, perched on the top of a pillar and eating flies, might be completely, indeed literally, detached from the world; but the fact that people were coming from miles around to see him live this way created temptations and difficulties of another kind.

One of the reasons for the original monastic movement was to gather these people out of the desert and let them live together, under supervision. Living in a group, even living in an enclosure, even under a rule of silence, prevents people from going off the deep end into their own private practices, which may prove harmful to them and scandalous to the larger community. The rules developed by the founders of these communities strove for balance between the legitimate needs of the body, on one hand, and renunciation for the sake of the higher goods, on the other.

The monastic life does indeed assist people to reduce their consumption of material goods, and many people chose this life for that reason. At the same time, however, monastic discipline also keeps people from going too far in the direction of underconsumption, and thus destroying the body.

There have been and continue to be numerous ascetic communities and movements, throughout the world and within various religious traditions. The Benedictine order, the oldest monastic order in Western Christianity, has been in existence since the year 529. This is obviously a very stable institution. For nearly fifteen hundred years, a small but noticeable number of people have chosen this life. The model I am proposing gives a reasonable account of this consumption decision.

X. The Rational and the Unpredictable

The model developed in this essay gives an account of disappointment in the outcome of one's decisions. The point of this discussion is to provide a motivation for the rational calculating person to become the rational reflecting person. For in the aftermath of disappointment, the person may well feel motivated to alter some aspect of his beliefs about himself.

A more complete theory of this problem might speculate about when a person becomes motivated to reflect. We might hypothesize, for instance, that a person would be so motivated when the disparity between the expectations about an experience and the actual realization of that experience becomes great enough. We might hypothesize about a primal discomfort that people feel when their beliefs crash into reality. Perhaps it is this discomfort that the person seeks to relieve by the reflective process, and the subsequent reordering of beliefs, values, and priorities. We might construct a theory about how great a disjunction between expectations and belief a person can stand. This more complete theory would have to take note of the fact that reconstructions of the preferences, indeed, reconstructions of the self, are costly, and therefore relatively rare.

The cost of changing one's beliefs about oneself may be higher than the expected benefit from doing so. Thus, the person may refuse to view himself—his behavior or his beliefs—as the cause of his own disappointment, even though he may have evidence that this is the case. Rather, the person may postpone the reevaluation, until such time as the accumulated costs of disappointment have grown large enough to make it worthwhile to bear the discomfort and other costs associated with reflection and change. Then, he will finally have his "moment of truth," or his "day of reckoning."

We might also speculate that some people cast off this discomfort by seeking to blame other people, or events outside themselves, for the disparity between expectation and reality that they experience. In this way, the person is spared the necessity, sometimes difficult, of rethinking his or her belief system. The person has found a cause, or at least an explanation, for his disappointment. And this cause, since it lies outside himself, allows the person to continue with the same belief system as before, and avoid all the costs associated with changing it. This provides an understanding of the very common phenomenon of rationalization. We might say, somewhat ironically, that we have provided a rationalization for rationalization.

But it is not my purpose to provide such a full theory at this juncture. We can surely discover exceptions to most any generalization we would care to make, and with those exceptions, we would find ourselves in an area of unpredictability. This is an area that economists are most loath to venture into; for we fancy ourselves scientists, and accurate prediction and falsifiable hypotheses are the hallmark of our trade.

Yet our unwillingness to entertain the unpredictable in human events is exactly what makes us the most suspect in the eyes of our more humanistically inclined colleagues. Our friends in history and literature and philosophy, while they admire our predictive capability in our own sphere, chuckle at us as we overlook the vast sphere of human life that is dominated by the idiosyncratic, the ironic, the whimsical, dare we say it, the personal.

Perhaps, then, it is a virtue for an economic theory of disappointment that it points to an area that seems to be the domain of chance. Of course, at one level, it is not a matter of chance at all that some people face their disappointments squarely, while others evade them at all costs. These individual differences could perhaps be understood, if only we knew enough about the individual person and his context. But unpacking every aspect of these differences is beyond the scope of my ambitions here. Rather, what I have done so far is to spell out the structure of certain kinds of errors that might be the cause of disappointments.

We can see, from the way we have structured the problem, that the person's lack of knowledge could be profound, in the sense that he has only a limited understanding of what it is that he does not know. He knows he did not get what he expected. He might know the level of utility he actually received. He might know the slope of the indifference curve that he actually landed on: that is, he might know the trade-off between the two goods that he actually faced, rather than the trade-off he expected to face. This knowledge is a very local and particular knowledge, however, and does not necessarily reveal to him everything he needs to know about the trade-offs between those two goods in every other context.

It is because of this very limited knowledge that our capacity to specify the person's next move is so limited. We cannot know how he will interpret his experience, or even how he ought to interpret his experience. Thus, under the theory proposed here, we have a place for the unpredictable, what our colleagues in the humanities call "the human element." Nonetheless, we have narrowed the problem somewhat, since we have moved beyond the realm of simply asserting that everyone maximizes his utility function, given from somewhere, based on fixed price and technology information, discovered somehow.

XI. Conclusion: The Mystery of Influence

In the earliest version of this essay, I was tempted to write down a model of people's speech and memories of speech as inputs into a person's reinterpretation of his preferences. The messages one receives, the intensity of the messages, the frequency with which each message is received—all of these would be inputs into the talk which a person constructs for his own internal dialogue.

But I discarded the idea of constructing such a model, for this is one place in which I certainly do not want to offer a deterministic account. I do not want to even remotely suggest that the influence people have on each other can be accounted for in a mechanical, cause-and-effect, push-button way. For this process, which goes on in the interior of each person, in the privacy of the mind, is one that cannot be reduced to a mechanized relationship between causes and effects. It is here, I believe, that the real mystery of human autonomy lies.

We live in a universe of cause and effect. Yet we ourselves have the capacity for independent action and thought. We have influence upon other people; other people influence us; but this whole process is shrouded in mystery. Why do some people respond to a given set of circumstances in a manner so different from the way others do? Why do the siblings in a family, responding to such similar external constraints, having a very similar genetic endowment, often react to the family's life so very differently? When we make an argument, or present a case, or offer an idea, why do people in the audience respond in such a wide variety of ways?

The fact is that we cannot control the influence we have on others. We can see ourselves as inputs into a process that is unique to each person, and whose final outcome is not up to us. At the same time, we can realize that while others do influence us in significant ways, we continue to exercise some discretion over the process. We have an influence of our own, over the thinking and choosing process that is uniquely our own responsibility, in spite of the influence of so many other people.

This mystery of influence is one that is familiar to everyone, especially those who are deeply engaged in the life of the mind. Some ideas become so familiar to us that they become part of the furniture of our minds. We can hardly remember when that thought was not present. Sometimes we use an idea and cannot remember its origins: How did I know that? Who told me that? Where did I read that? And yet there it is, part of our inner dialogue, part of our interior world.

At the same time, we often hope to influence other people, knowing full well that we have only limited control over their responses. We do the best we can to make ourselves clear to others. In spite of our best efforts, however, we know that we frequently will be misunderstood, misinterpreted, or disagreed with, even when we know we have made an argument that is perfectly sound and reasonable to us. I daresay that many of us enter academic life precisely for the chance to participate in this mystery of influence. We know that the people who read and hear our words will take them in, and will process our thoughts in their own ways and for their own purposes. Often our purposes will be completely thwarted by the use to which others put our efforts. Still, we persist. We believe, or maybe we just hope, that our influence will serve some greater good, in spite of all the slippage between our intentions and those of our listeners.

The cellist on the sidewalks of Sarajevo is not a stimulus-response machine. Neither is he a selfish gene, acting in some preprogrammed, complicated, and subtle way for survival. He is one unique and irreplaceable example of the human person, in all of his mystery, and all of his glory.

Economics, George Mason University

HAPPINESS AND MEANING:
TWO ASPECTS OF THE GOOD LIFE

By Susan Wolf

The topic of self-interest raises large and intractable philosophical questions—most obviously, the question "In what does self-interest consist?" The concept, as opposed to the content of self-interest, however, seems clear enough. Self-interest is interest in one's own good. To act self-interestedly is to act on the motive of advancing one's own good. Whether what one does actually is in one's self-interest depends on whether it actually does advance, or at least, minimize the decline of, one's own good. Though it may be difficult to tell whether a person is motivated by self-interest in a particular instance, and difficult also to determine whether a given act or decision really is in one's self-interest, the meaning of the claims in question seems unproblematic.

My main concern in this essay is to make a point about the content of self-interest.[1] Specifically I shall put forward the view that meaningfulness, in a sense I shall elaborate, is an important element of a good life. It follows, then, that it is part of an enlightened self-interest that one wants to secure meaning in one's life, or, at any rate, to allow and promote meaningful activity within it. Accepting this substantial conception of self-interest, however, carries with it a curious consequence: the concept of self-interest which formerly seemed so clear begins to grow fuzzy. Fortunately, it comes to seem less important as well.

I. Theories of Self-Interest

In *Reasons and Persons*,[2] Derek Parfit distinguishes three sorts of theories about self-interest—hedonistic theories, preference theories, and what he calls "objective-list theories." *Hedonistic theories* hold that one's good is a matter of the felt quality of one's experiences. The most popular theory of self-interest, which identifies self-interest with happiness, and happiness with pleasure and the absence of pain, is a prime example of a hedonistic theory. Noting that some people do not care that much about their own happiness, however—and, importantly, that they do not even regard their own happiness as the exclusive element of their own good—

---

[1] The view described and defended here shows the influence of and my sympathy with the views of Aristotle and John Stuart Mill throughout. I cannot individuate my debts to them; they are pervasive.

[2] Derek Parfit, *Reasons and Persons* (Oxford: Oxford University Press, 1984).

has led some to propose a *preference theory* of self-interest, which would identify a person's good with what the person most wants for herself. Thus, for example, if a person cares more about being famous, even posthumously famous, than about being happy, then a preference theory would accord fame a proportionate weight in the identification of her self-interest. If a person cares more about knowing the truth than about believing what it is pleasant or comfortable to believe, then it is in her self-interest to have the truth, unpleasant as it may be.

A person's preferences regarding herself, however, may be self-destructive or otherwise bizarre, and it may be that some things (including pleasure) are good for a person whether the person prefers them or not. It is not absurd to think that being deceived is bad for a person (and thus that not being deceived is good for a person) whether or not the person in question consciously values this state. Friendship and love may also seem to be things whose goodness explains, rather than results from, people's preferences for them. The plausibility of these last thoughts explains the appeal of *objective-list theories*, according to which a person's good includes at least some elements that are independent of or prior to her preferences and to their effect on the felt quality of her experience. On this view, there are some items, ideally specifiable on an "objective list," whose relevance to a fully successful life are not conditional on the subject's choice.

The view that I shall be advancing, that meaningfulness is an ingredient of the good life, commits one to a version of this last kind of theory, for my claim is that meaningfulness is a nonderivative aspect of a good life—its goodness does not result from its making us happy or its satisfying the preferences of the person whose life it is. Thus, it follows that any theory that takes self-interest to be a wholly subjective matter, either in a sense that identifies self-interest with the subjective quality of a person's experiences or in a sense that allows the standards of self-interest to be set by a person's subjective preferences, must be inadequate. At the same time, it would be a mistake to think that the objective good of a meaningful life is one that is wholly independent of the subject's experience or preferences, as if it could be good for a person to live a meaningful life whether or not it makes her happy or satisfies her preferences. Indeed, as we will see, the very idea that activities can make a life meaningful without the subject's endorsement is a dubious one.

II. MEANING IN LIFE

What is a meaningful life? Spelling it out will constitute the bulk of my essay, for my hope is that once the idea is spelled out, it will be readily agreed that it is an element of a fully successful life.

A meaningful life is, first of all, one that has within it the basis for an affirmative answer to the needs or longings that are characteristically described as needs for meaning. I have in mind, for example, the sort of questions people ask on their deathbeds, or simply in contemplation of their eventual deaths, about whether their lives have been (or are) worth living, whether they have had any point, and the sort of questions one asks when considering suicide and wondering whether one has any reason to go on. These questions are familiar from Russian novels and existentialist philosophy, if not from personal experience. Though they arise most poignantly in times of crisis and intense emotion, they also have their place in moments of calm reflection, when considering important life choices. Moreover, paradigms of what are taken to be meaningful and meaningless lives in our culture are readily available. Lives of great moral or intellectual accomplishment—Gandhi, Mother Teresa, Albert Einstein—come to mind as unquestionably meaningful lives (if any are); lives of waste and isolation—Thoreau's "lives of quiet desperation," typically anonymous to the rest of us, and the mythical figure of Sisyphus—represent meaninglessness.

To what general characteristics of meaningfulness do these images lead us and how do they provide an answer to the longings mentioned above? Roughly, I would say that meaningful lives are lives of active engagement in projects of worth. Of course, a good deal needs to be said in elaboration of this statement. Let me begin by discussing the two key phrases, "active engagement" and "projects of worth."

A person is actively engaged by something if she is gripped, excited, involved by it. Most obviously, we are actively engaged by the things and people about which and whom we are passionate. Opposites of active engagement are boredom and alienation. To be actively engaged in something is not always pleasant in the ordinary sense of the word. Activities in which people are actively engaged frequently involve stress, danger, exertion, or sorrow (consider, for example: writing a book, climbing a mountain, training for a marathon, caring for an ailing friend). However, there is something good about the feeling of engagement: one feels (typically without thinking about it) especially alive.

That a meaningful life must involve "projects of worth" will, I expect, be more controversial, for the phrase hints of a commitment to some sort of objective value. This is not accidental, for I believe that the idea of meaningfulness, and the concern that our lives possess it, are conceptually linked to such a commitment.[3] Indeed, it is this linkage that I want to defend, for I have neither a philosophical theory of what objective value is nor a substantive theory about what has this sort of value. What is clear to me is that there can be no sense to the idea of meaningfulness without a distinction between more and less worthwhile ways to spend one's time, where the test of worth is at least partly independent of a subject's ungrounded preferences or enjoyment.

[3] This point is made by David Wiggins in his brilliant but difficult essay "Truth, Invention, and the Meaning of Life," *Proceedings of the British Academy*, vol. 62 (1976).

Consider first the longings or concerns about meaning that people have, their wondering whether their lives are meaningful, their vows to add more meaning to their lives. The sense of these concerns and resolves cannot fully be captured by an account in which what one does with one's life doesn't matter, as long as one enjoys or prefers it. Sometimes people have concerns about meaning despite their knowledge that their lives to date have been satisfying. Indeed, their enjoyment and "active engagement" with activities and values they now see as shallow seems only to heighten the sense of meaninglessness that comes to afflict them. Their sense that their lives so far have been meaningless cannot be a sense that their activities have not been chosen or fun. When they look for sources of meaning or ways to add meaning to their lives, they are searching for projects whose justifications lie elsewhere.

Second, we need an explanation for why certain sorts of activities and involvements come to mind as contributors to meaningfulness while others seem intuitively inappropriate. Think about what gives meaning to your own life and the lives of your friends and acquaintances. Among the things that tend to come up on such lists, I have already mentioned moral and intellectual accomplishments and the ongoing activities that lead to them. Relationships with friends and relatives are perhaps even more important for most of us. Aesthetic enterprises (both creative and appreciative), the cultivation of personal virtues, and religious practices frequently loom large. By contrast, it would be odd, if not bizarre, to think of crossword puzzles, sitcoms, or the kind of computer games to which I am fighting off addiction as providing meaning in our lives, though there is no question that they afford a sort of satisfaction and that they are the objects of choice. Some things, such as chocolate and aerobics class, I choose even at considerable cost to myself (it is irrelevant that these particular choices may be related), so I must find them worthwhile in a sense. But they are not the sorts of things that make life worth living.[4]

"Active engagement in projects of worth," I suggest, answers to the needs an account of meaningfulness in life must meet. If a person is or has been thus actively engaged, then she does have an answer to the question of whether her life is or has been worthwhile, whether it has or has had a point. When someone looks for ways to add meaning to her life, she is looking (though perhaps not under this description) for worthwhile projects about which she can get enthused. The account also explains why some activities and projects but not others come to mind as contributors to

---

[4] Woody Allen appears to have a different view. His list of the things that make life worth living at the end of *Manhattan* includes, for example "the crabs at Sam Woo's," which would seem to be on the level of chocolates. On the other hand, the crabs' appearance on the list may be taken to show that he regards the dish as an accomplishment meriting aesthetic appreciation, where such appreciation is a worthy activity in itself; in this respect, the crabs might be akin to other items on his list such as the second movement of the *Jupiter Symphony*, Louis Armstrong's recording of "Potatohead Blues," and "those apples and pears of Cézanne." Strictly speaking, the appreciation of great chocolate might also qualify as such an activity.

meaning in life. Some projects, or at any rate, particular acts, are worth-while but too boring or mechanical to be sources of meaning. People do not get meaning from recycling or from writing checks to Oxfam and the ACLU. Other acts and activities, though highly pleasurable and deeply involving, like riding a roller coaster or meeting a movie star, do not seem to have the right kind of value to contribute to meaning.

Bernard Williams once distinguished categorical desires from the rest. Categorical desires give us reasons for living—they are not premised on the assumption that we will live. The sorts of things that give meaning to life tend to be objects of categorical desire. We desire them, at least so I would suggest, because we think them worthwhile. They are not worth-while simply because we desire them or simply because they make our lives more pleasant.

Roughly, then, according to my proposal, a meaningful life must satisfy two criteria, suitably linked. First, there must be active engagement, and second, it must be engagement in (or with) projects of worth. A life is meaningless if it lacks active engagement with anything. A person who is bored or alienated from most of what she spends her life doing is one whose life can be said to lack meaning. Note that she may in fact be performing functions of worth. A housewife and mother, a doctor, or a busdriver may be competently doing a socially valuable job, but because she is not engaged by her work (or, as we are assuming, by anything else in her life), she has no categorical desires that give her a reason to live. At the same time, someone who *is* actively engaged may also live a mean-ingless life, if the objects of her involvement are utterly worthless. It is difficult to come up with examples of such lives that will be uncontro-versial without being bizarre. But both bizarre and controversial ex-amples have their place. In the bizarre category, we might consider pathological cases: someone whose sole passion in life is collecting rubber bands, or memorizing the dictionary, or making handwritten copies of *War and Peace*. Controversial cases will include the corporate lawyer who sac-rifices her private life and health for success along the professional ladder, the devotee of a religious cult, or—an example offered by Wiggins[5]—the pig farmer who buys more land to grow more corn to feed more pigs to buy more land to grow more corn to feed more pigs.

We may summarize my proposal in terms of a slogan: "Meaning arises when subjective attraction meets objective attractiveness." The idea is that in a world in which some things are more worthwhile than others, meaning arises when a subject discovers or develops an affinity for one or typically several of the more worthwhile things and has and makes use of the opportunity to engage with it or them in a positive way.

An advantage of the slogan is that it avoids the somewhat misleading reference to "projects." That term is less than ideal in its suggestion of

---

[5] See Wiggins, "Truth, Invention, and the Meaning of Life," p. 342.

well-defined and goal-oriented tasks. To be sure, many projects do add
meaning to life—mastering a field of study, building a house, turning a
swamp into a garden, curing cancer—but much of what gives meaning to
life consists in ongoing relationships and involvements—with friends,
family, the scientific community, with church or ballet or chess. These
ongoing strands of life give rise to and are partly constituted by projects—
you plan a surprise party for your spouse, coach a little league team,
review an article for a journal—but the meaning comes less from the
individuated projects than from the larger involvements of which they
are parts. The slogan, moreover, is intentionally vague, for if pretheoretical judgments about meaning even approximate the truth, then not only
the objects of worth but also the sorts of interaction with them that are
capable of contributing to meaning are immensely variable. One can get
meaning from creating, promoting, protecting (worthwhile) things, from
helping people one loves and people in need, from achieving levels of
skill and excellence, from overcoming obstacles, from gaining understanding, and even from just communing with or actively appreciating what is
there to be appreciated.

It is part of our job, if not our natural bent, as philosophers to be
skeptical—about the correctness of these pretheoretical judgments, about
our ability reliably to distinguish meaningful from meaningless activities,
and about the very coherence of the distinction. About the first two worries I am not very concerned. Assuming that the distinctions are coherent
and that some activities are more worthwhile than others, our culture-
bound, contemporary judgments of which activities are worthwhile are
bound to be partly erroneous. History is full of unappreciated geniuses,
of artists, inventors, explorers whose activities at their time were scorned,
as it is full of models of behavior and accomplishment that later seem to
have been overrated. Though we may improve our judgments, both particular and general, by an open-minded, concentrated, and communal
effort to examine and articulate the basis for them (a project that strikes
me as both worthwhile and intrinsically interesting), the hope or expectation that such scrutiny will yield a reliable method for generally distinguishing worthwhile from worthless activities seems overly optimistic.
Why do we respect people who devote themselves to chess more than
those who become champions at pinball? Why do we admire basketball
stars more than jump-rope champions? What is more worthwhile about
writing a book on the philosophy of language than writing one on Nicole
Brown Simpson's sex life? It is useful to ask and to answer such questions,
so far as we can, both to widen and correct our horizons and to increase
our understanding. But our inability to give complete and adequate answers, or to be confident in the details of our assessments, need not be a
serious problem. The point of recognizing the distinction, after all, is not
to give rankings of meaningful lives. There is no need, in general, to pass
judgment on individuals or even on activities in which people want to

engage. The point is rather at a more general level to understand the ingredients of our own and others' good, and to get a better idea of the sorts of considerations that provide reasons for living our lives one way rather than another.

The point, which I am in the midst of developing, is that meaningfulness is a nonderivative part of an individual's good, and that meaningfulness consists in active engagement in projects or activities of worth. Though it seems to me that the point and most of its usefulness can stand despite acknowledged difficulties with identifying precisely which projects or activities these are, it would be utterly destroyed if it turned out that there were no such things as projects or activities of worth at all—if it turned out, in other words, as Bentham thought, that pushpin were as good as poetry,[6] not because of some heretofore undiscovered excellences in the game of pushpin, but because the very idea of distinctions in worth is bankrupt or incoherent. If there are no projects of worth (in contrast to other projects), then there are no such things as what I have in mind by more and less meaningful lives, and so it cannot be a part of one's good to live a more meaningful rather than a less meaningful life. If the idea of a worthwhile project is just a fraud or a hoax, then my account of self-interest is undone by it.

Since I have no *theory* of worth by which to prove the coherence of the concept or refute all skeptical challenges, I can only acknowledge the vulnerability of my account of self-interest in this regard. That we do, most of us, believe that some activities and projects are more worthwhile than others, that we regard certain activities as wastes of time (or near wastes of time) and others as inherently valuable, seems undeniable. These beliefs lie behind dispositions to feel proud or disgusted with ourselves for time spent well or badly, and they account for at least some of our efforts to steer our children and our friends toward some activities and away from others. When I try to take up a point of view that denies the distinction between worthwhile and worthless activity, I cannot find it convincing. Still, it is an article of faith that these untheoretical judgments, or some core of them, are philosophically defensible. It is on the assumption that they are defensible that my views about meaningfulness and self-interest are built.

III. TWO CHALLENGES

My proposal so far has been that meaningfulness in life arises from engagement in worthwhile activity. I have argued for the plausibility of this account on the grounds that it fits well both with the needs that are typically referred to as needs for meaning and with the concrete judg-

---

[6] This remark was made famous by John Stuart Mill, who quoted it in his essay on Bentham. See J. M. Robson, ed., *Collected Works of John Stuart Mill*, vol. 10 (Toronto: University of Toronto Press, 1969), p. 113.

ments of meaningful and meaningless activity that are most commonly
made. Before proceeding with an examination of the relation between
meaning and self-interest, two challenges to this account of meaning
should be answered.

The first objects that, contrary to my claims, my account of meaning
fails to meet the requirements I have set up for it. It fails, more particularly, to answer to the needs of at least one type of longing for meaning
that members of our species tend to have. Traditional worries about the
meaning of life, often set off by reflections on our own mortality and on
the indifference of the cosmos in which we occupy so tiny a place, are
rarely appeased by the reflection that one can actively engage in projects
of worth. At least, they are not appeased by reflection on the availability
of the kind of projects I have been talking about, like taking up the cello,
writing a novel, volunteering at a child's day-care center or a nursing
home. Tolstoy, the publicly acclaimed author of some of the greatest
works of literature ever written, the father and spouse of what he described (perhaps inaccurately) as a loving and successful family, could
have had no doubt that, relatively speaking, his life was spent in projects
as worthwhile as any. Yet he was plagued by the thought that it was all
for naught.[7] Nothing he did seemed to save his life from meaninglessness. Like Tolstoy, such philosophers as Albert Camus[8] and Thomas Nagel[9] see the meaning or meaninglessness of life as an issue relating to the
human condition. The difference between a person who wastes her time
in frivolous or shallow pursuits and one who makes something of herself
and serves humanity cannot, on their views, make the difference between
a meaningful and a meaningless life.

To try to give a wholly adequate answer to this challenge would take
us too far afield from the purposes of this essay. The issue of The Meaning
of Life is too obscure and complex, and the differences among the philosophers whose views seem to pose a challenge to the one I am offering
call for different responses. Some brief remarks, however, will at least
indicate what a more detailed answer might look like and will give some
reason for thinking that the challenge can be met.

Among those who think that meaning in life, or the lack of it, is primarily concerned with facts about the human condition, some disagree
not with my general account of meaning but with, if you will, its application. Their position, in other words, shares my view that meaning comes
from engagement in projects of worth, but assigns certain facts about the
human condition a crucial role in settling whether there are any such
projects. If God does not exist, they think, then nothing is any more

[7] See Leo Tolstoy, "My Confession," in E. D. Klemke, ed., *The Meaning of Life* (New York:
Oxford University Press, 1981).
[8] Albert Camus, *The Myth of Sisyphus and Other Essays* (New York: Vintage Books, 1955).
[9] Thomas Nagel, "The Absurd," in Nagel, *Mortal Questions* (Cambridge: Cambridge University Press, 1979).

worthwhile than anything else. Within this group, some believe that God is the only possible standard for judgments of nonsubjective value. If God does not exist, they think, then neither does moral or aesthetic value or any other sort of value that could distinguish some projects as better than others. Others believe that though there may be a difference between great literature and junk, and between virtue and vice, there is no point in bothering about which you occupy yourself with. Nothing lasts forever; the human race will be destroyed; the earth will crash into the sun. Only God, and the promise of an eternal life either for ourselves or for the universe in which our accomplishments have a place, can give a point to our living lives one way rather than another. Only God can make meaningful life so much as a possibility.

My own view about this position is that it expresses an irrational obsession with permanence; but it is enough for the purposes of this essay to note that it does not really challenge the account of meaning I have offered. I have already acknowledged that the usefulness of my account rests on the assumption that the distinction between worthwhile and worthless projects is defensible, and on the assumption that at least a core of our beliefs about what is worthwhile and what is worthless is roughly correct. Those who think that God is a necessary grounding for these assumptions and who believe in Him may still find my account of meaning acceptable. Those who think that God is a necessary grounding that unfortunately does not exist will reject my substantive claims about meaning for reasons we have already admitted.

Others, including Nagel and arguably Camus, think that there are differences between better and worse ways to live our lives. Evidently, they think that projects and activities can be more and less worthwhile, and that we have some sort of reason to favor the more worthwhile. They do not, however, see these facts as supplying a basis for meaning. Like the group just discussed, they link meaning inextricably to facts about our place in space-time and in the order of the cosmos. In an indifferent universe, they think, our lives are unavoidably meaningless no matter what we do with them. On the other hand, there may be some other point to choosing to do something good or worthwhile. This view disagrees explicitly with my own proposal—indeed, it appears to be in outright contradiction to it. However, it seems to me to be largely a disagreement in the use of words. *The* issue of meaning, which these philosophers tie essentially to issues about our significance (or lack of it) in the universe, seems to me to be really a tangle of issues with overlapping strands. Though talk about meaning sometimes expresses a concern about our relation to the cosmos, the use of the term and its cognates to refer to differences among human lives and activities is no less common. I believe that there are relations between these different uses that have not been fully appreciated, and that philosophers like Nagel and Camus have insufficiently recognized the degree to which anthropocentric values can serve as a basis for addressing worries about our place in the universe.[10] However, this issue is not relevant to my present purpose. My purpose here is to advance the view that it is in our interest to live lives of a certain sort, and to explore some of that view's implications. Whether we should describe these lives as more meaningful than others, or describe the desire to live them as a desire for meaning, is relatively superficial and may in any case be left to another day. I shall continue to use my terminology, however, and hope that no one will be confused by it.

The second challenge to my account of meaningfulness is more directly relevant to the issue of the nature of self-interest. It consists of an alternative subjective account of meaning that is forcefully suggested, although not in quite the terms I shall use, by Richard Taylor's discussion of the meaning of life in his book *Good and Evil*.[11] According to this position, meaning is not a matter of one's projects in life being worthwhile from some objective point of view. (Taylor himself seems to think that no projects could meet this standard.) Rather, a person's life is meaningful, one might say, if it is meaningful *to her*, and it is meaningful to her if she thinks or feels it is.

The suggestion that something is meaningful to someone as long as she thinks it is can be of no help to us in developing an account of meaningfulness, for we cannot understand what it would be for someone to think her life meaningful until we have an account of what meaningfulness is. The view I want to discuss, however, is, strictly speaking, more concerned with a feeling or, better, a sense or qualitative character that some of our experiences have. We may use the term "fulfillment" to refer to it. It is pleasant to be or to feel fulfilled or to find an activity or a relationship fulfilling, but it is a pleasure of a specific sort, one that seems closely associated with the thought that our lives or certain activities within them are meaningful. Recognizing this, it may be suggested, gives us all the basis we need for an account of meaning that meets my requirements. We may understand people's longing for meaning as a longing for this particular feeling, a longing which other sorts of pleasure cannot satisfy. We can also explain why some activities characteristically answer the call of meaning better than others. Some yield the feeling of fulfillment while others do not. Chocolate is filling but not fulfilling; it gives pleasure but not of this particular kind. When a person steps back, wondering whether her life has had meaning, or searching for a way to give it more meaning, she may simply be surveying her life for its quotient of fulfillment or looking for ways to increase it.

The very close ties between meaningfulness and fulfillment on which this account of meaning relies are important for understanding both the concept of meaning and its value. That meaningful activity or a mean-

---

[10] I discuss this in my "Meaningful Lives in a Meaningless World," unpublished manuscript.
[11] Richard Taylor, *Good and Evil* (New York: Macmillan, 1970).

ingful life is at least partly fulfilling is, as this account suggests, a conceptual truth. To *identify* meaningfulness with fulfillment, however, neglects aspects of our use of the terms, and aspects of the experiences that are described by them, that my more objective account of meaningfulness better accommodates.

For one thing, fulfillment is not a brute feeling but one with some cognitive content or concomitant. That certain activities tend to be fulfilling and others not seems connected to features of the relevant activities that make this fact intelligible. There is a fittingness between certain kinds of activities and the potential for fulfillment. When a relationship or a job is fulfilling, there is something about it that makes it so. One feels appreciated or loved, or has the sense of doing good, or finds the challenge of the work rewarding. It is not just that the activities in question meet our expectations, though that is a part of it. Some things are fine but not fulfilling—my relationship with my hairdresser, for example, or my weekly trips to the supermarket.

These considerations suggest that we find things fulfilling only if we can think about them in a certain way. It is difficult precisely to identify a single belief that is always associated with the experience of fulfillment. Still, I propose that there is some association between finding an activity fulfilling and believing, or at least dimly, inarticulately perceiving, there to be something independently worthwhile or good about it.

In his discussion of the meaning of life, Richard Taylor considers the case of Sisyphus and imagines that the gods, by inserting some substance in Sisyphus's veins, give Sisyphus a love for stone-rolling. Sisyphus's life is thereby transformed from one of miserable bondage to one of ecstatic fulfillment. Taylor himself recognizes that the thought experiment is an odd one, and that the passion for stone-rolling will strike his readers as bizarre. Taylor, however, seems to think that the strangeness of the example comes simply from its being unusual. People do not characteristically get passionate about mindless, futile, never-ending tasks; nor is this the sort of disposition that drugs typically induce. To many, however, the example is not just surprising but somewhat horrifying. The state of being fulfilled by perpetual stone-rolling is not unreservedly enviable. Of course, for Sisyphus, who is condemned to roll stones in any case, there is a great benefit in being able to be happy with his lot. In general, however, I suspect that most people would think that stone-rolling (mere stone-rolling, that is, without any purpose or development of skill) is not the sort of thing by which one ought to be fulfilled.[12] That Sisyphus is fulfilled by stone-rolling suggests an understanding of Sisyphus as a victim (albeit a happy one) of a kind of drug-induced illusion. He finds something in stone-rolling that isn't really there.

[12] See Joel Feinberg, *Freedom and Fulfillment* (Princeton: Princeton University Press, 1992), ch. 13.

If we accept the idea that the feeling of fulfillment is necessarily connected with beliefs about its objects—if we accept that an activity or relationship can be fulfilling only if one believes it to be somehow independently good—then we can distinguish two hypotheses about the relationship between meaning and fulfillment. Does meaning come from the experience of fulfillment, no matter what its cause, or is a meaningful life one in which a subject is fulfilled by activities suitable to the experience? The subjective account suggested by Taylor opts for the former; but the latter seems to square better with our ordinary use of the concept.[13]

One test case is Taylor's version of Sisyphus itself. That Sisyphus finds his life fulfilling is built in by assumption. But should we describe his life as meaningful? This seems to me a misuse of the word. "It is meaningful to him," someone will say, and we understand what this means. It means that he finds his life fulfilling, and, perhaps, that he thinks it is meaningful (or would think it, if asked). But, for those who find the example horrifying, that is part of the problem: he thinks his life gets meaning from mindless, futile stone-rolling, but it does not.

We can construct a second test case by considering someone whose judgment of an aspect of her life has changed. A woman previously blissfully in love discovers that the man she loved has been using her. She had found the relationship fulfilling before she learned of his deceits. She would have said, had you asked her earlier, that the relationship contributed to the meaningfulness of her life. What would she say now, however, and what should we say about her? No one can take away the feelings of fulfillment she experienced during the period she was deceived; but it seems unlikely that she would say, after the fact, that the relationship truly had given meaning to her life. Indeed, part of what makes this sort of event so sad is that, in addition to the pain that is caused when the deception is discovered, it undermines the value of all the pleasure that came before.

Less fanciful than Sisyphus are cases of addicts or inductees of religious cults whose feelings of contentment are caused, but not justified, by the things that bring them about. Though we should be cautious about passing judgment on the activities that others take to be worthwhile, this is no reason to rule out the possibility that people are sometimes mistaken, that their finding something fulfilling can be wrongly induced, either through the establishment of false factual beliefs (such as belief in a loved one's fidelity or in the divine status of a charismatic leader) or by drugs or electrodes. If, moreover, they are led by such mind-altering means to spend their lives occupied by some equivalent of stone-rolling—watching endless reruns of *Leave It to Beaver* or counting and recounting the number of tiles on the bathroom floor—then it seems to me most in line with

[13] Robert Nozick makes a similar suggestion in *The Examined Life* (New York: Simon and Schuster, 1989). In addition to wanting happiness, Nozick writes, "[w]e also want this emotion of happiness to be *fitting*" (p. 112).

ordinary language to describe them as leading meaningless lives, however fulfilled they may feel themselves to be. If, further, such people wake up or snap out of it—if they come to occupy a point of view that devalues their former lives—then their later descriptions would not, I think, grant meaning to the things in which they had found contentment before.

IV. Meaningfulness and Self-Interest

So far I have been occupied with spelling out a conception of what meaningfulness in life is. My point in doing so, in the present context, is to bring it to bear on the idea of self-interest. Meaningfulness seems to me an important ingredient of a good life, and one that is too often either neglected or distorted by contemporary accounts of individual well-being.

I do not know what an argument for this claim would look like. My hope, as I mentioned before, is that the mere spelling out of the claim will be enough to incline most people to assent to it. Still, I think that without attending explicitly to our interest in meaning, we tend to misunderstand and misdescribe it, with the eventual result that the shapes our lives take have less meaning than may be good for us.

Most people—at least most people within a certain group, bounded perhaps by class or education as well as by culture and history—behave in ways that suggest that they are looking for worthwhile things to do with their lives. They actively seek projects or, more typically, happily seize upon activities, from among those to which they are attracted, that they believe to be worthwhile. Explicit thoughts about worth and meaning often occur in connection with major life decisions, in addition to those moments of crisis to which I referred before. Some people decide to have children because they think it will give meaning to their lives. Others decide not to have children because they fear that the attendant responsibilities will deprive them of the time and resources and peace of mind that they need for other things in which they do find meaning. Deliberations about whether to pursue a particular career, or any career, may similarly involve concerns about whether the job is worthwhile, or whether it would demand time and energy that would distract one from what is worthwhile. Even many who do not talk explicitly in terms of meaning or worth make choices that are best explained by reference to them. In other words, our behavior, including some of our speech, seems to reveal a preference for a meaningful life.

We are, however, more apt to explain our choices in terms of fulfillment than meaning. A man opts for the more challenging of two possible careers, even at the cost of stress and insecurity. A woman chooses to work for less pay at a job she believes is morally valuable. People arrange their lives so as to give a few hours a week to Meals on Wheels, or to practicing piano, or to keeping up with their book group, even though it means going with a little less sleep, less flexibility, less straightforward fun. Why? Because, they will say, they find these things fulfilling. They choose to live this way because they regard it as, in some sense, best for them.

To defend these choices in terms of fulfillment establishes them as choices made out of self-interest. Talk of fulfillment may, however, suggest a more hedonistic interpretation of what is going on than the one I have offered. To choose something because it is fulfilling is, after all, to choose it because of a qualitative character of one's experience—and though fulfilling activities are not always as much fun or as intensely pleasurable as some of the alternatives, it may be that in the long run, or the wide run (taking into account Mill's differences in the quality as well as the quantity of pleasure, as it were), a fulfilling life is qualitatively better, and thus happier in the truest sense, than a life with as many or more pleasures but no fulfillment. So at least must the people described in the paragraph above believe, and so must we believe if we think their choices are rational, and are rational for the reason they give.

It is no part of my aim to deny this suggestion. On the contrary, that fulfillment is a great qualitative good, and that it deserves an important place in an adequate theory of happiness, are important contributing factors to my claim that meaning is a component of our good. We have already seen that the links between meaningfulness and fulfillment are very tight. Since a meaningful life is necessarily at least partly fulfilling, and since fulfillment is a major component of happiness, a very important reason for taking meaningfulness to be in our interest is that it brings fulfillment with it. It would be misleading, however, to draw from this the conclusion that meaningfulness is an instrumental good for us. To think of meaning as good because it is a means to an independent good of fulfillment would be a mistake.

It is doubtful that fulfillment is an independent good, although feeling fulfilled is pleasant and feeling unfulfilled unpleasant. If fulfillment were an independent good, it would follow that the feeling of fulfillment would be desirable no matter what its cause. It would have to be better to be Sisyphus happy (or, more precisely, Sisyphus fulfilled) than Sisyphus unhappy (unfulfilled), even if this required that Sisyphus was perpetually stoned out of his normal mind. Opinion, however, divides on this matter. Many value fulfillment only on the condition that it be based on appropriate thoughts or perceptions. Moreover, even among those who believe that feeling fulfilled is unconditionally better than the alternative, many would still prefer that these feelings were suitably caused. Better to be Sisyphus happy than Sisyphus unhappy, they may say, but better still not to be Sisyphus at all.

A proponent of a purely hedonistic theory of self-interest may point out that reports of such intuitions prove nothing. People's thinking that justified or appropriate fulfillment is better than unjustified inappropriate fulfillment doesn't make it so. To those who have these intuitions, however, the burden of proof seems to lie with the hedonist. Unless one is committed to a purely hedonistic account of value ahead of time, there seems no reason to doubt that what is principally desirable is getting fulfillment from genuinely fulfilling activities, from activities, that is, whose accompanying feeling of fulfillment comes from the correct perception of their value. There seems no reason to doubt, in other words, that what is principally desirable is living a meaningful life and not living a life that seems or feels meaningful. Insofar as we prefer a truly meaningful life to one that merely seems or feels meaningful, a purely hedonistic theory of self-interest will not account for it.

A preference theory of self-interest, however, would not have to account for it—preference theorists simply accept our preferences and go on to compute our self-interest from there. This suggests an alternative account of the relation between meaning and self-interest. According to preference theories, meaning is important to our well-being if and only if meaning matters to us. Since many of us do want to live meaningful lives—since we think it is better for us if we do—preference theorists will agree that it is in our interest that our lives are meaningful. From their point of view, there is no need to make any more objective claims than that.

From a practical perspective, it matters little whether we accept this theory or a more objective one, particularly if you think, as I do, that the preference for a meaningful life is widespread and deep. If it is accepted as a fact of human nature (even a statistical fact, and even of a culturally created human nature) that people just do care about meaning in their lives, then this gives us reason enough to shape our lives in ways that will encourage not just fulfillment but meaningfulness, and it gives us reason enough to shape our social and political institutions in ways that will increase the opportunities for everyone to live not just happily and comfortably but meaningfully as well.

A preference theory does not, however, seem accurately to reflect the status a meaningful life has for most of us. Most of us, it seems, do not regard our preference for a meaningful life as an ungrounded preference we just happen to have. If we did think so, then we would judge it a matter of indifference whether anyone else had or lacked this preference, and indeed, we would have no reason to want to keep this preference ourselves if we were convinced that we would be better off without it. For most people, however, at least so it seems to me, having a meaningful life is a value and not just a preference. We do not just want our lives to be meaningful, we think it good that we want it. Indeed, our interest and concern for meaning is sometimes mentioned as a mark of our humanity, as an aspect of what raises us above brutes. We think that we would be diminished as a species if we lost the aspiration, or the interest, in living meaningful lives and not just happy ones. Individuals who lack the desire that their lives be meaningful we regard with regret or even pity.

Again it may be noted that our believing something is no proof of its being true, and again I must acknowledge that I have no proof of the value or objective desirability of meaningfulness. At the same time, the claim that a meaningful life is preferable (and not just brutely preferred) to a meaningless one may seem so nearly self-evident as to require no proof. Once one is willing to apply the terms of meaningfulness and meaninglessness at all, it may seem unstable to believe that a life that lacks meaning is no worse than one that possesses it. Even if we can logically distinguish the position that some lives are more meaningful than others from the position which adds that (some) meaningfulness is a good, this latter position seems more natural than one which denies it. Though we may be unable to argue for caring about meaning in a way that would convince someone who doesn't care to begin with, the concern or the desire for meaningful activity is, for those who have it, more rationally coherent with other values and dispositions than its absence would be.

In response to the question "Why care about living a meaningful life rather than a meaningless one?" the answer that I believe best expresses reflective common sense will begin with the connection between meaning and happiness: Nine times out of ten, perhaps ninety-nine times out of a hundred, a meaningful life will be happier than a meaningless one. The feelings of fulfillment one gets from interacting positively and support-ively with things or creatures (or "realms") whose love seems deserved are wonderful feelings, worth more, on qualitative grounds alone, than many other sorts of pleasure, and worth the cost of putting up with considerable quantities of pain. Moreover, the awareness, even dim and inarticulate, of a lack of anything that can constitute a source of pride or a source of connection to anything valuable outside of oneself can be awful, making one irritable, restless, and contemptuous of oneself.

Except in an academic philosophical context such as this, it is perhaps unnatural to press further. If we do press further, however, it seems to me that the strength and character of these feelings of pleasure and pain are not best explained as mere quirks of our natural or culturally conditioned psyches. Rather, that we feel so good or so bad in accordance with our sense of connection to value outside ourselves seems to me best explained in terms of an underlying belief that a life is better when it possesses such connections. What precisely is better about it is difficult to say. But perhaps it has to do with our place in the universe: since we are, each of us, occupants in a world full of value independent of our individual selves, living in such a way as to connect positively and supportively with some nonsubjective value harmonizes better with our objective situation than would a life whose chief occupations can be only subjectively defended.[14]

---

[14] I explore this in "Meaningful Lives in a Meaningless World."

V. The Deconstruction of Self-Interest

I have in this essay been concerned to defend, or rather to elaborate, what I take to be a deeply and widely held view about individual human good, namely, that a fully successful life is, among other things, a meaningful one. Further, I have urged that this claim is distorted if it is understood as an element of either a hedonistic or a preference theory of self-interest. Properly understood, it requires a rejection of both of these sorts of theories.

As a substantive claim, I do not expect that the point that a good life must be meaningful will be surprising. We are not used to thinking very explicitly or very analytically about it, however; and in popular unreflective consciousness, a substantive interest in a meaningful life often sits side by side with assumptions that are incompatible with it. How often have you heard someone say, "What's the point of doing something if it isn't fun, or if you don't enjoy it?" I hear this sentiment expressed quite frequently, despite living on the East Coast. To be fair, such expressions tend to be limited to contexts of self-interest. They are not intended as rejections of the rational authority of moral or legal obligation. Moreover, there is often a point behind such remarks that I would strongly endorse. Against a kind of workaholism and related neurotic obsessions with some forms of success and achievement, it can be useful to step back and reflect in the way these remarks would invoke. Still, the suggestion that there can be no point to things if they are neither duties nor fun is, strictly speaking, both false and dangerous.

Much of what we do would be inexplicable, or at least indefensible, if its justification depended either on its being a duty or, even in the long run, on its maximally contributing to our net fun. Relationships with friends and family, nonobligatory aspects of professional roles, and long-term commitments to artistic, scholarly, or athletic endeavors typically lead us to devote time and energy to things that are difficult and unpleasant, and to forgo opportunities for relaxation and enjoyment. It is arguable that many of these choices advance our happiness (in the broadest sense, our fun) in the long run, but such arguments are at best uncertain, and the thought that they are necessary for the defense of these choices puts a regrettable kind of pressure on the commitments that give rise to them. There is, however, a point—even a self-interested point—to doing things that fall outside the categories both of duty and of fun. One can find a reason, or at least a justifying explanation, for doing something in the fact that the act or activity in question contributes to the meaningfulness of one's life.

Once we have ceased to identify self-interest with happiness, however, other assumptions are also undermined. The concept of self-interest becomes more difficult to work with. Specifically, a conception of self-interest that recognizes the importance of meaning to a good life admits of much greater indeterminacy than the more traditional conceptions. This is partly a function of indeterminacy within the category of meaningfulness itself. Though meaningfulness is not an all-or-nothing concept— some lives are more meaningful than others, a person's life may not have *enough* meaning in it to be satisfactory—there is no well-formed system for making comparative judgments. The meaningfulness of a life may vary depending on how much of it is spent in meaningful activity, on how worthwhile the activities in question are,[15] or on how fully engaged (or attracted) the individual is. In many instances, however, it seems absurd to think there is a correct comparison to be made. Is the life of a great but lonely philosopher more or less meaningful than that of a beloved housekeeper? There seems to be no reason to assume that there is a fact of the matter about this. Moreover, from a self-interested point of view, it is unclear whether, beyond a certain point, it matters whether one's life is more meaningful. A meaningful life is better than a meaningless one, but once it is meaningful enough, there may be no self-interested reason to want, as it were, to squeeze more meaning into it. Finally, the mix between meaning and felt happiness may have no determinate ideal. A person often has to choose between taking a path that would strengthen or expand a part of his or her life that contributes to its meaningfulness (going to graduate school, adopting a child, getting politically involved) and taking an easier or more pleasant road. Once one has accepted a conception of self-interest that recognizes meaningfulness as an independent aspect of one's personal good, one may have to admit that in such cases there may be no answer to the question of what is most in one's self-interest.

Fortunately, as the concept of self-interest becomes more difficult to apply, it becomes less important to be able to apply it. In accepting the value of meaningfulness as an ingredient of our own interest, we necessarily also accept that meaningful activity has a value that is partly independent of our interest. We accept, in other words, the availability of a kind of reason for doing things that can compete with self-interest, a kind that will, at any rate, draw us away from a concern for our self-interest. What I have in mind is the sort of reason given by the worthiness of the meaningful activity (or its object) itself.

Meaningful activity, remember, involves engagement in projects of worth. It occurs where subjective attraction meets objective attractiveness. To acknowledge that an activity or a project is worthwhile, however, is to acknowledge, among other things, that there is a reason for doing it—a reason, at least, for doing it if you are attracted to doing it. A reason for writing a book on free will is to stimulate thought in a fruitful direction. A reason to plant bulbs and weed the garden is to maintain a place of

---

[15] The relevant scale of worth, however, will itself be a matter of contention. As my examples have probably made clear, there is no reason to identify the relevant kind of worth here with *moral* worth.

natural beauty. A reason to sew a groundhog costume for an eight-year-old girl is to make her happy.

To those who get meaning from the activities just mentioned, these sorts of reasons will dominate. Being suitably engaged in these activities in the way in which people who get meaning from them *are* engaged involves being drawn by their specific good or value. One so engaged is not likely to step back from the activity and ask, "Is this the best thing I can be doing *for me*?"

The point here is not just the one with which we are familiar from the paradox of hedonism. It is not just that, by not caring too much about whether her activities will be best for her, the agent is more likely to be living a life that is best for her. Rather, it is that she has a reason for her activities that is not conditional on their being best for her. Accepting a conception of self-interest that incorporates meaningfulness, then, involves rejecting too dominant a place for self-interest. Yet meaningful activity and self-interest cannot psychologically stretch too far apart. Activity is meaningful only if one can engage with it, be attracted to it, be in love with it or with the object around which it revolves. Such activity will always be somewhat fulfilling, and therefore will always make one somewhat happy. And as the fulfillment and happiness will be appropriate or deserved, that is all to one's good.

Philosophy, Johns Hopkins University

SELF-INTEREST AND VIRTUE*

By Neera K. Badhwar

Being happy . . . is found in living and being active. . . . The activity of the good person is excellent, and [hence] pleasant in itself.

Perceiving that we are alive is pleasant in itself. For life is by nature a good, and it is pleasant to perceive that something good is present in us. And living is choiceworthy, for a good person most of all, since being is good and pleasant for him.

—Aristotle, *Nicomachean Ethics*[1]

I. Introduction

The Aristotelian view that the moral virtues—the virtues of character informed by practical wisdom—are essential to an individual's happiness, and are thus in an individual's self-interest, has been little discussed outside of purely scholarly contexts. With a few exceptions, contemporary philosophers have tended to be suspicious of Aristotle's claims about human nature and the nature of rationality and happiness (*eudaimonia*).[2] But recent scholarship has offered an interpretation of the basic elements of Aristotle's views of human nature and happiness, and of reason and virtue, that brings them more into line with common-sense thinking and with contemporary philosophical and empirical psychology.[3] This makes it fruitful to reexamine the question of the role of virtue in self-interest.

* This essay has been vastly improved owing to the comments of the other contributors to this volume, its editors, and my colleagues at the University of Oklahoma who took part in a Faculty Workshop discussion of the essay. I owe special thanks to Ray Elugardo, James Hawthorne, Lester Hunt, Wayne Riggs, and Chris Swoyer for their extensive written comments.

[1] Aristotle, *Nicomachean Ethics*, ed. and trans. Terence Irwin (Indianapolis: Hackett, 1985), 1169b30-32 and 1179b1-4. All further references to the *Nicomachean Ethics* are to this translation, unless otherwise noted, and are abbreviated in the text as *NE*.

[2] See, e.g., Bernard Williams, *Ethics and the Limits of Philosophy* (London: Fontana Press, 1985); and David Gauthier, ed., *Morality and Rational Self-Interest* (Englewood Cliffs, NJ: Prentice-Hall, 1970), pp. 5-6. Some notable exceptions are N. J. H. Dent, *The Moral Psychology of the Virtues* (Cambridge: Cambridge University Press, 1984); John Casey, *Pagan Virtue* (Oxford: Clarendon Press, 1990); and David Brink, "Rational Egoism, Self, and Others," in *Identity, Character, and Morality*, ed. Owen Flanagan and Amélie O. Rorty (Cambridge: MIT Press, 1990), pp. 339-78. Brink gives a neo-Aristotelian, neo-Parfitian, egoistic justification of morality.

[3] See, e.g., Terence Irwin's discussion of the human function, rationality, and happiness in Irwin, *Aristotle's First Principles* (Oxford: Clarendon Press, 1988), sections 193-98; John M. Cooper, *Reason and the Human Good in Aristotle* (Cambridge: Harvard University Press, 1986); and Nancy Sherman, *The Fabric of Character* (Oxford: Clarendon Press, 1989).

Given the variability of human psychology, practically no claim about human nature, the nature of self-interest, or its connection to morality can apply without exception to all human moral agents, much less to all members of the human species. But this no more makes psychological or moral generalizations useless than the variability of human physiology makes generalizations about health, or its connection to diet and exercise, useless. For such claims still apply to, and thus have practical value for, most of us.

In this essay I will attempt to make a case for a broadly Aristotelian conception of self-interest and virtue, and for the centrality of virtue to self-interest so conceived. My aim is not to conclusively *prove* that a fully virtuous character is indispensable to self-interest, but to show that a far stronger case can be made for this claim than is usually supposed. Since this essay is not an exercise in Aristotelian scholarship, I will discuss Aristotle only as a launching pad for my own discussion. I will use Aristotle's insights about virtue as a psychological and practical disposition, and about self-interest as an objective psychological and practical condition of happiness or well-being (*eudaimonia*), to examine the connection between individual self-interest and some major virtues. But I will include in my discussion virtues not explicitly discussed by Aristotle if there are good reasons to think that they are, in fact, required for happiness. And I will reject Aristotle's assumption, shared by a strong strand in philosophical and common-sense morality, that someone who is just, or who has integrity, in one domain of her life (for example, as a judge), must be just, or have integrity, in all domains (for example, as a friend, mother, etc.). I believe that Aristotle is right that the virtues are interconnected, so that one virtue implies all the others; but I also believe that this is true only within domains, not globally. I have argued for these claims elsewhere, and will simply assume them here.[4]

The claim that individual well-being requires virtue is stronger than the claim that all that well-being requires by way of morality is a *commitment* to moral principles. It is stronger because (Aristotelian) virtue goes far beyond commitment to principle. Yet it is also more plausible, because both virtue and well-being are connected with the harmonious, effective functioning of our cognitive, emotional, social, and physical capacities — with what I will call "practical efficacy." Aristotle does not tell us in any detail exactly how virtue, practical efficacy, and well-being are connected. Doing this will be my main task in this essay. I will argue for the following claims: (1) virtue is essential to practical efficacy; (2) practical efficacy is essential to well-being or happiness; hence (3) virtue is essential to happiness. In other words, virtue not only makes us better, it also makes

---

[4] See my essay "The Limited Unity of Virtue," *Noûs*, vol. 3, no. 1 (September 1996). The empirical evidence against the assumption that the virtues are global is summarized in Owen Flanagan, *Varieties of Moral Personality* (Cambridge: Harvard University Press, 1991). My argument is made largely on the basis of philosophical considerations.

us better off. Virtue alone, however, is not sufficient for practical efficacy or for happiness—a degree of good fortune is also required. But virtue and a degree of good fortune are jointly sufficient for practical efficacy as well as happiness. Again, both practical efficacy and virtue are necessarily connected with the nature of our ultimate goals, and thus happiness is also connected with the nature of these goals. It is this connection with our ultimate goals that makes happiness an enduring, objective, psychological and practical state of well-being.

On this understanding of happiness, then, to say that happiness is objective is to say that happiness is not just a matter of pleasurable, tranquil, contented, or other positive feelings, but also a matter of leading a certain sort of life. A happy person, on the view I will defend, is a person whose positive feelings are a reflection of an efficacious life, and not only of a life marked by success and prosperity through the blessings of good fortune. For it is only insofar as positive feelings are a reflection of an efficacious life that they are firm and enduring, and it is only insofar as they are firm and enduring that they can be constituents of a firm and enduring thing like happiness.

It is worth noting that both practical efficacy and happiness come in degrees, so that, under circumstances of equally good fortune, someone with greater efficacy will also be happier. Further, goodness of character also comes in degrees, with virtue—moral excellence—representing the pinnacle of moral achievement. For these reasons, the claim that virtue is essential to practical efficacy and happiness should be read to mean "for the highest degree of practical efficacy and happiness." Someone whose character is good without being excellent—virtuous—in most domains may still, barring misfortune, be relatively efficacious and happy. These issues are further discussed in Section II below.

Some conceptions of moral virtue are, no doubt, incompatible with the attempt to show that virtue is a constitutive component of an agent's objectively conceived well-being. For example, conceptions that deny that virtue implies good ends, or that virtuous dispositions are, in part, emotional dispositions, are incompatible with the claim that virtue is a constitutive part of well-being. I have argued against these conceptions of virtue elsewhere;[5] in this essay, I will restrict myself to giving arguments in favor of the Aristotelian conception (Section II).

In Section II, I will give a brief overview of Aristotle's conception of human nature and human well-being, and of virtue and its role in well-being, to serve as a background to my own discussion. I will indicate which of his views are plausible on psychological or philosophical grounds, and which dubious. In the sections that follow, I will discuss the nature of practical efficacy and its role in well-being (Sections III and IV), and the

---

[5] See my "The Limited Unity of Virtue"; "The Rejection of Ethical Rationalism," *Logos,* vol. 10 (1989), pp. 99–131; and *Friendship: A Philosophical Reader* (Ithaca: Cornell University Press, 1993), pp. 20–25.

connection between well-being and virtue (Section V). I will conclude by restating the main thrust of my argument, and indicating some further directions for development (Section VI).

II. Aristotle's Theory of Human Nature, Well-Being, and Virtue

All men by nature desire to know. An indication of this is the delight we take in our senses; for even apart from their usefulness they are loved for themselves; and above all others the sense of sight.[6]

[W]e take the human function to be a certain kind of life, and take this life to be the soul's activity and actions that express reason. (*NE* 1098a12–13)

[T]hat man is more of a political animal than bees or any other gregarious animal is evident . . . [for] man is the only animal who has the gift of speech. . . . [T]he power of speech [*logos*] is intended to set forth the expedient and inexpedient, and therefore likewise the just and the unjust.[7]

As these passages show, Aristotle regards human nature as essentially rational *and* social *and* animal.[8] These are the three most fundamental psychologically and morally relevant facts about human beings. For together with the nature of the world we live in, they constitute "the circumstances of well-being and of virtue," in that they give rise to, and explain, the fundamental goals, pursuits, and pleasures that constitute our good and ground the virtues.

The fact that we are finite, fallible, and mortal *animals* explains why we have an interest in physical satisfactions and pleasures, and in preserving ourselves by gaining control of our environment and acting effectively. As *rational* animals, moreover, we are also intellectually exploratory, imaginative, capable of puzzlement, speculative, deliberative, and evaluative—and aware of ourselves as such. Hence, we seek to exercise our rational

---

[6] Aristotle, *Metaphysics*, 980a22–28, trans. W. D. Ross, in *The Complete Works of Aristotle*, ed. Jonathan Barnes (Princeton: Princeton University Press, 1984). Further references to *Metaphysics* are given parenthetically in the text. The thought expressed in this passage is put in a dramatic context in a description of one of the main characters of Ayn Rand's novel *Atlas Shrugged*: "[H]e looked as if his faculty of sight were his best-loved tool and its exercise were a limitless, joyous adventure, as if his eyes imparted a superlative value to himself and to the world—to himself for his ability to see, to the world for being a place so eagerly worth seeing" (Rand, *Atlas Shrugged* [New York: New American Library, 1957], p. 652).

[7] Aristotle, *Politics*, trans. Benjamin Jowett, in Barnes, ed., *The Complete Works of Aristotle*, 1253a7–15.

[8] At *Politics*, 1253a7–15, Aristotle tells us not only that a human being is a social or political animal, but also that he is more so than other social animals, and that this has to do with his possession of rationality. For only a rational (*logikon*) being can perceive and communicate the good and the bad, the just and the unjust.

faculties and gain knowledge of ourselves and our environment not only for the sake of further ends, but also for their own sake, i.e., for the sheer pleasure of knowing, and for experiencing ourselves as knowers (*Metaphysics* 980a22–28; *NE* 1170a32–b1, 1174b14–23). Similarly, we seek to exercise and enhance our agency for its own sake, i.e., for the sheer pleasure of acting and experiencing ourselves as agents; and the greater the complexity of the activity, the greater the pleasure.[9]

The fact that we are *social* rational animals explains why we have an interest in interacting with others. Like all social animals, we need others of our kind in order to meet our survival needs. Unlike other social animals, we also need others in order to share our imaginative, speculative, deliberative, and evaluative lives (*NE* 1097b12, 1170a16–19). This, too, is an intrinsically valuable activity, something we engage in for its own sake.

All of these intrinsically valuable activities are in evidence in early childhood: the eager delight in seeing and touching, in exploring one's surroundings, in exercising developing motor skills, and in communicating with others.[10] And when, in adulthood, these activities are informed and harmonized by reason, they are a constitutive part of living well. It is in this sense that we are "above all" our reason (*NE* 1168b27–33, cf. 1098a8–15).

Our self-interest as rational, social animals, then, is fundamentally both independent and interdependent, both a matter of our independent interactions with the world, and a matter of our shared life with others. These two sorts of goods, the independent and the shared, ground both the self-regarding virtues such as temperance or honesty with oneself, and the other-regarding virtues such as justice or generosity. The virtues, in turn, guide and help to specify the attitudes and goals essential to living a happy human life.

Since human beings are immensely complicated biological creatures— far more so than Aristotle realized—in an immensely complicated physical environment, we cannot take the claim about our nature being rational and social as applying to *all* members of the human species. And even with respect to those who *are* rational and social, the variability of human psychology and of social environments suggests that the conditions of human happiness can be specified only at a relatively abstract level, a level that leaves room for different individuals to fill in the details according to their different environments, experiences, interests, and tastes. The virtues specify the attitudes and goals essential to happiness at just

[9] Aristotle, *Nicomachean Ethics*, 1168a5–28, 1170a32–b3. Cf. John Rawls, *A Theory of Justice* (Cambridge: Harvard University Press, 1971), section 65 on the Aristotelian Principle, esp. pp. 426–27.

[10] Melanie Klein calls childhood curiosity a love of knowledge, *epistemophilia*, in her *Love, Guilt, and Reparation*; cited in Jonathan Lear, *Aristotle: The Desire to Understand* (Cambridge: Cambridge University Press, 1988), p. 3.

this level of abstraction. In this respect, virtue is to happiness as the most general and universal norms of physical health are to health. Just as many different sorts of diets and patterns of physical activity—many different lifestyles—are compatible with health norms, so many different patterns of activity involving different goals and pleasures—many different life-plans—are compatible with psychological and moral norms. Moreover, just as accidents and injuries can damage a person's physical functioning and health regardless of a healthy lifestyle, so great misfortunes, whether natural or caused by others' actions, can mar a person's practical efficacy and happiness despite virtuous dispositions. Thus, as noted in Section I, the virtues do not guarantee practical efficacy or happiness; they guarantee only the essential internal conditions of efficacy and happiness, namely, the appropriate ultimate goals and attitudes. In this way, they provide the best security available against the baneful effects of misfortune.

This is Aristotle's general picture of human nature, human well-being, and the role of virtue in well-being. But if we conjoin this general picture with other passages from his ethical works, we can derive a more concrete picture of happiness and virtue. From what has been said so far, we can see that a happy life must include both internal and external goods: goals worth pursuing, the mental and physical means to pursue them well, success (and more importantly, enjoyment) in the pursuit, and mental and physical security. We can also see, however, that not every way of incorporating internal and external goods is compatible with living well. For example, people who make the acquisition of external goods such as fame or political power their dominant aim in life, thinking these to be the chief sources of happiness, are easy hostages to fortune. For the acquisition and enjoyment of such goods depends too much on the opinions of others, whereas "we intuitively believe that the good is something of our own and hard to take from us" (NE 1095b25–26). The same is true of those who live under the direction of others, guided by *their* choices rather than their own. Nor do those who take their guidance from whim fare any better. All such people lack the security that characterizes a good life, the security that allows us to anticipate the future, and to strive to realize our hopes and dreams for the future. For such security is possible only with a degree of invulnerability to the vagaries of chance or whim or the choices of others, and such invulnerability is possible only if the central aspects of a person's life are under his own rational control.

Rational control, then, requires two things. It requires that a person be guided by his own reasoned choices (*prohaireseis*)—deliberative choices made in light of his overall ends—rather than by others' choices, or by whim.[11] And it requires that he choose as central to his life only those goals or goods whose acquisition or enjoyment does not leave him too

---

[11] See Sherman's discussion of *prohairesis* as a reasoned choice expressing a person's ultimate ends or values and, hence, character (Sherman, *The Fabric of Character*, pp. 79–84).

vulnerable to the decisions of others or the vagaries of chance. For the choice of certain goals—for example, money-making or popularity—as central to his life will undermine his future ability to live by his own choices. In short, rational control over his own life requires a person both to live by his own reasoned choices, and to choose goods that will not make him an easy hostage to fortune.

But what about those who do not *need* to live under their own rational control to anticipate, and extend themselves into, the future? That is, what about those who have the socially backed assurance of being completely cared for by their families, so that their future is entirely predictable—as is surely the case with some women in traditional societies, including Aristotle's own? Why do *they* need rational control over their own lives? Aristotle himself, of course, does not think that women need such control to the same extent as men, for the simple reason that with their naturally defective rationality, they *cannot* exercise such control.[12] But if we can separate this unfortunate assumption from his general answer to the question just asked, we can see why even someone who does not need to exercise rational control over her life for the sake of security still has a need for it. Aristotle's general answer suggests that the chief importance of exercising rational control over our lives is that doing so exercises our nature as rational agents with choice-making powers—in current terminology, as *autonomous* agents. Such activity is crucial to happiness, because in such activity we actualize ourselves and experience ourselves as the independent causes of our actions and makers of our individual selves. Indeed, such activity is "the pleasantest" and "most lovable" of all activities.[13] Those who fail to live autonomously fail to experience this deepest of pleasures.

Living the life of a rational agent whose dominant source of happiness is under one's own control is also necessary for forming deep friendships and fulfilling one's nature as a social animal. Such friendships, in which there is a sharing of lives, are possible, according to Aristotle, only between virtuous people.[14] Whether or not we accept this claim, we can reasonably accept that it is only insofar as we exercise and develop our

---

[12] Aristotle regards women's deliberative capacity as *akuron*, lacking in authority (*Politics*, 1260a12–30, 1261a14). Ironically, women are still the primary moral educators of the young child. See the discussion of this issue in Sherman, *The Fabric of Character*, pp. 154–55.

[13] Aristotle, *Nicomachean Ethics*, 1168a15. Aristotle has in mind all rational productive activity: fashioning crafts, writing poetry, benefiting others, and loving (1167b34–1168a22). Two of the features of rational productive activity that make it valuable—the effort of production, and the knowledge that what is produced is yours—also apply to the nonrational productive act of giving birth (1168a25ff.). And while what is actualized here is not the rational self, Aristotle suggests that it is still, in some sense, an act of self-actualization.

Cf. Lawrence Haworth's view that autonomous choice is an expression of a fundamental aspect of our human nature, because it expresses "the desires to stand out, to make a mark, and to be responsible" (Haworth, *Autonomy: An Essay in Philosophical Psychology and Ethics* [New Haven: Yale University Press, 1986], p. 190; see also ch. 11, esp. pp. 186–90).

[14] Aristotle, *Eudemian Ethics*, trans. J. Solomon, in Barnes, ed., *The Complete Works of Aristotle*, 1237a30ff.; *Nicomachean Ethics*, book VIII, ch. 3. Friendships between the virtuous are

capacity for rational choice, thinking our own thoughts, setting our own aims, shaping our selves, that we forge a life of our own to share with others. Moreover, a deep friendship results from a mutual choice of each other as "other selves," and it is only insofar as we do thus make our own selves that we can choose, and be chosen by, another person as a second but "separate self."[15] Those who fail to lead autonomous lives may well be moved by their own neediness to make utility friends, or by a desire for pleasant times to make pleasure friends (NE VIII 3; EE VII 2–4). But such friendships are insecure because they are based on incidental and transient qualities. Nor do they provide the satisfactions of the best kind of friendship, in which friends love, take pleasure in, and help, each other for themselves, i.e., for the sorts of persons they are, their character.

Hence, Aristotle concludes, a happy life is a life shaped by the choice and pursuit of goods that play a fundamental and enduring role in a human life, the sort of life in which we actualize ourselves as rational, social agents. Given the plurality of happy lives that are possible, we should, I think, reject some of Aristotle's candidates for fundamental goods. For example, political activity, insofar as this is distinct from merely social activity, is not an essential component of every happy life. We should also reject his claim that a truly happy life must contain all the fundamental goods—if this is, indeed, his claim. But we cannot reasonably reject his point that some goods play a more fundamental and enduring role in our lives than others, and that these fundamental goods have to do with our basic needs and abilities as rational and social agents. Nor can we reject Aristotle's point that one of the most basic of these needs is the need to be autonomous and exercise rational control over key aspects of our own lives. For as we have seen, rational control of our lives is the only alternative to control by whim, the choices of others, or chance. The story of paramedic Robert O'Donnell (the daring rescuer of Baby Jessica), who took his own life when he lost his short-lived spot in the limelight, because life without fame lost all meaning for him, is only a

---

called "primary" friendships in the *Eudemian Ethics*, and "character" friendships in the *Nicomachean Ethics*. Further references to the *Eudemian Ethics* in the text are abbreviated as *EE*.

[15] The phrase "separate self" is at *Eudemian Ethics*, 1245a35. The terms "other self," "another self," "another himself," and "second self" are used in various places, including *Nicomachean Ethics*, 1170b7; *Eudemian Ethics*, 1245a30; and *Magna Moralia*, trans. St. George Stock, in *The Complete Works of Aristotle*, book II, ch. 15. The importance of choice in the best sort of friendship is brought out in various places in the *Nicomachean Ethics* and the *Eudemian Ethics*. "[T]he primary friendship, that of good men, is a mutual returning of love and choice. . . . This sort of friendship, then, is peculiar to man, for he alone perceives another's choice" (*Eudemian Ethics*, 1236b3–6); and again, "the primary friendship is a reciprocal choice of the absolutely good and pleasant because it is good and pleasant" (*Eudemian Ethics*, 1237a30ff.). See also *Nicomachean Ethics*, 1170b6–7.

Cf. C. S. Lewis's observation that to love a friend is to "*care about* the same truth" (Lewis, *The Four Loves* [Glasgow: William Collins Sons and Co., 1960], p. 62). "The very condition of having friends is that we should want something else besides friends," for "[t]hose who have nothing can share nothing" (p. 63).

particularly dramatic example of the internal and external consequences of surrendering control of our lives to others.[16] Further, as numerous psychological studies and theories have indicated, the exercise of rational control over our lives is a key component of a satisfactory life, both because it is self-actualizing and intrinsically pleasurable, and because it is productive of further ends.[17]

The best assurance of rationally choosing and successfully pursuing fundamental goods is a sound conception of particular fundamental goods as well as of the proper way to pursue them, and a reliable disposition to act accordingly. But to have such a conception and such a disposition, according to Aristotle, is to have moral virtue, i.e., the virtues of character such as justice, temperance, et al., informed by the virtue of reason: practical wisdom (*NE* 1144a30). When we have moral virtue, we have emotions and desires that are informed by reason, and a reason that is informed by our emotional and desiring nature. Hence, what we desire or find pleasant is what we justifiably believe to be good, and what we justifiably believe to be good is based, in part, on our recognition of our nature as feeling and desiring beings. Since the virtues are grounded in our common human capacities and enable us to satisfy our common human needs, their exercise is necessary both for the agent's good, and for others' good. Even the virtues that find their occasion in others' legitimate claims or concerns, such as justice or generosity, are essential to our own good because, as social beings, we share our lives with others, and the virtues are both means to, and partly constitutive of, shared activities.

But what, more precisely, is Aristotle's view of the nature of moral virtue? Moral virtue, on his view, is an emotional and rational disposition to feel, deliberate, and act "at the right [i.e., appropriate] times, about the right things, towards the right people, for the right end, and in the right way" (*NE* 1106b21ff.). Virtue enables a person to do this in a wide variety of different circumstances, because virtue enhances a person's perceptiveness, attuning her to subtle moral nuances (*NE* VI 5, 7, 8, 11–13). A decision that expresses a virtuous disposition expresses "truth agreeing with correct desire" (*NE* 1139a30) or correct desire combined with correct thought (*NE* 1139b5), and the act that expresses it is a fine, or morally admirable,

---

[16] See Lisa Belkin, "Death on the CNN Curve," *New York Times Magazine*, July 23, 1995, p. 18. Eighteen-month-old Jessica McClure fell into a dry water well in October 1987; her plight, and her rescue by O'Donnell, were the focus of national media attention for months after the event.

[17] Some of these studies and theories are usefully summarized in Roger Brown and Richard J. Herrnstein, *Psychology* (Boston: Little, Brown and Co., 1975), pp. 177–82. Particularly noteworthy are the neurologist Kurt Goldstein's definition of self-actualization as the impulse to fulfill one's potentialities, Abraham Maslow's classification of self-actualization as a "growth motivation" in contrast to various sorts of "deficiency motivation," and the emphasis placed by the psychologist Henry Murray and the anthropologist Clyde Kluckhohn on the intrinsic pleasures of activity done for its own sake. This is not to say that every detail of the analysis of rational control (mastery) or of self-actualization given in these pages is compatible with Aristotle's views.

act. A virtuous person takes pleasure in the rightness of an act, even if the act is painful in certain respects and, in these respects, unwillingly done (*NE* 1099a15–17ff., 1104b7ff., 1117b1–2, 7ff.). Someone who characteristically does the right thing for the right reasons despite a painful struggle is, no doubt, an upright person; but his struggle reveals a conflict between his practical reason, on the one hand, and emotions and desires, on the other. Such a person is continent rather than virtuous, for his responses fall short of the integrated, wholehearted, pleasurable responses of the virtuous man. He is rational without possessing that excellence of practical reason which is practical wisdom, and he is rightly motivated without possessing that excellence of desire and feeling which is necessary for virtue of character.[18] Hence, he also lacks the kind of fine-tuned perceptiveness and responsiveness that is characteristic of the virtuous. He would be a better, as well as a happier, person if he were virtuous, rather than merely continent or strong-willed.

Virtue is the practical analog of knowledge. Just as knowledge of a subject involves the cognitive disposition to assent to true and rationally justified claims about that subject, so virtue involves the cognitive and emotional disposition to value, desire, and act on what is truly valuable in human life. This is the heart of Aristotle's conception of virtue. This conception explains wide-ranging features of common moral judgment and experience. For example, it explains the distinction we make between those who *struggle* to act justly, and those who act justly from a *passion* for justice. It also helps explain why we praise those who help or give gifts to others "spontaneously" and "in the right spirit," rather than those who help or give gifts with an air of performing a painful, externally imposed duty. And it sheds light on why, as Woody Allen puts it in his film *Crimes and Misdemeanors*, it is so "hard to get your heart and head together in life," why, in so many cases, as, purportedly, in his, "they're not even friendly." The idea that practical reason shapes, and is shaped by, emotion—an idea that underlies Aristotle's theory of moral development— is also in line with our best scientific and philosophical theories of the nature of emotion.[19] Further, the idea that such rational emotion and

---

[18] That the continent man lacks practical wisdom, even though he understands the true worth of pleasure, wealth, honor, and so on, and deliberates and acts correctly in a variety of circumstances, is implicit in Aristotle's view that practical wisdom implies, and is implied by, virtue. I discuss this in "The Limited Unity of Virtue."

[19] The cognitive nature of emotion is a common theme of much recent psychological and philosophical writing on emotion. Thus, the psychologist Nico H. Frijda, *The Emotions* (Cambridge: Cambridge University Press, 1986), argues that emotions express our evaluations of situations or events as good or bad for us. More broadly, Ronald de Sousa, *The Rationality of Emotion* (Cambridge: MIT Press, 1987), gives a philosophical defense of the claim that emotions apprehend real evaluative properties. The role of emotion in making us cognizant of evaluative facts is also a common feature of daily experience. For example, new mothers, once able to sleep through the sound of thunder, typically find that even the slightest whimper from the baby now has the power to wake them up: their concern for the child makes them susceptible to its needs.

emotional rationality are essential to virtue gets indirect support from empirical studies of the psychopath that show the importance of well-developed emotions for moral perception.[20] Thus, a variety of considerations converge to support Aristotle's conception of virtue.

Just as virtue is a disposition to desire, feel, and act rightly, so vice is a disposition to desire, feel, and act wrongly. It is a dispositional commitment to the bad, or indifference to the good. Someone who is wholly or partially vicious harbors inappropriate emotions toward others, emotions such as malice, spite, or envy, and has inappropriate aspirations for himself, such as the aspiration to dominate others. Indeed, his very perceptions of good and bad are distorted by his vice, as the sick man's perceptions of food and drink are distorted by his disease (NE 1113a26-29): "vice perverts us, and produces false views about the origins of actions" (NE 1144a35). Indeed, on Aristotle's view the vicious man sees the bad as good and the good as bad or, at least, as valueless.

We should not, however, conclude that the vicious man is completely ignorant of the good. For the fact that a vicious person can react with righteous anger or with resentment when *others* harm *him* shows that his "ignorance" of the good is compatible with a general, if schematic and stillborn, awareness of the difference between right and wrong.[21] Hence, it seems that a vicious person's "false view" of the good is not entirely the *effect* of his bad emotions and desires, as Aristotle seems to think, but is also, in part, a strategy of dispositional evasion or self-deception in the *service* of these emotions and desires.

Not all bad actions, however, are the result of vice: they can be the result of incontinence or weakness. The incontinent man will sometimes behave like the vicious man, but his cognitive state and psychological dispositions will be different. For unlike the vicious man, the incontinent man deliberates and decides correctly, but succumbs to his contrary desires out of weakness. Thus, incontinence is to vice as continence is to virtue: a trait that differs from vice in its constitutive thoughts, emotions, and desires, yet leads to similar behavior.

Even with these distinctions, however, Aristotle's taxonomy of character types is incomplete. There may be individuals who are "satanically wicked"—individuals who make evil their goal *because* it is evil, in full

[20] Hervey Cleckley, *The Mask of Sanity* (St. Louis: C. V. Mosby, 1964), argues that the psychopath's failure of moral agency is due to his stunted emotional capacity rather than any deficiency in his ability for logical thought. For the psychopath is able to make rational inferences like anyone else and, indeed, is often unusually intelligent. Yet he is incapable of seeing the *significance* of things, of grasping value. See also the summary of psychological research on the psychopath's lack of affectivity, and especially of empathy and self-awareness, in Daniel Goleman, *Emotional Intelligence* (New York: Bantam Books, 1995), ch. 7. Lack of empathy, however, is neither the only, nor the necessary, cause of criminality.

[21] See the discussion of "moral emotions"—emotions that express a sense of right and wrong, such as resentment or indignation—in Rawls, *A Theory of Justice*, pp. 487-88; and Bernard Williams, *Morality: An Introduction to Ethics* (New York: Harper and Row, 1972), pp. 3-4.

awareness of its evil.[22] Such individuals do not fit Aristotle's definition of vice. Nor do those who are committed to certain bad ends out of ignorance of some purely empirical fact. Such, for example, is the mistake made by D-503, the hero of Yevgeny Zamyatin's *We*, at least at the beginning of the story. D-503 believes that the One State is a noble institution because he mistakenly believes that it has rescued humankind from millennia of barbarism and has fostered an era of unprecedented scientific advancement, material prosperity, and close-to-perfect rationality and happiness. Analogously, Renaissance scientists who investigated alchemy and "natural magic" were simply mistaken in some of their empirical beliefs.[23] Hence, it is important to distinguish between being disposed to value bad ends for culpable reasons, and being disposed to value them from inculpable ignorance. In the former case the disposition is a vice, in the latter it is neither a vice nor a virtue, neither continence nor incontinence.

The variety of character traits allows for degrees of goodness or badness in a character. So does the fact that a person's traits can vary from one domain to another, so that she can be virtuous in one domain and continent or incontinent in another (though not, perhaps, virtuous in one domain and vicious in another).[24] Thus, if virtue is necessary for full happiness, then the degree of happiness in a life blessed by good fortune will also vary with the degree of goodness in that life. The best imaginable life, the life in which we successfully develop and effectively exercise— "actualize"—our independent and interdependent, mental and physical, capacities in all domains, is the life of virtue (and good fortune) in all domains. For virtue guarantees the chief internal condition of happiness, namely, the dispositions, goals, and perceptiveness necessary for living with the greatest amount of practical efficacy. The further we are from virtue in a particular domain, the further we are from efficacy and well-being in that domain; and the greater the number of domains in which we lack efficacy, the more widespread our lack of well-being.

In the sections that follow, I will analyze the notion of practical efficacy and the role it plays in independent and interdependent well-being (Sections III and IV), and justify the claim that virtue is necessary for practical efficacy and, thus, for happiness (Sections IV and V). I will start with a minimal notion of practical efficacy, and then show how an analysis of this notion leads to a fuller notion of efficacy and, thereby, to virtue.

---

[22] See Ronald Milo's discussion of satanic wickedness in his book *Immorality* (Princeton: Princeton University Press, 1984), p. 7.

[23] For an account of the fascination with alchemy and natural magic in the Renaissance, see Marie Boas, *The Scientific Renaissance: 1450–1630* (New York: Harper and Row, 1966).

[24] I argue against such a possibility in "The Limited Unity of Virtue," on the grounds that vice in any domain entails a general and culpable ignorance of the good, whereas moral virtue in any domain entails a general knowledge of the good. Thus, the political viciousness displayed by people like Mao Tse-tung or Himmler or Pol Pot reveals such a warped notion of human nature that it could not possibly coexist with wisdom in *any* domain.

III. Practical Efficacy and Independent Well-Being

Since we are purposive beings, we are efficacious to the extent that we act in a way conducive to our purposes, and seek purposes conducive to our needs as rational and social animals. And for this we need to satisfy certain psychological and practical conditions.

An efficacious agent is someone who can find appropriate means to her ends, and the appropriate ends given her means—her powers, abilities, and resources. Someone who adopts ends she has no capacity to fulfill, either because they outstrip human powers—for example, attempting to walk across the waters of the English Channel—or because they outstrip her individual talents or resources—for example, attempting to become a world-class violinist despite a tin ear and a history of clumsiness with the violin—is simply unrealistic. So is someone who, irrationally, tries to achieve all her many ends simultaneously instead of arranging them in a hierarchy, or who has incompatible ends. And someone who refuses to rationally choose her own ends at all, or chooses ends that undermine her future ability for rational control over her life, chooses a way of life that invites misfortune and deprives her of the pleasures of agency. Such a person lacks autonomy. If, on the other hand, she is both autonomous and realistic in her choice of goals, but neglects to discover or use the appropriate means to achieve them, she undercuts herself through incompetence. In either case, such a person courts failure, frustration, and disappointment—and, eventually, a serious breach of self-confidence.

In addition to being autonomous, choosing realistic ends, and pursuing them competently, someone who is practically efficacious must also find her ends *worth* achieving, as having genuine value. Without this sense of the worth of her ends, she will have little or no incentive to achieve them. Someone who is autonomous, realistic, and competent will, typically, also have self-regard, that is, will see herself as *worthy* of happiness and of other-regard, even if misfortune deprives her of happiness or of other-regard. But someone with unrealistic standards of self-worth may be prevented from feeling the self-regard she deserves to feel, and this, too, will affect her efficacy. If she feels unworthy of happiness, she will find little lasting pleasure or satisfaction in the exercise of her powers and talents, or in her achievements, whether in her personal relationships, or in her independent activities. If she feels unworthy of other-regard, she may be prevented even from *seeking* personal relationships. A fully efficacious person, then, will have self-regard in addition to the other components of practical efficacy. Together, the sense that she has control over her own life and that her ends are realistic and worthwhile, confidence in her ability to achieve them, and a sense of her own worthiness, add up to *self-esteem*.[25] Self-

---

[25] Cf. Rawls, *A Theory of Justice*, section 67; and Nathaniel Branden, *The Six Pillars of Self-Esteem* (New York: Bantam, 1994), esp. ch. 2.

esteem is thus an individual's perception of herself as an efficacious individual.

A radical deficiency in realism or competence or sense of the worth of her ends will tend to undercut a person's autonomy and sense of autonomy, because each of these elements affects her capacity for rational control of her life. A lack of autonomy, in turn, will undercut a person's sense of self-worth. Thus, a radical deficiency in any one of the elements of practical efficacy will undermine a person's overall efficacy and self-esteem.

The practical efficacy and self-esteem under discussion are needed both in the activities we undertake for our independent good, and in the activities we undertake for our interdependent or shared good. Someone who is efficacious in the independent realm will find pleasure in activities— intellectual, material, artistic, psychological, et al.—that she values as both expressing, and continually reshaping, her life as a separate individual. Someone who is efficacious in the interdependent realm will find pleasure in the joint activities of friendship and other relationships, relationships she values as both expressing, and reshaping, her life as a social individual. Someone who is efficacious, then, is engaged both in self-expression and in self-creation.

It is possible to satisfy the requirements of practical efficacy in the two realms to varying extents. For example, someone with a high degree of practical efficacy in the independent realm might be insecure in the social realm for reasons of inexperience or lack of skill. However, just as a radical deficiency in any one of the elements of practical efficacy within a realm will affect a person's overall efficacy and self-esteem, so a radical deficiency of efficacy and self-esteem in one realm will affect her efficacy and self-esteem in the other. Thus, a deficiency of efficacy and self-esteem in the independent realm will affect one's ability to form close friendships, the sort of friendships that involve a sharing of lives. For, as already noted, a necessary condition for such sharing is that we forge a life of our own to share (Section II). Conversely, the absence of close friends will leave one without the encouragement and support to build up one's efficacy and self-esteem in the independent realm.

Practical efficacy serves both our independent and our interdependent or social good. And, I will argue, the virtues—whether self-regarding (such as honesty with oneself, integrity, and temperance) or other-regarding (such as justice, generosity, and kindness) or both (such as courage)—are essential for a high degree of practical efficacy. At first blush, it appears that there is little need for argument here, given the obvious baneful effects of the corresponding vices. Thus, someone who is characteristically dishonest with himself about his abilities or the worth of his ends will undermine his self-confidence in his ability to act effectively, or his motivation to try to pursue his ends. Similarly, someone who lacks integrity will betray his more important values when they stand in the way of lesser, but more urgently desired, values such as professional success or social popularity. Again, an intemperate person will succumb to the temptation of easy pleasures whenever the going gets tough. Finally, an unjust or cowardly person will be untrustworthy, and an unkind or stingy person will be, at the very least, distinctly unpleasant and unwelcome company. And both untrustworthy and unpleasant people will tend to be excluded from contractual enterprises as well as friendships.

But the apparent simplicity of this argument from self-interest is called into question when we consider the implication of the claim that practical efficacy requires virtue, and virtue is necessarily directed at good ends. For with this understanding of virtue, the argument implies that bad ends rob us of practical efficacy. But surely, someone might object, there have been, and are, effective and successful tyrants, gangsters, and other less obvious sorts of vicious characters—effective not for accidental reasons, but precisely because they have the requisite qualities: autonomously chosen realistic ends, competence, and a sense of their own worth and the worth of their ends. For there is no reason, it might be thought, why such people cannot have a sense of self-worth and the ability to autonomously choose realistic goals that *they* find worthwhile, even if their victims do not. Nor is there any reason why they cannot be, and experience themselves as being, competent to fulfill their goals. Moreover, it is common knowledge (the objector might add) that members of the same gang often have strong ties of affection, loyalty, care, and concern. Thus, they seem to be efficacious not only in the independent realm, but also in the interdependent realm.

To answer this objection, we need to step back and reconsider the notion of practical efficacy. In this section I will concentrate on practical efficacy and self-esteem in the independent realm, and in the next section, in the interdependent realm. I will begin by asking whether those with dramatically vicious ends can have practical efficacy, then move on to discuss those whose lives are a mixture of good and bad.

To the extent that tyrants, gangsters, and others prefer to live by preying on others, they display an unwillingness to live by their own independent efforts to create value, and a willingness to live through violent, parasitic dependence.[26] Thus, they display a lack of other-regard: an indifference to the well-being of those they prey upon, or a malicious or

---

[26] See, for example, Stephen Cox, *Blood and Power: Organized Crime in Twentieth-Century America* (New York: William Morrow and Co., 1989); and Nathan McCall's autobiographical *Makes Me Wanna Holler: A Young Black Man in America* (New York: Random House, 1994). Cox relates how well-educated Mafia members, with opportunities for professional jobs, still chose to follow in their fathers' footsteps of a life of blood and power out of a general ineptitude and an aversion to "hard, honest work" (p. 371). He also cites Harvey Bonadonna, a mobster's son, as stating that his friends and relatives in the rackets simply "did not want to work," that they preferred "to go out and prey upon the community, to steal" (p. 382). McCall's opportunities for interesting work were far more limited, but not as limited, he realizes in hindsight, as he thought when he drifted toward the relatively easy life of crime (p. 402).

spiteful hostility toward them.[27] Even if one of these—lack of other-regard or of a willingness to engage in the effort to produce value—is the primary motivation to begin with, the two tend to be mutually reinforcing.[28] Regardless of which—if either—motivation is dominant, to the extent that someone prefers the life of a predator, he prefers to live off the productive efforts of others without making a return. Thus, he rejects the choice to live as an equal among others, giving value for value.

Since my concern in this section is the independent realm, I will focus on the implications of the unwillingness to live by one's own independent efforts to create value. To simplify matters, I will often talk as though all predators are predators without qualification, and likewise all creators. Since this is often not the case, however, I should be read as saying: "to the extent that someone is a predator" or "to the extent that someone is a creator."

Someone who is unwilling to produce value because of ineptitude or lack of confidence in his ability to produce anything of genuine worth already seems to be confessing to a certain lack of efficacy in the realm of independent action. So is someone who is unwilling because he gets little or no pleasure from any sort of value-creation (since efficacy is productive of pleasure). And whatever the social or psychological constraints or liabilities that contribute to the erosion of someone's competence, self-confidence, or pleasure in the production of value, the fact remains that insofar as someone is unwilling to engage in the production of value from any of these motives, he shows a certain lack of efficacy.

But the recently encountered defense of the predator as someone with all the qualities needed for practical efficacy implies that it matters little if a person lacks confidence in his *productive* abilities, or enjoyment in their exercise. What matters is that he have confidence in his ability to perform his chosen task, whether creative or destructive, and that he enjoy ex-

---

[27] McCall recalls his penchant for holding a grudge, for hatred and vengeance (*Makes Me Wanna Holler*, p. 106), not only toward the oppressive whites, but also toward other blacks, the chief victims of his predatory activities (p. 86). And nothing beats the cold indifference of mobsters Greg Scarpa and Lefty Ruggiero. According to Scarpa's former attorney, Scarpa had the intelligence and ability to become a lawyer "or run any big business," but chose not to because "it would be no fun to him" (cited in Cox, *Blood and Power*, p. 420). What was "fun," Cox adds, was to get "the pleasures of deference and opulence, without the bother of working hard and earning them" (p. 420). Noteworthy, too, is the exultant exclamation of Lefty Ruggiero: "As a wiseguy, you can lie, you can cheat, you can steal, you can kill people—*legitimately*. You can do any goddamn thing you want. . . . Who wouldn't want to be a wiseguy?" (p. 420).

[28] McCall notes the effect of their violent lives on his own and his friends' minds, which, through disuse, slip out of their control and start to go "from logic to illogic" without their realizing it, until they are left wondering why they are "being pushed into the backseat of life and . . . [cannot] get at the wheel" (*Makes Me Wanna Holler*, p. 119). Again, Goleman discusses the research that shows how aggressive children become inept at their work thanks to their "impulsivity" or poor self-control, and eventually become unwilling to work (*Emotional Intelligence*, pp. 236–37). The evidence also suggests that the (aggressive) impulsivity that leads to delinquency also contributes to low IQ scores (p. 335, n. 18), and that the ineptitude and the aggression reinforce each other (pp. 236–37).

ecuting *that*. And surely a predator can have such confidence, and enjoy the skillful, ingenious use of his faculties to reshape the raw material of others' lives for his own purposes: witness the expert jewel thief or art forger, or the Unabomber.[29] Or, in the realm of personal relations, witness the confidence and pleasure with which Shakespeare's Iago manipulates people's souls. To be efficacious, then, someone who chooses the life of predation must have confidence in his ability to control and get the better of others, must enjoy honing and exercising his powers of exploitation and manipulation, and must find his activities worth engaging in for his own benefit. That he is not creative in the sense of producing, promoting, or preserving value is a *moral* issue, not an issue of efficacy.

This reply, however, does not take the predator very far. The creation of value, that is, of some good or service, material, artistic, intellectual, psychological, et al., that can enhance or preserve human well-being, is an objective requirement of leading a good life. Such value-creation may take place entirely in the domestic realm, or it may also (and more typically) take place in the public realm. Some creative activity, such as psychological and philosophical self-exploration, may be directly aimed at self-development, at the project of making ourselves certain kinds of persons; the rest may also be aimed at the development of some external value. The important point is that it is through value-creation that we establish an independent relationship to reality and, thereby, to others. For as value-creators we are, and experience ourselves as being, the autonomous agents of our actions and makers of our individual selves, able to give value for value and relate to others as mutual beneficiaries. To fail at the task of value-creation, not through misfortune, but by choice, is to willingly fail at the task of becoming the autonomous agents of our lives, free of any need for a parasitic dependence on others. The multifarious ways in which such a failure is incompatible with efficacy and self-esteem can be illustrated by comparing the predator's life of parasitic dependence with the creator's life.

A physically coercive predator in the independent realm is someone who chooses to bypass the challenge of value-creation by a violent, parasitic dependence on those who face it and meet it. It is because a predator produces nothing to offer in exchange for value, and lacks other-regard to boot, that he lives by extorting or otherwise expropriating the values produced by others. By contrast, the producer qua producer has nothing to gain from the predator: indeed, in a world without predators he could be *more* productive. Further, the predator's basic life choice, the choice of leading a life of predation, is entirely dependent, both conceptually and practically, on others' choice to produce: if there were no production, there could be no predation.[30] Once again, the converse does not hold for

[29] Regarding Unabomber suspect Ted Kaczynski, see "Tracking Down the Unabomber," *Time*, vol. 147, no. 16 (April 15, 1996), pp. 38–46.
[30] This is the (often misunderstood) lesson of the producers' strike in Rand's *Atlas Shrugged*.

the producer: the choice of leading the life of value-creation is neither conceptually nor practically dependent on anyone's choice to expropriate one's values.

It might be thought that this is false, because certain kinds of productive activity, for example, criminal law enforcement and criminology, are immediately dependent, both conceptually and practically, on the existence of predators. But since predation is itself ultimately dependent on production, and since the criminal code and criminal law enforcement, which are studied by criminology, exist for the sake of protecting (among other things) productive activity, what stands at the end of the conceptual and practical chain of dependence is, once again, productive activity.

It follows, then, that the predator's relationship to the producer is fundamentally unequal. In making the basic choice to lead a life of predation instead of production, he makes the choice of letting his life be shaped, in the final analysis, by *others'* decisions, not his own. Thus, the predator's life displays a dismal lack of self-direction, of autonomy.

There is a sense, of course, in which the lives of most of us are shaped by others' decisions insofar as what, when, and how much we create depends on what, when, and how much others choose to create. Even the most independent, original minds depend on the material, intellectual, or artistic creations of others. There are, however, major differences between the dependence of creators on other creators, and the dependence of predators on creators, namely, the difference between *mutually beneficial interdependence* in the former case, and *destructive parasitic dependence* in the latter. The following considerations make this evident.

First, everyone who lives productively has something to offer in return for what she gets, and how much she gets from others is proportional to how much she has to offer. Thus, her relationship to other producers is one of equality and reciprocity (through exchange, cooperation, and so on), rather than one of inequality and parasitic dependence. In relation to each other, creators are both benefactors and beneficiaries, and their interdependence is an example of mutually beneficial social existence. Secondly, although particular *forms* of production depend on particular other *forms* of production—for example, scientific experiment on technology, perspectival painting on the science of optics—production as such does not presuppose production. Robinson Crusoe was the sole producer on his desert island before he rescued Friday (another solitary productive act), the Homeric poems were conceived without the benefit of paper, and many a solitary child has drawn original sand figures. Nor is the basic *choice* to be productive, to establish an independent relationship to reality and, thereby, to others, necessarily dependent on someone else's similar choice. By contrast with predators, then, producers are autonomous in their relationship to other producers, and they are autonomous in this respect because, through value-creation, they establish an independent relationship to reality and become the autonomous agents of their lives.

In his unwillingness to create value, and his choice to live off the decisions and productive efforts of others, a predator's mode of existence lacks genuine worth as well as autonomy. But autonomy and a worthy mode of existence are essential to practical efficacy and genuine self-esteem—a self-esteem reflective of the facts of one's life. At this bedrock level of an individual's relationship to the world, then, the predator is utterly inefficacious and lacking in genuine self-esteem.

The objection might be made that whether or not his self-esteem reflects reality, a predator may well *have* self-esteem. And given that self-esteem is an important component of practical efficacy, if he has self-esteem, he will also have a high degree of efficacy. Further, he will have self-esteem if he sees himself as an independent, autonomous agent because he defies society and manages to get the better of his victims, and if he regards his vicious ends as admirable and himself as worthy of happiness and other-regard.

The predator may well have these attitudes—these beliefs and feelings toward himself—but if so, he is also committed to certain other attitudes that, I will argue, cannot be harbored without mental contortions that are incompatible with self-esteem. Thus, if the predator sees himself as admirable because of the kind of person he is, he must also see productive people as pitiable or contemptible, seeking to live as they do because they are too cowardly to defy convention and feed off others, or too weak or stupid or lacking in self-regard to claim the best for themselves. Or again, perhaps he finds them pitiable or contemptible because they find pleasure in their slavish activity of production instead of in the free, spontaneous power-play of the predatory. Indeed, the very fact that he regards productive people as fair game for his predatory activities implies that he has these attitudes toward them. There are, however, two problems with the line of reasoning that leads him to the conclusion that he is admirable and that productive people are pitiable or contemptible.

First, the view that predation is admirable implies that if someone should victimize the *predators*, the latter would have to acknowledge, no matter how *angered* they might be by the act, that the victimizer has acted admirably. For by their own standards, someone who can get the better of others is admirable. As we know, however, intergang or intragang warfare or cheating is typically *not* regarded in this way by those who are attacked or cheated. Rather, it is regarded as "disrespect" and disgrace, an insult inviting retaliation to reestablish one's honor, often at great risk of serious injury or death.[31] Thus, their line of reasoning is internally inco-

---

[31] That respect or honor is all-important in gangs, is attested to by various sources. Thus, McCall tells of how the most admired member of the gang was the one who "would shoot anybody for looking at him the wrong way" (*Makes Me Wanna Holler*, p. 61). And in her book about the Los Angeles gangs, the Crips and the Bloods, Leon Bing writes about the infighting among Crips over questions of respect, and reports one of the Crips as saying, "You got to be ready to do anything if somebody dis' [disrespects] your 'hood" (Bing, *Do or Die* [New York:

herent. It might be said on their behalf that there is no incoherence here, because their reaction is based not on their belief that *predatory* skills and proclivities are admirable, such that anyone who possesses them is admirable, but on their conviction that *they* are inherently superior. But if their conviction in their superiority is not based on their central characteristics, the characteristics that make them what they are, then it is not merely false—it is deluded. Thus, their attitudes are either internally incoherent, or utterly deluded.

Second, the predator's view that the life and pleasures of the producers are slavish conflicts with the undeniable appearances to the contrary, namely, that unlike slaves, producers engage in voluntary production and exchange, and are at liberty to stop producing. Again, unlike slaves, producers engage in their chosen activities freely and openly, without fear or favor. Indeed, in this respect it is *predators* who are akin to slaves, for it is they who must keep their true desires secret and fear being found out. Further, the view that producers are slavelike and predators masters of their own fate runs afoul of the already-noted fact that it is predators who, like voluntary slaves, give up their autonomy.[32]

The only remaining ground for regarding the activities and pleasures of the productive as "slavelike," then, is the assumption that creative activity is a burden, a constraint on our nature, rather than a realization of it. On this view, it is parasitic activity that is a form of freedom and self-realization, a way of achieving our human potential. The problem with this view is that the *human* potential is something whose realization by different individuals is compossible (mutually compatibly realizable), and whose realization plays an essential role in human well-being. But on the view under discussion, if most people *did* realize their human potential, most people would perish. In other words, this view implies, absurdly, that the human potential is a potential for self-destruction, and that self-actualization is a form of self-annihilation. Even if we overlook the inherent absurdity of this claim, it is hard to see why, if freedom and pleasure lie in preying on others, most members of any functioning society attempt to lead productive lives, and teach their children to do likewise. The answer cannot simply be: "fear of being caught out and punished," for this merely raises the prior question of what sustains a social structure of punishment for predatory behavior and reward for productive behavior. It is because such a system rests on widespread social support that producers can conduct their business freely and openly, and predators cannot; and it is because a system of production and vol-

---

HarperCollins, 1991], p. 23). The importance of honor in all organized criminal societies is well described in Francis A. J. Ianni and Elizabeth Reuss-Ianni, *A Family Business: Kinship and Social Control in Organized Crime* (New York: Russell Sage Foundation, 1972), esp. ch. 7.

[32] Cf. Aristotle's conception of the "natural slave" as someone who does not have "a deliberative faculty" and, consequently, cannot make his own rational choices (*Politics*, book I, chs. 5 and 12).

untary exchange is a requirement of human well-being that it has widespread social support.

In short, insofar as predators deny that their ends are worthless and that they themselves are radically dependent and deficient in autonomy, their denial requires for its sustenance a whole array of "sleights of mind"—obfuscation, rationalization, evasion, self-contradiction, fantasy, and projection. And such a mental existence is not compatible with a sense of oneself as a freely thinking, freely acting, efficacious agent—that is, with self-esteem. On the other hand, if predators face the truth about themselves, they must see themselves as they are: dependent on the minds and productivity of others, and on their ignorance and mistaken trust, as on a crutch that might any day be yanked out from under them. Hence, whether they face the truth about themselves or not, they cannot have self-esteem. And this is true for anyone to the extent that he lives the life of a predator.

This analysis of the predator as radically lacking in efficacy and self-esteem helps explain another commonly noted feature of predators, namely, their other-directed, reactive, and mistrustful attitudes. Although these attitudes are not limited to physically violent predators—or, even, to aggressive people in general, whether physically violent or not—it is not hard to see why predatory behavior should reinforce and exacerbate them. Recall, first, that to the extent that the predator substitutes predation for a life of independent creation, he substitutes dependence on others for autonomy. Second, to the extent that he seeks to regain a sense of efficacy by controlling others, he makes himself further dependent on their actions and reactions. Thus, lacking a sense of his own worth, relying for his self-esteem entirely on the deference and honor afforded by others, and used to an unreflective mode of life, the predator, like the prototypical Nietzschean man of *ressentiment*, is constantly on the lookout for slights and insults, ever-ready to interpret innocent remarks as signs of "disrespect," ever-threatened and ever-vengeful.[33] And the more he indulges his anger and resentment, the more self-righteous his view of his own behavior.

The portrait of the predator presented so far is of someone whose mental existence is incompatible with even the successful pretense of self-

[33] See, for example, McCall's description of how his sense of powerlessness fed his fascination with the power of guns (*Makes Me Wanna Holler*, ch. 8), and of how his sense of his own vulnerability led him to look upon guns as "life's great equalizer" (p. 68). The psychology of *ressentiment*—the reactive, vengeful affects it involves, and the sense of powerlessness and insignificance it feeds on—is analyzed by Friedrich Nietzsche in, among other places, *On the Genealogy of Morals*, essay 1, trans. Walter Kaufmann and R. J. Hollingdale (New York: Vintage House, 1967). This analysis is further borne out by research on deeply insecure children, typically the products of parental mistreatment. Such children, whether they respond to their mistreatment by becoming bullies at school or withdrawn social outcasts, share a "deep perceptual bias," perceiving "slights where none were intended," interpreting an "innocent bump . . . as a vendetta" (Goleman, *Emotional Intelligence*, p. 235). Aggressive children, especially, proceed on the "presumption of malevolence rather than innocence," becoming more "muddled" in their thinking as they become more angry and hostile (pp. 235–36).

esteem. But is it not possible, even if highly unlikely, that someone might internalize his self-deceptions to such an extent that they become "second nature" to him, that he might embed them so deeply in his life that evasion and projection become, in Sartrean language, a way of "being in the world" that is hidden from him? On Sartre's own theory of the mind as a transparent unity, this is impossible. But this theory of mind is rather implausible, and nothing less seems to quite rule out the hypothesis under consideration here. Hence, the possibility that a person's self-deceptions might become second nature to him must be granted. But if so, then it follows that a person's self-deceptions can blot out any vestige of self-knowledge and free him from inner conflict and feelings of worthlessness. Aristotle suggests the possibility of this kind of amnesia when he contrasts the vicious with the incontinent person: "[T]he vicious person," he says, "does not notice that he is vicious, while the incontinent person notices that he is incontinent."[34] Taken in by his own facade, such a person may even project his own fraudulence on others, and bury his self-estrangement under a sense of estrangement from this putatively fraudulent world. He may then self-righteously see his viciousness as justified by the world's injustices toward him, or by its general moral decay. This may well be the case with the technology-hating Unabomber, and may have been the case with some Nazis. Whether or not such total self-unawareness is possible, however, the important point for the present discussion is that the absence of inner conflict and the measure of deluded self-esteem that it affords cannot protect a person from conflict with, or alienation from, the world. Thus, whatever he gains in practical efficacy from his deluded inner state, he loses through conflict with, and alienation from, the world, a conflict and alienation far greater than that of the self-conflicted predator. Nor can the self-estranged predator's moral amnesia make him any less reactive and other-directed, living as he does in an unjust world that is out to get him—or a decadent world that is out to destroy his most cherished ideals.

[34] Aristotle, *Nicomachean Ethics*, 1150b35; cf. 1144a3. Later, however, Aristotle tells us that a vicious person's "soul is in conflict" and that he hates and shuns himself (1166b14–20). So either Aristotle is of two minds about the nature of a vicious person, or he has two sorts of vicious persons in mind: people who are responsible for "many terrible actions" in the later passage (1166b14–20), and people who express their vice in less destructive ways in the earlier passage (1150b35, 1144a3).

The idea of such total loss of self-knowledge as a kind of amnesia is from the poet Adrienne Rich, who likens lying "as a way of life" to amnesia, "the silence of the unconscious" (Rich, "Women and Honor: Some Notes on Lying," *On Lies, Secrets, and Silence: Selected Prose, 1966–1978* [W. W. Norton and Company, Inc., 1979]; reprinted in *The Experience of Philosophy*, 2d ed., ed. Raymond Martin and Daniel Kolak [Belmont: Wadsworth Publishing Co., 1993], p. 563).

Jean-Paul Sartre also compares the initial act of self-deception to putting oneself to sleep, but likens the ensuing state of self-deception to a dreaming state that the self-deceiver continually perpetuates (Sartre, "Self-Deception," in Walter Kaufmann, ed., *Existentialism: From Dostoyevsky to Sartre* [New York: New American Library, 1975], p. 326).

I have talked only about those whose lives are dramatically deficient in practical efficacy, and who attempt to compensate for this deficiency through a policy of physically coercive control over others. Most of us, of course, are not so thoroughly deficient in practical efficacy that we are led to live a life of physically violent predation. But most of us do have good reason to entertain *some* self-doubt about our autonomy, or competence, or the worth of our ends, or all three, in *some* aspects of our independent lives. And many people may also sometimes experience such warranted doubt about their self-worth. That lack of self-esteem is a major cause of unhappiness, even among those possessed of abundant external goods, is evident not only from everyday experience, literature, and film, but also from reports of the clinical experience of the vast numbers of flourishing psychotherapists.[35]

To the extent that we have reason for such self-doubt, but refuse to acknowledge it to ourselves, attempting instead to gain a sense of efficacy by controlling others through psychological manipulation or exploitation, we, too, are engaged in predation. Hence our lives, too, must be characterized by the same sort of parasitic dependence on others and the same sort of reactive, other-directed, unself-reflective emotional and cognitive glitches, projections, and conflicts.[36] And even if we succeed in totally deceiving ourselves and escaping from inner conflict, we will be, for all that, no less reactive, other-directed, and alienated from self or others.

There may be yet other psychological possibilities. Thus, it is possible that some people are simply naturally deficient in the rational or emotional capacities required for growth to full efficacy and self-esteem. Such people might be able to prey on others with a kind of primitive innocence that prevents any need for self-deception or other mental contortions.

All the same, if we go by the evidence provided by clinical psychology and by literature, the sorts of psychologies I have described are the most plausible and widespread ones. And what they show is that, if we lack efficacy and self-esteem, the only self-interested course of action is to face our deficiencies and take the responsibility for overcoming them. Until we do, good fortune cannot protect us from unhappiness.

[35] See, for example, Carl Rogers, "Toward a Modern Approach to Values: The Valuing Process in the Mature Person," and Abraham Maslow, "The Good Life of the Self-Actualizing Person," both in *Moral Problems in Contemporary Society*, ed. Paul Kurtz (Buffalo: Prometheus Books, 1969); and Nathaniel Branden, *The Six Pillars of Self-Esteem*. Albert Ellis also sees lack of autonomy and lack of self-esteem as the major causes of unhappiness, and his Rational Emotive Therapy focuses on helping the patient to regain these. For a useful summary of his ideas, see Gregory Kimble, Norman Garmezy, and Edward Zigler, *Principles of General Psychology*, 4th ed. (New York: The Ronald Press Co., 1974), pp. 574–75; this book also summarizes the ideas of Rogers (p. 573) and Maslow (pp. 243–46).
[36] For a remarkable depiction of the cognitive and emotional state of mind of a man in self-deception, see Fyodor Dostoyevsky's *Notes from the Underground* (New York: Dover Publications, 1992). See also Sartre on the "opacities" and "evanescence" of a self-deceived consciousness, a consciousness that has convinced itself that "the metastable [unstable] structure is the structure of being and that non-persuasion is the structure of all convictions" ("Self-Deception," pp. 299–328).

IV. Practical Efficacy and Interdependent Well-Being

Practical efficacy in the independent realm both serves, and is served by, interdependent or social well-being. It serves interdependent well-being insofar as it enables us to express and actualize our social natures in multidimensional ways. In particular, it enables us to fulfill our need as social beings to love, trust, and admire others, to open our imaginative, speculative, evaluative, and deliberative lives to them, and to participate in theirs. And it enables us to do this because, as we have seen, a precondition of such mutual sharing is that we forge a life worth sharing, a life that is shaped by our own purposes and animated by our own aspirations, a life that justifiably inspires self-confidence and a sense of self-worth. Conversely, interdependent well-being serves practical efficacy in the independent realm in various ways. In particular, cooperative relations extend one's agency and enhance one's ability to achieve one's independent goals; and close friends do this in ways that mere contractual partners cannot. For one thing, in friendship—the shared life of "conversation and thought" (*NE* 1170b11–14)—we can participate vicariously in activities and interests we are unable to pursue on our own, discover and come to appreciate new sorts of activities and interests, and expand our stock of experiences.[37] Thus, our agency is extended both by vicarious action, and through an enrichment of our goals and of our imaginative lives. Again, close friends enhance our powers of deliberation and practical judgment, and thus our agency, by affirming—or questioning—the value of our goals and aspirations through ongoing, caring, and reliable feedback.

At least as importantly, in such a relationship a basic cognitive and emotional need—the need to be seen by, and to see oneself in, another self—is fulfilled more deeply and pervasively than is otherwise possible. There are several reasons why having this need fulfilled is intrinsically valuable and a constitutive part of our well-being.[38] To be seen as we are by another person, and to perceive oneself in another, are intrinsically valuable because they allow us to see ourselves from the outside, as it were, making us visible to ourselves by giving us an objective reality, a reality out there in the world. The experience of "visibility" through another's accurate perception of us is also intrinsically valuable for another reason: if our self-perception is accurate, and we have no reason to

---

[37] On this and the following point, see Aristotle, *Nicomachean Ethics*, 1169b5–6, 1170a5–7, 1170b12–14. See also Irwin, *Aristotle's First Principles*, pp. 393–95; Brink, "Rational Egoism, Self, and Others," pp. 355–57; and David Schmidtz, *Rational Choice and Moral Agency* (Princeton: Princeton University Press, 1994), ch. 5.

[38] Most of the points in this passage are derived from Aristotle, *Nicomachean Ethics*, book IX; and Nathaniel Branden, *The Psychology of Romantic Love* (New York: Bantam Books, 1980), pp. 68–85. Aristotle argues that perceiving oneself in another is pleasant because the good is pleasant, and if one's life is good or "choiceworthy," observing oneself will also be pleasant, and one can observe oneself better in another person. The notion of "visibility" is Branden's.

hide from ourselves, visibility is an important source of pleasure. Visibility of both forms—through being perceived by, and through perceiving ourselves in, another—is valuable for other reasons as well. It gives us a heightened sense of connection with others, thereby satisfying a basic need of our social natures; and it contributes centrally to self-knowledge and to self-growth, thus satisfying a basic need of our natures as rational, self-conscious, agents.[39]

To the extent that we lack self-esteem in our interdependent lives, but seek personal relationships with those who do not, we cannot see ourselves as their equals, but only either as willing tools for their purposes, or as parasitic dependents on their creative activities, pure consumers of the values they create. Or we can see ourselves both as tools and as parasites, like the narrator of Dostoyevsky's *Notes from the Underground*, who combines slavishness with a parasitic manipulation and exploitation in his relationships with people.

This is not to say that those who, in violent opposition to civil society, seek only the companionship of others like themselves, will succeed in forming close friendships. Although they may well forge emotional attachments, their reactive, mistrustful attitudes will undercut the possibility of friendships that constitute the shared life of "conversation and thought," the friendships of "privileged trust" and mutual disclosure in which people seek and find mutual visibility.[40] The quest for self-knowledge and self-growth cannot coexist with the quest for self-deception, self-gratification, and domination of others.

With rare exceptions, even the sort of goodwill that exists in lesser friendships—the desire for the other's independent well-being essential to any relationship of genuine caring—is absent in those who choose a life of predation.[41] For obvious reasons, the affective and cooperative ties of gang members are based almost entirely on the assumption of loyalty to the power-hierarchy of the gang, a loyalty that is enforced through violence or the threat of violence.[42] Hence, the care and concern of gang

---

[39] Cf. Aristotle, *Nicomachean Ethics*, 1172a13–14, on self-growth and self-knowledge; and John M. Cooper, "Aristotle on Friendship," in *Essays on Aristotle's Ethics*, ed. Amélie O. Rorty (Berkeley: University of California Press, 1980), pp. 301–40.

[40] The phrase "privileged trust" is from Laurence Thomas, *Living Morally: A Psychology of Moral Character* (Philadelphia: Temple University Press, 1989), ch. 4. Cf. Aelred of Rivaulx: "[O]nly those do we call friends to whom we can fearlessly entrust our heart and all its secrets; those, too, who, in turn, are bound to us by the same law of faith and security" (*Spiritual Friendship*, book I, 32, in Michael Pakaluk, ed., *Other Selves: Philosophers on Friendship* [Indianapolis: Hackett Publishing Co., 1991], p. 137).

[41] That there are rare exceptions is attested to by Bing in *Do or Die* (*supra* note 31). Bing describes how some of the same people who can torture outsiders to death for no worse fault than being outsiders can also, sometimes, help the younger boys go to school and get out of the gang.

[42] See, for example, Virgil W. Peterson, *The Mob: Two Hundred Years of Organized Crime in New York* (Ottawa: Green Hill Publishers, 1983), on the use of torture and murder to punish double-crossers, and the use of the fear of violence to maintain "rigid discipline" (p. 426). See also the minutes of the Oyster Bay Conference of organized-crime-control specialists,

members for each other, and their willingness to help in times of need, are highly defeasible. Even among the family-oriented Mafia, rarely do fathers encourage their sons to use their education and opportunities to seek a safer and more enriching life for themselves. Their affective ties, then, not only fail to enhance the agency of individual gang members, they constrain it.

Thus, despite the romantic portrait of gang life often found in movies and books, the overwhelming evidence is that gang culture is generally characterized by a dominate-or-be-dominated code, a love of "glory," and a competition for power that often erupt in violent rivalry not only between gangs but also within gangs. This is especially true of street gangs, whose ranks are filled by young people with reactive, other-directed, unself-reflective psychologies, and violent, short lives. Their lives thus tend to bear out Thomas Hobbes's observations about the internal and external condition of the life of individuals in the state of nature.

It is also possible for people with impoverished lives to form mutually exploitative and manipulative relationships, relationships based on a tacit consent to engage in subtle deceits and power-games and to use each other for their own agendas. Such would be an alliance of mutual deception between two people who need from each other, and are willing to give to each other, constant and uncritical reassurance of their worth. To a larger or lesser extent, such tacitly agreed-upon mutual deception is a feature of many "love" relationships. At their worst, such relationships can become like a drug addiction, as they progressively constrict the possibilities of self-knowledge and self-growth for both people, narrowing their world to each other at their lowest level of self-esteem.[43]

A relationship between two manipulative people can also be aimed at harming others. In the worst case, it might be a partnership in vicious aggression against others, as exemplified in the plotting and scheming relationship of the Marquise de Merteuil and the Vicomte de Valmont, the chief characters of Choderlos de Laclos's *Les Liaisons Dangereuses*.

In all these cases, those who seek to dominate and control the minds and actions of others do so because it is only or largely in the reactions of others that they can gain a sense of their own power and agency. Similarly, those who seek through tacit or explicit consent to be controlled and used by others do so because it is only or largely through their value to others that they can get a sense of self-worth. Thus, they live "secondhand," their relationship to the world and to themselves mediated by

---

describing the structure of various organized-crime groups: "They are totalitarian in nature. . . . The leader of the organization has absolute authority over the life and death of the organization's members" (cited in Dwight C. Smith, Jr., *The Mafia Mystique* [New York: Basic Books, Inc., 1975], p. 247).

[43] For an insightful discussion of the mutually exploitative and manipulative—and finally addictive—relationship of two such people, see Stanton Peele (with Archie Brodsky), *Love and Addiction* (New York: Taplinger, 1975).

others' perceptions and purposes.[44] What none of these relationships can do is satisfy the need for an independently forged life, or supply the joys of sharing such a life with another.

The fuller conception of practical efficacy and self-esteem provided in this and the previous section makes it clearer how and why efficacy and self-esteem are essential for well-being. Insofar as we are efficacious, we have the central component of personal well-being: a life of unimpeded active engagement with the world, based on a realistic appraisal of ourselves and others, and the accompanying awareness of ourselves as "fit" for the world. Such an awareness is pleasurable for the same kind of reason that the awareness of the healthy, unimpeded activity of one's body is pleasurable. And this is how we expect well-being or happiness to be, since, in Aristotle's words, we "all think the happy life is pleasant and weave pleasure into happiness" (NE 1153b13–15).

The analyses and arguments given in these sections also support the claim that virtue is both necessary and, in the absence of misfortune, sufficient, for practical efficacy and happiness. For they suggest that in the absence of external impediments to efficacy or happiness, the lack of efficacy in fundamental areas of human concern and, thus, the lack of happiness in a person's life, imply a lack of practical wisdom and virtue. Insofar as we lack autonomy, we either fail to live by our own reasoned choices, or we choose ends that rob us of the continued ability to live by our own reasoned choices. Insofar as we lack worthy ends, we lack either the ability to make sound value-judgments, or the ability to act on them. Insofar as we lack realism in our choice of ends, we lack either the ability to accurately gauge our capacities, or the ability to live by our perceptions. Insofar as we lack the competence to pursue worthy ends, we lack either the ability to deliberate rationally, or the ability to live by the results of such deliberation. If we have both competence and autonomously chosen realistic and worthy ends, but lack a sense of self-worth, we lack either sound standards of self-worth, or the ability to appraise ourselves by them. But the ability to realistically and autonomously choose and pursue worthy ends, using sound standards of value to appraise ourselves and others, is part and parcel of practical wisdom and virtue. Hence, lack of practical efficacy in the absence of external impediments implies a commensurate lack of practical wisdom and virtue.

When we are fully efficacious, we are not only rightly self-directed, acting in ways conducive to our natures as rational and social animals and, thus, to our well-being, we also take pleasure in our power of right self-direction—our autonomy. It is then that autonomy becomes a virtue, and our autonomous choices exhibit wisdom and virtue, for it is then that

---

[44] The term "second-hand" is Ayn Rand's. The nature of the independent individual versus the nature of the second-hander is the central theme of her novel *The Fountainhead* (New York: New American Library, 1968). The addictive lovers described by Peele and Brodsky in *Love and Addiction* are also examples of two second-handers.

our emotions and desires become integrated with reason. And it is only when our choices exhibit virtue that we are fully rationally self-interested.[45] For it is only then that we are appropriately responsive to our own human and individual capacities and needs, and take pleasure in exercising our capacities, expressing our emotions, and satisfying our appetites, in the right circumstances, in the right manner, at the right time, and to the right extent. Further, in recognizing our own human capacities and needs, we recognize our commonalities with others and, thus, the capacities and needs of others.[46] In this way, the virtues put us in touch with various aspects of reality, our own and others', free us of the control of skewed perceptions and irrational emotions, and enable us to feel at home in the world. The virtues, in other words, empower us.

A deeper analysis of practical efficacy supports a picture of the virtues as "emergent properties," qualities of character that emerge hand-in-hand with increasing efficacy and self-esteem, qualities that represent excellence in the functioning of our cognitive, emotional, and social capacities.

In the next section I will use extended examples to show this connection between virtue and happiness—as well as the connection between lack of virtue and lack of happiness.

V. Self-Interest, Well-Being, and Virtue

What was I created for, I wonder? Where is my place in the world? . . . Is there not a terrible hollowness, mockery, want, craving, in that existence which is given away to others, for want of something of your own to bestow it on?[47]

The sort of giving away of one's existence to others that Caroline, in Charlotte Brontë's novel *Shirley*, has in mind here, is the giving away in self-sacrificial service that is often taught to women.[48] But there are many other ways of giving away one's own existence to others, and many ways of not having a life of one's own that do not involve others. In each case, some ways are more culpable than others. In all of them, however, as the following examples show, there is a hollowness and mockery, a deficiency

[45] Cf. Aristotle's remark that the virtuous person is a self-lover because "he acts for the sake of his reasoning part, which is what each person seems to be" (*Nicomachean Ethics*, 1166a16–17); and: "[T]he excellent person, in so far as he is excellent, enjoys actions expressing virtue, and objects to actions caused by vice, just as the musician enjoys fine melodies and is pained by bad ones" (1170a8–10).

[46] I argue for this in my "Moral Agency, Commitment, and Impartiality," *Social Philosophy and Policy*, vol. 13, no. 1 (Winter 1996), pp. 22–25.

[47] Charlotte Brontë, *Shirley*, ed. Herbert Rosengarten and Margaret Smith (New York: Oxford University Press, 1979), p. 174.

[48] For a fascinating discussion of this sort of self-abnegation, see Jean Hampton, "Selflessness and the Loss of Self," *Social Philosophy and Policy*, vol. 10, no. 1 (Winter 1993), pp. 135–65.

of rational self-direction and of self-love. Hence, in all such ways of life there is lack of both virtue and well-being, with the extent and depth of the first lack reflected in the extent and depth of the second.

As we have seen, the very vicious, those who live a life of aggression against others, whether through physical violence or through psychological manipulation, are also radically lacking in the willingness to be the autonomous agents of their own lives and establish an independent relationship to reality. Whatever the initial cause of their vice, their extreme injustice and deceitfulness toward others express their lack of autonomy and self-esteem, and strengthen and exacerbate their unhappiness. For the more they aggress and scheme against others, the less they live lives of their own; and the more they succeed in rationalizing their behavior to themselves, the less they see a reason to make lives of their own. Their callous attitude toward others' well-being is reflected in a like attitude toward themselves, an attitude of indifference to their moral selves, their characters.[49] Thus, they rob themselves not only of the pleasures of living lives of their own, but also of the pleasures of friendship.

The callousness, and the deliberate, cultivated purposelessness, of the lives of the Marquise de Merteuil and the Vicomte de Valmont serve as a case in point. The destruction of others' reputations and lives through sexual intrigue, seduction, and betrayal is the leitmotif of their liaison, and amusement and diversion from boredom are its only purpose. Every victory over others confirms them in their sense of superiority to others — yet every victory leaves them dissatisfied and in search of an ever-greater variety of amusement and refinement of cruelty. For the Vicomte, this search culminates in the project of seducing and destroying Madame de Tourvel, a woman who stands aloof from the surrounding intrigues and scandals, and whose greatest charm is her radiant virtue. She must be seduced and destroyed *precisely because* she is self-possessed and virtuous. When, contrary to his own expectations, he starts to fall in love with her, experiencing the first genuine passion and love and happiness he has ever felt, he is led by the shallowness of his own character, as by a destiny, to reject his feelings as pusillanimous. His project comes to an end only when he has destroyed her — and his own happiness.

Similar considerations apply to those who, in lesser and more limited ways, attempt to manipulate or exploit others instead of living through their own agency. Whatever the initial cause of their (more limited) vice, their attempts to use others as mere means to their own ends perpetuate their lack of autonomy, and hence their lack of well-being. For example, the narrator of Dostoyevsky's *Notes from the Underground* seeks

[49] Such indifference to the self may also be called the vice of *sloth* or *acedia*, from the Greek *akedeia*, "without care." Thomas Aquinas discusses sloth in the form of "spiritual apathy," which he defines as "sorrow over spiritual good," and in particular, the divine good; see Aquinas, *Summa Theologiae* (New York: Blackfriars and McGraw-Hill Book Co., 1972), 2a2ae, question 35, article 2.

ever more elaborate—and ever more absurd—techniques to prove his worth to himself and others. When such manipulation and exploitation are mutual, each party is caught in a spiral of escalating game-playing to gain a sense of his or her own agency and value through the other's actions and reactions. For every success prompts further attempts, and every failure creates a need to invent a new technique for outwitting each other.

There are also other ways of living through others that involve only a willingness to *be* manipulated and exploited. Such is the case of someone who sacrifices his autonomy and integrity for the sake of pleasing others and being liked by them. The character of Leonard Zelig, in Woody Allen's film *Zelig*, is the epitome of someone who has taken self-surrender to its logical conclusion. In countless acts of phony agreement with others' opinions and tastes, in innumerable shifts of preference and belief to tailor his personality to "fit in" with the crowd, Zelig ends up a chameleon-like personality whose identity, and sense of identity, become entirely dependent on the identity of those around him. As he perfects the skill of blending in with the environment, he loses all sense of his own separateness and distinctness: when with doctors, he becomes a doctor, when with actors, an actor—and when with fascists, a fascist.

Like the Marquise, the Vicomte, and the Underground Man, Zelig's failure of autonomy and integrity is also a failure of courage, the courage to confront the feelings of insecurity and worthlessness that lead him to try to gain the esteem of others through utter conformity to their values. Insofar as he denies these feelings, it is also a failure of honesty with himself. Like the others, too, Zelig shows a lack of spiritual ambition, a lack of concern for his moral self, and, thus, for his own well-being.

But feelings of insecurity and worthlessness are not the only starting points on the route to such conformity and cowardice and dishonesty. Someone brought up on the wrong moral code, a code that preaches self-sacrifice and service to others as the highest moral ideals, can, if she fails to challenge this code, end up where Zelig starts: radically heteronomous, cowardly, and compromised—her life a pretense in the name of an ideal.

A person might also live in an uneasy balance between total self-surrender and autonomy, self-betrayal and integrity. Consider a woman who, like Brontë's Caroline, has been raised in a culture that devalues independence and rationality for women, and severely constrains their opportunities for discovering the value of these traits. But unlike Caroline, who questions her culture's code, this woman unthinkingly accepts it as right and tries to act on it. She tries this, but never fully succeeds, because she never fully internalizes the "womanly virtues" of abiding by the decisions of the male authority, and of defining her interests in terms of his. And she never fully internalizes them because she cannot quite surrender her own vision of things or see herself as inferior. Thus, she sacrifices the virtues of autonomy and of pride without ever quite acquiring the vices of slavishness and humility.[50] Likewise, she sacrifices the virtues of integrity, and of a truthful view of herself in her self-presentations to others, without falling into total self-betrayal and self-deprecation.[51] Hence, she retains some sense of her own potentialities and of self-worth, without ever forging a life of her own.

All of these are ways of not having a life of one's own because one has given it away to others. But a person can also lack a life of his own not necessarily (or even primarily) because he has given it away to others, but because he has given it up for the easy pleasures of immediate gratification or inertia—the "false pleasures," as Plato would call them, of avoiding pain by avoiding gain. Such a person might be simply incontinent or weak-willed, rather than indifferent to, or committed to, the bad. Unlike some of the cases discussed above, an incontinent person knows well the difference between the good and the bad, in principle and in application. But he lacks the wherewithal to act on this knowledge, because he lacks the strength to counteract his inertia or his desire for immediate gratification. And so he fails in temperance, integrity, and spiritual ambition. Thus, he fails to pursue the ends he recognizes as worth pursuing and, rationally, wishes to pursue, in favor of ends that seem more immediately pleasing or in some way easier. He aspires to make something of himself, but his aspirations remain a blueprint buried under the pleasures of immediate gratification, or of effort-avoidance. His self-indulgence reinforces his weakness of will, creating a gulf between his aspirations and his actions, and leading to derailed goals, recurring regrets, a sense of failure, and an ever-lower self-esteem.

If and when he becomes continent, he will regain much of the self he has frittered away in easy pleasures, or create the self he has never had. He will not only have a general understanding of what is humanly important, he will also have a more realistic understanding of his own strengths and weaknesses, and will act resolutely on his well-considered decisions. Thus, he will accomplish the goals he rationally wishes to accomplish, regain much of his lost (or never-gained) self-trust, and have reason to feel pride instead of regret.

Nevertheless, even a continent person does not have the psychological prerequisite for a high degree of well-being. For a continent person lacks the depth of conviction and fullness of purpose that come only with an

---

[50] A person who claims less than he should, says Aristotle, "would seem to have something bad in him because he does not think he is worthy of the goods" he is worthy of, and "he would seem not to know himself" (*Nicomachean Ethics*, 1125a20–23). Again, someone who never gets angry when insulted and, thus, never defends himself, but is willing "to accept insults to . . . [himself] and to overlook insults to . . . [his] family and friends is slavish" (1126a6–8).

[51] Cf. Aristotle, *Nicomachean Ethics*, 1127a32–b35, where Aristotle contrasts the virtue of truthfulness about oneself with the deficiency of self-deprecation and the excess of boastfulness.

integration of understanding and judgment with emotion and desire. When nearby or easy pleasures beckon, he needs to struggle to resist their beckoning. He does what he judges to be important, but wishes it could be otherwise and looks for reasons that might justify making an exception. His deliberations and actions, though finally successful, are still impeded by his wayward feelings and desires. Hence, he lacks the enjoyment inherent in activity that engages one's emotions and desires. Thus, even in the event of good fortune, his well-being is impeded by his lack of virtue: his inability to wholeheartedly desire what he rationally wishes to do, and does. Conversely, to the extent that he is happy, he is happy for the same reason that he is morally upright: he perceives what is important in a human life and in his own life, and why, and he commits himself to living up to this perception.

A high degree of well-being—*eudaimonia*—requires the virtues, the virtues of character informed by practical wisdom. For, as argued in Section II above, it is only insofar as someone is virtuous that she has not only the correct general conception of the things worth striving for and the best means to them, but also the perceptiveness to see the subtle shadings of value in the particularities of their daily manifestation. And it is only insofar as someone is virtuous that she possesses the wherewithal to create a life of her own, in a world of her own: freedom from the blandishments of rejected desires, independence of the temptations of conformity, and equanimity in the face of misfortunes. For it is only insofar as she is virtuous that she feels and desires in harmony with her reason (and reasons in harmony with her feelings and desires) and is able to act wholeheartedly and pleasurably in ways that express her understanding, perceptions, and emotions. Thus, it is only insofar as someone is virtuous that she possesses the dominant internal source of full efficacy and happiness.

Charlotte Brontë's portrait of Jane Eyre, in her novel of the same name, is in many ways the portrait of such a person. In one scene in the novel, we get a description of Jane Eyre by Edward Rochester, the novel's other main character. We are told that Jane Eyre has eyes that are "soft and full of feeling," yet also proud and reserved; a mouth that is "[m]obile and flexible," that "delights at times in laughter," and is "meant to speak much and smile often"; yet also a brow that declares that she can live alone if necessary, for she has "an inward treasure" which can keep her alive "if all extraneous delights should be withheld; or offered only at a price" she "cannot afford to give."[52] She also has "passions" that "may rage furiously," but her judgment always has "the last word in every argument, and the casting vote in every decision."[53] And as the events of the novel, and Jane Eyre's own words, reveal, she has also yearned for

[52] Charlotte Brontë, *Jane Eyre* (1847), ed. Sandy Lesberg (New York: Peebles Press International, Inc., n.d.), p. 242.
[53] *Ibid.*, pp. 242–43.

"an original, a vigorous, an expanded mind" such as Rochester's, and delighted in it when she has found it.[54]

The picture we get is of a person who is firmly independent, courageous, proud, and resourceful, gentle, sympathetic, and giving, delighting in conversation and the life of the mind, passionately loving, and passionately rational. For such a person, doing wrong by others is as much an anathema as the idea of doing wrong by herself for the sake of "extraneous delights" (including, as the story reveals, the delights of a life with the only man she has ever loved). For being just or honest with others is as much a part of her sense of who she is, as is having the self-regarding virtues. Indeed, being just and honest with others follows from her self-regarding virtues, and conversely. Because she is autonomous, she does not wish for any value from others that she cannot get in a fair exchange, or as a freely given gift. Hence, she lacks any reason to exploit or manipulate others. Moreover, because she has a justifiable sense of self-worth—the virtue of pride—she would disdain becoming a dependent on the mistaken trust of the victims of her deception. Because she has courage and pride, she neither fears the judgment of others, nor needs their unearned approval. Hence, she has reason neither to flatter others, nor to deceive them about herself. Since she is honest with herself, she knows herself well and wishes to know herself better; and therefore she seeks honest interaction with others. Because she has self-regard, she approaches others with the same presumption of self-regard; and therefore she extends the same honesty to others. Each of these dispositions is a part of her sense of who she is; hence, her sense of integrity requires that she live in truth to all of them. And in so doing, she succeeds in living a life of full engagement with the world.

Her success, however, is not achieved without a degree of good fortune. Everything turns out well in Charlotte Brontë's story: Jane marries Rochester when she can do so without compromising her principles. But circumstances *could* have conspired to deprive her of a life worth living, thanks to her unwillingness to compromise. Hence we must now consider the possibility of conflict between the internal and external conditions of well-being—i.e., between virtue and good fortune—and their relative weight in well-being in case of such a conflict.

If Jane Eyre's virtues had invited disaster, would she have had a self-interested reason to *change* who she was, if she could? Would it be true to say that she would have been better off if she had had less integrity, so that, in case of conflict, she *could* have compromised it for the sake of gaining or preserving some of those "extraneous delights"? Since certain sorts of external goods are also essential for human happiness, it is entirely possible for someone with less integrity to do better in terms of external goods than someone with the integrity of a Jane Eyre, and thus

---

[54] *Ibid.*, p. 306.

to preserve a life worth living where the other fails. But this in itself does not imply that the person with less integrity will do better overall than the person with more integrity. For the intensity of happiness of a short-lived life might outweigh the paler pleasures of a longer life. It is only in cases where virtue invites the sort of disaster that leads not to death but to extreme lifelong suffering, the sort of suffering that breaks down a person's inner resources, that it is clear that (other things being equal) a person of lesser virtue would have done better overall.

But if someone retains her virtue even in catastrophic circumstances, then neither she, nor those who know and admire her, can think that she would have been better off if she had been a different sort of person. She cannot think this because her conception of her self-interest cannot be prised apart from her conception of herself, and her conception of herself cannot be prised apart her moral virtues. A person's virtues are deep-seated dispositions that she identifies with and loves, expresses in her thoughts, feelings, and actions, has produced by her actions, and is partly the product of. Most importantly, however, she cannot wish to be without her virtues because she recognizes them as the source of her most cherished possessions: her sense of freedom and her capacity for enjoyment. Likewise, those who admire her and wish her well also cannot wish her to be without her virtues. For when they have a full-enough conception of her life to admire her, they can see how her virtues have enhanced her life, and cannot conceive of any life as a good life for her independently of her virtues.

To take a real-life example: it was largely Socrates' virtues that led to his execution, but it would be false to say that Socrates would have been better off without his passion for self-knowledge or his honesty in the quest for it, or without the sense of justice that led him to refuse to participate in the unjust trial of the Athenian Generals or to cooperate with the Thirty Tyrants. For these are the intellectual and moral virtues that made the life of Socrates what it was. And it is hard to imagine a fuller life than Socrates', combining as it did the harmonious exercise of all his human capacities—rational, emotional, social, and appetitive—and his intense pleasure in such exercise.[55] Even if he had been killed at, say, the age of forty, instead of at the age of seventy or seventy-one, his life would have been fuller than most people's lives anywhere. It is also hard to imagine how someone whose virtues are confined to fewer areas of life could have as rich a life as Socrates'. For it is only too clear how Socrates' virtues made for the richness of his life—and for the fascination of his character for his friends and admirers, past and present. It is hardly surprising, then, that neither Socrates nor his well-wishers regretted his courageous, just, or other virtuous dispositions or actions.

[55] Such, at least, is the portrait of Socrates presented in Plato's *Symposium*, trans. Michael Joyce, in *The Collected Dialogues of Plato*, ed. Edith Hamilton and Huntington Cairns (Princeton: Princeton University Press, 1961), especially in Alcibiades' speech at 219e–222a.

Do similar considerations apply to a vicious person as to a virtuous one? Must a vicious person find it impossible to conceive of himself as better off without his vices?[56] Just as the virtuous person identifies with his virtues, a vicious person will identify with his vices. But unless he is totally self-deceived and self-alienated, he cannot see himself as efficacious or happy, and thus he cannot see his vices as promoting his well-being—even if he also cannot quite see how virtue can promote anyone's well-being. If he *is* totally self-deceived, however, he will see others, rather than his own character, as the cause of his problems, and live in a state of self-alienation, as well as of alienation from, and conflict with, others. Insofar as a vicious person cannot conceive of himself as better off without his vices, then, it is either because he cannot conceive the possibility of better people than himself, or because he cannot conceive the possibility of better people having better lives. But if he is, in rare moments, capable of conceiving these possibilities, then he is also capable of conceiving of himself as better off without his vices. For at such moments he is aware that it is his vices that deprive him of efficacy, cause his resentments, and create the constant need to posture and try to outwit others. Thus, he is aware—as are those who observe him—that it is his vices that deprive him of freedom and the enjoyment of life.

Furthermore, the salience of the fact that heroic figures are sometimes struck down by those who fear or envy or resent them should not lead us to forget that those who are wholly or largely lacking in moral virtue are also subject to certain sorts of misfortunes, precisely on account of this lack. This is the chief moral lesson of *Zelig*. In the movie, Zelig starts by sacrificing assorted opinions and preferences, proceeds to sacrifice his very identity and capacity for moral judgment, and eventually becomes the prey of fascist propaganda. History shows that lack of integrity and autonomy and pride do not have to reach Zelig-like proportions before we make ourselves vulnerable to such propaganda: the Nazis succeeded in attracting millions of ordinary human beings to their cause by playing on their feelings of impotence and worthlessness. And experimental psychology and everyday experience show that this historical lesson has relevance beyond its time and place, because the habits of conformity, and of obedience to authority, are widespread and deep, much deeper by far than integrity or justice or goodwill.[57]

Nor does the possibility of becoming the tool of another exist only where there are individuals with totalitarian aspirations. For individuals with aspirations to control us exist everywhere—in the school, the streets,

---

[56] I thank Daniel Shapiro for raising this question.

[57] For experimental evidence of the depth and scope of habits of conformity and of obedience to authority, see Solomon Asch, *Social Psychology* (Englewood Cliffs, NJ: Prentice-Hall, 1952); and Stanley Milgram, *Obedience to Authority* (New York: Harper and Row, 1974), respectively. Conformity also plays a role in the phenomenon of "the unresponsive bystander"; see the description of the experiments conducted by Bibb Latane and John Darley in their book *The Unresponsive Bystander: Why Doesn't He Help?* (New York: Appleton, 1970).

the office, the home, the government—and come in many forms—school bullies, gang leaders, autocratic bosses, fathers, or husbands, cult leaders, organizers of paramilitary groups, politicians with loyal fiefdoms, et al. Given the right circumstances—and the circumstances are only too often right—the step from "ordinary" conformity to the status of victim—or victimizer—is only a short one. As victim, one may be the passive object of another's cruelty, or the eager self-abnegator who sacrifices her or his own perceptions and goals in the hope of finding salvation or meaning in life through submission to another; as victimizer, one may be the reluctantly obedient subject who visits cruelty on others, or the eager conformist to the group's norms of brutality.[58] Whatever the case, the result is the same: the loss of a self and a world of one's own. Only those who wholly or largely lack virtue are struck by such misfortune; and only those who have the virtues of autonomy, integrity, pride, justice, goodwill, et al. are assured of averting it.

Even in the absence of such misfortune, there is the daily grayness, or the frequently recurring anxiety, of many lives. As I noted in Section III, the psychological and other evidence points to widespread unhappiness even among people blessed by good fortune—unhappiness resulting from self-doubt and low self-regard, from a sense of inauthenticity, of not being one's own person, and so on—in short, from lack of autonomy, integrity, pride, and honesty. Since most people are not vicious, since they do not endorse the obviously immoral, the lack of these virtues can only take the form of the daily moral shortcuts—the compromises, the surrenders, the evasions, the petty manipulations and injustices—that characterize so many people's actions and affect so many relationships, at home and in the workplace. It is true for vast numbers of us, then, as many psychologists have recognized, that moral virtue is an indispensable part of our self-interest.[59]

[58] In Philip Zimbardo's disturbingly fascinating "prison experiments," college students assigned to play prisoners and guards soon started to exhibit alarming levels of self-abnegating obedience as prisoners, or cruelty and brutality as guards. This happened spontaneously, without pressure from the experimenters. What sufficed for the extreme results were the deliberate creation of an atmosphere of degradation in the "prison camp" by Zimbardo, his tacit permission to the students to do as they liked within the parameters of the experiment, and conformity on the part of the students to their respective peer groups. Owing to the unexpected brutality, Zimbardo had to call off a planned two-week experiment after six days. This experiment, and the Milgram and Asch experiments cited in note 57, are well discussed in John Sabini and Maury Silver, "On Destroying the Innocent with a Clear Conscience: A Sociopsychology of the Holocaust," in their book *Moralities of Everyday Life* (Oxford: Oxford University Press, 1982).

[59] Since the virtues just *are* rational and emotional dispositions to recognize and respond to value, and since such recognition and response are part and parcel of practical efficacy and happiness, this is hardly surprising. Thus, in "Toward a Modern Approach to Values" (*supra* note 35), Rogers talks about the psychologically mature person as being "sensitively discriminating" (p. 87) and "accurate" in his responses because he is in touch with the "totality of himself" (p. 89), i.e., his perceptions, feelings, and thoughts, and in touch with "the realities of the objective world" and of other people (p. 92). Such a person comes to value being "real," tolerant, and self-accepting, and acquires pride. Thus, he moves toward the "universal values" (p. 93) of "sincerity, independence, self-direction, self-knowledge,

Hence, even though a person's virtue might invite unusual misfortune, a misfortune that deprives him of a great part of happiness and that would not strike someone with a more accommodating character, we cannot wish, for any future person to whom we wish happiness, that she grow up to be less than morally admirable. For to wish a person to grow up to lack virtue is to wish her to acquire less of the most essential resource for a truly happy life, for the sake of avoiding an unusual—and, therefore, unlikely—circumstance. It is only in the event of a misfortune so great that it tears down a person's inner resources, that goodwill must lead us, in retrospect, to wish that she had had the ability for moral compromise.

I have assumed all along that the virtues need not extend, and typically do not extend, across all domains of a person's life. This means that even the most morally admirable people are likely to fall short of virtue in some area of their lives. Socrates, for example, despite his courage and his sense of justice, seems never to have spoken out against the injustice of slavery in his society. Yet this moral limitation did not, as far as we know, tarnish his happiness. It is possible that Socrates did not even *notice* the injustice of slavery, that he had a culturally induced blind spot regarding its injustice.

This suggests that if a person's injustice in certain domains of his life is due to blind spots, and the victim of injustice does not protest or resist it, the injustice of the partially unjust person will not undermine his sense of rectitude. And since a sense of rectitude is a major component of a person's self-esteem, and thus of his well-being, it follows that his limited injustice will not undermine his overall well-being. But even if the injustice *is* due to evasion, if a person's life is otherwise full enough and rich enough owing to his virtues, then the injustice will not affect it so significantly that he is robbed of his overall happiness. Such might have been the case with Thomas Jefferson. Jefferson seems to have combined great courage and justice and integrity in many areas of his life with a shocking lack of these in at least one area: slavery. He spoke out against slavery, and was clearly troubled by his own involvement with it, apparently spending sleepless nights over it. Yet he was not troubled enough (or principled enough) to free his slaves during his lifetime or, indeed, even after his death, when he had them sold to pay off his debts. Although his happiness was tarnished by his injustice, it was not tarnished enough to deprive him of a fairly rich and satisfying life.

---

social responsivity, social responsibility, and loving interpersonal relationships" (p. 95). Similarly, in "The Good Life of the Self-Actualizing Person" (*supra* note 35), Maslow talks about the self-actualizing person as moving toward "truth, justice, beauty, and virtue," and thereby coming to feel "loving and admiring" toward herself (pp. 73–74). Again, in *The Six Pillars of Self-Esteem* (*supra* note 25), where Branden discusses why self-esteem is an indispensable component of happiness, he includes "personal integrity" as the "sixth pillar" of self-esteem, and lists the following virtues as the main components of personal integrity: practicing what one preaches, promise-keeping, honoring one's commitments, and "dealing with other human beings fairly, justly, benevolently, and compassionately" (p. 165).

None of this should be surprising. If happiness is analogous to physical health, then given the fact that some people can stay healthy despite their violation of certain health norms, it is to be expected that some people will lead more or less happy lives despite their violation of certain moral norms. Hence, they will not have sufficient—or, if the violation is due to blind spots, any—motivation to do the right thing, independently of appropriate reactions by their victims. In such cases, the importance of each of us standing up to those who do injustice to us is both self-regarding and other-regarding. Moreover, if we are truly concerned to stay in touch with ourselves and others, we will be concerned about the possibility of our own blind spots and injustices. Hence, it is important that each of us also want others to stand up to us when we do injustice to them, and that we heed them when they do.

VI. Conclusion

I have argued that virtue is essential to practical efficacy—to our ability to function well as beings with certain sorts of rational, social, and physical powers and needs—and hence, that virtue is central to well-being. For both well-being and virtue involve facing ourselves and others and the circumstances of our world realistically, and taking pleasure in acting accordingly. But virtue is neither identical with, nor sufficient for, well-being. Great misfortunes can mar a person's well-being by impeding her practical efficacy, regardless of her virtues. The virtues guarantee only the essential internal condition of practical efficacy and well-being, namely, the appropriate ultimate goals and dispositions.

I have suggested some ways in which the self-regarding and other-regarding virtues (and vices) are connected; but there is much more to be said about the connections. In particular, the suggestion that the other-regarding virtues are required for an adequate conception of, and concern for, ourselves requires development. What I hope to have shown, however, is that most of us have as much reason to develop the virtues as we do to seek happiness.

Philosophy, University of Oklahoma

THE VIRTUE IN SELF-INTEREST*

By Michael Slote

As a motive, self-interest is constituted by a certain kind of concern for oneself; but we also use the term "self-interest" to refer to the object of such a motive, to the well-being or good life sought by a self-interested agent. In this essay, I want to concentrate on self-interest in the latter sense and say something about how self-interest or well-being relates to virtue. One reason to be interested in this relationship stems from our concern to know whether virtue pays, i.e., is in the moral agent's self-interest, a question which Plato notably asks in the *Republic* and which has been of concern to moral philosophers ever since. But the importance for ethics of notions like virtue and self-interest is hardly exhausted by their role in the debate over whether virtue pays; indeed, any large-scale ethical theory will presumably have something to say about how these major notions relate, so we have reason to want to understand this relationship independent of the particular desire to show that morality or virtue is in the self-interest of the (virtuous) agent.

It will be a background assumption of this essay that some ways of connecting virtue and well-being/self-interest redound to the advantage of the larger theories that incorporate them. If, in particular, we believe in the bona fides of ethical *theory*, then unifying power is a desideratum in ethics and it stands in favor of utilitarianism (and Epicureanism) that it offers us a way of unifying our understanding of virtue and well-being. To be sure, that advantage may to some extent or ultimately be undercut if unification leads to counterintuitive ethical consequences. But if theory is appropriate in ethics, then utilitarianism stands to gain from its ability to *reduce* all notions of virtue to the coinage of well-being and self-interest.

In what follows, however, I hope to show that the ability to unify is not unique to reductive theories like utilitarianism. Many other ethical views may be "dualistic" about the categories of virtue and self-interest and thus at an initial disadvantage vis-à-vis utilitarianism, but certain forms of virtue ethics are also capable of unifying virtue and self-interest; and what I have in mind here is not reductive virtue-ethical theories like Epicureanism, but forms of virtue ethics that effect the unification in a

* For helpful comments and suggestions, I want to thank Jerry Levinson, Ellen Frankel Paul, Georges Rey, Christine Swanton, and the other contributors to this volume.

manner entirely different from the way in which both utilitarianism and Epicureanism proceed.[1]

I. UNIFICATION IN UTILITARIANISM

One of the main strengths or attractions of act-utilitarianism is that it allows for a reduction of all our ethical ideals and standards to the ethical notion of well-being or welfare. Actions count as right, roughly speaking, to the extent that they bring about the greatest possible well-being. And utilitarianism also reduces other moral notions to the notion of well-being suitably supplemented by appropriate causal and other concepts. An act counts as blameworthy, for example, if the act of blaming or negatively reinforcing it will have best or good-enough consequences for human or sentient well-being, and a trait counts as a virtue if it generally leads to well-being rather than to its opposite. In addition, utilitarianism tends to treat terms of *rational* appraisal like "prudent," "rationally acceptable," and "good choice" as reducible to the category of personal good or well-being taken together with other, nonethical concepts (though different utilitarians effect this reduction in different ways); so it is, I think, safe to say that utilitarianism reduces all prominent ethical notions to concepts of well-being or self-interest.

The reduction does not end there, however. The fundamental ethical category of well-being is treated by the utilitarian as further reducible to empirical or nonethical notions like preference-satisfaction or pleasure/pain. Thus, utilitarianism not only reduces the major concepts of ethics to a single ethical notion, but then reduces the whole realm of ethical value and evaluation to naturalistic or value-free terms. However, this unifying reduction occurs at a considerable price, since utilitarianism notoriously clashes with common-sense judgments about what is morally right or admirable. (It typically holds, for example, that duty can require one to kill one innocent person in order to save the lives of innocent others, and to give up one's career and family life if one can do more good, say, as a medical missionary.) Even apart from this "price," I think we also need to be a little clearer about the character of the double reduction that utilitarianism seeks to effect.

In philosophic parlance, one kind of reduction occurs or is attempted when one seeks to understand the macro in terms of the micro (the whole in terms of its elements or parts), as, for example, when we identify salt with sodium chloride. But another form of reduction takes place when an attempt is made to understand what is "higher" in terms of what is

---

[1] "Virtue ethics" refers to ethical views that focus on the character or motives of agents rather than on good consequences or conformity to rules. Virtue ethics predominated in the ancient world, and Plato, Aristotle, the Stoics, and the Epicureans are all good examples of this approach; but there are also some modern instances, and very recently there has been a strong resurgence of interest in virtue ethics.

"lower."[2] Thus, when the utilitarian identifies well-being or doing well in life with pleasure or desire-fulfillment, this is plausibly regarded as a *reduction*, because the realm of value seems in some way *higher* than the merely empirical and natural. (Is that perhaps because it involves *standards for judging* what actually occurs or might occur in human life?) For the same reason, it makes sense to say, for example, that Freud and Alfred Adler *reduced* all higher activities and aspirations, respectively, to mere sexual strivings and desire for power.

When utilitarianism seeks to understand all rationality, virtue, and morality in terms of facts about well-being, that also counts as a reduction, because it is natural to think of the ethical category of well-being as in some sense *lower* than the ethical categories utilitarianism seeks to understand in terms of it. To that extent, the unification utilitarianism seeks *within* the realm of the ethical is reductive in character quite apart from the further attempt to reduce well-being (and thus all other ethical concepts as well) to naturalistic concepts; but I think we need to say a bit more about why well-being is regarded as *lower* than virtue, etc.

The most important point to be made in this connection, I think, is that what counts as an element in our well-being or as good for us may in no way be admirable. For example, in the *Eudemian Ethics*, Aristotle makes the common-sense point that unlike the virtues, health is good but not praiseworthy (1248b17–27). And a similar point can be made about pleasure and common enjoyment. These involve something good happening to us, but because they do not seem to require any virtue, rationality, or morality on our part, there seems to be nothing admirable about the capacity for and occasions of pleasure, enjoyment, or, for that matter, health.

But the distinction between what is *merely* enjoyable, pleasurable, and good (for us) and what is admirable seems to involve a distinction between lower and higher ethical values (what else can the word "merely" be doing in this sentence?). Claims about rationality, morality, and what is admirable in other spheres express *ideals*, and in becoming generous or prudent or trained in physics or philosophy, we would normally be thought to be realizing certain actual or possible ideals of character or human aspiration, in a way that experiencing enjoyment or feeling secure or having a healthy constitution do not require. Thus, in understanding rationality, virtue, and moral obligation/blameworthiness as (mere) means to human or sentient well-being, utilitarianism is reducing (what is intuitively and antecedently taken to be) the ethically higher to (what is intuitively and antecedently taken to be) the ethically lower, what is admirable to what is (merely) desirable or good for us. And to that extent utilitarianism deflates ethics internally by telling us that there is nothing

---

[2] One can also try to reduce the number of entities or concepts one refers to or makes use of in a theory, but this notion of reduction cuts across the distinctions I am making in the text, and I shall ignore it in what follows.

to the apparent distinction between higher and lower ethical values—
telling us that what we tend to think of as higher than mere or sheer
well-being is really at the same level as (what we regard as) the lower.

But isn't this an inevitable effect of any attempt to unify the major
concepts of ethics, a price we have to and should be willing to pay, if we
value theoretical systematization and unification highly and are willing to
pay the price of rejecting many of our ethical intuitions? I think not. There
is another mode of intra-ethical unification that involves just the opposite
of reductionism, and it will be my main purpose here to try to demonstrate its philosophical promise. In order to understand how such a different mode of unification is possible and even plausible, we would do
well first to consider the difference between Stoicism and Epicureanism.

II. ELEVATION VERSUS REDUCTION

Epicureanism is reductive in the manner of utilitarianism, though on an
(arguably) egoistic, rather than universalistic or agent-neutral, basis. What
is antecedently regarded as higher is understood in terms of what is
antecedently thought of as lower via Epicureanism's claim that practical
rationality and (the) virtue(s) generally are nothing more than effective
means to—and thus exist at the same level as—a person's well-being.
(Like utilitarianism, Epicureanism then effects a second reduction by treating well-being as a matter simply of pleasure or, more accurately, freedom
from pain.)

But if Epicureanism, like utilitarianism, assimilates the admirable and
putatively higher to the desirable and putatively lower, Stoicism works in
just the opposite direction, understanding the putatively lower values of
well-being or self-interest in terms of the supposedly higher ones of rationality and virtue. If the term "reduction" is useful for conveying the
first sort of assimilation, we need a convenient term for the opposite
mode of assimilation or identification that Stoicism advocates, and there
is none readily available in the philosophical literature. (It is quite odd
that there should be no such generally available expression, since, as we
shall see in a moment, many kinds of theories both inside and outside
ethics assimilate levels in the manner of Stoicism.) The best we can do, I
think, is to say that Stoicism *elevates* human well-being to the level of
human virtue/morality/rationality (unfortunately, I have been unable to
find any more idiomatic or attractive way of conveying the opposite of
reduction).

For the Stoics, human well-being *consists* in being virtuous. Virtue or
the virtues taken together are the sum and substance of human well-
being: nothing beyond (the attainment of) rational virtue is required for
us to be well-off or have good lives, and nothing that fails to improve us
in virtue/rationality can be, therefore, of any real benefit. A virtuous
individual bereft of wealth, friends, bodily pleasure, and good health—

indeed even on the rack and in great pain—can be as well-off as it is possible to be, and thus on a Stoic account human well-being is regarded very differently from the way it ordinarily is. On a common-sense view, whether or not virtue, or various virtues, are part of a good life, there are certain enjoyments and activities which seem neither admirable nor means to anything admirable yet which are definitely seen as constituents of living well, of a good life, of personal good or well-being. But Stoicism denies the intrinsic personal goodness of so-called worldly and appetitive goods, and it doubts even the universal instrumental goodness of such things, because it questions whether they usually contribute to the virtue of those who enjoy them. And therefore the following contrasts can be drawn between the Stoic and Epicurean treatments of the relation between personal goods/well-being and the virtues.

The Epicurean deflates our ideas about virtue and admirability, by regarding the latter as simply a matter of what is conducive or not conducive to the well-being (or happiness) of individuals. What is normally seen as higher than mere personal well-being (as being, e.g., admirable in a way well-being or enjoyment isn't) turns out, on the Epicurean account, to be of a piece with, at the same level as, facts solely about human well-being and its causes or effects.

Rather than reducing virtue/admirability to personal well-being (or happiness), however, the Stoic inflates or elevates our ideas about personal good (or well-being or happiness) by regarding the latter solely in terms of (what constitutes) human virtue or admirability. What is normally seen as lower than (ideas of) virtue turns out, on the Stoic account, to be of a piece with facts about virtue. And if, for the Epicurean, virtue is nothing more than a factor in the individual's personal good or happiness, then, for the Stoic, happiness and well-being are nothing *less* than virtue or virtuous living, and these contrasts should at this point make it understandable that Stoicism should be deemed a form of elevationism if Epicureanism is regarded as a form of reductionism.

But having set elevationism and reductionism at odds, I think it is important to note what they have in common. It is well-known, for example, that reductions need not preserve meaning—"salt is sodium chloride" is not an analytic or *a priori* truth. Similarly, neither utilitarian nor Epicurean reductionism need claim for itself an analytic status, and the same holds true for Stoic elevationism. These are *theories*, and they can be true in the way theories are true rather than definitionally or by virtue of some form of ethical mathematics.

In addition, the idea of reducing one kind of entity or property, say, to another, is often clarified by invoking the notion of certain *distinctions* being reducible to certain others. For example, we naturally think of the mental as in some sense higher (evolutionarily? spiritually?) than the purely physical; and if the mental then turns out to be reducible to the physical, then every valid mental distinction can be reduced to or identified with some distinction made in physical terms. According to such reductionism, then, where no physical distinction obtains, no distinction will (be able to) occur at the mental level either. But none of this entails that every physical distinction will be accompanied by some mental one. As long as the mental is a function of the physical, the reducing relation can obtain even if no function from the mental to the physical can be found; and thus, more briefly, we can characterize typical reductions of the mental to the physical as claiming that physical distinctions are *necessary but not sufficient* for the existence of mental distinctions.

By the same token, when Epicureanism (or utilitarianism) reduces virtue to well-being, it treats all distinctions of virtue as accompanied by distinctions in (causal, relational, and other) facts about individual well-being or happiness. It need not claim, however, that every distinction relating to the production of well-being (distinctions, e.g., about *who* certain dispositions benefit) will be accompanied by or give rise to a distinction in regard to virtue.

Elevation can be understood in essentially similar terms. When the Stoic elevates the personally good (up) to the virtuous or admirable, he or she is committed to saying that every distinction with regard to the former can be thoroughly understood or accounted for in terms of distinctions relating to the latter, just as, when the Epicurean reduces the virtues or virtue (down) to matters of well-being, he or she is committed to saying that every distinction with regard to the former can be thoroughly understood or accounted for in terms of distinctions involving the latter. The only difference between the two processes or results lies in the respective *heights* of "the former" and "the latter" in the two cases. In elevations, distinctions with regard to the presumptively lower are always correlated with distinctions that involve the presumptively higher, but the reverse need not be true. In reductions, distinctions regarding the presumptively higher are always accompanied by distinctions relating to the presumptively lower, though, again, the reverse need not be true. In some sense, then, reduction and elevation are the same thing operating in *opposite* (vertical) directions.

Moreover, the distinction between reduction and elevation also applies well beyond the confines of ethics. For example, just as in ethics we can be dualistic about virtue and well-being or else identify these concepts either reductively or elevatively, one of our main choices in metaphysics is between mind-body dualism and monism of either a reductive (materialist) or an elevative (idealist or phenomenalist) character. Indeed, quite a number of disputes outside the domain of ethics allow of historiographic clarification through these categories. We think of concepts, for example, as higher (as depending on more highly evolved capacities) than percepts or sensations, yet British Empiricism basically reduces all concepts to percepts, whereas Continental Rationalism treats sensation/perception as a matter of obscure conception and thus counts as a form of elevationism. Kant's insistence on the distinction between percepts and concepts would then represent the "dualistic" option in this area of philosophical thought.

Similarly, thinking now in terms of wholes and parts, the choice among reduction, elevation, and dualism can also be seen to apply in the area of social philosophy. Social atomism is the reductionist option regarding the relation between individuals and the societies of which they are members, whereas an organicism that treats the individual as a mere aspect or reflection of society constitutes a form of elevationism, and the view that the social and individual levels need to be differentiated represents dualism in this area. But however historiographically significant these extra-ethical applications of our distinction may be, we have more than enough to occupy us in considering its relevance, and, in particular, the relevance of elevationism, to the field of ethics.

III. Is Elevationism Viable?

Stoic elevationism is implausible as a theory of human well-being. It notoriously considers ordinary appetitive pleasures to constitute no part of human well-being, and it regards (nonmoral) pain as in no way intrinsically contrary to human well-being or good. Such conclusions about human good and ill are highly counterintuitive, perhaps more counterintuitive than anything utilitarianism commits us to, and although the Stoics offer a variety of arguments for their views, those arguments are widely regarded as unpersuasive and will not concern us here. Let us see, rather, whether any other kind of virtue-ethical elevationism can avoid the excesses of the Stoic view of human good and ill.

At first glance, this might seem to be impossible. If a virtue ethics is to be elevationist, it must understand all distinctions relating to well-being in terms of distinctions having to do with virtue. Doesn't this mean that how well-off one is will depend on how virtuous one is, and doesn't this precisely deliver us up to the forbidding conclusion that pain is no evil for the virtuous person on the rack? It is certainly natural to think so. It is natural to think that if virtue and well-being do not, so to speak, coincide, then neither can be understood in terms of the other (suitably supplemented by nonevaluative notions), and it is interesting, in this connection, to consider what Kant says about Stoicism and Epicureanism in the *Critique of Practical Reason*.[3]

Kant recognizes that these ancient views are not merely inconsistent with one another, but are in an important respect opposites—his discussion to some extent anticipates, though in a less general fashion, the distinction I am making between elevationism and reductionism. Kant holds that individual virtue cannot be identified with what effectively

---

[3] See especially Immanuel Kant, *Critique of Practical Reason*, 3d ed., ed. Lewis White Beck (New York: Macmillan, 1992), part I, book I, ch. ii.

serves the well-being or happiness of the individual, in the manner of Epicureanism, but also that individual well-being or happiness cannot, in the Stoic manner, be identified with the individual's (consciousness of his or her own) virtue. (He refuses to accept the Stoic's claim that pain is for him no evil.) Kant is in fact a dualist about our higher and lower values, about the admirable and the personally desirable, and he claims that well-being and virtue are "entirely heterogeneous" concepts.

Yet even if we assume, as Kant does, that virtue and well-being do not coincide either in the way Stoics believe or in the way Epicureans believe, it does not follow that these notions are entirely heterogeneous. Kant does not say that this follows, and he seems to have independent reasons, to be discussed briefly in a moment, for holding that we cannot understand virtue in terms of well-being or vice versa. But what is most important at this point is to see why "entire heterogeneity" does not follow from noncoincidence, since that will precisely leave open the possibility of an elevationism that avoids the problems of Stoicism. And we can see this most easily, I think, if we consider utilitarianism (which is not mentioned in Kant's discussion).

Utilitarianism simultaneously denies the coincidence of virtue and well-being and insists that the former can be understood in terms of the latter, taken together with nonethical, empirical notions. For under utilitarianism, the virtuous individual is one who contributes to the general well-being at the possible *expense* of her own, and the familiar criticism that utilitarianism is too demanding is based on the realization that utilitarian morality puts at considerable risk, rather than ensuring, the well-being of the virtuous individual. Yet utilitarian reductionism treats virtue and morality as understandable in terms of well-being rather than as "entirely heterogeneous" with the latter notion, and in that case there is room in ethical/conceptual space for an elevationist (virtue) ethics that understands well-being in terms of virtue without assuming, in the way so damaging to Stoicism, that virtue and well-being coincide in individuals. It must be possible for there to be a view or views that bear to Stoicism something like the relation that utilitarianism bears to Epicureanism, a possibility that I myself have previously ignored in writing about elevationism and that Kant does not seem to regard as a serious option for ethical theory.

I believe that the overall Critical Philosophy gives Kant a reason to ignore this option and to look askance at all monistic theorizing about virtue and personal well-being, a reason emerging from the approach to metaphysics and epistemology taken in the *Critique of Pure Reason*. Kant thinks that in ethics well-being represents or corresponds to sensibility and virtue represents or corresponds to the understanding; and to the extent that the Critical Philosophy rests on a dualism of sensibility and understanding (and of percepts and concepts), Kant seems to want a corresponding dualism in ethics; and that may be why he insists that well-being and virtue are entirely heterogeneous. Thus, Kant's larger or more systematic dualism seems to predispose him not only against any form of reductionism, but also against the possibility I want to defend here: the possibility of understanding well-being in elevationist terms but not as *coincident* with virtue.

But doesn't the drive for a unifying system actually favor the Kantian ethical dualism at this point over any form of elevationist monism? To be sure, monism allows us a greater unification within ethics than dualism does; but to the extent that Kant's ethical dualism allows him to dovetail his ethics with his metaphysics in a way that ethical elevationism does not claim to do, doesn't Kant's *ethical* dualism come out ahead of any monistic elevationism that virtue ethics can deliver?

It depends, I think, on what one says about the *Critique of Pure Reason*. If one has doubts about the way Kant treats concepts and percepts and about his general metaphysical and epistemological conclusions in that context, then that may actually redound *against* the approach Kant takes in ethics. Basing an ethics on an epistemology-cum-metaphysics is a double-edged sword, but rather than attempting here to investigate all the epistemological and metaphysical issues that we would need to examine in order to determine which way the sword cuts, it seems reasonable to explore the possibilities of a monistic, elevationist virtue ethics in order to see whether, quite apart from any connection to metaphysics and epistemology, such an ethics can fulfill the (somewhat independent) criteria of a good systematic ethical theory. Those criteria are demanding and interesting enough, so that it seems worth our while to see whether any form of elevationist virtue ethics can meet them, and I shall proceed accordingly.

IV. ARISTOTELIAN ELEVATIONISM

A more plausible example of virtue-ethical elevationism than Stoicism offers us can be found, I think, in a certain way of understanding Aristotle's views in the *Nicomachean Ethics*. The so-called "function argument" of Book I of the *Ethics* concludes that the good life for human beings consists in a long and active life of virtue. But Aristotle immediately qualifies this claim by pointing out that how pleasant or painful, successful or unsuccessful one's life is also helps to determine how good it is. This further point seems to take Aristotle away from any attempt to understand human well-being in terms of the higher categories of virtue and rationality and toward some sort of dualistic conception of the ethical. But that interpretation is not actually forced on us, because of some of the things Aristotle says later about pleasure. In Book X (chapters 3 through 5), he says that pleasures deriving from perverted or morally unworthy sources are not good, not desirable; and it is possible to interpret this as meaning that a person who gains money or certain enjoyments through injustice or betrayal gains nothing good for himself, fails to have his well-being (even momentarily) enhanced. Sarah Broadie interprets the relevant passages in something like this manner,[4] and once one does so, there is an obvious way to treat Aristotle as an elevationist monist.

For if Aristotle is saying that pleasure and success count as elements in our well-being only if and when they can be obtained consistently with being virtuous, then his conception of well-being or the good life will at every point have to refer to virtue. The good or best life will then, roughly, be a life full of virtuous activity and of pleasures and successes that are consistent with virtue—and a life lacking in pains and failures that virtue does not require. On such a picture, there are no purely natural personal goods and evils: that is, everything that adds to or subtracts from our well-being must do so *in relation to higher moral or ethical values*. We have ended up with a form of elevationist monism, but one that is less extreme and less implausible than Stoicism, because it allows many ordinary pleasures and achievements a role in constituting human well-being, and many ordinary pains and failures a similar role in making lives worse than they otherwise could or would be.

However, as I indicated earlier, this is not the only way one can interpret Aristotle's views about the good of pleasure and achievement. In Book X of the *Nicomachean Ethics*, Aristotle also says, for example, that the good man is the measure of what is truly pleasurable, so that what appears pleasant only to a spoiled or perverted taste is not really pleasant. Perhaps he is here making the quasi-linguistic point that what is pleasant only to a perverted taste cannot properly be called pleasant *tout court*, while at the same time being willing to grant that such things can be pleasant to—and perhaps then even good for—the perverted individual. On such a reading, a vicious person can get something good-for-himself, something that enhances *his* well-being at least, from vicious actions, and this then leaves some natural or lower human good outside the orbit of (specification in terms of) virtue. It makes Aristotle into a dualist about virtue and well-being.

No matter. We are trying to see whether any plausible form of elevationist monism can be found, and the form of monism we have just unearthed—whether it is actually in Aristotle or not—seems more promising in its own right than Stoic elevationism. Let us consider, then, whether it enables virtue ethics to achieve a unification of virtue and well-being that can rival anything utilitarianism has to offer.

Because "Aristotelian" elevationism, as I shall call it, allows individual well-being to depend on more than virtue and virtuous actions, it claims no coincidence between individual virtue and individual well-being and avoids the worst implications of Stoicism. But it has other implications that I think ought to bother us. It entails that the pleasures (or achievements) that a vicious person obtains only through being vicious are no

---

[4] See Sarah Broadie, *Ethics with Aristotle* (Oxford: Oxford University Press, 1991), p. 376.

part of her good, so that, for example, the pleasure of eating food she has stolen is no sort of good for the thief. But intuitively, and here I am following Kant as well, one wants to say that though it is not a good thing *that* someone should benefit from wrongdoing, what is bad here is precisely that a person actually *benefits* from acting viciously.

Aristotelian elevationism will also seem implausible for what it has to say about personal evils. To maintain a thoroughgoing and essential connection to virtue in each aspect of its account of human well-being, the view has to maintain that the pain that virtue requires an individual to suffer involves no diminution of her well-being. If virtue requires someone to remain silent under torture, then the pain and suffering that occur during and result from such an episode will count as in no way making the individual's life worse, and, if anything, this seems even more implausible than what the Aristotelian theory has to say about the irrelevance to well-being of pleasures gained through vicious actions. In the end, I think Aristotelian elevationism is seriously counterintuitive, though certainly less extreme and counterintuitive than Stoic elevationism. (Here I ignore what these views have to say about the content of virtue and refer only to how they connect virtue with well-being.)

The possibilities of elevationist ethical monism are not yet exhausted, however; and if we take the proper lesson from the assumed failure of Aristotelian elevationism, we may yet learn how to construct a plausible form of elevationist virtue ethics. At this point I would like to see if we can avoid the unwelcome consequences of Stoic and Aristotelian elevationism by *weakening our assumptions about the connection between well-being and virtue*. Stoicism says that virtue and well-being coincide in the individual; Aristotelian elevationism says, in effect, that all elements of personal well-being must be compatible with *virtue taken as a whole*; and we have reason to criticize both these assumptions. But what if we say, instead, that every element of human well-being must be compatible with or involve at least some *part* of virtue or one or another *particular* virtue? Such a claim might be entirely in keeping with the goal of elevationism and yet enable us to avoid the untoward implications of both Stoic and Aristotelian elevationism. For it allows us to deny that virtue and well-being coincide and to hold that a pleasure that a virtuous individual would not choose or desire, a pleasure incompatible with *virtue as a whole*, might still count as part of someone's well-being *as long as it bore an appropriate relation to some particular virtue or part of virtue*. Better still, I believe that the beginnings of a theory that actually meets these requirements can be found in Plato's *Gorgias*.

V. PLATONIC ELEVATIONISM

Plato notably holds that all good things possess a common element or exemplify a common property or pattern, and Aristotle famously criticizes this fundamental view in the *Nicomachean Ethics*. But Plato makes a somewhat more specific claim about the things that are good in a rather neglected passage in the *Gorgias* (S. 506), where he says that "all good things whatever are good when some virtue is present in . . . them."[5] Leaving aside judgments about functional goodness (but remembering that good knives and good doctors are commonly spoken of as having their "virtues") and focusing solely upon judgments about intrinsic personal good or well-being, Plato's claim implies that all personal good or well-being contains an element of virtue and thus has something in common with the virtues themselves. If this thesis were correct, then we would have all the help we need in establishing elevationism, but what Plato is saying clearly sounds odd, to say the least, so let me at this point attempt to make a persuasive case for it.

In order to have any chance of doing so, I think we must find a plausible way of arguing that even common pleasures and enjoyments, in order to count as an intrinsic part of our well-being, must contain or be accompanied by some form or instance of virtue, and at this point such a view seems perilously close to the idea, previously rejected, that pleasure is a good thing in someone's life only if it is achieved compatibly with the dictates of moral virtue. However, the Platonic view mentioned above in fact allows that a person who viciously steals food and then enjoys it may, contrary to the Aristotelian and Stoic views, have his well-being enhanced *as long as he exemplifies one virtue in the course of that enjoyment*; and what I want to argue in what follows is that appetitive pleasures and enjoyments must be accompanied by at least some degree of moderation, a quality we admire and think of as a virtue, in order to count toward a person's well-being.[6] The idea that appetitive goods demand some sort of virtue is far from obvious and represents the largest stumbling block to any acceptance of the Platonic approach I am proposing. But before we consider more closely what can be said about the relations between appetitive satisfactions and the virtue of moderation, let me say a bit more about other sorts of personal good or well-being whose connection to one or another virtue seems far less problematic. (Later on, I shall also say something about how Platonic elevationism treats personal ills or evils.)

In what follows I shall simply assume some relatively plausible "objective-list" theory of personal well-being. An objective-list view assumes that not all aspects of well-being are reducible to subjective factors like pleasure or desire-satisfaction, and it treats a plurality of things in human life as intrinsically (rather than merely instrumentally) adding to the goodness of lives. What I hope to show is that if one assumes some such

---

[5] Plato, *Gorgias*, in *The Dialogues of Plato*, trans. Benjamin Jowett (New York: Random House, 1937), S. 506.

[6] Actually, I shall only argue that appetitive goods require that one not be *totally immoderate* (and similarly for the other goods to be mentioned), but for simplicity's sake I shall continue to speak as I have in the text above.

reasonable or intuitive pluralism about personal goods, about the sorts of things that inherently contribute to human well-being, one ends up with a short list of highly plausible candidates all of which (with the exception of appetitive and other pleasures and enjoyments) have an obvious and essential relation to particular virtues.

Different objective lists of intrinsic personal goods have been offered by different philosophers, but it seems to me that almost everyone who favors this sort of approach will include certain conspicuous examples: enjoyment/pleasure; certain kinds of achievement; love and friendship; and certain kinds of knowledge or wisdom. Now the connection between putative goods of social relationship (goods like love and friendship, but also less intimate forms of social interaction) and various virtues is not difficult to see. Love and friendship essentially depend on some sort of unselfishness or generosity toward one's friend or loved one. Intuitively, a relationship does not count as love or friendship if its participants are entirely selfish in their relations toward one another. Even some of the less intimate social ties we might regard as elements of a given individual's well-being seem to require some connection to virtue. Merely companionable relationships, relationships in which things are shared but only at a fairly superficial level, entail some degree of the virtue of reciprocity, of the desire to give and take, to share, rather than try to keep everything for oneself. Without such reciprocity and genuine sharing, we simply have people using one another, and though, arguably, various personal goods can *come from* such interaction, the interaction itself is not commonly regarded as an independent and substantial personal good on its own, the way friendship, love, and even superficial companionship tend to be.

The goods of personal interaction or relationship—goods like love and friendship—thus seem to require certain virtues, and the virtues in question are other-regarding ones like reciprocity and unselfishness (or generosity). Other goods on our objective "short list" are not essentially interpersonal and, therefore, not surprisingly connect only to more self-regarding virtues. Almost anyone who thinks there are elements of personal well-being other than pleasure would mention achievement or accomplishment as an example. Notoriously, achievements can require great suffering and great personal sacrifice in the course of their accomplishment, and anyone who believes achievement represents a personal good in itself will want to hold that despite all the suffering and sacrifice, a life can be made good or better through the achievement of the goals that required all the suffering and sacrifice.

But what kind of virtue or virtues does achievement require? A certain degree of talent or aptitude is certainly necessary to most achievements, but talent and aptitude are arguably not virtues, whereas strength of purpose, or perseverance, pretty clearly is a virtue, and I think any genuine achievement will essentially depend on the presence of some degree of perseverance. Even Mozart, in whom musical invention seems to have arisen spontaneously, had to write down the tunes that occurred to him, and orchestrate and develop them, in order to produce his actual compositions. Talent itself does not depend on effort and perseverance; indeed, one needn't develop a talent one knows one has, but, interestingly, most of us are much less inclined to treat the presence of raw talent as in itself a personal good in someone's life. If the talent is not developed, is left fallow, then it does not seem to represent any sort of good in the life of the individual who has it, and thus the case of talents contrasts intuitively with what we think about achievements, about successfully making something out of and with a talent or ability. Achievements seem to qualify a life as better in a way mere unused talents do not, and I think part of what leads us to such a distinction is our sense of the effort and perseverance that go into actual achievements. Talent does not require any application of virtue, but achievement always requires some degree of perseverance, and the latter fact influences, I think, our willingness to treat achievement, but not sheer talent, as a genuine good in life, one which is somewhat independent of pleasure and enjoyment.

But what about knowledge or wisdom? Do these putative personal goods also require the presence of virtue? Now knowledge, at least of deep or important facts, and wisdom may themselves be thought to be virtues, intellectual virtues; so once again, and fairly straightforwardly, there is a connection between what we tend to think of as personal goods and certain virtues, in this case a relation of absolute identity. But more can be said about the connection between wisdom or deep knowledge and at least one familiar *moral* virtue: courage.

Nowadays we tend to think that some of the deepest and most important facts about the universe and our relation to it are frightening or at least highly unpalatable when we first come to be acquainted with them. In consequence, we also think that it takes a certain kind of courage to face those facts rather than deceive ourselves or think wishfully about them (or avoid thinking at all about certain topics). I say nowadays, because (for reasons it would be very interesting to pursue on another occasion) very little of this attitude is to be found, e.g., in ancient thinkers like Plato and Aristotle, despite all their emphasis on the virtue of wisdom.

Consider one famous example of the courage it takes to face facts about the universe. In the nineteenth century (though not merely then), accumulating evidence of the age of the earth and cosmos and of the evolutionary origin of plants and animals led many people to doubt the biblical account of things and reexamine their religious beliefs. But it took some courage to face and "take in" this evidence against the biblical account of human life and human destiny. It is much easier and more comfortable, in the main, to believe that there is a God who has a plan for human beings; and one (Whiggish, I admit) way to interpret the struggle that occurred in the nineteenth century (and is not over yet) between secular

MICHAEL SLOTE

science and religious tradition is to see it as a test of the courage of human beings.

But the test of courage versus self-deception and wishful thinking occurs in a host of other areas. It takes courage to face some of one's own deepest fears and desires, and to the extent that wisdom as a life good requires facing one's inner demons, the important connection between wisdom and courage is further underscored. Finally, it can take courage to face the results of philosophical argument. What we initially hope for from philosophy, philosophy in many instances proves itself incapable of providing: David Hume, Nelson Goodman, W. V. Quine, and Ludwig Wittgenstein all show us that philosophy can run out of justifications more quickly and more irrecusably than we hope or desire. And it is interesting that Wittgenstein himself seems to be noticing the connection between philosophical understanding or wisdom and moral virtue when he says: "You could attach prices to thoughts. Some cost a lot, some a little. And how does one pay for thoughts? The answer, I think, is: with courage."[7] I think Wittgenstein is basically right here. Many of the conclusions philosophy tends toward are unsettling and uncomfortable, and it requires courage rather than wishful thinking to accept them. More generally, Platonic elevationism will say that knowledge constitutes a distinctive form of personal good, and counts as wisdom, only when it takes courage to acquire it.[8]

It would seem, then, that some of our best candidates for status as personal goods have an intimate connection to one or another virtue or set of virtues; thus, to make good on the form of elevationism I think most promising, we must now establish a similar connection between appetitive (or other) pleasures and human virtue. We can do this if we can show that someone totally lacking in the virtue of moderation, someone insatiably immoderate in her desires, gains no personal good from the pleasures she frenetically or restlessly pursues and obtains.

A moderate individual who is enjoying food or drink will at a certain point decide that she has had enough (enjoyment) and stop pursuing, perhaps even turn down, further gustatory enjoyment(s). But the totally insatiable person will never feel she has (had) enough and will remain thoroughly unsatisfied no matter how much she has had or enjoyed, and it is not counterintuitive to suppose that such an individual gains nothing good (at least noninstrumentally) from her pursuit of pleasure or power or whatever. We feel sorry for someone who is never even partially satisfied with what she has or has obtained, and in feeling this way, I don't

---

[7] See Ludwig Wittgenstein, *Culture and Value* (Oxford: Basil Blackwell, 1980), p. 52e.

[8] We are then committed to saying that sheer information, however instrumentally valuable, is not intrinsically good for people. Note, however, that where knowledge does not require courage *but is difficult to attain*, it can still count as a personally beneficial *achievement*. (Something similar may even be true of the insatiable person who gains more and more power or pleasure through persistent efforts.)

think we are necessarily assuming that the insatiable pursuit of power, gustatory sensations, sexual pleasure, or whatever is automatically frustrating and painful; rather, it seems somewhat plausible to suppose that we feel sorry for such people because their frenetic pleasure and desire for pleasure are never "rounded off" by any sense of satisfaction with what they have or have had. When people gain something good for themselves from pleasure, it is, I am arguing, because the pleasure is part of a "package" containing both pleasure and satisfaction with that pleasure. (I shall say more just below about how the elements in this package relate to one another and to the personal good that requires them.) If this is the case, Plato's claim in the *Gorgias* appears to be vindicated. For the idea that some degree of moderation is a requirement of all pleasure-related good or well-being, while never explicitly stated by Plato, is one that resonates both with the statement I quoted from the *Gorgias* and with Plato's frequent invocation of the virtue of moderation in his discussion of the appetites and of the desire for power, etc. The total elevationist view I am maintaining may not be explicit in Plato, but I think it gains impetus from things Plato says.

Moreover, I am assuming that there is nothing *unintuitive* about the supposition that (some substantial degree of) satisfaction with pleasure is necessary for an appetitive (or any other pleasure-related) good to occur in someone's life. I am assuming, in effect, that the pleasure or enjoyment we take from an activity in some (perhaps metaphorical or analogical) sense *anticipates* some measure of satisfaction, and that where the satisfaction, the sense of having had enough, never comes, the pleasure seems empty, the activity not worth it. There is something pitiable about insatiability that reminds us of Sisyphus but also of Tantalus. (Everyone knows about Sisyphus, but Tantalus, according to Greek mythology, was condemned by the gods to stand under luscious grapes that always eluded his reach and in water that always receded when he tried to drink it.) For surely we can say that the insatiable individual wishes to have or obtain something good in his life, yet, on the view I wish to defend, personal good seems always to recede from the insatiable individual as she seeks to approach and attain it. Thus, the appetitively insatiable individual may not only fail to be admirable, because of her immoderate, indeed unlimited, need for and dependence on appetitive (or other) pleasures, but, in addition and as a result of that lack of virtue, may act self-defeatingly in regard to her own good.[9]

---

[9] The elevationist view I am proposing must insist that the virtue status of moderation, unselfishness, generosity, and the other character traits said to be essential to various personal goods does not depend on their having good consequences for human life. Otherwise it would be saying, circularly, that these virtues both ground and are grounded in facts about human well-being. But it is not implausible to hold that generosity, for example, is morally admirable even if, despite the best of efforts (and perhaps unbeknownst to everyone), it fails to achieve its aims; and the courage to face and not deceive oneself about unpleasant

But why not say, rather, that the insatiable individual does get something good out of her restless and insatiable pursuit of more and more pleasure, namely, whatever pleasure she obtains along the way? Is this view really so contrary to common sense? I think not; but neither, as I have been saying, is the claim that the appetitively insatiable individual gets nothing good from his appetitive pursuit. I do not think common sense is really decisive on this issue, and so I propose to let theoretical considerations resolve the issue for us. If we say that pleasure needs to be accompanied by some measure of satisfaction with it in order for an appetitive good to occur in someone's life, then there is some chance for an overall elevationist account of human good to suceed.[10] Such an account unifies ethics in a desirable way, and in the name of such unity we may wish to make assumptions which, though not counterintuitive, are not overwhelmingly obvious apart from such theoretical considerations. (Compare the way linguists like Noam Chomsky have allowed considerations of theory, sometimes in different directions, depending on the theory then being espoused, to decide the syntactic status—i.e., grammaticality or nongrammaticality—of "don't care" sentences like "Colorless green ideas sleep furiously.") If we assume in appetitive cases that virtue needs to accompany personal good, we can easily make a similar assumption across the entire range of goods that objective-list pluralism tends to accept, and we end up with a more satisfactory elevationist account of human well-being than Stoicism or Aristotelianism provides. In that case, accepting the idea that pleasure is not a sufficient condition of personal good seems a small price to pay for the unification we achieve as a result (smaller, one could certainly say, than what utilitarian reductionist monism forces us to relinquish in the form of lost intuitions).[11]

---

facts seems an inherent part of being rational, rather than depending on its consequences for its status as a virtue. (Indeed, the courage, e.g., to face the fact that one has cancer may easily tend to make things harder, worse, for oneself and for those around one, but that does not undercut what we find admirable about such courage. On this point, see my book *From Morality to Virtue* [Oxford: Oxford University Press, 1995], p. 130f.) In a similar fashion, finally, I think an insatiable dependence on or greed for, say, gustatory pleasures seems inherently less than admirable (Aristotle calls people who are like this "belly gods"). We needn't be making assumptions about the *consequences* of such traits to have this opinion.

[10] Of course, someone might claim that nothing *counts as pleasure* unless the individual is in some degree satisfied with it. But this assumption clearly makes it easier for Platonic elevationism to hold that appetitive goods require some degree of virtue, and it is in any event very questionable. The French use the term "alumette" (literally "match") to refer to hors d'oeuvres that are supposed to inflame one's appetite, and this more than suggests that such appetizers are pleasurable yet the very opposite of satisfying.

[11] The elevationist theory I am proposing entails not only that pleasure may fail to give rise to an appetitive (or other) good, but that appetitive desire-fulfillment may also fail to result in any good for an individual. Someone insatiably seeking a certain kind of pleasure may have an open-ended desire that is never fulfilled, but will certainly have particular desires along the way: the desire for a given piece of foie gras, for example. That desire is certainly fulfilled, but on the account offered here, the insatiable person gains nothing good thereby. (We also speak of the desire being "satisfied," but if the *individual* is in no way satisfied with the resultant state of affairs, then she has gained nothing good from the

If we accept this kind of Platonically inspired elevationism, we have to reject hedonism, of course; but, more interestingly perhaps, we have to reject an idea that many hedonists and nonhedonists *share*, namely, that if pleasure is not the sole personal good, it is the *most typical* of personal goods, and that friendship, achievement, wisdom, and the like are at best somewhat *problematic* examples of such goods. This view represents a kind of halfway house in the direction of hedonism, and the elevationist account I have offered constitutes a direct challenge to it. For Platonic elevationism regards it as essential to and characteristic of human well-being that it should involve an intimate connection to virtue, and personal goods like friendship and achievement show their connection to virtue *much more clearly* than do appetitive goods. Thus, the present view requires us to renounce the somewhat tempting belief that pleasure is the most typical of human goods and indeed *to learn about the character of appetitive goods from the example of other, more spiritual forms of well-being.*

In addition, we still have not settled some important issues about the metaphysics of human goods. We have said, for example, that appetitive (or pleasure-related) goods require both pleasure and satisfaction with pleasure, but that does not yet tell us whether the satisfaction with pleasure that is necessary to the emergence/existence of an appetitive good is part of that good or merely its necessary accompaniment. One might hold, in other words, that when appetitive goods occur they consist merely in a certain kind of pleasure or enjoyment, but that such an enjoyment does not constitute a personal good for someone unless it possesses the relational property of being accompanied by satisfaction with it on the part of the person in question. But there is also the alternative of saying that appetitive goods *contain* both pleasure and satisfaction with pleasure.

Similarly, with regard to the personal good of achievement, one can say that it consists merely in the attaining of the goal one has sought, but that that attaining does not count as a good unless its way is paved by a virtuous perseverance or persistence that makes it possible. Or one can say that both the attaining of one's goal and the persistence one shows in doing so are elements in (the good of) any achievement. However, if we say that satisfaction with pleasure is part of any appetitive good and likewise say that persistence is part of (the good of) achievement and so on for the other goods on our short list, then Plato may turn out to have been right in claiming that for something to be good, there must be virtue *in* it. Wouldn't it be interesting and lovely if, in such an unexpected way, Plato turned out to be correct on this issue? But there are also some good philosophical reasons for agreeing with Plato.

If pleasure and satisfaction with it do not merely accompany one another, but *interpenetrate* one another, so that the character of pleasure

---

fulfillment or satisfaction of the particular desire. I am indebted here to discussion with Richard Wollheim.)

differs to the extent that one is satisfied with it (or the pleasure one has already had), then it does not make much sense to separate the two phenomena and say that the pleasure constitutes an appetitive good, when one is satisfied with it, but the satisfaction lies outside the good thus constituted. Even if such interpenetration cannot be assumed, however, we have reason to regard "satisfaction with" as part of appetitive goods, on grounds of the seemingly nonrelational character of attributions of appetitive goodness. If we say that pleasure constitutes the whole of an appetitive good when, but only when, it is externally accompanied by the individual's satisfaction with his pleasure, then whether an appetitive good exists will depend on facts metaphysically external to that good. This directly challenges the idea that appetitive goods are intrinsically good, and such goods are supposed to be paradigm cases of intrinsic goods. However, if pleasure and "satisfaction with" are externally related to one another, but together constitute (are both elements in) appetitive goods, then the *goodness* of such goods is not relational; and since this assumption fits in better with our intuitions and philosophical traditions concerning appetitive goods, I shall assume that some exemplification of virtue is an element in, rather than merely a necessary condition for, appetitive goods and the other kinds of personal goods I have spoken of.

Having focused almost exclusively on personal well-being, it is time I said something about the Platonic elevationist account of personal ills or evils. That account, in fact, works symmetrically with what I have said about personal goods, and it holds, in particular, that nothing counts as intrinsically bad for a person unless it involves and includes some degree of vice (or an absence of total virtue). Thus, on such a view, pain is a constituent of a personal evil only if there is something less than fully virtuous or admirable about how one takes or reacts to the pain, and just as it is best to be in some degree *satisfied* with substantial pleasure, so too does it seem appropriate and admirable—a kind of strength—not to be *dissatisfied* with, but, rather, to *accept* (unavoidable) pain. For that reason, I want to claim that when (a) pain is totally accepted, it does not constitute anything intrinsically bad for a person. Only when someone *minds* his pain or is *bothered* by it, does the pain enter into something intrinsically bad for the individual. (Of course, there may be kinds of pain that no human being is capable of accepting, and the view I am offering will regard such pains as personal evils.)

Thus, it takes a "package" of pain (or discomfort) and the vice or nonvirtue of nonacceptance to constitute a personal evil, and this implication of Platonic elevationism strikes me as by no means implausible. Certainly, it is far less implausible than saying, with the Stoics, that pain is never (part of) a personal evil, but it also seems somewhat intuitive to suppose that a person who so totally accepts a pain that he does not (any longer) mind it is suffering no intrinsic ill. (Of course, if one wants to claim that something cannot count as a pain if it is totally accepted, that makes things easier, not harder, for the view that every personal ill requires some measure of vice.)

Moreover, when one applies Platonic elevationism to more spiritual forms of human ill, one arrives at a view with some obvious attractions. Given present assumptions, failure to succeed in one's goals does not count as in itself (and apart from the pain, e.g., that it causes one) a personal ill *unless some vice was part and parcel of the failure.* But this means that if someone fails, despite valiant efforts and through no fault of her own, that failure constitutes merely the absence of something good rather than a positive personal evil; whereas if someone fails through a total lack of virtuous effort and perseverance, the failure really does amount to a personal evil. And this distinction has some intuitive force, since it is natural to think there is something far more pathetic and unfortunate about a life in which failure results from fecklessness than about one in which it is due to bad luck. By the same token, it seems acceptable to suppose that a lack of wisdom that results from sheer cowardice is to that extent more unenviable and pathetic than a lack of wisdom that results from the cultural unavailability of certain kinds of knowledge, and this is precisely what is claimed under the Platonic elevationist view I am offering.

VI. Conclusion

If the above discussion has been on the right track, then intra-ethical elevationism in a form inspired by Plato is capable of avoiding the problems that beset Stoic and Aristotelian versions of elevationism, while at the same time offering us an account of the relation between virtue and well-being or ill-being that has some of the unifying power we find in reductive utilitarian (and Epicurean) accounts of that relationship. I say "some" because Platonic elevationism of the sort I have discussed leaves virtue in a more pluralistic condition than that in which the utilitarian account leaves the notion of well-being. (For simplicity's sake, let us again leave ill-being to one side.) If well-being is understood as pleasure or desire-satisfaction, then utilitarianism is capable of reducing all virtue (as well as rationality and morality) to well-being conceived in a unitary fashion, whereas Platonic elevationism relates different goods to different virtues and offers no immediate prospect of treating all those virtues — moderation, unselfishness, perseverance, and courage — as forms of some underlying single "master virtue." Nevertheless, the present account does allow us to see all forms of well-being as dependent on and containing forms of virtue, and such a conception of well-being substantially unifies our ideas about what well-being really is.

Many objective lists of what constitutes human well-being have been based simply on intuitions about what things count as goods, but the objective list we get from Platonic elevationism at least offers us the beginnings of an explanation of why some things count as personal goods and others do not. Its insistence that all personal goods essentially involve some virtue explains, for example, why unused talent and frenetic pleasure are naturally thought of as making no inherent contribution to human well-being; and the theory also helps to explain why, unlike virtue-involving love and friendship, forms of personal interaction in which people are merely useful (or just plain indifferent or hostile) to one another are not typically thought to contribute as such to the well-being of those involved in them. This is hardly a complete story, but at least it takes the objective-list approach beyond its usual aspirations and grounds a particular objective list in a more general understanding of what makes things good for us. (I also suspect that if advocates of an objective-list approach wanted to expand the list offered here, the most plausible candidates they could propose would turn out to involve a connection to virtue along the lines I have been discussing.)

In the way they deal with virtue and self-interest, ancient ethical theory and modern moral philosophy often seem like ships passing in the night. Modern views (and here I am thinking not only of utilitarianism, but of Kant and certain virtue ethicists, like James Martineau, as well)[12] tend to separate well-being from virtue and understand the former on largely hedonistic lines. So understood, well-being and virtue have *nothing in common*, but most ancient views of ethics have the opposing tendency of making it difficult to understand how well-being can consist of *anything but virtue*. The present form of elevationism avoids the extremism of Stoic conceptions of well-being and the exaggerated role in the constitution of well-being that even Aristotelian elevationism imputes to virtue. Rather than assuming that virtue is well-being or that what is incompatible with total virtue makes no contribution to well-being, the present form of elevationism assumes only the weakest of connections between virtue and well-being. By supposing only that well-being in all its instances has to involve some particular virtue or other, Platonic elevationism scales down the aspirations and avoids the implausibilities of more extreme versions of elevationism. This leaves the basic enterprise of elevationism intact, but accommodates our strongest modern-day intuitions about the importance of pleasure and enjoyment in constituting human well-being. We have to sacrifice the idea that every instance of pleasure constitutes a human good, but that is an idea whose hold over most of us is tenuous at best, and the theory we arrive at by rejecting it thus represents a kind of compromise between extreme forms of elevationism, on the one hand, and reductionism, on the other.

In recent centuries we have faced a choice between reductionism and dualism in regard to the relationship between virtue and well-being:

[12] See James Martineau, *Types of Ethical Theory*, 2 vols. (Oxford: Clarendon Press, 1891).

ancient forms of elevationism, to the extent that we have been aware of them, have seemed too wild and implausible to be taken seriously in our attempts to understand that relationship. The weaker, milder, more intuition-friendly version of elevationism offered here may show not only that the options we have been considering in this area are too narrow and limiting, but that a revival of the ancient idea of treating self-interest or well-being as a function of virtue has much to recommend it.[13]

Philosophy, University of Maryland, College Park

---

[13] I have here been speaking of intra-ethical elevationism; but an elevationism that seeks to understand well-being in terms of virtue might ultimately attempt to understand or account for the virtues in purely naturalistic terms. Thus, elevationism within the ethical is compatible with reductionism respecting the entire sphere of the ethical.

SELF-INTEREST, ALTRUISM, AND VIRTUE*

By Thomas Hurka

My topic in this essay is the comparative moral value of self-interest and altruism. I take self-interest to consist in a positive attitude toward one's own good and altruism to consist in a similar attitude toward the good of others, and I assess these attitudes within a general theory of the intrinsic value of attitudes toward goods and evils. The first two sections of the essay apply this theory in a simple form, one that treats self-interest and altruism symmetrically. The third section examines whether the theory can be revised to accommodate an apparent asymmetry in our common-sense thinking about self-interested and altruistic attitudes.[1]

I. Loving One's Own and Others' Good

I will start by assuming that each person has a good, or that certain states of the person are intrinsically desirable and others undesirable. Of course, philosophers have disagreed for centuries about what this good consists in, or what particular states are desirable. Welfarists take each person's good to consist in pleasure, the fulfillment of her preferences, or something describable as "welfare" or "happiness." Perfectionists hold that certain states of a person are good apart from any connection with happiness. Thus, some perfectionists hold that knowledge, achievement, and deep personal relations are good independently of how much a person wants or enjoys them. For the purposes of this essay it does not matter much which initial claims about the good we accept. To discuss issues about self-interest and altruism we need only *some* initial theory of each person's good, whatever its specific content. Consequently, and to cover as many bases as possible, I will start by assuming a mixed welfarist-perfectionist theory of the good, one claiming that pleasure, knowledge, and achievement are all intrinsically good. Though any comparable theory would do as well, I will work with this initial characterization of each person's good.

* For helpful comments I am grateful to Ellen Frankel Paul and to the other contributors to this volume.

[1] By "common-sense" moral thinking I mean those informal beliefs about right and good that are affirmed by most people in Western (and perhaps other) societies. I do not assume that these beliefs are incontrovertible; sometimes philosophical argument can show that they need to be reformed. But I take it to be (other things equal) a merit in a moral theory if it can affirm common-sense beliefs.

In the first two sections of the essay, I will take this theory to have an agent-neutral form. This means that it makes each person's pleasure, knowledge, and achievement good not only from his point of view but from that of all persons, so all persons have the same moral reason to pursue these aspects of his good. As we will see in the third section, we can also consider agent-relative claims about the good, such as that each person's pleasure is good only from his point of view, giving only him reason to pursue it. But at this point I will assume an agent-neutral theory, one giving each person as much reason to care about the good states of other people, whatever they are, as about his own.

Given this concept of each person's good, we can distinguish between positive and negative attitudes toward that good, or between what I will call "loving" and "hating" it "for itself." By "loving" a good I mean being positively oriented toward it in desire, action, or feeling. This has three main forms. One can love a good by desiring or wishing for it when it does not obtain, by actively pursuing it to make it obtain, or by taking pleasure in it when it does obtain. Thus, if pleasure is a good, one can desire pleasure, pursue pleasure, or take pleasure in pleasure. "Hating" a good involves the opposite, negative orientation: desiring or pursuing the good's not obtaining or being pained by its obtaining. By loving or hating a good "for itself" I mean loving or hating it apart from its consequences or for its own sake, that is, loving or hating instances of the good because they are instances of the good. Thus, one loves pleasure for itself if one loves instances of pleasure because they are pleasures or for their pleasantness, and one loves knowledge for itself if one loves instances of knowledge because they involve knowledge. This loving "for itself" has two more-specific forms. One can love a good for itself because one believes that it is intrinsically good and loves whatever one believes is good. Thus, one can believe that pleasure, either in oneself or in another, is intrinsically good, and one can desire, pursue, and take pleasure in pleasure because of that belief. Alternatively, one can, without depending on any belief about goodness, simply desire, pursue, and enjoy pleasure as an end in itself, from an immediate emotional attraction to pleasure. To take another example, one can desire knowledge for itself either because one believes that knowledge is part of an ideal human life and because one wants to lead that life, or because, without any sophisticated thoughts about ideals, one simply wants to know, or is naturally curious.

We can now use these concepts to define self-interest and altruism: self-interest is the love for itself of one's own good, and altruism the love for itself of another's good. According to this definition, both self-interest and altruism have three forms, namely those of desire, active pursuit, and pleasure, so there are self-interested and altruistic desires, actions, and feelings. One can self-interestedly desire one's own good, that is, desire one's own pleasure, knowledge, or achievement; one can self-interestedly pursue that good; and one can self-interestedly take pleasure in it. Both self-interest and altruism can also either be derived from beliefs about the good or be independent of such beliefs. Self-interested and altruistic attitudes must be directed at goods for their own sake, or independently of their consequences, but they can spring either from beliefs about ideals or from immediate emotions.

This definition restricts what can count as an object of self-interest or altruism. Any object of self-interest must be a state of oneself, and any object of altruism a state of some other person. Desiring for itself some feature of the natural environment is neither self-interested nor altruistic; nor is desiring for itself some global fact about a group of people, such as that income be distributed equally among them. (Desiring equal incomes as a means to the good of the group's members is, however, altruistic.) If an attitude derives from a belief about what is good, there is no further restriction on its object. Loving what one believes to be good, in oneself or in another, automatically counts as self-interested or altruistic. If one desires fame for itself because one believes fame to be good, then even if fame is not good, one's desire for fame is self-interested. If an attitude is independent of beliefs about the good, however, it can be self-interested or altruistic only if its object is in fact good. Desiring for itself one's own humiliation, assuming one's desire does not derive from the belief that humiliation is good, is not self-interested, because its object is not good. Nor is desiring for itself that another suffer pain altruistic. Only states either believed to be or in fact good can be objects of self-interested or altruistic attitudes.

This definition allows us to evaluate self-interest and altruism within an attractive general theory of the value of attitudes toward goods and evils. This theory was developed by several philosophers of the late nineteenth and early twentieth centuries, Franz Brentano, G. E. Moore, Hastings Rashdall, and W. D. Ross, and has also been discussed by some contemporary philosophers.[2] The theory holds that if a state of affairs is intrinsically good or evil, then appropriate attitudes toward it are also intrinsically good and inappropriate attitudes intrinsically evil. If a state is intrinsically good, the appropriate attitude toward it is loving it for itself, in the sense defined above, and the theory holds that this loving for itself is intrinsically good. Thus, if pleasure, knowledge, and achievement are intrinsic goods, desiring, pursuing, and taking pleasure in these goods for themselves is a further intrinsic good. If states such as pain are intrin-

---

[2] Franz Brentano, *The Origin of Our Knowledge of Right and Wrong*, trans. Roderick M. Chisholm and Elizabeth Schneewind (London: Routledge and Kegan Paul, 1969); G. E. Moore, *Principia Ethica* (Cambridge: Cambridge University Press, 1903); Hastings Rashdall, *The Theory of Good and Evil*, 2 vols. (London: Oxford University Press, 1907); and W. D. Ross, *The Right and the Good* (Oxford: Clarendon Press, 1930). For contemporary treatments, see Robert Nozick, *Philosophical Explanations* (Cambridge, MA: Harvard University Press, 1981); Roderick M. Chisholm, *Brentano and Intrinsic Value* (Cambridge: Cambridge University Press, 1986); Michael J. Zimmerman, "On the Intrinsic Value of States of Pleasure," *Philosophy and Phenomenological Research*, vol. 41 (1980–81), pp. 26–45; and my "Virtue as Loving the Good," *Social Philosophy and Policy*, vol. 9, no. 2 (Summer 1992), pp. 149–68.

sically evil, what is appropriate and therefore intrinsically good is hating them for themselves—for example, trying to relieve pain. In some cases these appropriate attitudes lead to actions that produce good or prevent evil, in which case the attitudes are instrumentally good. But the theory holds that, independently of any effects, the attitudes are intrinsically good, because they are appropriate to a good or evil object. The attitude that is inappropriate toward an intrinsic good is hating it for itself, and this hating is intrinsically evil, as is loving for itself something evil. Thus, being pained by another person's pleasure or desiring his pain are both intrinsically evil. The theory that generates these claims has a recursive structure, and I will therefore call it the *recursive theory*. Starting from initial claims such as that pleasure is intrinsically good, it adds that loving a good for itself is also intrinsically good. This makes not only the love of pleasure intrinsically good, but also the love of the love of pleasure, the love of the love of the love of pleasure, and so on. To an initial set of base-level goods and evils the recursive theory adds an infinite hierarchy of higher-level goods, each consisting in an appropriate attitude toward a lower-level good or evil. It is attractive to describe these higher-level goods as *moral* goods, as against the nonmoral base-level goods of plea-sure, knowledge, and achievement, and in what follows I will often speak in this way. It is also attractive to describe the higher-level goods as *virtues* and the higher-level evils as *vices*, so that, for example, desiring another's pleasure for itself is virtuous and desiring his pain for itself is vicious. In what follows I will also speak in this way, taking the recursive theory to imply that some attitudes toward intrinsic goods and evils are both in-trinsically good and virtuous, while others are evil and vicious.

The recursive theory implies that both self-interest and altruism as I have defined them are intrinsically good. Each involves loving for itself an intrinsic good, either in oneself or in another, and on that basis is a further intrinsic good. More specifically, both self-interest and altruism are moral (because they are higher-level) goods and constitute virtues. The theory therefore values self-interest and altruism positively, since it holds that they are good in themselves, and it also values them symmetri-cally, since it holds that they are good to the same degree and for the same reason. This symmetry of treatment results from the agent-neutrality of the theory's initial claims about value. If from each person's point of view the pleasure, knowledge, and achievement of others are good in the same way as her own, then, given the recursive principles, her loving their good is good in the same way as her loving her own is good. This symmetry marks a certain departure from common-sense morality. As I will explain more fully below, common-sense morality agrees that altru-istic attitudes are always intrinsically good, but it does not make the same claim about self-interested attitudes, since it does not hold that failing to care about one's own good is always a moral flaw. The symmetry is unavoidable, however, if the recursive theory is built on a foundation of agent-neutral claims about value. Given that starting-point, the theory has to hold that all forms of self-interest and altruism are in the same way intrinsically good.

There is one possible qualification to this conclusion, arising from a modification to the classical versions of the recursive theory. Brentano, Moore, and the others held that all instances of loving good are good and all instances of hating good are evil. But these claims imply that the intermediate state of being indifferent to a good—of neither loving it nor hating it for itself when, given one's beliefs, one could—is of intermediate or zero value, so that indifference to a good or evil is intrinsically indifferent. Though not completely unacceptable, this implication is not, on reflection, very attractive. Imagine that a person knows that another is suffering intense pain but is entirely unmoved by this fact, feeling no compassion for the other. Surely his indifference to another's great evil is not just not good, but evil; it manifests callousness, which is a vice. And surely a person's being entirely unmoved by another's great good, or apathetic about it, is likewise evil. If we share these intuitions, we will want to supplement the recursive theory with principles holding that indifference to intrinsic goods and evils is intrinsically evil.[3] Moreover, assuming a continuous scale of value for attitudes, these principles require that some instances of loving good and hating evil, namely those of the very lowest intensity, also be judged intrinsically evil. If complete apathy about a good is evil, then concern about that good so weak that it verges on apathy must also, albeit to a lesser degree, be evil. Given the principles about indifference, then, the recursive theory does not hold that all instances of self-interest and altruism are intrinsically good. Those that involve only very weak loves of the good are not good but evil. Yet the theory does imply that all instances of self-interest and altruism above a minimum threshold of intensity are intrinsically good, and it also maintains its symmetrical treatment of the two kinds of attitude. When self-interest and altruism are sufficiently intense to be intrinsically good, they are good for the same reason and to the same degree.[4]

II. PROPORTIONAL DIVISION: SELFISHNESS AND SELF-ABNEGATION

To say that self-interest and altruism are intrinsically good is to say that they are good when considered on their own. But self-interested and altruistic attitudes do not occur on their own. People have them in con-

---

[3] These principles are proposed in Zimmerman, "On the Intrinsic Value of States of Pleasure," p. 35; Thomas L. Carson, "Happiness, Contentment, and the Good Life," *Pacific Philosophical Quarterly*, vol. 62 (1981), p. 387; and Noah M. Lemos, *Intrinsic Value: Concept and Warrant* (Cambridge: Cambridge University Press, 1994), p. 37.

[4] A related issue concerns the value of loving or hating for itself what is intrinsically indifferent in value. The recursive theory holds that both these attitudes are also indifferent in value: loving or hating what is neither good nor evil is likewise neither good nor evil. By the proportionality principle introduced in Section II below, loving something indifferent much more than one loves some good can make for a combination of attitudes that is intrinsically evil as a combination and even on balance; this constitutes the vice of fetishism. Considered on their own, however, all attitudes toward the indifferent are indifferent in value.

junction with other attitudes, or in combinations of different loves and hates for different goods and evils. What is more, some of these combinations are intrinsically better than others, and some, though composed only of good attitudes, are intrinsically less good. This raises the possibility that a self-interested or altruistic attitude that is intrinsically good may nonetheless be instrumentally evil, and even evil all things considered, because it makes for a less good combination of attitudes than if the person had a different attitude in its place. A complete theory of the value of attitudes must address this possibility by considering the values not just of individual attitudes but also of combinations of them.

More specifically, a complete recursive theory must address what I will call the *problem of division*. Even if it is always good to love what is good, we humans cannot love all good things with infinite intensity. We have just finite capacities for desiring, pursuing, and taking pleasure in what is good, and we therefore face the question of how it is best to divide our love between good objects. If there are two good states of affairs, one better than the other, what is the best division of love between them? If the two good states are pleasures, for example, and do not obtain, how intensely should we desire the one as against the other? If the two pleasures do obtain, how intensely should we be pleased by each? Nor does this problem of division arise only because of our limited capacities. Imagine that a person is not giving as much love as he could to two goods; though he cares a little about each, he could care more about both. It would clearly be better if this person loved the two goods more intensely; if he can make himself do so, he should. Even if he does not, however, we can ask whether the love he does give to them is divided in the best possible way. Taking his total concern for the two goods as fixed, would his attitudes be improved if he shifted some love from one good to the other? This problem of division can arise for goods within the life of a single person. Thus, we can ask what is the best division of love between two good states of oneself, or between two good states of some other individual. But the problem can also arise for the goods of different people. In particular, we can ask what is the best division of love between a good in one's own life and a good in the life of another person, or between self-interested and altruistic attitudes. A complete account of the values of self-interest and altruism must address this last aspect of the problem of division, considering their contribution to the values of combinations of attitudes with both self-interested and altruistic components.

One general view about the problem of division seems overwhelmingly intuitively appealing. This *proportionality view*, as I will call it, holds that the best division of love between two goods is proportioned to their degrees of goodness, with the ideal relative intensity of love for each good determined by its relative degree of goodness. If two goods are equal in value, this view holds, it is best to love them equally intensely. If one good is greater than the other, however, one should love it with as much more intensity as its goodness exceeds that of the other. Thus, if one pleasure is twice as great as another, one should love it twice as much. Assuming agent-neutral initial claims about the good, this proportionality view implies that the ideal division between a self-interested and an altruistic attitude is the same as between two self-interested or two altruistic attitudes. Given a good of oneself and an equal good of another person, one should love the former no more but also no less than the latter. Given a good of oneself and a greater or lesser good of another person, one should love the former by as much less or more as its relative goodness makes appropriate. One should love one's own greater pleasure more than another's lesser pleasure, and one's own lesser pleasure less. Since the goods of different people are all good in the same way, one's division of love should take no account of their location in different people but instead should be guided only by their relative degrees of goodness.

A word of caution is necessary here. My talk of "proportionality" in attitudes should not be taken to imply that issues about the division of love can be pursued in anything like a mathematically precise way. On the contrary, I believe our judgments about the values and intensities of attitudes, and also about the values of their objects, can at best be rough and imprecise. But we can still talk meaningfully about proportionality and departures from it. We can, for example, judge that one good is only slightly greater than another but that, despite this, a person loves the first good much more intensely than the second. These rough judgments are enough to establish that the person's love is disproportionate and therefore not ideal.

The proportionality view should also not be taken to be more demanding than it is. If a person has attitudes that are slightly out of proportion, the view says they are not as good as they could be, but it does not say they are evil. It allows that they can be good, even significantly good, and that their being good can be the most salient fact about them. Compare a person who feels intense compassion for another's pain, but not quite as much compassion as he could. On most views it would be better if he felt more compassion, but that does not stop his actual attitude from being good. If few other people feel that much compassion, the attitude's being good can be what is most salient about it. Just as we can have an ideal of the deepest compassion without condemning all who fall even slightly short of it, so we can have an ideal of proportionality without condemning all departures from it.[5]

---

[5] Does the proportionality view not imply that people with slightly disproportionate attitudes have acted wrongly in not making them fully proportional? It does not when people cannot control their attitudes, as they often cannot. And when they can control their attitudes, the implication follows only given a maximizing principle of right action, one telling people always to produce the most good possible. But this principle is not mandatory. As Michael Slote has pointed out, an alternative "satisficing" principle requires people only to produce outcomes that are reasonably good, in the sense of being above a minimum threshold of goodness; see Slote, *Common-Sense Morality and Consequentialism* (London: Routledge and Kegan Paul, 1985), ch. 3. Given this principle, people whose attitudes are reasonably close to proportionality need have done nothing wrong in not making them fully proportional.

If the proportionality view is as intuitively appealing as I have suggested, we should try to incorporate it in the recursive theory. The sim-
plest way to do so is within a framework that is *atomistic*, in the sense of
taking the value of a combination of attitudes to equal the sum of the
values of its component attitudes. Assuming this atomistic approach, the
proportionality view can be derived from either of two views about the
degrees of value in individual attitudes.

Both these views take the value of an attitude to depend on two factors:
its intensity and the value of its object. Both views also hold that loving
a greater good is always better than loving a lesser good. More specifically, they hold that the relation between the value of an attitude and that
of its object is constant or linear, so that loving an object twice as good
with intensity m is always twice as good as loving an object half as good
with intensity m. For example, if pleasure x is twice as good as pleasure
y, then desiring x with intensity m is twice as good as desiring y with
intensity m. The first view, which I will call the *asymptotic* view, holds that
loving a good more intensely is always better than loving it less intensely,
but denies that this second relation is linear. It holds that the value of a
fixed increase in the intensity of love for a good gets smaller as that love's
intensity increases, and diminishes asymptotically toward zero. The more
intensely one loves a good, the less value additional love for it has. As a
result, loving a good twice as intensely is never as much as twice as good,
and at high levels of intensity is only infinitesimally better. The second, or
optimality view, takes this last claim further. It denies that loving a good
more intensely is always better than loving it less intensely, holding instead that the value of a fixed increase in the intensity of love for a good
not only diminishes but eventually becomes negative. For every good,
there is an optimal intensity of love, and just as an attitude can be less
than the best because it is not as intense as it could be, so it can be less
than the best because it is too intense.[6] The asymptotic and optimality
views are represented in Figures 1 and 2, where each curve shows how
the value of an attitude toward a good of a given magnitude varies with
its intensity.[7] In Figure 1, which represents the asymptotic view, the curves
rise steadily to the right, though eventually only infinitesimally, whereas
in Figure 2 they turn down after passing an optimal point. But in both
diagrams the curves are spaced so that attitudes toward objects that are
twice as good are themselves always twice as good. Combined with the
shape of the curves, this last feature ensures that the best division of love
between two goods is always proportioned to their degrees of goodness.

If the recursive theory includes either the asymptotic or the optimality
view, it implies that a self-interested or altruistic attitude, though intrin-

[6] This optimality view is proposed in Nozick, *Philosophical Explanations*, pp. 431–32.

[7] For simplicity's sake, these diagrams do not reflect the principles making indifference to
intrinsic goods and evils intrinsically evil. Instead, the lines in each diagram all pass through
the origin or zero-zero point, implying, as in the classical versions of the recursive theory,
that indifference to goods and evils is intrinsically indifferent.

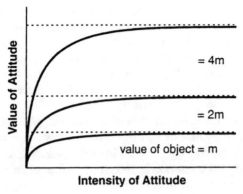

FIGURE 1. Asymptotic view.

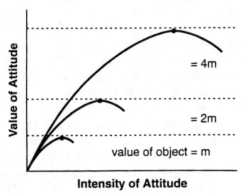

FIGURE 2. Optimality view.

sically good, can be instrumentally evil and even evil all things considered if it prevents the existence of a better combination of attitudes. More
specifically, the theory implies that there are two traits of combinations of
self-interested and altruistic attitudes that can make them less than ideally good. The first such trait is *selfishness*. It consists in loving one's own
good with disproportionate intensity, that is, in loving goods in one's own
life more than equal or greater goods in the lives of other people. The
second trait I will call *self-abnegation*, though it can equally well be called
selflessness, abjectness, or, in a certain sense, a lack of self-respect. It
consists in loving goods in one's own life less than equal or lesser goods
in the lives of other people, or caring about one's own interests less than
those of others. Both selfishness and self-abnegation are traits of combinations of attitudes, but their values affect those of individual attitudes.
If a person is selfish, his intense love of his own good is intrinsically good,

and at least on the asymptotic view is intrinsically better than any less intense love of his own good. But the person's intense love of his own good is instrumentally evil because, taking his total quantity of love as fixed,[8] it prevents his having a more intense love of the good of other people that would be intrinsically even better. A parallel claim holds for the self-abnegating person's intense love of the good of others. Even if it is intrinsically better than any less intense love of the good of others, this love prevents his having an intrinsically even better love of goods of his own. In line with its generally symmetrical approach to self-interest and altruism, the recursive theory treats selfishness and self-abnegation as parallel moral failings, each involving a departure from the same ideal of proportionate division. This marks a departure from common-sense morality, which, as I will argue below, does not always treat self-abnegation as a moral failing. Of course, selfishness and self-abnegation are distinct psychologically, and a person who is prone to one may not be at all prone to the other. Carol Gilligan suggests that boys in Western societies tend to grow up selfish, with too much concern for their own good, while girls are typically self-abnegating, with too little concern for themselves.[9] Despite their psychological distinctness, however, selfishness and self-abnegation are on the recursive view morally parallel, since they involve a similar departure from full proportionality, and the corrective for each is the same move to the intermediate state of equally proportioned self-interest and altruism.

The account of selfishness and self-abnegation just given is plausible as far as it goes, but it is limited. The account implies that selfish and self-abnegating attitudes are instrumentally evil, because they prevent the existence of intrinsically better attitudes. But it holds that the combination of attitudes of a selfish or self-abnegating person is always on balance intrinsically good; though not ideally good, the combination of attitudes still has positive value. Consider a person who is extremely selfish, caring much more about lesser goods of his own than about much greater goods of other people. The first component of his extreme selfishness, his intense love of his own good, is intrinsically good, and on at least the asymptotic view is intrinsically better than any less intense love of his good. The second component of his extreme selfishness, his mild love of others' good, is likewise intrinsically good if it is above the minimum threshold for love of others' good, as it surely can be. Given this latter assumption, the person's extreme selfishness involves two components each of which on its own is good. Assuming the atomistic view that the value of a combination of attitudes equals the sum of the values of its

---

[8] If the person's quantity of love is not fixed, but could be greater, there is another instrumental evil, namely his failure to love as much as he could. Even here, however, his selfishness remains one instrumental evil, or one factor that makes his attitudes less good than they could be.

[9] Carol Gilligan, *In a Different Voice* (Cambridge, MA: Harvard University Press, 1982).

components, it follows that the selfish person's combination of attitudes is good. It may not be as good as it could be, but it is not intrinsically evil. In the language of virtue, even extreme selfishness and self-abnegation involve, at most, *shortfalls in virtue*, or traits that make an attitude or combination of attitudes less good than it might be. But extreme selfishness and self-abnegation do not involve vices, or any element of intrinsic evil.

I find this implication counterintuitive. The recursive theory holds that any inappropriately oriented attitude is evil, even a very mild love of another's minor evil. It also holds that indifference to another's minor evil is evil. But surely if these mild forms of malice and callousness are evil, then extreme forms of selfishness and self-abnegation can be evil; if the former traits are moral vices, the latter should be too. To capture this view, however, we must abandon an atomistic account of the values of combinations of attitudes and supplement the asymptotic or optimality view, which gives the values of individual attitudes on their own, with a different principle concerned with combinations of attitudes *as combinations*.[10]

I will call this additional principle the *proportionality principle*. It says that any disproportion in one's division of love between two goods or evils is, as that disproportion, intrinsically evil. The individual attitudes in a disproportionate combination may have their own intrinsic values, which must be considered in an overall evaluation. According to the proportionality principle, however, any mismatch between the ratio of one's intensities of love for two goods and the ratio of the goods' values is a separate intrinsic evil. If a combination of attitudes is perfectly proportioned to its objects, the principle says that it contains no intrinsic evil, and the value of the combination equals, as before, the sum of the values of its component attitudes. Once there is a disproportion, however, the proportionality principle finds this a separate intrinsic evil, and we should understand the magnitude of this evil to be greater when the disproportion is greater. If state x is half as good as y, loving x much more than half as intensely as y is a greater evil than loving x a little more than half as intensely. Given this last assumption, slightly disproportionate combinations of attitudes involve small intrinsic evils, and extremely disproportionate ones involve great evils. Mild selfishness and self-abnegation, where one loves one's own good a little more or less than proportionally, involve small evils, whereas extreme selfishness and self-abnegation involve great evils. This implies that the former combinations can be on balance intrinsically good whereas the latter are on balance intrinsically evil. If a person is mildly selfish or self-abnegating, the disproportion between her loves is to a small degree evil, and this evil may be outweighed by the positive goods in her two loves considered on their own.

[10] The importance of evaluating combinations of attitudes as combinations, rather than just atomistically, is stressed in Holly M. Smith, "Varieties of Moral Worth and Moral Credit," *Ethics*, vol. 101 (1991), pp. 279–303.

As her selfishness or self-abnegation becomes more extreme, however, the evil of the disproportion increases until her combination of attitudes is on balance evil. Whereas mild selfishness and self-abnegation involve just shortfalls in virtue, extreme selfishness and self-abnegation are vices.

A recursive theory that includes the proportionality principle embraces Moore's principle of "organic unities," according to which "the value of a whole must not be assumed to be the same as the sum of the values of its parts."[11] The theory's operation can therefore be clarified by Moore's distinction between intrinsic value "as a whole" and intrinsic value "on the whole."[12] A whole's intrinsic value *as a whole* is its intrinsic value just as a whole or a complex, independently of any values present in its parts. Its intrinsic value *on the whole* is its intrinsic value on balance or all things considered, that is, the value that results from adding its intrinsic value as a whole to any intrinsic values in its parts. In this terminology, the proportionality principle gives the value as a whole of a combination of attitudes such as mild selfishness; it says this value is slightly negative. The value on the whole of mild selfishness is then arrived at by adding this slight negative value to the positive values in the component attitudes of the selfishness, and this value on the whole is positive. Though mild selfishness is, as a whole, of negative value and therefore a vice, it involves, on the whole, only a shortfall in virtue. Extreme selfishness, by contrast, is evil and vicious not only as a whole but also on the whole, that is, considering all factors relevant to its intrinsic value.

Variant versions of the proportionality principle are possible. Thus, some may argue that the evil in a disproportionate combination should depend not just on the ratio of intensities it involves but also on their absolute levels. Imagine that persons a and b are both selfish in the same ratio; imagine, for example, that they both care twice as much about their own good as about other people's. But b cares more intensely about all goods than a does, so that, whereas a has, say, 10 units of love for his own good and 5 for others', b has 20 for her own and 10 for others'. (We could call a's a more anemic and b's a more passionate selfishness.) The original proportionality principle implies that b's combination of attitudes is on balance intrinsically better than a's. It involves the same evil of disproportion, but better, because more intense, individual loves of the good. (On neither the asymptotic nor the optimality view are these loves twice as good as a's, but they are still better.) Some may find this implication counterintuitive, holding that a's and b's kinds of selfishness should be on balance equally evil. To capture their view, the recursive theory must revise the proportionality principle to find a greater intrinsic evil in the same disproportionate ratio among more intense attitudes. I myself do not find this revision attractive. If a and b both divided their loves in

[11] Moore, *Principia Ethica*, p. 28.
[12] *Ibid.*, p. 214f.

perfect proportion, but b's loves were more intense, then b's attitudes would surely be on balance better. (Compare a human's ideally proportioned loves with God's.) The parallel claim about a's and b's kinds of selfishness seems to me plausible. That b loves his own and especially others' good more intensely than a does, makes b's more passionate selfishness on balance less of a vice. Nonetheless, a version of the proportionality principle that makes b's vice equal to a's is also possible.[13]

Whatever its exact formulation, the proportionality principle completes an initial recursive account of the values of self-interest and altruism. This account makes three central claims about the two kinds of attitudes, running from the positive to the potentially more negative. The first claim is that both self-interested and altruistic attitudes, since they involve a positive orientation toward a good in oneself or another person, are intrinsically good. This claim follows from the general recursive idea that appropriate attitudes, which include loving for itself what is good, are intrinsically good. The second claim is that, though intrinsically good, both self-interested and altruistic attitudes can be instrumentally evil if, by being disproportionately intense, they prevent a person from having another, intrinsically better attitude. This second claim, which follows from the asymptotic or optimality view about individual attitudes, underwrites the first, weaker diagnosis of selfishness and self-abnegation as shortfalls in virtue, that is, as traits that make on-balance good combinations of attitudes somewhat less good. The final claim, which follows from the proportionality principle, is that self-interested and altruistic attitudes can also be instrumentally evil in the stronger sense of making for intrinsic evil in one's combination of attitudes as a combination and even, given a sufficient disproportion, on balance. This claim underwrites the stronger diagnosis of selfishness and self-abnegation as not just shortfalls in virtue but also, in some circumstances, vices. The three claims all apply symmetrically to self-interest and altruism, and this symmetry derives from the agent-neutrality of the recursive theory's initial claims about the good, the claims that each person's pleasure, knowledge, and achievement are equally good from the point of view of all persons. But common-sense moral thought affirms a striking asymmetry in the values

---

[13] Another version of the proportionality principle changes the zero-value point for divisions of love. The original principle holds that the best division of love, a perfectly proportioned one, has zero value as a division or combination, and that any disproportionate division has negative value. An alternative principle says that a perfect division of love has positive value, as (to a lesser degree) do mildly disproportionate ones, and that only seriously disproportionate divisions have negative value. Given this principle, the zero-value point for divisions of virtuous love is not perfect proportion but some moderate disproportion. The revised principle makes perfect divisions of love intrinsically better on balance, since they involve not only the intrinsic goods in their component attitudes but also the further intrinsic good of proportionate division. It also raises the level of disproportion at which traits such as selfishness and self-abnegation switch from shortfalls in virtue to vices, so that a degree of selfishness or self-abnegation that would be on balance intrinsically evil given the original principle is still on balance good. It is an arbitrary matter where one places the zero-value point for divisions, and though my original choice of perfect proportion is one possibility, there are others.

of self-interested and altruistic attitudes. The question is whether this asymmetry can be captured by applying the same recursive structure to different, partly agent-relative, claims about value.

III. Agent-Relativity and Asymmetry

Agent-relative claims about value hold that what is good, or at least the degree to which it is good, differs from one person's point of view to another's. Henry Sidgwick used an agent-relative claim about goodness to formulate a consequentialist version of egoistic hedonism. Egoistic hedonists, he suggested, hold that each person's pleasure is good only "for him," or from his point of view, rather than agent-neutrally, and they combine this claim with the standard consequentialist principle that each person ought to maximize what is good from his point of view.[14] This appeal to agent-relative goodness was challenged by Moore, who denied its intelligibility. States cannot, Moore argued, be good "for" one person but not another; they are good either agent-neutrally or not at all.[15] Before we consider combining the recursive principles with agent-relative claims about value, we must decide whether those claims are indeed intelligible.

The answer depends on what we take goodness, whether agent-neutral or agent-relative, to consist in. One view, associated with Moore, holds that goodness is a simple, unanalyzable property had by some states of affairs.[16] A different view, versions of which were endorsed by Brentano and Sidgwick, holds that claims about goodness are reducible to claims about which states it is appropriate to love, or which states people have reason to desire or pursue, as ends in themselves.[17] Those who take the first view do not deny that the second view's reducing claims are true. Thus, they do not deny that it is appropriate to love what is good, or that people have reason to desire and pursue what is good. They just deny that a state's goodness consists in this appropriateness or in the existence of this reason; on the contrary, the goodness is something prior that explains them.

Given the first view about goodness, it is indeed hard to see how agent-relative goodness is possible. If goodness is a simple property, how can a state of affairs have it from one "point of view" but not another? Surely it either has the property or not. It is therefore no surprise that Moore, who accepted the first view, rejected agent-relative goodness. But there is no difficulty about agent-relative goodness given the second view. If goodness consists in what it is appropriate for persons to feel, or what

---

[14] Henry Sidgwick, *The Methods of Ethics*, 7th ed. (London: Macmillan, 1907).

[15] Moore, *Principia Ethica*, pp. 97–102. The debate between Sidgwick and Moore has been taken up more recently, with Amartya Sen defending agent-relative goodness and Donald H. Regan challenging it. See Sen, "Rights and Agency," *Philosophy and Public Affairs*, vol. 11 (1982), pp. 3–39; and Regan, "Against Evaluator Relativity: A Response to Sen," *Philosophy and Public Affairs*, vol. 12 (1983), pp. 93–112.

[16] Moore, *Principia Ethica*, ch. 1.

[17] Brentano, *The Origin of Our Knowledge of Right and Wrong*, p. 18; Sidgwick, *The Methods of Ethics*, p. 112.

they have reason to feel, then what is appropriate or a reason for one person can be different from what is appropriate or a reason for another. Egoistic hedonism, for example, can say that what it is appropriate for each person to care about, or what she has reason to pursue, is only her own pleasure. In the absence of a compelling argument that goodness must be understood in the first, Moorean way, I will assume with Sidgwick that claims about agent-relative goodness are coherent, and ask how they may affect the recursive account of self-interest and altruism.

Given its starting-point in agent-neutral claims about value, the recursive theory developed in the previous two sections expresses, within the theory of good and evil attitudes, a strict impartialism. It holds that what is intrinsically best is caring impartially about the goods of all people, no one person's any more or less than any other's. This impartialist view is inspiring, and it may even be correct. But it is not the view of common-sense morality, which holds that the best attitudes do or can involve certain asymmetries of concern. The question is whether we can capture these asymmetries by combining the general recursive idea that it is good for each person to love what is good from his point of view with agent-relative initial claims about goodness.

There is one place where this combination looks promising. Common-sense morality holds, against impartialism, that it is not best to care equally about the good of all other persons. On the contrary, one should care more about those people who stand in certain special relationships to one, such as one's children, spouse, and friends. It is both right to act in ways that favor these people and intrinsically good to care more about their interests. Both these asymmetric claims can be derived from agent-relative claims about goodness—for example, that from each parent's point of view, the pleasure, knowledge, and achievement of her children are intrinsically better than the equal pleasure, knowledge, and achievement of strangers. Common sense does not hold that there are no grounds for concern about strangers, and it would be going too far to say that, from each parent's point of view, only her own children's states are good. What is called for is only the weaker claim that her children's states are better, or from her point of view more important. And combining this weaker claim with the original recursive principles captures the asymmetries in the common-sense view of concern for other people. Given the asymptotic or optimality view, it is now better for a parent to care about her child's pleasure with intensity m than to care about a stranger's equal pleasure with intensity m. In addition, the best division of a parent's love between her child's and a stranger's pleasure is not equal but weighted toward the child. The modified recursive theory still leaves room for a moral failing of nepotism, or of favoring one's children too much, but it also affirms a contrary failing of favoring them too little. In particular, the impartial combination of equally intense loves for one's child's and a stranger's equal pleasures is not the best possible combination and may even, given the proportionality principle, be on balance evil.

This appeal to agent-relative goodness concerns the values of different forms of altruism, and is therefore tangential to our central topic of self-interest and altruism. But common-sense morality also recognizes an asymmetry in the values of these two attitudes, though the asymmetry is subtler and more difficult to capture.

In its theory of right action, common-sense morality grants each person an agent-relative permission to pursue lesser goods of himself rather than somewhat greater goods of other people, for example, a lesser pleasure of his own rather than a greater pleasure of another. This permission is not unqualified; it is by common-sense standards wrong to produce an utterly trivial good of oneself rather than a very great one of another.[18] Given this qualification, however, people are permitted, though not required, to show some preference in their actions to their own interests.[19] I do not believe, however, that this permission in the common-sense theory of right action is accompanied by a parallel permission in the common-sense theory of good and evil attitudes. Thus, I do not believe common sense holds that the attitudes of a person who cares more about his own good are as intrinsically good as those of a person who divides his concerns impartially. The former person, even if he does not act wrongly, is selfish, and selfishness remains a moral failing. The common-sense theory of right action may permit people to act from moderate selfishness, but that only means that it permits them to act from what common sense still regards as less than the best motives.[20]

The common-sense theory of right action also contains a parallel permission allowing each person to pursue lesser goods of others rather than somewhat greater goods of himself, for example, a lesser pleasure of another rather than a greater pleasure of himself. This action too, though not required, is not morally wrong.[21] But here I believe the agent-relative permission about right action is accompanied by a parallel permission about attitudes. A person who loves a pleasure of another more than an equal pleasure of his own does not by common-sense standards have intrinsically better attitudes than if he loved the two pleasures equally. Nothing is better than dividing self-interest and altruism equally. But in certain circumstances his attitudes can be just as intrinsically good. For

---

[18] This qualification may need some refining. Common sense certainly holds that it is wrong to prefer a trivial good of one's own to a much greater good of a person immediately present before one. It is not so clear that it condemns a similar preference for one's lesser good over the greater good of someone far away, e.g., in a distant country. Still, there is clearly some qualification on the common-sense permission to prefer one's own lesser good.

[19] See Samuel Scheffler, *The Rejection of Consequentialism* (Oxford: Clarendon Press, 1982).

[20] Is it not inconsistent for common-sense morality to allow this disparity between its claims about right action and its claims about good attitudes? I do not believe it is. In granting the agent-relative permission, common-sense morality already holds that an act which it is permissible (i.e., not wrong) to perform has consequences that are intrinsically less good than those of some alternative act. It can likewise hold that the former act, if performed, will issue from motives that are intrinsically less good than some alternative. In both cases the permissive claim about the right is partly independent of claims about the good.

[21] See Slote, *Common-Sense Morality and Consequentialism*, ch. 1.

example, if he believes that his own pleasures are as morally significant as other people's but chooses freely to prefer another's pleasures, his doing so is not objectionable. It is not that common sense never condemns preferring another's lesser good. In other circumstances, which I will specify below, this involves a moral failing of self-abnegation. In circumstances like those just described, however, this preference is by common-sense standards not a failing, but consistent with attitudes as good as any others. Common sense holds that it can be not worse, though also not better, to care less about one's own good. It is this subtle asymmetry that I want to try to capture using agent-relative claims about goodness.

To illustrate the complexity of this task, consider a relevant proposal of Ross's. Ross believed that there is no moral duty to pursue one's own pleasure, though he did think that there is a duty to pursue the pleasure of others. In *The Foundations of Ethics*, he proposed grounding this asymmetry in an agent-relative claim about goodness: that from each person's point of view his own pleasure is not intrinsically good, though the pleasure of other people is.[22] Given a general duty to promote what is good from the agent's point of view, this claim implies that each person has a duty to promote others' pleasure but not his own. The agent-relative claim also introduces an asymmetry into the recursive theory of attitudes, which Ross defended. Because he believed that other aspects of a person's good, namely knowledge and virtue, are good agent-neutrally, Ross believed that it is good and a form of virtue to love knowledge and virtue either in oneself or in others. But he held that only the love of others' pleasure is a virtue. Since from one's own point of view one's own pleasure is not intrinsically good, loving it for itself is likewise not good.

As I have indicated, Ross made his agent-relative claim only about the one good of pleasure, but we may wonder whether the common-sense asymmetry does not extend to other goods. Ross may have been right that the asymmetry does not extend to base-level perfectionist goods such as knowledge and achievement. Common sense may not hold that it can be as good to care more about others' achievement of these goods than about one's own. But the asymmetry does seem to extend to the higher-level perfectionist good of virtue. Imagine that person *a* acts virtuously in pursuit of person *b*'s pleasure and successfully produces that pleasure. There are then two intrinsic goods present in this situation: *a*'s virtuous pursuit of pleasure and *b*'s pleasure. How it is best for *a* to divide his love between these goods depends, in an agent-neutral theory, on the relative values of the virtuous pursuit and the pleasure at which it is aimed. I have argued elsewhere, following Moore, that the goodness or evil of an attitude toward an object is always less than the goodness or evil of that object, so that, for example, the goodness of compassion for another's pain can never outweigh the evil of that pain. A situation containing one person's pain and another's compassion for it is always on

---

[22] Sir W. David Ross, *The Foundations of Ethics* (Oxford: Clarendon Press, 1939), pp. 282–84.

balance evil.[23] Given this view about comparison, and assuming agent-neutrality, it is best for *a* to care more about *b*'s pleasure than about his own virtuous action, though he should still care to some extent about the virtuous action. (He can do this either by desiring the pleasure more than the virtuous action before he acts, or by being more pleased by the pleasure afterward.) I believe that common-sense morality says this proportional division of *a*'s love makes for a combination of attitudes that is as good as any other, but not for a uniquely best combination. Imagine that *a* cares only about *b*'s pleasure and not at all about his virtuous action, so his concern is focused entirely on the object of his virtue. If he does this in the right way, which I will again specify below, his division of love seems by common-sense standards to be no less good. It is not a failing in him not to attend lovingly to his own good attitudes. In some cases, not appreciating one's own virtue involves a morally suspect form of self-abnegation, but in other cases, common sense holds that it makes for a combination of attitudes as good as any other.

Can these asymmetries be captured by Ross's kind of agent-relative claim? They cannot, because the claim is too crude. Consider just Ross's claim that from each person's point of view his own pleasure is not intrinsically good. This claim indeed implies the common-sense view that self-abnegation is not always a moral failing, but it goes beyond it to imply that self-abnegation is never a moral failing. If one's own pleasure is not at all a good, how can not loving it ever be a shortfall in virtue? But common sense does hold that self-abnegation can be objectionable; only in certain circumstances is it not. Ross's claim also implies the common-sense view that a self-abnegating combination of attitudes can be on balance as good as one that is impartially divided. The claim again goes further, however, implying that self-abnegation is intrinsically better than impartiality. If one's own pleasure is not at all good, then caring as much about it as about the equal pleasures of others involves caring as much about something of no value as about something good, which is disproportionate and a moral flaw. But this is again not the common-sense view. Common sense holds that impartiality about one's own and others' pleasure, while not the uniquely best combination of attitudes, is nonetheless as good as any other. Ross's claim is too crude to capture this view.[24]

Because of these difficulties, the recursive theory needs a more subtle agent-relative claim. As a first approximation I propose the following. Each person's pleasure and virtue are good from the point of view of other people, and they are also good from her point of view *if but only if*

[23] See my "Virtue as Loving the Good," pp. 160–63; and Moore, *Principia Ethica*, pp. 219–20.
[24] Ross's claim has an equally unacceptable implication in the theory of right action. As Michael Stocker points out, it implies that a person who acts to produce a greater pleasure of himself rather than a lesser pleasure of someone else always acts morally wrongly; see Stocker, "Agent and Other: Against Ethical Universalism," *Australasian Journal of Philosophy* vol. 54 (1976), p. 208.

she loves them intrinsically or for themselves. Since claims about the good are, in an agent-relative context, claims about what it is appropriate for people to love or what they have reason to love, this claim implies that if a person does love her own pleasure or virtue, her doing so is appropriate and therefore also appropriate to love. If she does not love her own pleasure or virtue, however, this is not inappropriate or any moral failing. For the specific objects of a person's own pleasure and virtue, both her loving and her not loving them are equally morally good. If she has or chooses to have love for these states, that is good; but it can be equally good if she does not. The same permissiveness extends to issues about division. If a person does love her own pleasure or virtue, what is best is her dividing her love impartially between her own pleasure or virtue and that of others. If she does not love those states of herself, however, it is best for her to concentrate her love on the pleasure or virtue of others. Given the biconditional agent-relative claim, there are, as common-sense affirms, two equally ideal combinations of attitudes toward one's own and others' goods.

The agent-relative claim needs to be refined to distinguish between the cases where self-abnegation is and is not a moral failing. This distinction turns initially on the role played by beliefs about the good within a combination of attitudes. If a self-abnegating combination of attitudes is independent of beliefs about value, and involves just an immediate lesser concern for one's own pleasure or virtue, then it is, as on the agent-neutral theory, a moral failing. Caring less about one's own good states, without a belief that justifies doing so, always makes one's attitudes less good. But a self-abnegating combination of attitudes is not a moral failing if it involves belief in the agent-relative claim I have just formulated. If a person believes that his own pleasure is good from the point of view of other people, so that they have as much reason to care about it as about anyone else's pleasure, and would also be good from his point of view if he chose to care about it, then his choosing not to care about it is not morally objectionable. It does not involve any abjectness or lack of self-respect, because it is based on the belief that his pleasure counts as much in principle as anyone else's, and does not count in practice for him only because he chooses that it not count. Surely in these circumstances his lesser degree of self-interest is not a flaw. I think it a mistake to hold, as a purely altruistic morality would, that self-abnegation is never a moral failing. It is important to emphasize that people's attitudes can be less than the best, and even on balance evil, because they care too little about their own good. But I think it also a mistake, or at least false to common sense, to go to the opposite extreme and hold that self-abnegation is always a moral failing.[25] We can avoid this false alternative by refining

[25] Michael Slote comes close to this extreme claim in *From Morality to Virtue* (New York: Oxford University Press, 1992), pp. 106–7.

the agent-relative claim formulated above by reference to a person's beliefs: caring less about one's own pleasure or virtue, though sometimes a
moral failing, is not a failing if one believes that one's pleasure or virtue
matters morally as much to other people, and would matter morally as
much to oneself if one did in fact care about it.

There are more complex cases of self-abnegation, involving not what I
am taking to be a true belief in the agent-relative claim stated above, but
certain false beliefs about the good. For example, imagine that a person
believes that her own caring about her pleasure or virtue is a condition
not only for its being good from her point of view but also for its being
good from the point of view of other people, so that if she does not care
about her pleasure or virtue they have no reason to either. (Perhaps saints
think this way.) She believes a biconditional agent-relative claim, though
one stronger than that which I have formulated. I believe this agent-
relative claim is false; no matter how a person views her own pleasure or
virtue, it is appropriate and good for others to desire, pursue, and take
pleasure in it for itself. But if a self-abnegating person has this false belief,
is her self-abnegation a failing? I do not believe so, for two reasons. First,
the person is forming attitudes on the basis of her beliefs about the good,
and, as I said in introducing the recursive theory, loving what one believes to be good is always good. Attitudes that fit one's beliefs about
value are appropriate to their objects as perceived.[26] Second, the person's
self-abnegation still does not involve any abjectness or lack of self-respect.
She still believes her pleasure or virtue has the same moral importance in
principle as anyone else's, and would have the same importance in practice if she chose to grant it that importance. Her self-abnegation, therefore,
though it denies a reason which others in fact have to care about her
good, does not seem morally objectionable.

A more difficult case is that of someone who believes that his pleasure
and virtue matter less agent-neutrally than other people's, that is, matter
less to all people, and matter less not just when he chooses not to love
them, but unconditionally, in all circumstances. This person does not
think that his own good counts less than others' merely in practice but
also in principle; he assigns his own states unconditionally less weight.
His self-abnegation therefore involves a more comprehensively false belief. Is it then a moral failing? If we believe that forming attitudes on the
basis of one's beliefs about the good is always good, then we have to
conclude that his self-abnegation is not in principle a failing. On the
contrary, it is a positive virtue. But we can temper this unattractive-
sounding conclusion in two ways. First, a person who believes falsely that
his pleasure matters less agent-neutrally may also have, independently of
that belief, a lesser immediate emotional concern for that pleasure than

[26] For a similar view, though applying to beliefs about right action, see Ronald D. Milo,
Immorality (Princeton, NJ: Princeton University Press, 1984), pp. 18, 251–53.

for other people's. In this case, the combination of his immediate emotional concerns for people's pleasures embodies a moral failing, and possibly an on-balance evil, that weighs against the goodness of the attitudes derived from his false belief. Second, in many cases the person's agent-neutral belief derives causally from the immediate emotions, as a rationalization of them. He has not formed the self-abnegating belief by independent reflection but in order to fit his preexisting attitudes. In these cases, it is reasonable to deny that any further attitudes deriving from the belief have, given the belief's origins, positive value. So in these cases it is reasonable to deny that there is anything good in his self-abnegation. For a related example, consider a Nazi who pursues the extermination of the Jews because he believes this extermination is agent-neutrally good. In normal circumstances a pursuit derived from beliefs about the good is good. If the Nazi formed his belief only to rationalize a preexisting hatred of Jews, however, it is reasonable to make the value of his pursuit depend entirely on the values of the attitudes from which it ultimately springs. And those attitudes, which do not involve beliefs, are entirely evil.[27]

As finally refined, the agent-relative claim says that each person's pleasure and virtue are good from the point of view of other people, that they are also good from her point of view if she loves them for themselves or fails to love them because of immediate emotions, but that they are not good from her point of view if she fails to love them because of a belief about their goodness that does not derive from immediate emotions. This claim is complex, and in some eyes that may count against it. The complexity is necessary, however, if the recursive theory is to capture common-sense morality's subtle view about self-abnegation and impartiality: that self-abnegation can be as good as impartiality though it cannot be better, and is as good only in some circumstances and not others.

IV. CONCLUSION

In this essay I have considered the moral values of self-interest and altruism within a general theory of the value of attitudes developed by

---

[27] The recursive theory does imply that the Nazi's pursuit of extermination could in certain imaginable circumstances be intrinsically good. First, the pursuit would have to derive only or primarily from his evaluative belief and not from immediate emotional hatred of Jews. Second, his belief could not have been formed by rationalization or in a way that manifests indifference to Jews and their moral standing. (Recall that indifference to a good is intrinsically evil.) These conditions could perhaps be satisfied if the Nazi was encouraged to form his belief as a child by parents whom he had other reasons to trust and believe, and was not subsequently exposed to sufficient reasons to change his belief. (This would presumably involve his never meeting any Jews.) I think it is correct to say that in these very special circumstances a Nazi's pursuit of the extermination of the Jews could be intrinsically good, even though it would also be enormously instrumentally evil and therefore evil all things considered. But the circumstances are highly unusual and probably did not apply to any actual Nazi. In a similar way, it is very hard to imagine any actual circumstances in which self-abnegation resulting from the belief that one's own good matters less agent-neutrally is intrinsically good.

Brentano, Moore, and several of their contemporaries. This theory has three main components. The first is a set of recursive principles holding that appropriate attitudes toward intrinsic goods and evils, including the love of intrinsic goods for their own sake, are intrinsically good, and inappropriate attitudes are intrinsically evil. The second is a view about the degrees of value in individual attitudes, either the asymptotic or the optimality view, that implies that the best division of love between any two goods is proportioned to their degrees of goodness. The third component is a stronger proportionality principle which implies that disproportionate combinations of attitudes can be not only intrinsically less good than proportionate ones, but on balance intrinsically evil. When this recursive theory is combined with agent-neutral initial claims about the good, it implies a symmetrical treatment of self-interest and altruism. Both self-interested and altruistic attitudes are intrinsically good, because they involve love of a good, but they can also be instrumentally and even on balance evil if, by being too intense, they cause a departure from strict impartiality between self and other. When self-interest is too strong, the result is the moral failing of selfishness; when altruism is too strong, the result is the parallel failing of self-abnegation. But the recursive theory can also be combined with more complex, agent-relative initial claims about value, and if it is, it can capture the common-sense view that in some cases self-abnegation, or caring less about one's own good, is not a moral failing. Given different initial claims about value, the recursive theory's implications about self-interest and altruism are different. In both cases, however, it is the same recursive theory, with the same three components, that yields the differing assessments of self- and other-concern.

Philosophy, University of Calgary

INDEX

Abstractions, and concretes, 7, 17–18
Achievement, 276–77, 281, 286–88, 300
Adeimantus, 125–26, 146
Adler, Alfred, 266
Aelred of Rivaulx, 250 n. 40
Affection, 14, 176. *See also* Love
Agency, 230, 249–50
Alcoholism, 193–94
Alienation, 17
Allen, Woody, 210 n. 4, 235, 255, 260
Altruism, 3–4, 7, 9–10, 12–13, 60–62, 159, 286–91, 293–94, 298, 301, 304, 306–7. *See also* Other-regard
Annas, Julia, 107–9, 117
Appetitive goods (Appetites), 185–92, 196–98, 201–2, 268, 275, 278–82
Aquinas, Thomas, 254 n. 49
Aristotle, vii, 8–9, 17, 19 n. 44, 20, 113, 167–17, 124–26, 136, 142–43, 153, 177, 245 n. 32, 246, 249 n. 38, 252, 253 n. 45; on friendship, 129–33, 144–51; on virtue, 227, 229–37, 266, 272–75
Arrogance, 24
Arrow, Kenneth, 103
Asceticism, 202–3
Associations, 135
Authority, 121, 260–61
Autonomy, 10–11, 79–80, 89–90, 205, 231–34, 238–40, 242–44, 246, 248, 252–56, 258, 260

Baby Jessica, 233–34
Badhwar, Neera, 13
Baier, Kurt, 2, 4
Beauty, 186–87, 195
Beliefs, 141–43, 203–4; about the good, 288, 304–6
Beneficence, 19 n. 44, 83
Benevolence, 12–13, 129, 135
Bentham, Jeremy, 12, 213
Bing, Leon, 244, 250
Blackburn, Simon, 113
"Bliss point," 198–201
Blum, Lawrence, 1 n. 3
Bradley, F. H., 133
Brain transplant, 137
Branden, Nathaniel, 262 n. 59
Brandt, Richard, 57 n. 7, 72, 77, 84
Brentano, Franz, 288, 290, 299, 307
Brontë, Charlotte, 253, 255, 257–58
Burroughs, Edgar Rice, 158–59
Butler, Joseph, 4 n. 13, 13, 66

Calculation, economic, 182–84
Callicles, 125
Camus, Albert, 214–15
Care, 176. *See also* Benevolence
Careers, 26, 201, 219
Categorical imperative, 78–80
Character, 117, 148; traits of, 237
Charity, 19–20. *See also* Beneficence; Generosity
Choice, rational, 179, 184, 188, 196, 231–33, 238; and self-interest, 64–68, 82, 170–73. *See also* Deliberation
Chomsky, Noam, 280
Christianity, 202–3
Citizenship, 150–51
Cleckley, Hervey, 236 n. 20
Coherence, of ends, 52, 68–70, 82
Common good, 120, 129–30, 133–35, 149–52, 155
Common sense: and morality, 54–64, 129, 153, 265, 268, 280, 286, 289, 295, 298–304, 306; and practical reason, 64–75, 81–85
Compassion (Sympathy), 9, 40, 118 nn. 20 and 22, 181, 302–3
Competence, 238–41, 252
Compromise, moral, 261–62
Concepts, 269–70, 272
Concern: object of, 13, 43–44; for others, 109–10, 143, 145–46, 148–54, 158, 173–76, 178, 300. *See also* Other-regard
Conflict, inner, 247–48
Conformity, 261
Consequentialism, 34, 53, 70–75, 83, 85, 119–20; act versus rule, 74 n. 41
Constraints, 116–17, 119, 188
Consumer theory, 180–81, 187–89
Consumption, 185–87, 189–91, 198–200, 203
Continence, 235, 256–57. *See also* Incontinence
Contractarianism, 50
Cooperation, 123, 135, 144–45
Cottingham, John, 17, 20
Counting principles, 68–69
Courage, 6, 8, 258, 277–78, 279 n. 9
Cox, Stephen, 240 n. 26, 241 n. 27
Criminals, 16. *See also* Gangs; Predation
Crusoe, Robinson, 2–4, 8, 243

Darwin, Charles, 3
DeBruin, Debra, 111

309

Hume, David, 1, 8 n. 20, 9, 66, 68, 70, 77, 118 nn. 21 and 22, 278
Hurston, Zora Neale, 22, 27, 48, 50
Hutcheson, Francis, 10
Hypothetical imperative, 69, 76–77

Ideas, transmission of, 205–6
Identity, personal, 124, 127–28, 136–43, 149. *See also* Psychological continuity
Immortality, 127, 148
Impartiality, 17–19, 73, 115, 300–301, 303, 306. *See also* Partiality
Inclinations. *See* Preferences
Income, 198–200
Incontinence, 236, 247, 256. *See also* Continence
Independence, 243, 255, 258. *See also* Autonomy
Indifference, 290
Indifference curves, 189–95, 198
Influence, interpersonal, 205–6
Injustice, 262–63
Insatiability, 278–80
Instincts, 180
Institutions, social, 119
Integrity, 239–40, 255–56, 258–60
Interdependence, 243
Interest: theories of, 158–65, 167–68, 175–76; scope of, 160–65; and worth, 177–78
Interests, 15, 26, 61, 63, 73, 124; conflict of, 135
IQ scores, 241 n. 28
Irrationality, 59, 195–96

James, William, 16–18
Jane Eyre (Brontë), 257–58
Jefferson, Thomas, 262
Jones, Bill T., 31
Judgments, moral, 81
Justice, 125–27, 130, 133, 146–47, 150, 262–63

Kant, Immanuel, 11 n. 27, 45, 47–49, 69, 89, 270–73, 284; on deliberative rationality, 75–85; on the Moral Law, 33–34; on practical reason, 53–55; on value, 28–30
Kavka, Gregory, 163
Knowledge, 104, 194, 204–5, 235, 256, 278, 286–88, 300, 302; of the self, 17–19, 247, 250–51
Korsgaard, Christine, 118 n. 20

Law enforcement, 243
Lee, Harper, 30–31
Legislation, moral, 79–84
Les Liaisons Dangereuses (De Laclos), 251, 254

Lewis, C. S., 233 n. 15
Life: control over, 231–34; meaningful, 208–13, 215–16. *See also* Good life; Meaning
Locke, John, 136–37
Longings, 185–92, 197–202, 208–10, 214
Love, 9, 146–47, 186, 200, 208, 276, 284; of the good, 287–90, 293–95, 297–98, 303–4, 307; Platonic, 126–28. *See also* Self-love
Loyalty, 250–51
Luck, 228, 231, 237, 258, 260–63, 283

Mandeville, Bernard, 9 n. 25
Martineau, James, 284
Maslow, Abraham, 262 n. 59
McCall, Nathan, 240 n. 26, 241 nn. 27 and 28, 244 n. 31, 246 n. 33
Meaning, in life, 208–15, 223–24, 259; and fulfillment, 216–21; judgments about, 212–13; and self-interest, 219–22
Medea, 15
Mental, and physical, 268–69
Middlemarch (Eliot), 36, 39, 41, 43, 46, 48
Milgram, Stanley, 121
Mill, John Stuart, 23–24, 30, 32–34, 220
Mind, 247
Misfortune, 263, 283. *See also* Fortune
Mobsters, 240 n. 26, 241 n. 27, 251
Moderation, 278–79
Monasticism, 202–3
Monism, 272–73
Moore, G. E., 77–78, 288, 290, 297, 299–300, 302, 307
Moral education, 106, 194
Moral point of view, 45, 114–15, 118 n. 22, 119
Moral rationalism, 96
Morality, 12, 32, 71, 102, 111, 160, 266, 271; nature of, 1–2, 5–7, 10–11, 14, 19–22, 35, 41, 47, 51, 113–14; personalized, 40–42, 51; and rationality, 107, 122–24, 156–57; and self-interest, 86–90, 97, 105–7, 112, 116–17, 118 n. 21, 119–20, 179–80. *See also under* Common sense
Motherhood, 26. *See also* Parents
Motivation, 9–13, 108, 112, 235, 241, 263
Mysian, remotest, 151–52

Nagel, Thomas, 1 n. 3, 156 n. 47, 214–15
Narcissism, 110
Naturalistic fallacy, 78
Nazis, 260
Needs, human, 5, 106, 253
Nepotism, 300
Nicomachean Ethics (Aristotle), 129
Nietzsche, Friedrich, 246
Norms, moral, 123